بسم الله الرحمن الرحيم

Qawāʿid fī ʿUlūm al-Ḥadīth

UNDERLYING PRINCIPLES OF THE SCIENCES OF ḤADĪTH

Qawāʿid fī ʿUlūm al-Ḥadīth

UNDERLYING PRINCIPLES OF THE SCIENCES OF ḤADĪTH

Also known as

Muqaddima Iʿlāʾ as-Sunan

The Introduction to *Iʿlāʾ as-Sunan*

Originally known as

Inhāʾ as-Sakan ilā man Yuṭāliʿ Iʿlāʾ as-Sunan

Complete Relief for Whosever Studies the *Iʿla as-Sunan*

By

The critical ḥadīth scholar

MAWLĀNĀ ẒAFAR AḤMAD

AL-ʿUTHMĀNĪ AT-THĀNAWĪ

(1310/1892–1394/1974)

Translated by

Abdassamad Clarke and Aisha Bewley

Edited and revised by

Mawlana Shamsudduha and

Mawlana Dr Mansur Ali

Introduction by

Mawlana Dr Mansur Ali

TURATH PUBLISHING

2014

ISBN: 978-1-906949-28-0

Published by
Turath Publishing
79 Mitcham Road   +44 (20) 8767 3666
London SW17 9PD   www.turath.co.uk

Author Mawlānā Zafar Aḥmad al-ʿUthmānī
Translation Abdassamad Clarke, Aisha Bewley
Editor Shamshudduha, Mansur Ali
General editor Yahya Batha

British Library Cataloguing in Publication Data
ʿUthmānī, Zafar Aḥmad
Qawāʿid fī ʿUlūm al-Ḥadīth
I. Title

Cover Design & Typesetting ARM (www.whitethreadpress.com)
Printed by Megaprinters, Istanbul, Turkey (export@mega.com.tr)

Distributors for UK and Europe
Azhar Academy Ltd.
54–56 Little Ilford Lane   +44 (20) 8891 19797
Manor Park   sales@azharacademy.com
London E12 5QA   www.azharacademy.com

Distributors for America and Canada
White Thread Press
www.whitethreadpress.com
inf@whitethreadpress.com

Distributors for South Africa
Darul-Ihsan Research and Education Centre
www.darulihsan.com/shop   +27 (31) 577 7868
bookshop@darulihsan.com

For

Mufti Shabbir Ahmad Patel

of Darul Uloom Bury

CONTENTS

PUBLISHER'S NOTE

First and formoest all praises are due to Allah ﷻ for helping us through the transaltion and publication of this book. In line with Prophetic tradition, "He who is not grateful to fellow people is not grateful to Allah ﷻ" we would like to thank the many people who have toiled and troubled to see this project from beginning to publication. We would like to acknoweldege and thank Sister Aisha Bewley and sidi Abdassamad Clarke for the translation of this difficult text. We would also like to show our appreciation to Brother Zameelur Rahman for providing us with a translation of Shaykh ʿAbd al-Fattāḥ Abū Ghudda's commendation of the *Iʿlāʾ as-Sunan* as well has his translation of Mufti Taqi Usmani's introduction to the *Iʿlāʾ as-Sunan*. Special graditude is shown to Mawlana Shamsudduha and Mawlana Dr Muhammad Mansur Ali for painstakingly editing and proof-reading the text. The latter for also providing an introduction to the history of *uṣūl al-ḥadīth*, which originally formed a part of his PhD thesis. The Cambridge Muslim College warrants our sincere appreciation for providing Mawlana Mansur Ali with the time, space, resource and finance to edit the translation. Finally, the publishers, the translators and the editors would like to express their awe and gratidude to the four people in the shadow of whose minds they had the honour of working: Shaykh ʿAbd al-Fattāḥ Abū Ghudda, Shaykh Ẓafar Aḥmad al-ʿUthmānī, Shaykh Ashraf ʿAlī at-Thānawī and our liege-lord the Holy Prophet ﷺ.

Yahya Batha

EDITOR'S FOREWORD

PRAISE BELONGS to Allah, hallowed be his name, who created the heavens and the earth and made darkness and light; yet the disbelievers set up equals to their Lord! Praise be to Him, who guided us to this: had He not guided us, We would never have found the way. May he shower a thousand bouquet of blessings and salutations upon his beloved and messenger, the apple of our eyes, and on his blessed family and on the stalwart imams of this ummah through whom we received the sacred knowledge. May Allah ﷻ give them the best of rewards from our behalf.

The current work is a translation of the ḥadīth introduction to the *Iʿlāʾ as-Sunan* known as *Inhāʾ as-Sakan ilā man Yuṭāliʿ Iʿlā as-Sunan.*[1] It is commonly known as *Muqaddimat Iʿlāʾ as-Sunan* and has been rendered by Shaykh ʿAbd al-Fattāḥ Abū Ghuddah as *Qawāʿid fī ʿUlūm al-Ḥadīth*. We have greately benefitted from Shaykh Abū Ghudda's edition of the text and extensively quoted him in the footnotes. We will have the opportunity to discuss the content of the *Muqaddimah* and the different stages of its authorship in more details further on in this introduction. Here we will suffice by saying that we have not provided a biography for the author, as the respected Mufti Taqi Usmani sahib has done us great service by providing us with the biography of the author in his introduction to his edition of the *Iʿlāʾ as-Sunan.*[2] In his introduction, Mufti sahib, includes the biography of Mawlana Ashraf ʿAlī at-Thānawī, the biography of Mawlana Ẓafar Aḥmad al-ʿUthmānī, Shaykh Abū Ghudda's biography of the author, Mawlana at-Thānawī's forward to the second edition of the *Iḥyāʾ as-Sunan* and Mawlana at-Thānawī's forward to the second volume of the *Iʿlaʾ as-Sunan*. This introduction has been kindly translated by Brother Zameelur Rahman and can be found in appendix two of this book.[3]

---

1 There is also a *fiqh* introduction to *the Iʿlāʾ as-Sunan* written by Mawlana Ḥabīb Aḥmad al-Kirānawī.

2 *Iʿlāʾ as-Sunan*, Idarat al-Qur'an wa al-'Ulum al-Islamiyyah, Karachi: Pakistan, 1427 H, 1:9–33.

3 P. 253.

TRACING THE *SUNNA* THROUGH TEXTUAL AND NON-TEXTUAL SOURCES

The science of ḥadīth (*uṣūl al-ḥadīth*) is the technical subject which is concerned with the rules, methods and principles for the preservation, audition, reception, transmission and understanding of the ḥadīth. Like all sciences, it has evolved and developed over the centuries with inputs from some of the finest minds history has witnessed. The current work is a continuation of this collective endevour. Therefore it is in order that we discuss some of the history of this development so that the current work can be situatuated in its correct context.

By way of illustration we will start this section by referring to a divorce case that took place during the time of the Prophet ﷺ. Abū ʿAmr ibn Hafṣ al-Makhzūmi irrevocably divorced his wife Fāṭima bint Qays. When al-Makhzūmī did not allocate any lodging (*suknā*) or maintance (*nafaqa*) for her, she complained to the Prophet ﷺ who agreed with the decision of al-Makhzūmī and ordered her to spend her waiting period (*ʿiddat*) in the house of the blind Companion ʿAbdullāh ibn Umm Maktūm. Years later when some ḥadīth scholars where discussing this issue, Ibrāhīm, told his colleagues about the opinion of ʿUmar ibn al-Khaṭṭab who said regarding this case 'we will not leave the Words of Allah ﷻ and the *sunna* of the Prophet ﷺ for the words of a woman regarding whom we are not sure if she remembers properly or has forgotten.' The narrator says, "ʿUmar used to allocate [for the triply-divorced women] both lodging and maintainance.'[4] After narrating this ḥadīth imam at-Tirmidhī presents the opinion of three groups of scholars who differed regarding the allocation of maintenance and lodging for a triply-divorced woman.

1. Al-Ḥasan al-Baṣrī, ʿAṭāʾ ibn Abī Rābāḥ, ash-Shaʿbī, imam Aḥmad, and Ishāq are of the opinion that the triply divorced woman is not entitled to maintenance or lodging.
2. ʿUmar ibn al-Khāṭṭāb, ʿAbd Allāh ibn Masʿūd, Sufyān ath-Thawrī and the people of Kūfa[5] are of the opinion that she is entitled to maintenance and lodging.
3. Imām Mālik, Layth ibn Saʿd and ash-Shāfiʿī are of the opinion that she is entitled to lodging only and not maintenance.

Sayyidunā ʿUmar's opinion is based on the Qurʾānic verse, 'House the wives you are divorcing according to your means, wherever you house yourselves, and do not harass them so as to make their lives difficult.'[6] The verse is explicit in providing lodging for her and implicit in providing maintenance. He also comes to this conclusion by

4 At-Tirimidhī, *Sunan*, ḥ. 1180.
5 This is also the opinion of imam Abū Ḥanīfah.
6 Surat aṭ-Ṭalāq, 65:6.

observing the general practice of the Prophet ﷺ which is in line with this verse thus his words, 'we will not leave the Words of Allah ﷻ and the *sunna* of the Prophet ﷺ [...].' Imam Abū Ḥanīfah concurs with this opinion. Imām Aḥmad's main source for his opinion is the ḥadīth of Faṭima bint Qays. For Imām ash-Shāfiʿī, lodging is proven from the Qurʾān and not providing maintenance from this ḥadīth. As for her not getting lodging in this ḥadīth, he says that it's due to Allah's ﷻ Words, 'Do not make them leave their homes, nor should they leave themselves-unless they commit a flagarant indecency (*fāḥishah mubayyina*).[7] *Fāḥisha mubayyina*, according to imam ash-Shāfiʿī means to be foul-mouthed (*al-badhāʾ*). Since Fāṭima bint Qays used harsh language towards her in-laws, as established from many narrations of this ḥadīth, according to ash-Shāfiʿī, this is why she lost her rights to lodgining. Imām Mālik basis his opinion on the Qurʾān and the practice of the people of Medina. Thus he says in the *Muwaṭṭāʾ*, 'This is what is done among us (*wa hādha 'l-amr ʿindanā*).'[8]

At first blush it may seem a bit odd to introduce an *uṣūl al-ḥadīth* book with this ḥadīth unless one is to assume that by *uṣūl al-ḥadīth* I mean the differences of the ʿulamāʾ in *fiqh*. However, upon closer inspection, it may dawn upon the reader that the issue here is not mere differences of opinion, but rather deep methodological differences. In other words, this ḥadīth is a good prism to look at the different methodlogical frameworks and hermeneutical devices that the ʿulamāʾ employ in their understanding of the shariʿah. The following table with help understand the point being made.

Name of Imam	Fiqh Position	Main source for opinion
Imam Abū Ḥanīfah	Lodging and maintenance	Qurʾān/*sunna*/ʿUmar
Imam Mālik	Lodging only no maintenance	Qurʾān/practice of the people of Medina
Imam ash-Shāfiʿī	Lodging only no maintenance	Qurʾān/Ḥadīth
Imam Aḥmad	No lodging and no maintenance	Ḥadīth

Table 1.1 Position of ʿulāmā on Fāṭima bint Qays Ḥadīth

What can be gleaned from the above is that the scholars' attitude towards the sources has a direct bearing on the way they arrive at a *fiqh* position. After the Qur'ān it's the *sunna* of the Prophet ﷺ which is the major source of the sharīʿah. But how is one to accurately ascertain what constitutes the *sunna* of the Prophet ﷺ? This question is pertinent since (a) there are no video or audio recordings of the Prophet's ﷺ words and actions or any original documents extant which are contemporaneous to the

7 Ibid., 65:1.

8 Mālik, *Muwaṭṭāʾ*, h. 2156.

Prophet ﷺ which can be resorted to and (b) if salvation depends on a precise following of the *sunna* of the Prophet ﷺ, then Muslims need to be certain what these *sunna*s were.

Muslim scholars have always understood the importance as well as the difficulty in tracing the Prophetic *sunna*. Right from the time of the Companions they set about formulating a method and formula, albeit primitive and rudimentary at its inception, for preserving the *sunna*. This method developed in complexity and precision as the distance in time and place between the Prophet ﷺ and the Muslim community grew. However, the underlying features of the method are simple and natural and something that we use in our everyday life. The method depends on transmitting information honestly and accurately and then corroborating this information by comparing it with others who have also transmitted the same information. The information that is transmitted takes the form of a simple statement that a Companion heard the Prophet ﷺ say such-and-such words or saw the Prophet ﷺ do such-and-such an action. The names of the transmitters are prefixed to the statement, which then function as a bibliography as well as an attestation for the narrator. These simple statements came to be known as ḥadīth. In this manner the scholars made an attempt to preserve and trace the *sunna* of the Prophet ﷺ through a text-based medium. The text-based medium originated initially as oral transmissions, supplemented with written notes for memory aid, and later became fixed as written texts in books.[9]

However, the *sunna* has not always been traced through a text-based medium (i.e. ḥadīth). In early Islam two other methods which grew simultaneously with the textual (ḥadīth) approach were employed to seek out the Prophetic *sunna*: (1) the practice of the Muslim community and (2) the spirit of the law. Due to the efforts of some scholars such as imam ash-Shāfiʿī and the incentive to bring some uniformity to the disparate behavior of Muslims the textual (ḥadīth) approach gained prominence and ossified into becoming the sole repository of the *sunna*. Henceforth *sunna* and ḥadīth became synonymous to the extent that Zubair Siddiqi states that any

---

9 This view is in contrast to what some Muslim scholars have put forward that right from its inception ḥadīth was written down and documented in books. Shaykh Dr. M. Muṣṭafā Aʿzamī has mentioned the written works of fifty Companions and forty-nine Followers from the first century, eighty-seven from the end of the first and the beginning of the second century and a further 251 works of second century scholars who all predate al-Bukhārī. See M. Muṣṭafā Aʿzamī, *Studies in Early Ḥadīth Literature with a Critical Edition of Some Early Texts*, 3rd ed., (Indiana: American Trust Publication, 1992), pp. 28–182. However, it seems that shaykh Aʿzamī has granted too much power to ink and paper. His approach was shaped by the allegations that were leveled against ḥadīth by Orienatlists. The Orientalists claimed that historicity cannot be granted to ḥadīth because there are no contemporary written works available from the time it is claimed they originate. The textual fetish (a term coined by Dr. Iftikhar Zaman) of the Orientalists and shaykh Aʿzamī's aggressive defense do not take into consideration that reality has more to it than what has been registered with ink and paper.

attempt to draw a distinction between them has remained highly theoretical.[10] The collections of ḥadīth known as *Sunan* (plural of *sunna*), such as *Sunan at-Tirmidhī* and *Sunan Abī Dawūd,* are yet further proof that the connotations of both words have become one. The *Sunan* collections are a special type of ḥadīth book which only deal with the legal aspect of a Muslim's life, and yet not surprisingly the *sunna*s are derived from ḥadīth texts. Nonetheless, the earlier scholars did understand a difference between ḥadīth and *sunna,* and this is why we find imam ʿAbd ar-Raḥmān ibn al-Mahdī (d. 198/814) saying that the Kufan scholar imam Sufyān ath-Thawrī (d. 161/778) is an imam of ḥadīth and not of *sunna* and the Syrian scholar imam al-Awzāʿī (d. 157/774) is an imam of *sunna* and not of ḥadīth, whereas the Medinan scholar imam Mālik ibn Anas is an imam of both ḥadīth and *sunna*.[11]

We will now engage the two alternative approaches to the *sunna*, as these have direct bearings on shaykh al-ʿUthmānī's *Qawāʿid fī ʿUlūm al-Ḥadīth*. When one starts to read the *Qawāʿid*, one will begin to realize that the author conforms to a pre-Shāfiʿī *uṣūl al-ḥadīth* and yet brialliantly proves his case from post-Shāfiʿī *uṣūl al-ḥadīth* texts. Before we proceed, it should be said that there are no strict demarcations between these approaches and there is a level of osmosis going on between them. To think otherwise is misleading and ahistorical.

Imam Mālik and Medinan ʿAmal

Imām Mālik ibn Anas al-Aṣbaḥī (93–179/711–795) is the person after whom the Mālikī school of thought takes its name. Imam Mālik lived, grew up and died in Medina. Unlike his contemporaries who went out into the world to seek knowledge, Imam Mālik remained in Medina and sought knowledge from the teachers there and subsequently went on to become one of the greatest teachers that Medina, or indeed the whole of Islam, has ever witnessed. Thus, the appellation that was designated to him *imām dār al-hijra* and *ʿālim al-Madīna* although fitting is in reality an understatement.

For imam Mālik the city of Medina and its scholars held a sentimental value because he saw that the essence of the true *sunna* lies in the practice of the people of Medina. This is because Medina was the city where the Prophet ﷺ and his Companions migrated to and where most of the Companions lived out their lives. In a letter addressed to his contemporary in Egypt, al Layth ibn Saʿd (d. 175/791), advising him regarding the true meaning of the *sunna* after finding out that Layth was issuing religious verdict contrary to the practice of the people of Medina. Imam Mālik writes:

10 M. Z. Siddiqi, *Ḥadīth Literature, Its Origin, Development and Special Features,* ed. by and rev. by Timothy Winter, (Cambridge: The Islamic Text Society 1993), p. 2.

11 Qāḍī ʿIyāḍ, *Tartīb al-Madārik wa Taqrīb al-Masālik li Maʿrifat Aʿlām Madhhab Mālik*, ed. by Aḥmad Bākir Maḥmūd (Beirut: [n. pub.], 1967) 1:132.

It has come to my notice that you give decisions on religious matters which go against the position of the scholars of this city of ours. You are a leading scholar, a man of position and eminence in your area. People need you and trust you in your decisions. Because of this you must fear for yourself and tread the path that is likely to take you to safety [. . .].

All people are subordinate to the people of Medina. To it the *hijra* was made and in it the Qurʾān was revealed, the lawful made lawful and the forbidden made forbidden. The Messenger of Allah ﷺ, was living amongst them and they were present during the very act of revelation. He would tell them to do things and they would obey him, and he would institute *sunnas* for them and they would follow him, until Allah ﷻ took him to Himself and chose for him what is in His presence ﷺ.

[. . .] So, if there is something which is clearly acted upon in Medina *(idhā kāna al-amr bi ʾl-Madīna ẓāhir maʿmūl bih)*, I am not of the opinion that anyone may go against it, because of this inheritance that [the Medinans] have which it is not permissible for any other to ascribe to, or claim for, themselves. Even if the people of other cities were to say, 'This is the practice (*ʿamal*) in our city', or 'This is what those before us used to do', they would not have the same authority for that, nor would it be permissible for them in the way that it is for [the people of Medina].[12]

The observation that can be made from the above paragraphs is that for imam Mālik the blessed presence of the Prophet ﷺ and the Companions and the revelation of the Qurʾān in it has endowed Medina with a divine authority and sanctity which no other city can boast or claim. His mode of writing almost has a superior tone when he writes, 'All people are subordinate to the people of Medina', and where he writes in the last paragraph that no one is allowed to go against the opinions of the people of Medina, nor are they to claim any kind of authority for their own provinces.

As an important side-note, which will help us understand imam Mālik's approach better, it should be mentioned here that as far as the epistemic value of ḥadīth is concerned all ḥadīth fall into three categories: (1) that which carries an epistemic certainty is known as *mutawātir,* (2) the pseudo-ḥadīth which is certainly fallacious is called *mawḍūʿ* and (3) finally the ḥadīth whose epistemic value is probable is known as *āḥād* (lone). The *mutwātir* ḥadīth, in the words of Ḥanafī scholar ʿĪsā ibn Abān (d. 221/836) is that which

is related by a large group of people whose opinions and concerns are so different that it would have been impossible for them to collude [. . .].[13]

---

12 Ibid., 1:64–5, cited in Yasin Dutton, *The Origins of Islamic Law: The Qurʾān, the Muwaṭṭāʾ and Madinan ʿAmal,* (London: RoutledgeCurzon, 2002), pp. 37–38.

13 ʿĪsā ibn Abān quoted in Murtaza Bedir, "An Early Response to al-Shāfiʿī: ʿĪsā ibn Abān on the Prophetic Report (*Khabar*)", *Islamic Law and Society,* (2002), p. 11.

In contrast to this an *āḥād* ḥadīth is the one whose number of conveyors falls short of the number of a *mutwātir.* Therefore a *mutawātir* ḥadīth yields *a priori* necessary certain (*ḍarūrī/yaqīnī*) knowledge on part of the listener and denying it is viewed as blasphemous. Examples of *mutawātir* are universal truths about Islam such as the Qurʾān being the book of God, Muḥammad ﷺ is the last Prophet, and worship such as prayer, and fasting and giving alms are mandatory. On the other hand the *āḥād* report only yields *a posteriori* probable (*ẓannī*) knowledge as a result of which a denier of this category cannot be charged with blasphemy. Another point that needs to be clarified here is that there are no contradictions between a ḥadīth being āḥād and *ṣaḥīḥ* at the same time because *āḥād* is in respect to the quantity of people narrating a ḥadīth whereas *ṣaḥīḥ* is in respect to the quality of the narrators involved. This is why no one has a problem with at-Tirmidhī compounding both the terms and saying this is a *ṣaḥīḥ gharīb* (another synonym for *āḥād*) ḥadīth. *Mutawātir* ḥadīth are very few in number, and most of the ḥadīth available are from the category of *āḥād.*

After understanding the different epistemic values that a ḥadīth can yield we can carry on with Mālik's approach to the *sunna* and ḥadīth. As has been mentioned above, the scholars tried their uttermost best to find the best channel to trace the *sunna* of the Prophet ﷺ. It goes without saying that the more epistemic certainty that an approach can guarantee the greater the confidence can be put in the *sunna* that is extracted through it. In his pursuit in finding the *sunna,* imam Mālik believed that by observing the practices of the people of Medina better results can be distilled than by attempting to trace the *sunna* through lone ḥadīth texts. There are many examples in the *Muwaṭṭāʾ* where the text of the ḥadīth says something which Mālik disregards on the basis that it is not a known practice of the people of Medina, even though the ḥadīth *is* prefixed with a perfectly reliable *isnād.* A famous example is that of the ḥadīth *of* the Prophet ﷺ regarding conditional sales (*bayʿ al-khiyār*). Mālik reports:

> Mālik—from (*ʿan*)—Nāfiʿ—from—Ibn ʿUmar that the Prophet ﷺ said, 'The parties to a sale are at liberty to withdraw from the sale as long as they do not separate, except when they themselves specify a period within which such withdrawal must take place.[14]

Imam Mālik concludes the chapter by making the following remark, 'There is no fixed limit for this [conditional sale] according to us nor is it an established practice (*laysa li hādhā ʿindanā ḥadd maʿrūf wa lā ʾl-amr maʿmūl bih*).'

---

14 Malik, *Muwaṭṭāʾ* with commentary *Awjaz al-Masālik,* 13:128. Translation of ḥadīth by Ghassan Abdul-Jabbar, *Bukhari,* (New Delhi: Oxford University Press, 2007), p. 77.

What this ḥadīth means is that a buyer and a seller have the right to make void a transaction as long as they have not departed and gone their own ways. Scholars such as ash-Shāfiʿī have taken this ḥadīth *literally,* thus they say that a transaction is not complete until the parties involved do not physically depart from each other. However, Mālik declines to accept this ḥadīth *on* the basis that it is not a known custom of the people of Medina, although the narrators in the *isnād* of the ḥadīth *are* not only authentic but this particular *isnād* has been dubbed as the golden chain (*al-isnād adh-dhahabī*) by the likes of al-Bukhārī.[15] Ghassan Abdul-Jabbar further elaborates on this point by saying:

> From numerous individual ḥadīths, from the practice of the business in Medina and reports regarding this practice, it is clear that conditional sales are legal, but the conditions must be specific. Mālik's comment was: 'We are not aware of any known limit for this. . . ' How long will this option to withdraw remain? If two people are together for a long time, say in a boat, must they find a way to separate before the sale will be final? Of the hundreds of sales Mālik must himself have witnessed and read about, he did not find that people felt the need to separate to finalise a sale.
>
> In addition, if a person were to make a sale conditional upon something without a known limit, such a condition would be void. How could religious law itself specify such a condition?[16]

This is only one example out of a plethora of examples which can be produced from Mālik's *magnum opus* the *Muwaṭṭāʾ* to demonstrate that it is the practice of the people of Medina that dictates the meaning and acceptance of ḥadīth and not the other way round.[17]

Imam Abū Ḥanīfah and the logic of God

The second channel for tracing the sunna of the Prophet ﷺ that was prevalent symbiotically with the Medinan *ʿamal* as well as the text-based ḥadīth approach is the conviction that there is an underlying logic in God's command. This logic is not to be sought in isolated statements but rather is derived from looking at patterns and similarities in thousands of specific cases of law as well as a close reading of the Qurʾān and *sunna.*[18] This is a very tedious approach and is only accessible to someone who not only possesses a sharp acumen but who has also spent years researching every possible aspect of a Muslim's life that relates to religious law, even hypotheti-

15 Ibn aṣ-Ṣalāḥ, *ʿUlūm al-Ḥadīth*, p. 23.

16 Ghassan Abdul-Jabbar, *Bukhari*, pp. 77–78.

17 For more on this see Yasin Dutton's excellent study on the *Muwaṭṭāʾ*; *The Origins of Islamic Law: The Qur'an, the Muwaṭṭāʾ and Madinan ʿAmal*, (London: RoutledgeCurzon, 2002).

18 See Akram Nadwi, *Abū Ḥanīfah: His Life, Legal Method and Legacy*, (Leicester, Kube Publishing Ltd., 2010); and Mansur Ali's review of the book in *Muslim World Book Review*, 31:4, 2011, pp. 29–31.

cal ones that do not exist, and who is also well versed in issuing religious verdicts and *fatwās*. Colin Imber, an expert on Ottoman history, eloquently summarizes the effort exerted by scholars to find the logic of God, he writes:

> A further characteristic of Islamic law is its tendency to devote energy and space to discussions of cases which have no application in reality. Jurists frequently take a practical rule of law and then discuss its hypothetical ramifications in ever more minute detail. This concern with details which often have little or no bearing on reality is an important element in Islamic jurisprudence. Law, in fact, was seen only in part as offering a practical legal system. Taken as a whole, it represents God's will, or at least man's effort to discover God's will. It is therefore an act of piety to examine every tiny aspect of a legal rule, however remote from the real world, because it is by doing so that man comes to know God's infinity. There has never been an expectation that mankind can, in practice, conform to the law in every detail. This remains a pious aspiration, but never a present reality.[19]

The approach to seeking the *sunna* in God's logic in his law is a salient characteristic of the scholars of Iraq in general and imam Abū Ḥanīfah (80–150/699–767) in particular. Imam Abū Ḥanīfah, a Persian by descent is the eponymous fountain-head of the Ḥanafī School of law. He was born in Kufa where he started out as a merchant and then later devoted himself to religious knowledge, first as a theologian and then as a jurist-consult.

The incentive for seeking the wisdom underlying religious ordinances had it influence in the intellectual and political situation of Iraq in imam Abū Ḥanīfah's time. The metropolitans of Iraq, due to influences from within and outwith Islam, were a more complex and advanced society than that of the unadulterated society of Medina. Hence, resorting to ḥadīth texts to seek out the *sunna* proved to be a daunting task because the ḥadīth texts were too raw and circumstantial to fulfill the daily religious needs of the people as well as to provide fresh answers for newly-emerging issues and problems. Therefore an attempt was made to understand the *sunna* through a holistic reading of the Qurʾān and ḥadīth thus formulating universal formulae on the basis of this reading. These formulae then became the standard and basis for tackling arising problems. The concoction of these formulae resulted in any lone reports that went against the standards to be rejected as anomalous (*shādhdh*) or modified (*taʾwīl*) to fit in with the general sense of the Qurʾān and *sunna*. Imam Abū Ḥanīfah's apologist and disciple imam Abū Yūsuf (d. 180/798) writes:

> Stay away from unusual ḥadīths. Hold fast to those ḥadīth that the community of

19 Colin Imber, *The Ottoman Empire, 1300–1640: the Structure of Power*, (New York: Palgrave Macmillan, 2002), p. 221.

> scholars has accepted, which the people of *fiqh* recognise, which are in harmony with the Qurʾān and the *sunna*. A ḥadīth that goes against the Qurʾān is not from the messenger of God even if [sound] narrators narrate it![20]

In another place he writes:

> Ḥadīth multiplies so much so that some ḥadīths which are traced back through chains of transmission are not well-known to legal experts, nor do they conform to the Qur'an and *sunna*. Beware of solitary ḥadīths and keep close to the 'collective spirit (*al-jamāʿah*)' of ḥadīth.[21]

For imam Abū Ḥanīfah Islamic law is like an edifice. Before removing or replacing any of the bricks or making changes to the structure, imam Abū Ḥanīfah will always ask what effect this change will have on the structure as a whole. If by removing a single brick the whole building is left in jeopardy, imam Abū Ḥanīfah will leave the brick in place keeping in mind the interests of the whole edifice. It was due to his deep understanding of the workings of the shari'ah that the ḥadīth scholar Sulaymān ibn Mahrān al-Aʿmash (d. 148/765) said to imam Abū Ḥanīfah 'you (the *faqīhs*) are the physicians of ḥadīth and we (the *muḥaddith*) are only pharmacists.'[22]

At the heart of the matter is an attempt to accurately follow the *sunna* through means which will yield epistemic certainty (*yaqīn*) as opposed to probable knowledge (*ẓann*). For imam Abū Ḥanīfah, the principles induced (*istiqrāʾ*) through a wide range of reading of the Qurʾān and ḥadīth is certain knowledge, whilst the narration of a lone narrator (*khabr wāḥid*), even though it may be *ṣaḥīḥ*, does not hold the same surety and certainty. Hence in the case of a conflict between the two, the certain is given preference over the probable. Or to put it in another way, the *sunna* (spirit of the prophetic teaching) is given preference over the ḥadīth (the literal words of the Prophet ﷺ).[23] The author discusses this point in many places of the book,[24] and in one place he has a whole sub-heading which reads 'The basis of the Ḥanafī position that when a single report contradicts the well-known *sunna* it is irregular (*shādhdh*), it is the same when it is reported about a general need.'[25] The following are some examples which will help to comprehend this point better.

---

20 Abū Yūsuf, *ar-Radd ʿalā Siyar al-Awzāʿī*, cited in Ghassan Abdul-Jabbar, *Bukhari*, p. 76.

21 Ibid., citied in Fazlur Rahman, "The Living *Sunna* and Ahl-Sunna wa'l Jamāʿah", in P. K. Koya (ed.), *Ḥadīth and Sunna: Ideals and Realities* (Kuala Lumpur: Islamic Book Trust, 1996), pp. 152–53.

22 Al-Khaṭīb al-Baghdādī, *Naṣīḥat Ahl al-Ḥadīth*, (Maktabat al-Shamela: digital print), p. 45.

23 See, al-Kawtharī, *Fiqh ahl al-ʿIrāq wa ḥadīthuhum*, with Shaykh Abu Ghudda's footnotes, (Beirut: Muʾassasat ar-Rayyān, 1997), pp. 45–50. This booklet can be found in the introduction to Shaykh ʿAwwāma's edition of az-Zaylaʿī's *Naṣb ar-Rāyah*.

24 Pp. 44, 44, 62, 62, 162.

25 P. 162.

Imam Abū Ḥanīfah rejects the ḥadīth, 'A Muslim will not be killed in retribution for the murder of a non-Muslim,'[26] on the basis that it goes against a higher authority with stronger epistemic value i.e. the Qurʾān. His rejection of this otherwise perfectly sound ḥadīth is on the basis that it holds no sanctity for human life which is in contrary to the teachings of the Qurʾān and the established *sunna*, as Allah ﷻ says in the Qurʾān 'You who believe! Fair retribution is proscribed for you in the case of murder,'[27] and 'We prescribed for them in it: a life for a life.'[28]

Imam Abū Ḥanīfah also rejects lone ḥadīth if it goes against an established practice. This established practice is not only confined to the practice of the people of Medina as imam Mālik would want us to believe. On the contrary, every major city had its own established practice. In his response to imam Mālik's, above mentioned letter, al-Layth ibn Saʿd writes:

> When something that the Companions of the Prophet ﷺ [residing] in Egypt, the Levant and Iraq practiced during the reign of Abū Bakr, ʿUmar and ʿUthmān, and they [the Companions] left this world whilst still practicing this point, they [the caliphs] did not order [the people] to act on the contrary. We do not see it permissible for the Muslim mass to innovate an act upon which their predecessors from the Companions of the Prophet e and the Successors did not practice although the Companions of the Prophet e differed greatly whilst issuing religious verdicts.[29]

Concerning combining two prayers in one time during heavy rain (which imam Mālik's teacher Ibn Shihāb az-Zuhrī deemed to be correct), he further writes:

> The rain in the Levant is much more than the rain in Medina, the extent of which only Allah ﷻ knows. However not a single imam from them [i. e. the *imams* of the Levant] have combined [the prayers] on a rainy night although amongst them were Abū ʿUbayda ibn al-Jarrāḥ, Khālid ibn Walīd, Yazīd ibn Abī Sufyān, ʿAmr ibn al-ʿĀṣ and Muʿādh ibn Jabal. It has reached us that the Prophet ﷺ, said, 'The most knowledgeable amongst you regarding the lawful and unlawful is Muʿādh ibn Jabal... [Also amongst them were] Sharahbīl ibn Ḥasana, Abū'd-Dardāʾ and Bilāl ibn Rabāḥ. In Egypt there were Abū Dharr, Zubayr ibn al-ʿAwwām and Saʿd ibn Abī Waqqāṣ. In Ḥimṣ there were seventy Companions [who fought in the battle of *Badr*]. In Iraq there were ʿAbd Allah ibn Masʿūd, Ḥudhayfa ibn al-Yamān and ʿImrān ibn Ḥusayn. The leader of the believers ʿAlī ibn Abī Ṭalib, with whom there were other Com-

---

26 Al-Bukhārī, at-Tirmidhī.

27 *Sūrat al-Baqara*, 2:178.

28 *Sūrat al-Māʾida*, 5:45.

29 *Risālat al-Layth ibn Saʿd ilā Mālik ibn Anas*, incorporated fully by Ibn al-Qayyim al-Jawziyya in his *Iʿlām al-Muwaqqiʿīn*. See Ibn al-Qayyim al-Jawziyya, *Iʿlām al-Muwaqqiʿīn*, ed. by ʿIṣām ad-Dīn, (Cairo: Dār al-Ḥadīth, 2002), 3:66.

> panions of the Prophet ﷺ, also took up residence there. None ever combined the Maghrib and ʿIshāʾ prayer ever [during heavy rain].[30]

If the *ʿamal* of the people of Medina holds the same level of epistemic value as the *mutawātir* ḥadīth for imam Mālik, then for imam Abū Ḥanīfah, an action that involve the life of the whole community (*ʿumūm balwā*) holds similar value. Hence if an action that affects the whole community is only being reported by lone ḥadīths, this ḥadīth immediately comes under suspicion. The reason for this being, if the action being discussed was so prevalent in the community, why is only one person reporting it? An example of this is the ḥadīth concerning *rafʿ al-yadayn* (the raising of the hands in prayer other than at the beginning) which are all *āḥād* reports.

These three examples should suffice for the time being. The author will discuss this point in a myriad places in the book. Not understanding imam Abū Ḥanīfah's overall methodology has led some, who have a very superficial knowledge of the inner workings of Islamic law, to maintain that he either did not know any ḥadīth or gives more preference to analogy (*qiyās*) over ḥadīth. Nothing can be further from the truth.

The Ḥadīth Movement

As the distance between the time of the Prophet ﷺ and the Muslim community became wider the possibility of observing the *sunna* in the practices of the community became remote. One of the reasons for this was the widespread dispersion of knowledge. Specific regional knowledge and the practices of the Companions and early Muslims were disseminated through *riḥla* (travels) to the extent that it was no longer possible for a person to observe and extract the *sunna* from local practices.

An unrestrained use of analogy and syllogism led to granting too much importance to the intellect and, contrary to what imam Abū Ḥanīfah ؓ had advocated, this initiated free thinking which, at times, disregarded any kind of fidelity to the letter of the scriptures. The wide dissemination of knowledge and the unrestrained use of analogy gave way to a number of contradictory views and doctrines. Scholars concerned with persevering the Prophetic *sunna* saw a strong urgency to unify the Muslim community under one umbrella.[31] They believed that if consistency could be imposed in the method of formulating doctrines then the assumption was that uniformity in doctrines would follow. The point of reference, about which no Muslim would disagree, was the Prophet Muḥammad ﷺ. They believed that resorting solely to the Prophet ﷺ would ensure uniformity. Thus, this time the ḥadīth was chosen to become the sole repository of the *sunna* and henceforth became identical with the word *sunna*. Imam Ash-Shāfiʿī writes:

---

30 Ibid.

31 Eerik Dickenson, *The Development of Early Sunnite Ḥadīth Criticism*, (Leiden: Brill, 2001), p. 1.

> If a tradition is authenticated as coming from the Prophet ﷺ, we have to resign ourselves to it, and your talk and the talk of others about why and how is a mistake... The question of how can only be applied to human opinions which are derivative and devoid of authority; if obligatory orders, by asking why, could be subjected to analogy or to the scrutiny of reason, there would be no end to arguing, and analogy itself would break down.[32]

Coming back to the issue of wide-spread dissemination of ḥadīth-knowledge), it seems that the great ḥadīth scholar ʿAlī ibn al-Madīnī (d. 234/849) noticed its implications in his discussion of the pioneers of ḥadīth in his book *Kitāb al-ʿIlal*. He lists the names of twenty-four scholars who played a pivotal role in receiving and transmitting ḥadīth. These twenty-four scholars have been grouped into four chronological categories: six in the first, twelve in the second, three in the third and three in the fourth. It is interesting to note that for the scholars of the first two categories (i. e. the first eighteen scholars), Ibn al-Madīnī mentions their place of residence alongside their names. From the third category onwards he does not provide any geographical information. These two categories (i. e. third and fourth) span the course of a century starting from the second half of the first/eighth century (Yaḥyā ibn Zakariyya Abī Zāʾida (119–182/737–798)) and ending in the first half of the third/late eighth century (Yaḥyā ibn Ādam (130s–203/740s–818)). It is in this particular era that knowledge of the *sunna* was dispersed into different regions of the Muslim world through *riḥla* travels until it became no longer possible to trace it through local collective practice (*ʿamal*). The following tables will help put what has been said above in focus.

ʿAlī ibn al-Madīnī says, 'Upon reflection [on ḥadīth] I saw that chains of narrations rely on six people':

	Place of origin	Name of scholar	Date of birth and death
1	Medina	Ibn Shihāb az-Zuhr	50–124/670–741
2	Mecca	ʿAmr ibn Dīnār	46–126/666–743
3	Basra	Qatāda ibn Diʿāma	60–117/679–735
4	Basra	Yaḥyā ibn Abī Kathīr	?-132/?-749
5	Kufa	Abū Isḥāq as-Sabīʿī	32–127/652–744
6	Kufa	Sulaymān al-Aʿmash	61–148/680–765

He then says, 'The authors of topical (*muṣannaf*) collections who composed books and gathered the knowledge of these six are':

32 Ash-Shāfiʿī, *Ikhtilāf al-Ḥadīth*.

	Place of origin	Name of scholar	Date of birth and death
1	Medina	Mālik ibn Anas	93–179/711–795
2	Medina	Muḥammad ibn Isḥāq	85–152/704–769
3	Mecca	Ibn Jurayj	86–150/705–767
4	Mecca	Sufyān ibn ʿUyayna	107–198/725–813
5	Basra	Saʿīd ibn Abī ʿArūba	70–157/689–773
6	Basra	Ḥammād ibn Salama	c. 89–167/707–783
7	Basra	Abū ʿAwāna	?-175/?-791
8	Basra	Shuʿba ibn al-Ḥajjāj	82–160/701–776
9	Basra	Maʿmar Rāshid	95–153/713–770
10	Kufa	Sufyān ath-Thawrī	97–161/715–777
11	Wasit	Hushaym ibn Bashīr	104–183/722–799
12	Syria	ʿAbd ar-Raḥmān al-Awzāʿī	88–157/707–773

As has been iterated above, Ibn al-Madīnī provides geographical information for all eighteen scholars hitherto mentioned. But for the following names he does not provide this information. This supports the theory that it was in this particular era that knowledge of the *sunna* became widely dispersed to the extent that it was no longer possible to trace it through observing the actions of regional scholars. He further says, 'Then the knowledge of those six and the knowledge of these twelve came to:'

	Names of Scholars	Date of birth and death
1	Yaḥyā ibn Saʿīd al-Qaṭṭān	120–198/738–813
2	Yaḥyā ibn Zakariyya Abī Zāʾida	119–182/737–798
3	Wakīʿ ibn al-Jarrāḥ	129–197/746–812

Finally he says, 'Then the knowledge of these three came to':

	Names of Scholars	Date of birth and death
1	ʿAbd Allāh ibn al-Mubārak	118–181/736–797
2	ʿAbd ar-Raḥmān ibn al-Mahdī	135–198/752–813
3	Yaḥyā ibn Ādam	130s–203/740s–818

Table 1.2: ʿAlī al-Madīnī's taxonomy of ḥadīth Scholars[33]

The generation after the fourth category is known as the era of the *ṣaḥīḥ* movement. It was in this era that a serious effort was made to separate the accepted ḥadīth from the spurious ones. This was also the generation of al-Bukhārī and other authors of the canonical collections.

33 ʿAlī al-Madīnī, *kitāb al-ʿIlal*, ed. by M. M. Aʿzamī, (Beirut: al-Maktab al-Islāmī, n. d.), p. 5.

Two Examples of the Effects of the Wide Dispersion of Knowledge

The effect of the wide dissemination of knowledge not only had an effect on the way the *sunna* was sought solely from the ḥadīth texts but it also affected the scholars' attitude towards some of the technical terms that were used transmit and receive ḥadīth. We may elaborate on two of them: *mursal* and the early use of the preposition *ʿan*.

Example 1: The *Mursal* Ḥadīth

The term *mursal* is used when a Follower omits the name of a Companion and reports directly from the Prophet ﷺ. This is seen as a flaw in the *isnād*, as it can happen that a Follower might have been narrating from another Follower and not necessarily a Companion. Imam Ibn Ḥajar al-ʿAsqalānī (d. 852/1448) through his analysis of ḥadīth has managed to show the possibility of seven Followers narrating from each other horizontally in the same *isnād*.[34] Scholars who came after the widespread dispersion of knowledge such as imam ash-Shāfiʿī (d. 204/820) and Aḥmad Ibn Ḥanbal (d. 241/855) held the view that *irsāl* (the verbal noun of *mursal*) is a defect in the *isnād* which renders a ḥadīth *weak*. However, omission through *irsāl* did not pose a problem for scholars who came before this period such as imam Abū Ḥanīfah and Mālik, and accepting such ḥadīth was perfectly sound according to them. As-Suyūṭī writes:

> Ibn Jarīr [aṭ-Ṭabarī] says: 'All the Followers were unanimous on the point that a *mursal* ḥadīth *is* accepted, and it has not been transmitted from any of them that they have disputed its [validity] nor from the scholars who came after them until the beginning of the 3rd century.' Ibn ʿAbd al-Barr says, 'By this he means ash-Shāfiʿī was the first to have rejected it. . .'[35]

Imam Abū Dawūd as-Sijistānī (d. 275/888), the author of *Sunan Abī Dawūd*, writes in his epistle (*risāla*) to the people of Mecca:

> The scholars of the past such as Sufyān ath-Thawrī, Mālik ibn Anas and Awzāʿī [note that these names occur in Ibn al-Madīnī's second category] used to deem the *mursal* [ḥadīth] as authoritative until ash-Shāfiʿī came along and voiced his opposition regarding it and Ibn Ḥanbal followed suit.[36]

The reason why the early scholars such as imams Mālik and Abū Ḥanīfah accepted these ḥadīths was because they were students of the scholars who were narrating

34 Ibn Ḥajar, *Nuzhat an-Naẓar Sharḥ Nukhbat al-Fikir*, (Cairo: Maktabat al-ʿIlm, [n. d.]), p. 52.

35 As-Suyūṭī, *Tadrīb ar-Rāwī*, p. 104.

36 Abū Dāwūd, *Risāla ilā Ahl al-Makka*, in *Thalāth Rasāʾil fī Muṣṭalaḥ al-Ḥadīth*, ed. by ʿAbd al-Fattāḥ Abū Ghudda, 2nd ed., (Beirut: Dār al-Bashāʾir al-Islāmiyya, 2005), p. 32.

them directly from the Prophet ﷺ and they knew them personally. They interacted with them in their everyday life, they learnt from them by observing the *sunna* being practiced and were fully aware of their probity and erudition. As for imam ash-Shāfiʿī and Aḥmad ibn Ḥanbal, they could not claim this personal allegiance; therefore their approach to such ḥadīth was scientific, objective and skeptical. The question now remains why did the Followers practice *irsāl* (omitting the names of Companions from the *isnād*)? There may be many reasons why they did this, from simply forgetting the name of the Companion who narrated to them to fear of political oppression. For example Yūnus ibn ʿUbayd, a student of imam al-Ḥasan ibn Abī al-Ḥasan al-Baṣrī (d. 110/728) asked him why he omits the names of his sources from the *isnād*:

> O Abū Saʿīd [i. e. al-Ḥasan al-Baṣrī], why is it that you say *qāla rasūl Allāh* ﷺ (the Prophet ﷺ said), whereas you have never met the Prophet ﷺ? [al-Ḥasan replied] 'my nephew, you have asked me about something that I have never been asked before, and had you not been dear to me I would not have informed you. I am living in such a time, as you can see for yourself' [the narrator says]—It was the reign of Ḥajjāj ibn Yūsuf—that 'whenever you hear me saying, 'the Prophet ﷺ said', [in reality I am reporting it] from ʿAlī ibn Abī Ṭālib, but I am living in times where I can not mention the name of ʿAlī.'[37]

Another instance as to why the Followers practiced *irsāl* is documented by imam at-Tirmidhī in *Kitāb al-ʿIlal al-Ṣaghīr* that al-Aʿmash asked Ibrahīm an-Nakhaʿī (d. 108/726) to report something from the Companion Ibn Masʿūd without a break in the *isnād*. An-Nakhaʿī replied that whenever he narrates from a person from Ibn Masʿūd by mentioning the name of that person, then he has truly heard from him. However, when he directly narrates from Ibn Masʿūd, whom he did not meet, then it could be from a number of people but he has forgotten the names.[38]

Example 2: The *Muʿanʿan* Ḥadīth

The second example in which the effects of wide dispersion of knowledge can be viewed is in the use of the preposition *ʿan* in the *isnād* to indicate transmission of a ḥadīth from one person to the other, such as 'Mālik—from (*ʿan*)—Nāfiʿ—*ʿan*—Ibn ʿUmar.' The preposition ʿan used in the ḥadīth serves as a good example because through its usage we can see the transition of the Prophetic *sunna* from practice to

---

37 Yūsuf al-Mizzī, *Tahdhīb al-Kamāl*, ed. by Bashshār ʿAwwād Maʿrūf, (Beirut:Muʾassasat ar-Risāla, 1985), 6:124. Al-Ḥasan's reporting from ʿAlī ibn Abī Ṭālib has been disputed by the scholars. See as-Suyūṭī's article, *'Ittiḥāf al-Firqa bi Rafʿ al-Khirqa'*, and its refutation by ʿAbd Allāh ibn aṣ-Ṣiddīq al-Ghumārī, found in *Majmūʿ min Rasāʾil as-Suyūṭī*, (Beirut: Dār al-Kutub al-ʿIlmiyya, 2003), pp. 337–44, for a discussion for and against this view.

38 At-Tirmidhī, *Kitābal-ʿIlal al-Ṣaghīr*, p. 1079.

text. The preposition *ʿan,* in the context of ḥadīth studies, implies receiving ḥadīth from a narrator. However the mode of reception cannot be verified by looking at this preposition. The contention here is that *sunna* was passed down practically and scholars expressed it by using the preposition *ʿan.* On the other hand, post ash-Shāfiʿī we find a whole hoard of sophisticated terminologies through which it can be exactly pinpointed how a ḥadīth has been received. Therefore the term 'he reported to us'[39] means the student received the ḥadīth *from* the shaykh in the presence of other students. 'He reported to me'[40] means the student received the ḥadīth from the shaykh without anyone being present, and 'he informed us'[41] means that the student read the ḥadīth to the teacher in front of other students, 'he informed me'[42] means that he read the ḥadīth to the teacher without anyone being present. 'He granted me'[43] means that the shaykh has granted permission through a letter permitting the student to narrate ḥadīth from him and finally 'he permitted me'[44] means that the shaykh has given the student a license to narrated ḥadīth verbally.[45]

It is noticeable that in early ḥadīth narrations the use of the preposition *ʿan* is excessively used in the *isnād*. Indeed Mālik and Abū Ḥanīfah do not use anything other than it in their narrations. Similarly, in the latter part of the *isnād* (that part which refers to earlier narrators such as the Prophet ﷺ and is closest to the text of the ḥadīth) of most ḥadīth *isnād* the preposition *ʿan* can be excessively seen in comparison to the other terms such as *ḥaddathnā* and *akhbaranā*.[46] This is no coincidence since the earlier portion of the *isnād* corresponds with the first and second category of Ibn al-Madīnī's taxonomy. It was only afterwards, post ash-Shāfiʿī, when ḥadīth became the sole repository of the *sunna* that it became important to specify the mode of reception, audition, and transmission. An example from the *Muwaṭṭāʾ* of Mālik and the *Sunan* of at-Tirmidhī will help to illustrate this point better. The narrator of the *Muwaṭṭāʾ* says:

> Yaḥyā ibn Yaḥyā al-Laythī has reported to me (*ḥaddathanī*)—from (*ʿan*) Mālik—from (*ʿan*) Ibn Shihāb—that (*anna*) ʿUmar ibn ʿAbd al-ʿAzīz delayed the prayer one day[. . .].[47]

---

39 *Ḥaddathanā.*

40 *Ḥaddathanī.*

41 *Akhbaranā.*

42 *Akhbaranī.*

43 *Nāwalanā.*

44 *Ajāzanī.*

45 Ibn aṣ-Ṣalāḥ, *ʿUlūm al-Ḥadīth,* pp. 128–80.

46 See the article by Amin Kamaruddin, 'Nāṣiruddīn al-Albānī on Muslim's *Ṣaḥīḥ*: A Critical Study of his Method', *Islamic Law and Society,* 11/2, pp. 149–76, for a good discussion on the early use of the preposition *ʿan.*

47 Mālik ibn Anas, *al-Muwaṭṭāʾ*, with commentary *Awjaz al-Masālik ilā Muwaṭṭāʾ Imām Mālik* by al-Kāndhlawī, (Damascus: Dār al-Qalam, 2003) 1:260.

It can be seen in this *isnād* that from Mālik onwards, the only term that is being used to describe the ḥadīth being passed on from one person to another is *ʿan*. Since Ibn Shihāb az-Zuhrī not only met ʿUmar II but was also employed by him, the chances are that az-Zuhrī saw ʿUmar II delaying the prayer one day rather than ʿUmar II telling az-Zuhrī that he did so.

In a second example given below from the *Sunan at-Tirmidhī*, it will be evident from the *isnād* that the part closest to at-Tirmidhī is replete with sophisticated technical terms for the reception and transmission of the ḥadīth, whilst its latter portion only uses a simple *ʿan*. At-Tirmidhī says:

> Qutayba and Maḥmūd ibn Ghaylān have reported to us (*ḥaddathanā*)—[who said that] Wakīʿ has informed us (*akhbaranā*)—from (*ʿan*) Sufyān. . .—from (*ʿan*) ʿAbd Allah ibn Muḥammad ibn ʿAqīl—from (*ʿan*) Muḥammad ibn al-Ḥanafiyya—from (*ʿan*) ʿAlī—from (*ʿan*) the Prophet ﷺ [. . .].[48]

It is evident from this *isnād* of *Sunan at-Tirmidhī* that the preposition *ʿan* was used from Sufyān ath-Thawrī onwards. Ath-Thawrī was a contemporary of imam Mālik and Abū Ḥanīfah and is number ten in al-Madīnī's second table.

From the above two examples and al-Madīnī's taxonomy of ḥadīth scholars it can be concluded that by imam ash-Shāfiʿī's time, due to his efforts and the wide dissemination of knowledge, ḥadīth became the sole repository of the *sunna* to the extent that this had an effect on the way scholars employed ḥadīth terminology. The illocutionary force of imam ash-Shāfiʿī's argument for the centrality of ḥadīth had such an impact that henceforth all ḥadīth *usūl*, broadly followed the themes that he devised in his *Risālah*. His method took such root among the scholarly community that it was essentialized to the level of a global super-methodology. Scholars developed and refined it further, and it became the standard methodology for ḥadīth research. People gradually forgot that this was *a* method from other competing methods available for understanding the *sunna*, in other words they forgot that it is Shāfiʿī *uṣūl al-ḥadīth*, like Shafiʿī *uṣūl al-fiqh*, in contrasat to Mālikī *uṣūl al-ḥadīth*, like Māliki *uṣūl al-fiqh* and Ḥanafi *usūl al-ḥadīth* like Ḥanafi *uṣūl al-fiqh*. The author in this book endeavours to prove just that.

ABOUT THE BOOK *IʿLĀʾ AS-SUNAN* AND ITS INTRODUCTION

The *Iʿlāʾ as-Sunan* is from the genre of *sharḥ* (commentary). It is not a commentary of a particular ḥadīth collection, but of a number of ḥadīths found in a myriad of

48 At-Tirmidhī, *Sunan*, (Deoband: Kutub Khana Rashidiya, [n. d.]), lithographic print, p. 5.

sources which form the basis for the Ḥanafī *madhhab*. Traditionally the commentaries were not only seen as plain depositories for Islamic knowledge, but they also functioned as discursive works which were employed to promote a partisan view or for settling scores.[49] A good example of such polemical use of the commentary can be seen in a series of commentary on the *Sunan at-Tirmidhī*. The *Tuḥfat al-Aḥwadhī* a commentary on the *Sunan at-Tirmidhī* written by the Indian *ahle ḥadīth* scholar ʿAbd ar-Raḥmān al-Mubārakpūri was not only a simple explication of the ḥadīths of *Sunan at-Tirmidhī*, but also a refutation of Shaykh Rashīd Aḥmad Gangohi's commentary on the *Sunan* called *al-Kawkab ad-Durrī*. The author of *Tuḥfa* in his commentary tries to prove that the Ḥanafī *madhhab* has no real association with ḥadīth. This was challenged and refuted by ʿAllāmah Kashmīrī's student Shaykh Yūsuf Binnori in the latter's commentary of the *Sunan* called *Maʿārif as-Sunan*. Although, ḥadīth was studied extensively in pre-colonial India, the Deobandi insistence on ḥadīth and writing large volumes of commentaries was a scholarly reaction to the *ahle ḥadīth* claim that the Ḥanafī *madhhab* was not rooted in the Prophetic *sunna*. In other words, ḥadīths were taught in the Deobandi schools not for extracting points of law (*ijtihād*) from them, but to prove that the already extracted Ḥanafī law has a basis in the ḥadīth.[50] This is why when one reads commentaries of ḥadith written in post-colonial India, one finds that the authors have gone to length to bring the ḥadīths in line with the Ḥanafī *madhhab* through the use of certain interpretive methods. By way of example one may refer to the ironically named 20 volume *Awjaz al-Masālik*, by hazrat Shaykh Mawlana Zakariyya al-Kandhlawī or the commentary of his teacher hazrat Shaykh Khalil Ahmad Sahāranpurī on the *Sunan Abī Dawūd* called *Badhl al-Majhūd*. Mawlana Zafar Aḥmad al-ʿUthmānī's *Iʿlāʾ as-Sunan* is by far and large the most exhaustive and ambitious work in this genre.[51]

One may get misled by the name *Qawāʿid fī ʿUlūm al-Ḥadīth* that this book is an introduction to the science of ḥadīth. This is definitely not the case. The book is an attempt to challenge current notions of the science of ḥadīth whilst it attempts to develop a Ḥanafī narrative of the science. Hence, it would have been less confusing if the title was qualified by adding 'according to the Ḥanafī School'.

---

49 Qasim Zaman, The Ulama in Contemporary Islam: Custodians of Change, (Princeton: Princeton University Press, 2002), pp. 38–50.

50 My statement here refers strictly to the use of ḥadīth in Islamic law. It goes without saying that ḥadīth was also studied to learn and practice the moral and ethical mores of the Prophet ﷺ.

51 Alongside a response to the *ahle ḥadīth* criticism against the Ḥanafī's, the author takes the opportunity to settle some inter-Deobandi issues through the *Iʿlāʾ as-Sunan* (see end of *kitāb as-Siyar*) such as his refutation on 'Composite Nationalism' which clearly is a refutation of Mawlana Husayn Aḥmad Madanī's (May Allah ﷻ have mercy on him) position. See Qasim Zaman, *The Ulama in Contemporary Islam*, pp. 41–50, for more details.

THE WRITING PROCESS OF THE *IʿLĀʾ AS-SUNAN* AND ITS EVOLUTION

The work *Iʿlāʾ as-Sunan* is the end product of a multi-layered work. Below we will give a brief summary of these different layers. A more detailed explanation of this can be found at the end of the book in the second appendix.

1. *Iḥyāʾ as-Sunan*: This was originally authored by Mawlana Ashraf ʿAlī at-Thānawī as a response to the allegations leveled against Ḥanafī *fiqh* that it has no basis in ḥadīth. This manuscript got lost before the Mawlana could send it for print.
2. *Jāmiʿ Al-Āthār*: This was hazrat Thānawī's second attempt to write a vindication for Ḥanafī *fiqh*. The style of this book was slightly different from the previous.
3. *Tābiʿ al-Āthār*: This was the footnote to *Jāmiʿ Al-Āthār* where hazrat Thānawī responds to ḥadīth that apparently goes against the Ḥanafī *fiqh*. Both the *Jāmiʿ* and its footnotes did not go beyond the book of prayers.
4. *Iḥyāʾ as-Sunan*: Due to his busy schedule, hazrat Thānawī entrusted Mawlana Aḥmad Ḥasan as-Sanbhalī to complete the remainder chapters of the *Jāmiʿ*. Hazrat Thānawī carefully monitored Mawlana Sanbhalī's work, making critical suggestions and ammendments. Mawlana Sanbhalī managed to write upto the book of Ḥajj.
5. *At-Tawḍīḥ al-Ḥasan*: is the footnote that Mawlana Sanbhalī wrote to his *Iḥyāʾ as-Sunan*. After the work was checked by hazrat Thānawī, Mawlana Sanbhalī added some of his own comments and thoughts and then published the book. Some of these comments were not to hazrat Thānawī's liking who stopped all further volumes of the book to be published.
6. *Al-Istidrāk al-Ḥasan ʿalā Iḥyāʾ as-Sunan*: This was a rejoinder that hazrat Thānawī asked his nephew Mawlana Ẓafar Aḥmad al-ʿUthmānī to write on Mawlana Sanbhalī's work.
7. *Iʿlāʾ as-Sunan* (first edition): Hazrat Thānawī instructed Mawlana Ẓafar Aḥmad al-ʿUthmānī to write the remainder of the book from where he left off (book of prayers),[52] till the last chapter of *fiqh*.
8. *Isdāʾ al-Minan*: Is the commentary of ḥadīths of *Iʿlāʾ as-Sunan*. In summary, the first volume (already published) was known as *Iḥyāʾ as-Sunan* and the remainder of the book was known as *Iʿlāʾ as-Sunan* with its commentary *Isdāʾ as-Sunan*.
9. *Itfāʾ al-Fitan*: This was the translation of the ḥadīths of *Iʿlāʾ as-Sunan* in Urdu found in the first edition of the *Iʿlāʾ as-Sunan*. This was removed in the second edition.
10. *Inhāʾ as-Sakan ilā man Yuṭāliʿ Iʿlāʾ as-Sunan*: was the name of the ḥadīth and

52 A decision was made to no longer publish the remainder of Mawlana Sanbhalī's work.

fiqh introduction to the *Iʿlāʾ as-Sunan*. The first authored by Mawlana Ẓafar al-ʿUthmānī is also known as *Muqaddimat Iʿlāʾ as-Sunan fi 'l-Ḥadīth*, and was renamed by its editor, Shaykh ʿAbd al-Fattāḥ Abū Ghudda with the permission of the author to *Qawāʿid fi ʿUlūm al-Ḥadīth*. The *fiqh* introduction was written by Mawlana Ḥabīb Aḥmad al-Kirānawī.

11. *Injāʾ al-Waṭan ʿan al-Izdirāʾ bi Imām az-Zaman*: Is a book by Mawlana Ẓafar al-ʿUthmānī on the biography of Imam Abū Ḥanīfah.
12. *Iʿlāʾ as-Sunan* (second edition): In the second edition to the book, Mawlana Ẓafar al-ʿUthmānī incorporated the *al-Istidrāk al-Ḥasan* into the actual text, got rid of the *Itfāʾ al-Fitan* and renamed the whole book as *Iʿlāʾ as-Sunan*.

IʿLĀʾ AS-SUNAN AND ITS CRITICS

The *Iʿlāʾ as-Sunan* did not go unchallenged. A certain Irshād al-Haqq al-Atharī, wrote a refutation on the *Iʿlāʾ as-Sunan* in 8 volumes called *Iʿlāʾ as-Sunan fi 'l-Mīzān*. A line to line rebuttal of the *Inhāʾ as-Sakan* was written by the Sindi *ahle ḥadīth* scholar, Shaykh Badīʿ az-Zamān ar-Rāshidī (1926–1996) called *Inmāʾ az-Zakan fi Tanqīd Inhāʾ as-Sakan*, which was later titled *Naqḍ Qawāʿid fi ʿUlūm al-Ḥadīth* by its editor.[53] However, both the author and the editor have missed the central argument of Shaykh Ẓafar al-ʿUthmānī upon which the whole of the *Inhāʾ as-Sakan*, nay the whole of the *Iʿlāʾ as-Sunan* pivots. This is the claim that since *uṣūl al-ḥadīth* is not an absolute science, no one group has the right to claim ownership of it. Hence the critics' atomistic rebuttal holds no force.

SUMMARY OF THE BOOK *QAWĀʿID FĪ ʿULŪM AL-ḤADĪTH*

This is a highly specialist and complicated book to understand; therefore a short overview of the book will help readers understand it better. It should be kept in mind that first and foremost this book was originally written for scholars and not the general public. The book is highly elliptical as the author assumes that his readers will already have had some exposure to the science of ḥadīth. It is a tedious book to read as the author very often interrupts his narrative by quoting large passages of texts from other sources. Obviously his purpose for doing this is to bolster his opinions by falling back onto the shoulders of the giants of this science. Readers

---

53 Badīʿ az-Zamān ar-Rāshidī, *Inmāʾ az-Zakan fi Tanqīd Inhāʾ as-Sakan,* ed. By Ṣalāh ad-Dīn Maqbūl Aḥmad called *Naqḍ Qawāʿid fi ʿUlūm al-Ḥadīth,* (Kuwait: Dār Gharās publication, 2003).

may notice that references to books have been given both in the text as well as the footnotes. Where a book is referred to in the text, this has been done by the author. The translator and the editors have kept this in the text without relegating it to the footnotes. One final general point that needs to be kept in mind is that this book is exclusively written to vindicate the Ḥanafī School from the criticisms of the *ahle ḥadīth*, hence this underpins everything that the author writes. To give just one example, the author writes on p. 232:

> *Muslim's distinction over al-Bukhārī by preserving the exact words in narration*
> Al-Ḥāfiẓ also said in *al-Fatḥ* about the ḥadīth, "No one should pray ʿAṣr except at Banū Qurayẓa": "Al-Bukhārī wrote it from memory and did not take care to preserve the exact words as is known that his position allows [not preserving] that, which is not the case with Muslim who often preserved the words literally. I did not allow the opposite because I agree with those who agree with Muslim about the wording in which he differs with al-Bukhārī."
>
> I say this is an immense virtue by which Muslim is distinguished as he is also distinguished by the excellence of his presentation of the ḥadīth and collecting of all its paths of transmission in one place. It is from this perspective that some people prefer Muslims' book to that of Al-Bukhārī.
>
> *Al-Bukhārī allows transmission of the ḥadīth by meaning; the basis of Mālik in preferring the practice of the people of Madina over single reports is when they contradict*
> In it there is also evidence that al-Bukhārī permitted transmission of ḥadīth by meaning without concern for the exact wording. That may be the basis of Mālik's opinion what one should abandon single reports if they differed from the *ʿamal* of the people of Madina because the *ʿamal* of the people of Madina in the best generations has a stronger *isnād* going back to the Prophet ﷺ than the report of a single person about whom we do not know whether he accurately recorded or not, and whether he narrated the ḥadīth with the exact wording or with the meaning, and whether he understood it or not?
>
> *The basis of the Ḥanafī position that when a single report contradicts the well-known sunna it is irregular (shādhdh), it is the same when it is reported about a general need*
> It [the above] is [also] the basis of the Hanafī position that single reports are accepted when they do not contradict the well-known *sunna*. If they contradict it, then they are irregular (*shādhdh*). That is also the case when they are reported by the transmission of solitary narrators in matters of general need (*balwā*). This is because one solitary person having knowledge of the ruling of such an occurrence is unlikely. We already indicated all of that when we discussed the fundamental principles (*uṣūl*).

What the author tries to achieve from this paragraph and the next is to make the case for the Ḥanafi's that an established practice (*sunna*) has prominence over a lone report (*khabr wāḥid*). He does this by first establishing that Muslim is more scrupulous than al-Bukhārī when it comes to ascertaining the correct wording of particular ḥadīth since al-Bukhārī mostly paraphrases (*riwāya bi al-maʿna*). The scholars say that this has given Muslim an edge of al-Bukhārī. Moving on from this, the author makes the case that since paraphrasing ḥadīth is deemed to be less scrupulous than ascertaining the correct wording of the ḥadīth, on the same token something which has a more epistemic certainty (*yaqīn*) over paraphrasing ḥadīth such as the collective practice of the scholars of Madīna will be more authorative than the actual paraphrased lone report. Once the author makes this case, by analogy and appropriation the case is made for the Ḥanafi's rejection of lone reports due to the presence of evidence which has an epistemic edge over it i.e. the established practice (*al-Sunna al-Mashhūra*).

The *Qawāʿid* originally had 10 chapters and an introduction. We split chapter 9 into two chapters, due to its length as well as the disparate themes in it. We have further added two appendices. Appendix 1 is a translation of Shaykh ʿAbd al-Fattāḥ Abū Ghudda's commendation of the *Iʿlāʾ as-Sunan* and appendix 2 is a translation of Mufti Taqi Usmani's introduction to his edition of the *Iʿlāʾ as-Sunan*. Both of these have been translated by Zameelur Rahman. Chapter 11 is the author's glossary for some terminologies he used in the book. In the introduction the author defines ḥadīth and the related terms associated with it. He explains the meaning of basic ḥadīth terminologies such *ṣaḥīḥ, ḥasan, ḍaʿīf, irsāl, tadlīs, inqiṭāʿ* etc. There is nothing unusual about this introduction as the author does not digress from the definitions given in the classical books of ḥadīth terminologies (*muṣṭalaḥ al-ḥadīth*). This introduction is the only fixed point of reference in the book and the rest of the book is speculative. The author does not have a problem with the conventional definitions of these terms but, to take one example, if it is a condition for a *ṣaḥīḥ* ḥadīth that the narrator is morally upright (*ʿadl*), who is to decide how one arrives at a decision that a particular narrator is morally upright? What criteria are to be used to judge this narrator? Is there a check list which is unanimously accepted that one can tick? Are there any universal standards for this? The author thinks not. For the author, these terminologies are empty abstract concepts which need to be concretized.

If the introduction was the theoretical backbone to the book, then chapter one is its methodological framework. In this chapter the author develops his master theory, which runs throughout the whole book. Without understanding this master theory, the book will not make any sense. It is the author's claim in this chapter that the science of ḥadīth is not an absolute science with hard fast binding rules. It is speculative and realative (*ijtihādī*) and is left at the discretion of the scholars. The implication of the author's theory is far-reaching. In other words, if the science of ḥadīth is *ijtihādī* and is left to the experts' discretion then no one group can lay claim to it. If the Ḥanāfī's scrutinize ḥadīth according to their own methodology, then this should be their prerogative.

After developing his master theory in chapter one, the author goes on to write about specific ḥadīth terminologies in the next five chapters (chapters 2–6). In chapter two, he writes about the *ṣaḥīḥ* and *ḥasan* ḥadīth. He writes that the *ṣaḥīḥ* ḥadīth is only probably *ṣaḥīḥ* (not definitely) and that the *ḍaʿīf* ḥadīth is probably *ḍaʿīf*, and that it is possible to act upon the *ḍaʿīf* ḥadīth because of other reasons. For example a weak ḥadīth does not remain weak if it is corroborated by a verse of the Qurʾān. The *ṣaḥīḥ* ḥadīth is not only confined to the quality of the *isnāds*, but to other factors such as the sheer number of narrators (*tawātur*), or the fact that a *mujtahid* has used a ḥadīth as proof, is *ṣaḥīḥ* according to him. He argues that the *Ṣaḥīḥ al-Bukhārī* and *Ṣaḥīḥ Muslim* are not the only depositories of *ṣaḥīh* ḥadīths and when the scholars disagree about the status of a ḥadīth whether it is *ṣaḥīḥ* or *ḍaʿīf* then at the least it is *ḥasan*.

Chapter three is regarding the status of weak ḥadīth. What are the conditions for acting upon a weak ḥadīth? What does imam Aḥmad ibn Ḥanbal mean when he says that there are no weak ḥadīths in the *Musnad*? If a *mujtahid* imam acts upon a weak ḥadīth what should one do?

Chapter four discusses the status of the *isnād* with regards to its continuity. There is an interesting discussion on internal inconsistencies (*inqiṭāʿ*) in the ḥadīth. For example if a hadith goes against the definitive meaning (*qaṭʿī ad-dalāla*) of the Qurʾān this is assumed to have internal discontinuation (*inqiṭāʿ*) and thus the hadith is to be rejected. Similarly if the ḥadīth goes against the general understanding of the *sunna*, or the general practice (*ʿumūm balwā*) of the community it is regarded as having internal inconsistencies. As the author himself says,

> The upshot of that is that along with the trustworthiness and exactness of the narrator it is preconditional in our view for the authenticity of a ḥadīth that the the ḥadīth does not contradict a definite [*āyah*] of the Book or a well known Sunna and that it should not be overlooked or action by it abandoned in the first generations, and that it should not be an irregular text (*shādhdh*) concerning a matter of general concern, but is on the contrary conspicuous and widespread.

In chapter five, the author introduces an interesting discussion on the status of the *mursal ḥadīth*. A mursal ḥadīth is when a follower (*tābiʿī*) omits the name of the Companion and narrates directly from the Prophet. This is accepted in the Ḥanafī School of *fiqh*. The author brings convincing arguments to prove the Ḥanafī point of view for example he points out that ḥadīth scholars generally accept the narration of earlier scholars who practiced *tadlīs* (i.e. giving the impression that one has narrated from an authority, whereas in this instance he has not). He brings evidence to prove that there isn't any essential difference between *tadlīs* and *irsāl* and places the burden of proof on the shoulders of the scholars to prove why they accept the former for earlier authorities and not the latter. Chapter six is a very short chapter on confusion in ḥadīth (*iḍṭirāb*).

Chapters seven and eight are very long chapters and the most difficult from all the chapters. Chapter seven is mainly related to the principles of narrator criticism (*jarḥ* and *taʿdīl*) and the ranking of its terminologies. Alongside the old-age debate regarding whether validation takes precedence over invalidation or vice versa, the author posits some interesting points. For example he writes that if the imamate of a person has been universally accepted, no amount of criticisms harms his integrity. The allusion here is made to imam Abū Ḥanīfah and his critics. He discusses whether innovation tarnishes the character of a scholar or not and makes apology for imam Abū Ḥanīfah that the *irjāʾ* belief attributed to him is different from the *irjāʾ* belief of murjiʾites.

Chapter eight is mainly related to *uṣūl al-fiqh* and what to do when there are apparent textual contradictions. This chapter is very important since knowledge of it will pacify many puzzled minds as to what to do when faced with contradictory Qurʾān verses or ḥadīths which seem to cancel each other out.

Chapter nine, documents the biography of the three imams of Ḥanafī *fiqh*. Chapter 10 is supplemented by further technical Ḥadīth points and further apologies for Ḥanafī *fiqh*. Such as refuting the claim that imam Abū Ḥanīfah did not live to see the codification of ḥadīth, or refuting objections to *taqlīd*. Again the conviction that the science of ḥadīth is not an absolute science is reiterated here. At first glance, this chapter seems confusing and convoluted as we find the author repeating the same point in a myriad of places over and over again. Such as a point regarding unclear depreciation (*jarḥ mubham*) is mentioned six times in six different places,[54] or the point about uncertainty at to whether a transimitter listened to a report before or after he began to muddle things is mentioned no less than four times.[55] Upon careful scrutiny, one finds that the author is carrying out an exhaustive reading of imam Ibn Ḥajar al-ʿAsqalānī's *Tahdhīb at-Tahdhīb*, from beginning to end, and when he finds something in the biographical notices of any of the ḥadīth scholars which corroborates his arguments in the rest of the book he quickly creates a sub-chapter heading for it and discusses it under this sub-heading even though he has discussed it many times before.

In this introduction, I have tried to situate the author's book within the devel-

54 Pp. 212, 213, 217, 219, 222.

55 Pp. 208, 214, 215.

opments of the science of ḥadīth. I tried giving an accurate picture of the book's biography as well as its content as to facilitate easier reading. It goes without saying that this is a very technical subject and one has to approach the book with already some understanding of the science of ḥadīth. I hope that readers will benefit from this work as much as I have benefitted from it. And all perfection belongs to Allah ﷻ, who is perfect in his essence and qualities, and salutation on his Prophet, our liege-lord and his pure family, as long as the night follows the day and the sun kisses the earth with its radiant light.

Mansur Ali
Cambridge Muslim College
October 2012

AUTHOR'S INTRODUCTION

PRAISE BELONGS to Allah ﷻ Who expanded the breasts of the people of Islam to the *sunna* and so they submitted to following it and gladly listened to it. He killed the selves of those people who transgressed in innovation after they persistently argued about it and excessively engaged in innovating. I witness that there is no god but Allah ﷻ alone without partner, Who knows submission of the hearts and their refusal, Who is well aware of the secrets of the hearts both in the state of communion and of separation.

I witness that Sayyidunā Muḥammad is His slave and His messenger because of whom the word of falsehood was diminished after it had been uplifted, and by whose countenance the lights of guidance shone and their proofs strengthened after having been severed. May Allah ﷻ bless him and grant him peace as long as the heavens and the earth endure, the former in its elevation and the latter in its expansiveness; and [blessings and peace] on his family and Companions ﷺ who broke the troops of the rebellious extreme people and conquered their fortresses and strongholds, and who safeguarded for their followers his sayings, deeds and states until the noble *sunna* was safe from loss.[56] And [blessings and peace] be upon their followers in excellence and good treatment (*iḥsān*), and in particular upon our Great imam Abū Ḥanīfah an-Nuʿmān, may Allah ﷻ, be pleased with him and make him contented and single him out for an extra portion of His overflowing favour and for His good pleasure, on whom all people are dependent in *fiqh* as the great notables have said, and who would have attained the dīn even if it had been in the Pleiades as the Master of the descendants of ʿAdnān ﷺ indicated, as long as the sun and the moon rise and as long as night and day follow each other.

The most appropriate matter on which valuable days should be spent, and the highest of the things that should receive special concern is to be occupied with the sciences of the Sharīʿah which are received from the best of creation. No intelli-

56 This sermon (*khutba*) is taken from the introduction to *Fatḥ al-Bārī* by Ibn Ḥajar al-ʿAsqalānī (may Allah ﷻ have mercy on him).

gent person will doubt [that the sciences of the Sharīʿah] pivot around the Book of Allah ﷻ which is to be followed and the *sunna* of His chosen prophet. All other sciences are either instruments for understanding the two of them and they two are the sought after lost property,[57] or foreign to them and they are harmful and vanquished.

One of the trials of this age is the effort expended by some extremists to destroy the *sunnas* which are the sources (*uṣūl*) for the derivative rulings (*furūʿ*) of imam Abū Ḥanīfah an-Nuʿmān. They extended their tongues against him casting aspersions, forging lies and slander, and against his school with the accusation that there was no argument and no proof for it from out of the authentic *sunna* or the Qurʾān. By Allah ﷻ, this is doubtless a defamation, and claim without foundation or basis.

Thus necessity dictated establishing proofs from the ḥadīth for important matters regarding derivative rulings of the school of the Ḥanafī masters. To disprove the argument of this wrongdoing party and to besiege the hearts of the group that exceeds the proper bounds. Moreover to expand the hearts of the people of the *sunna* with brilliant lights from strong arguments whose lights shine forth with exalted chains of transmission and precious texts about which 'no prattle is ever heard',[58] indeed as if it were a garden whose pickings were easy.

Furthermore [necessity dictated] authenticating ḥadīth or verifying that they are fair [*ḥasan*] according to the principles (*uṣūl*). Those [principles] which have received acceptance with the scholars of narration, and along with confirmation of the elicitation of needed judgements according to the principles confirmed by the *fuqahāʾ* of deep understanding (*dirāyah*).

So the sulṭān of knowledge and of action in his age, the frequent champion (in the races of knowledge and excellence), possessor of the signs [*āyāt*], the sage of the Muhammadan Ummah, the renewer of the Islamic way of life, the noblest of the perfect *awliyāʾ*, the most bold and daring against the enemy of the people firmly established in knowledge, the man of pure *taqwā*, the Qurʾānic commentator and *faqīh*, the close friend of Allah ﷻ, my master the Shaykh, the Ḥāfiẓ, the firm and trustworthy narrator, the noted scholar Mawlana Ashraf ʿAlī, who is the unqualified proof of Allah ﷻ in his age, and to whose far-reaching wisdom and outstanding intelligence the people of knowledge of the whole world submitted, embarked on this important matter.

Some years previously, he had drafted some of that in all of the categories of *fiqh* and had called it *Iḥyāʾ as-Sunan*, but it was lost and the hands of the age carried it away. Then after a short time he began to write it again, but not according to his previous method, and he called it *Jāmiʿ al-Āthār*, and it became circulated everywhere, and Allah ﷻ be praised, but it never exceeded the chapters on the prayer.

---

57 Referring to the ḥadīth, 'wisdom is the lost property of the believer . . .' al-Tirmidhī, ḥ. 2687.

58 *Sūrat al-Ghāshiya*, 88:11.

He—may Allah ﷻ lengthen his life for the benefit of those who come to him and those who issue from out of his company and those of the travellers of the path and the people of *dhikr* who seek to be reunited with Allah ﷻ—never got the time to complete this book, and so he told some of his attendants with him who are occupied in the service of knowledge to complete it quickly and to show him whatever they wrote so that he could correct it, and improve it. So one of those people who served him fulfilled his order and wrote numerous volumes which did not concur with what the Shaykh had intended, because he had entered some of his own refutations and conclusions.

Then after that, he told me to undertake this heavy burden and important matter and so I obeyed his command seeking support from the oceans of his knowledge and taking light from the lights of his full moons and stars, and I wrote some volumes on that which fortunately he accepted and which agreed with his intention and expectation. He named them *Iʿlāʾ as-Sunan* and commanded that a volume of them should be printed, and it previously became widespread, with praise of Allah ﷻ.

Then he told me to redress some mistakes and slips that had occurred from some people in their authorship,[59] and to quickly write an introduction to this book which would be insightful for whoever should study it. A foundation for our discourse in declaring ḥadīth as *ṣaḥīḥ* (authentic) and *ḥasan* (fair), and everything connected to the area, comprising the principles which ḥadīth scholars accepted or recommended. Explaining the principles in which our Ḥanafī scholars differ from the ḥadīth scholars; since each person has a perspective which he takes in the area of declaring [ḥadīth] *ṣaḥīḥ*, *ḥasan*, or weak (*ḍaʿīf*).

If you know this, then the reality of the discreditors' aspersions against our Ḥanafī scholars that they use weak ḥadīth in their proofs will be unveiled to you. This is in addition to the fact that the origins of their allegations is due to their heedlessness of their (the Ḥanafī's) fundamentals (*uṣūl*) and ignorance of their principles (*qawāʿid*); for often something regarded by ḥadīth scholars as weak is regarded as authentic by others, and vice versa.

There is no doubt that the fundamentals of authentication and declaring weak are a matter of opinion which mostly pivot on the taste of the ḥadīth scholar and the mujtahid.[60] Therefore, there can be no blame on a ḥadīth scholar and mujtahid for arriving at a judgement which disagrees with other ḥadīth scholars and mujtahids. Do you not see that Muslim differed from al-Bukhārī in some of his fundamentals such as the fact that one of them (al-Bukhārī) stipulated in accepting a narration through the use of the preposition *ʿan* (*ʿanʿanah*)[61] that the two narrators had to have

59 Most likely he is referring to al-Sanbhalī the author of *Iḥyāʾ as-Sunan* here.

60 The expert scholar who exerts his knowledge and intellect to arrive at unprecedented *fiqh* judgements.

61 *ʿAnʿanah* is when a narrator uses the relatively more ambiguous word "*ʿan*" (from) when narrating a

met one time and been in direct contact, but the other (Muslim) did not stipulate that but was contented with their being contemporaries with the possibility of their having met with. The dominant majority of the outstanding people of knowledge agreed with him on this.

Similarly, Ibn Ḥibbān differed with the dominant majority of the ḥadīth scholars in accepting and using as proof the narration of someone unknown if the person narrating from him (the unknown person) and his (the unknown person's) shaykh are both trustworthy narrators and if the ḥadīth is not unfamiliar (*munkar*). So what blame is there on the Ḥanafis if they differ in some fundamental matters? Every man apart from the Messenger ﷺ is both refuting and refuted as long as the East and West winds blow.

So I wrote this introduction after finishing the corrections of some people concerning his authorship which the Shaykh named *al-Istidrāk al-Ḥasan ʿalā Iḥyāʾ as-Sunan*, and he named this introduction *Inhāʾ as-Sakan ilā man Yuṭāliʿ Iʿlāʾ as-Sunan*[62] and it comprises an introduction and some sections. I ask Allah ﷻ for success and acceptance, and He is the Best to grant success and the Most Generous of those who are asked, and His good pleasure is what is sought and most hoped for.

ḥadīth instead of clearly stating that he had heard, or been told it.

62 Shaykh ʿAbd al-Fattāḥ Abū Ghuddah changed its title with the agreement of the author to *Qawāʿid fī ʿUlūm al-*ḥadīth in his edition of the text.

FUNDAMENTAL CONCEPTS AND DEFINITIONS

KNOW THAT EVERY science has its subject (*mawḍūʿ*), fundamental concepts (*mabādī*) and topics (*masāʾil*).

The subject is that which is studied in that science in terms of its essential propositions.[63]

The fundamental concepts are those matters on which the science is built, and they are either conceptualisations (*taṣawwurāt*) or assents (*taṣdīqāt*). Conceptualisations are the (basic) definitions of the things used in that science, and assents are the premises (*muqaddimāt*) from which the reasonings of the science are composed.

The topics are what the science comprises.

In a nutshell, if that which constitutes the science is that which is the main objective in the science, then this is the topics [*masāʾil*]; that which is not the main objective of the science but related to the topics is the subject matter [*mawḍūʿ*], otherwise it is the fundamental concepts [*mabādī*] which are its definition [*ḥadd*], its utility [*fāʾidah*] and its support (*istimdād*).

The definition of the science of ḥadīth with respect to transmission (*riwāyah*) is: the science by which the sayings, deeds and states of the Messenger of Allah ﷺ are known and their narration, their [oral or written] capture[64] (*ḍabṭ*) and the precise formulation of their wordings (*alfāẓ*) are recognised.

The [definition of the] science of ḥadīth with regards to comprehension (*dirāyah*) is: a science by which one recognises the true state of narration, its preconditions, its types and its rulings, the state of the narrators and their preconditions and the varieties of narrated traditions and what is connected with them.

Its utility is: gaining the bliss of the two abodes and distinguishing what is *ṣaḥīḥ* from other types (and recognizing evidences for the legal judgements, the majority of which derive from the science of ḥadīth).

---

63 *Aʿrāḍ* possibly a mistake for *aghrāḍ* 'goals'.

64 Capture through oral memorization and in writing.

Its support (*istimdād*) is from the sayings of the Messenger of Allah ﷺ and his deeds.

His sayings are in Arabic speech so whoever does not recognise Arabic speech in all its aspects (*jihāt*), he is far afield from this science. They (his sayings) are both literal and metaphorical, allusive and unambiguous, universal and particular, unqualified and qualified, containing ellipsis and reference by means of personal pronouns, clearly articulated or implicitly understood, containing required and indicated meanings, explicit and inferred meanings, warnings and gestures and the like, along with the fact that it is according to the canon of Arabic which the grammarians have explained in all detail and according to the principles of the usages of the Arabs, which are expressed as the science of linguistics (*lughah*).

His deeds are those matters which issued from him in which he ordered us to follow him as long as they were not natural constitutional matters or something particular to him.

The subject of the science of ḥadīth is the chain of transmission and the text, and some say it is the person (*dhāt*) of the Messenger of Allah ﷺ with respect to the fact that he is the Messenger of Allah ﷺ,[65] but as-Suyūṭī and his shaykh[66] considered the former weightier.

Its issues are those things intended in it (for study), for example, "The Messenger of Allah ﷺ said such-and-such" and "he ordered thus," and "he forbade thus," and "he did thus."

Its fundamental concepts are criterion upon which its topics are based on, and they are the states of the ḥadīth and its attributes (and the definitions of things employed in the science of ḥadīth) as is stated in *ʿUmdat al-Qārī* and *Tadrīb ar-Rāwī*.

DEFINITION OF THE TERMS USED IN THIS SCIENCE

ḥadīth [*lit.* new or originated] in the ordinary usage of the Sharīʿah is that which is ascribed to the Prophet ﷺ. It is as if (in its literal sense) it is meant to be placed opposite the Qurʾān which is without beginning and unoriginated (*qadīm*).[67] At-Ṭībī said, "ḥadīth is general which includes the statements of the Prophet ﷺ, or the Companions, or the Followers, their doings and their tacit approvals."

Al-Ḥāfiẓ said in the commentary of *an-Nukhba*, "*Khabar* [*lit.* a piece of information] according to the scholars of this science is a synonym for ḥadīth and they are

65 This is the opinion of al-Kirmānī quoted by as-Suyūṭī. Jalāl ad-Dīn as-Suyūṭī, *Tadrīb Ar-Rāwi Sharḥ Taqrīb-Nawāwī* (Al-Maktabat al-ʿIlmiyya, 1379), p. 9.

66 Referring to ʿAllāmah Muḥyi 'd-Dīn al-Kafījī, as-Suyūṭī, *Tadrīb ar-Rāwi*, p. 5.

67 ḥadīth means 'new' or 'originated' and is the opposite of *qadīm* which indicates that which has no beginning or origination.

both used unqualifiedly for the raised ḥadīth (*marfūʿ*)[68] the halted ḥadīth (*mawqūf*)[69] and the cut-off ḥadīth (*maqṭūʿ*).[70] Some have said that ḥadīth is what is narrated from the Prophet ﷺ and *khabar* is what is narrated from someone else. Some have said that [the difference] between them is of that between a general term and a particular, so that every ḥadīth is a *khabar* but not the reverse. ḥadīth scholars call the *marfūʿ* and *mawqūf* ḥadīth *athar*.[71] The jurists of Khurāsān call *mawqūf* ḥadīth *athar* while they call the *marfūʿ* ḥadīth *khabar* and ḥadīth. The ḥadīth scholar is called *atharī* (traditionist) by ascription to *athar* (tradition), and it is said, "*athartu al-ḥadīth*," meaning, "I narrated (*rawaytu*) it."

The *matn* (text) is the wording of the ḥadīth by which meanings are formed.

The *sanad* (chain) is the route which leads to the text, i.e. the names of its narrators set out in a structured fashion.

Isnād is [the act of] reporting the chain of the text. By this it is clear that the text is the point at which the chain of transmission ends. Ibn Jamāʿah said, "Ḥadith scholars use sanad and *isnād* for one single thing."

As for the *Musnad*, there are a number of points of view.

First, [that it is] the ḥadīth whose chain is continuous from its narrator to its end, thus comprising the ḥadīth which are *marfūʿ*, *mawqūf* and *maqṭūʿ*. However, it is first and foremost used for what is narrated from the Prophet ﷺ rather than from anyone else. Al-Ḥākim and others said, "primarily it is not used except for a *marfūʿ* uninterrupted ḥadīth (*muttaṣil*) ascribed by a Companion to the Messenger of Allah ﷺ" And al-Ḥāfiẓ was positive about that in the commentary of *an-Nukhbah*.

Second, [that it is] the book in which are gathered that which the Companions ascribed i.e. narrated, thus it is a passive participle.

Third, that it is used unqualifiedly and what is meant by it is the chain of transmission (*isnād*), and thus it is a verbal noun (*maṣdar*).

Musnid [the one who ascribes] is the person who narrates the ḥadīth with its chain of transmission whether he has knowledge of it or has nothing but the simple act of narrating it.

As for *muḥaddith* (ḥadīth scholar) he has a higher rank than him, for he is the person who knows the pathways to authenticating the ḥadīth, and knows the reliability of its narrators and their flaws [which would detract from their reliability] rather than someone whose knowledge is simply confined to having heard it.

---

68 ḥadīth which are ascribed by a Companion to the Messenger of Allah ﷺ

69 Narration from a Companion without mention of the Prophet ﷺ

70 Narration from a Follower without mention of the Prophet ﷺ

71 ʿAllamah al-Laknawī in *Ẓafar al-Amanī*, p. 4–5 mentioned that an '*athar*' is that which is narrated from the Messenger of Allah ﷺ, or a Companion or a Follower (*tābiʿī*), whether it is *marfūʿ* or *mawqūf*, this is the position of the majority of the scholars of ḥadīth from the early muslims (*salaf*) and the scholars that came after (*khalaf*), and this is the position of the majority as was stated by al-Nawawī in *Sharḥ Ṣaḥīḥ Muslim*, (al-Miṣriya, 1347), 1:63.

Ibn Sayyid an-Nās said, "The *muḥaddith* in our age is whoever is occupied with ḥadīth both in narrating them and understanding them, who brings together its transmitters, and knows many of the narrators and the narrations in his own age, and becomes distinguished in that until his mark is recognised in that and his accurate retention of it becomes well known.[72]

"If he becomes vastly learned in that until his shaykhs and their shaykhs are recognised, generation after generation, to such an extent that what he knows about each generation is greater than that about which he is ignorant, then this person is *Ḥāfiẓ* [guardian and memoriser of ḥadīth]."[73]

In *Kashshāf iṣṭiliḥāt al-funūn* by the noted scholar Qāḍī Muḥammad Aʿlā at-Thānawī, may Allah ﷻ have mercy on him, there is a useful point: the people of ḥadīth are in degrees the first of which is the interested student who is the absolute beginner. Then later there is the ḥadīth scholar (*muḥaddith*) who is the perfect master, and similarly Shaykh and Imam have the same sense, and then later the *Ḥāfiẓ* who is the one whose knowledge encompasses one hundred thousand ḥadīth with their texts and chains of transmission, the states of the narrators in terms of criticism, authentication, and their histories. Then later there is the *Ḥujjah* whose knowledge encompasses three hundred thousand ḥadīth, as Ibn al-Matari said.

Al-Jazarī, may Allah ﷻ have mercy on him, said, "A narrator (*rāwī*) is someone who transmits the ḥadīth with its chain of transmission. A ḥadīth scholar (*muḥaddith*) is someone who undertakes its narration and is concerned with understanding its meaning. A *Ḥāfiẓ* is someone who narrates what reaches him and retains what is necessary in his view in his memory."[74]

I say that the differences of terminology in that are to do with the differences of convention in each age. [In my view] the *Ḥakīm* is above the *Ḥujjah* and is the one whose knowledge encompasses all of the ḥadīth in terms of their texts, their chains of transmission, the states of their narrators in terms of criticism authentication, and their histories. This is how I remember it, and I did not at first find anywhere in which it was stated, but then later I found it like that in the margins of *Sharḥ an-nakhbah* transmitted from *Sharḥ ash-sharḥ*.[75]

72 Shaykh Abū Ghuddah, pp. 27–28, quotes some beautiful advice for the one seeking to become a *muḥadīth* from imam adh-Dhahabī from his work *Tadhkirat al-Ḥuffāẓ*, 1:4.

73 The words of Shaykh Taqī ad-Dīn as-Subkī are mentioned in *Tadrīb Ar-Rāwi*, p.10, that the definition of a *ḥāfiẓ* returns to the custom of the people. Shaykh Abū Ghuddah agrees with this quoting his teacher ʿAllāmah al-Kawthar who mentioned something similar.

74 At-Thānawī, *Kashshāf Iṣṭalāḥāt al-Funūn*, (Kokota, 1279), 1:27. ʿAllāmah ʿAbd al-Ḥayy al-Kattānī has a more detailed discussion regarding the *muḥaddith*, *musnid* and *ḥāfiẓ*. ʿAbd Al-Ḥayy Kattāni, *Fihris Al-Fahāris wa 'l-Athbāt* (Fez 1346), 1:41–47.

75 ʿAlī al-Qārī, *Sharḥ Sharḥ an-Nukhbah*, (Istanbul, 1327), p. 3.

CATEGORIES OF ḤADĪTH

Know that the text of the ḥadīth itself only rarely enters into the discussion of ḥadīth masters. On the contrary, it earns its description of strength or weakness and the intermediate states according to the characteristics of the narrators such as integrity (*ʿadalah*), accuracy (*ḍabṭ*) power of retention (*ḥifẓ*) or lack of these things. [It also earns its description of strength or weakness according to attributes such as] the scarcity of narrators or abundance of them, and according to whether the chain of transmission is uninterrupted (*ittiṣāl*), interrupted (*inqiṭāʿ*), loose (*irsāl*) or disrupted (*iḍṭirāb*) etc. Hence, ḥadīth are categorised as sound (*ṣaḥīḥ*), fair (*ḥasan*), weak (*ḍaʿīf*), and as those which are widespread (*mutawātir*), famous (*mashhūr*) and lone (*aḥād*).

The *mutawātir* (widespread) is: that which such a number narrates, based on sensory perception rather than pure intellect, that ordinary experience would consider their concurring on a falsehood impossible; or they narrate from those like them from beginning to end, the last of them also basing themselves on sensory perception in their narration. The first type has no gradations to it, but the second has two grades or more. Then moreover with both types it render definite knowledge rather than speculative knowledge, and is not confined to a specific number and exists plentifully and is not nonexistent or only exists in small amounts contrary to those who claim that. Whenever its conditions exist in full but it fails to yield knowledge, it is because of some other obstacle not because of itself. Another aspect of it is that the reliability of its narrators is not a precondition in contrast to other types of narration.

The *mashhūr* (famous) is: that whose paths of transmission are limited but are more than two without reaching to the degree of being widespread (*mutawātir*), i.e. it does not in itself give [certain] knowledge. It is [also known as] widely dispersed (*mustafiḍ*) according to the view of a group of the imams who are *fuqahāʾ*. Some said that the *mustafiḍ* has an equal number of [transmitters in] at both ends [of the chain] and the middle and that the *mashhūr* is more universal than that. *Mashhūr* is sometimes used for what is well known on people's tongues i.e. even if it does not have a single chain of transmission.

The *ʿazīz* (scarce) is: that which no less than two people transmit from no less than them in each generation, and its precondition is not also a precondition for the *ṣaḥīḥ* contrary to those who claim so.[76]

The *gharīb* (rare, isolated) is: that which one person alone narrates (from a trust-

76 Such as al-Ḥākim. Here *Ṣaḥīḥ* is referring to al-Bukhārī's book and not the technical term meaning 'authentic'.

worthy narrator or not) in whatever point of the chain of transmission he alone occurs. If the isolation (*taffarud*) is at the end of the chain of transmission, i.e. in the [position of the] Follower who narrates it from the Companions then it is absolutely unique (*fard muṭlaq*), but if it occurs somewhere in the chain of transmission in that more than one narrate from the Companion and then a single person narrates it from one of them, then it is relatively unique (*fard nasabī*). Most often [the term] fard (isolation) is used unqualifiedly for the absolutely unique and [the term] *gharīb* (rare) for the relatively unique.

A *gharīb* ḥadīth is either authentic if the person who uniquely narrates it is a trustworthy narrator such as the isolated ḥadīth in the authentic collections or it is not authentic which is more likely.

A *gharīb* ḥadīth is either unusual in its chain and in its text and that is in the case where a single person alone transmits a certain text, or it is unusual in the chain only and not in the text. For example a ḥadīth whose text is recognised [as transmitted] from a group of Companions but a single person alone narrates it from another Companion. The verdict of al-Tirmidhī, "rare in regard to this line of transmission" (*gharīb min hādha al-wajh*) is from this [category]. There are no [ḥadīth] to be found that are isolated in text but not in chain of transmission except where the ḥadīth of a certain individual become famous and many people transmit from the person, in which case it becomes a rare famous (*gharīb mashhūr*). The ḥadīth "Actions are only by intentions. . ."[77] is described as isolated in its earlier part but is considered famous in its latter part.

All of them apart from the widespread ḥadīth (*mutawātir*) are *āḥād* [trasmitted by individual narrators at some of point of the chain] and,—in contrast with the widespread ḥadīth, which are all accepted—there are accepted narrations among them, which are those in which it is more probable that the informant is truthful; and there are rejected narrations among them, which are those in which it is more probable that the informant is untruthful. Furthermore there are those where one has to hesitate to accept or reject because accepting them as proof is dependent upon research into the states of their narrators.

There are a number of types of acceptable *āḥād*:

Aṣ-ṣaḥīḥ li-dhātih (intrinsicly authentic) is the narration of an individual with an uninterrupted chain of transmission transmitted by upright narrators (*ʿadl*) of accurate retention, and not weakened by any defects or irregularities.

If its retention and other attributes are not so strong then it is in intrinsicly fair (*ḥasan li-dhātih*).

If there are numerous pathways of the intrinsicly *ḥasan li-dhātih* in that it is nar-

77 Al-Bukhāri, 1:2, 8:175, 9:29.

rated by another pathway which is stronger or the equal or by other pathways even if they are of lower quality, then it is externally authentic (*ṣaḥīḥ li-ghayrih*).

The narration of a single person which is narrated by someone whose memory is bad even confused so that he does not distinguish between what he narrated before he became confused, or his circumstances are obscure (*mastūr al-ḥāl*), or someone who narrates a loose ḥadīth (*mursal*),[78] or he is someone who misrepresents ḥadīth (*mudallis*) without knowing who the omitted narrator is in both of these cases, but then, any one of these narrators, is corroborated by someone who is the equal of him or above him in degree in narration, then it is *ḥasan li-ghayrih*.

If there arise evidence which then renders the acceptability more probable of what one is hesitating to accept then that is also *ḥasan* but not intrinsicly (*li-dhātih*).

The gist of it is that if the weak [narration] has a number of paths of transmission or is supported by something which makes its acceptability more probable, then it is *ḥasan li-ghayrih*.[79]

Both *ṣaḥīḥ li-dhātih* and *ḥasan li-dhātih* have degrees some of which are higher than others. That which has all of the attributes of the *ṣaḥīḥ* ḥadīth without any disagreement has priority over that in which they (i.e. the attributes of the *ṣaḥīḥ*) exist but with disagreement, whether or not the disagreement is over the existence or absence of one of the attributes or over whether it is a condition of soundness or not.

As for that about which some of the imams have said that it is the soundest of chains of transmission [*isnād*], then it has priority over others, even though the reliable position is not to say that unrestrictedly because a specified few have been checked. Similarly those which the two shaykhs concurringly compiled have priority over those which one of them alone narrated; and that which al-Bukhārī alone narrated has priority over that which Muslim alone narrated (i.e. in the view of ḥadīth scholars, but according to the *fuqahāʾ* what is pivotal is the presence of all of the conditions of soundness irrespective of who compiled the ḥadīth as you will soon learn).

The *ḥasan* ḥadīth is the one where a number of ḥadīth scholars have regarded its chain of transmission as being sound and have described it as the lowest grade of *ṣaḥīḥ*. It has priority over [the ḥadīth] whose chain no one has declared authentic. That [*ḥasan* narration] whose chain no one has declared *ṣaḥīḥ* or *ḍaʿīf* has a higher rank than the *ḥasan* ḥadīth which some declare *ḍaʿīf*.

At-Tirmidhī said, "The *ḥasan* is that in which there is no [narrator] suspected [of lying], and which is not anomalous (*shādhdh*), and the like of which is narrated in more than one way." This is that about which one says that it is fair without further

78 Such a person is called a *mursil*.

79 If there are a number of paths of transmission it is raised from *ḥasan* due to others (*li-ghayrih*) to the level of *ṣaḥīḥ* due to others (*li-ghayrih*). Taqī ad-Din as-Subkī, *Shifāʾ as-Siqām fī Ziyārat Khayr al-Anām*, (Būlāq, 1318), p.11; Ibn aṣ-Ṣalāḥ citied by Ibn Kathīr in *Ikhtiṣār ʿUlūm al-*ḥadīth, (Ṣabīḥ, 1377), p. 43.

qualification. But as for the one about which one says fair-authentic (*ḥasan ṣaḥīḥ*) or fair-isolated (*ḥasan gharīb*) or fair-authentic-isolated (*ḥasan ṣaḥīḥ gharīb*), then it does not fit his definition. Combining *ḥasan* and *ṣaḥīḥ* together is either because of hesitation over the state of the transmitter whether or not the conditions of authenticity are found in him or whether he falls short in them, or because of taking into account two chains.[80]

The *ḍaʿīf* (weak) is that which does not hold the attributes of *ḥasan* [ḥadīth] and its weakness is in degrees of severity or slightness just as in the soundness of the *ṣaḥīḥ*, so that in it is the weakest (*awhā*) just as the *ṣaḥīḥ* has the most authentic (*aṣaḥḥ*).[81]

According to the people of knowledge it is permissible to be lenient in [the use of] the chains of the *ḍaʿīf* [ḥadīth] without declaring its weakness for the purposes of admonitory talks (*mawāʿiẓ*), stories, and for [sourcing] the merits of actions (*faḍāʾil al-aʿmāl*) but not for [establishing] the attributes of Allah ﷻ, nor for legal rulings on halal and haram.[82]

It is not permissible to narrate fabricated ḥadīth (*mawḍūʿ*) except to make clear their condition.

It has been said that it was a part of an-Nasāʾi's method to narrate from everyone about whom there was not a consensus that he should be abandoned. Abū Dāwūd used to go by his verdict and narrate weak ḥadīth if he could not find anything else in that chapter, and he would regard it weightier than the opinions of men.

The *musnad* (supported) is that whose chain is connected right back to the Prophet ﷺ.

The *muttaṣil* (uninterrupted) is that whose chain is uninterrupted whether or not it goes right back to him ﷺ or goes back to a companion or the like.

The *marfūʿ* (raised) is that which is specifically ascribed to the Prophet ﷺ [through his] words, deeds or tacit approvals whether or not it is uninterrupted [*muttaṣil*] or interrupted [*munqatiʿ*].

The *muʿanʿan* (ḥadīth transmitted with the preposition *ʿan*) is that in whose chain it is said [to be narrated by] 'so-and-so *ʿan* (from) so-and-so' (*fulān ʿan fulān*).[83] The normative position is that it is [to be deemed] uninterrupted (*muttaṣil*) if it was possible [for the two narrators] to meet providing that [they are] free from misrepresentation (*tadlīs*). They (the *muʿanʿan* ḥadīth) are included in the two *Ṣaḥīḥ* books.

The *muʿallaq* (hanging) is that in the beginning of whose *isnād* one or more narrators are omitted. Al-Bukhārī used this type a great deal in his *Ṣaḥīḥ* and it does not prevent it being *ṣaḥīḥ* if he quoted it decisively as we will see.

---

80 *Sharḥ an-Nukhbah*, pp. 34,35.

81 *Tadrīb ar-Rāwī*, p.106.

82 ʿAllamah ʿAbd al-Ḥayy al-Laknawī has a detailed discussion surrounding acting upon weak ḥadīth. ʿAbd al-Ḥayy al-Laknawī, *Al-Ajwibah al-Fāḍilah* (Aleppo, 1384), pp. 36–59.

83 i.e. the two narrators are connected using the preposition *ʿan*, which means from. Ed.

The *munqaṭiʿ* (broken) is that in the middle of whose *isnād* someone is omitted.

The *mursal* (loose) is that at the end of whose *isnād* there is someone omitted,[84] and it is the statement of a Follower, "The Messenger of Allah ﷺ said such-and-such or he did such-and-such." Sometimes *mursal* is used for any omission in whatever place it occurs.

The *mudraj* (interpolated) is that ḥadīth in which some words of one of the narrators are inserted, so that one thinks that it is a part of the ḥadīth; or in which someone takes two texts with two separate chains and narrates them with a single chain; or if someone hears a single ḥadīth from a group of people who differed about its chain or its text and then one narrates it as if they agreed without mentioning the differences. To deliberately intend any one of the three is impermissible.

The *musalsal* (enchained) is that in which the narrators, when narrating the ḥadīth, successively maintain a single state up to the Messenger of Allah ﷺ. [This succession is maintained] either orally in the narrator such as in the *musalsal bi 's-simāʿ* (the enchainment through audition) in which every narrator says, "I heard so-and-so saying, 'I heard so-and-so saying...'" up to its end, and [such as] the *musalsal bi 't-taḥdīth* (enchainment using the term ḥaddathanā) or the *musalsal bi 'l-Ikhbār* (enchainment using the term *akhbaranā*) in which its [every] narrator says, "So-and-so informed us, by Allah ﷻ!" etc. [The enchainment is also maintained] in action such as *al-musalsal bi 't-tashbīk bi 'l-yad* (enchainment in the intertwining of the hands); or [the enchainment maintained] in word and deed such as in the narration of Abū Dāwūd, Aḥmad and an-Nasāʾī in which the narrator said,[85] "The Messenger of Allah ﷺ took my hand and said, 'I love you, so say, "O Allah ﷻ aid me to remember You and be grateful to You and to worship You well."'" And thus each narrator acted with each one to whom he narrated and told him to say [those words]. [Enchainment] can also be in its description such as *musalsal bi 'l-fuqahāʾ* (enchained with narrators who are *fuqahāʾ*] or [*musalsal bi*] *'l-khulafāʾ* (enchained with narrators who are caliphs] and the like.

The *muṣaḥḥaf* (misreading) is that in which some diacritical points in [letters in] the chain or the text has been changed. An example of it in the chain is [of the name] al-ʿAwwām ibn Murājim (with a *rāʾ* and *jīm*) which Ibn Maʿīn misread when he said, "Muzāḥim," (with a *zāʾ* and *ḥāʾ*). An example [of misreading] in the text is the ḥadīth, "Whoever fasts six of Shawwal," (in which there is a *sīn* and a *tāʾ*) which aṣ-Ṣūlī changed into "something [*shayʾ*]" (in which there is a *shīn* and a *yāʾ*).[86]

84 Meaning the companion is omitted from the chain.

85 [The narrator] is our Master Muʿādh ibn Jabal May Allah ﷺ, the ḥadīth is narrated by Abū Dāwūd 2:86, an-Nasāʾī 3:53 and Aḥmad in his *Musnad* 5:245.

86 It should be observed that the misreading (*taḥrīf*) is not strictly specific to the alteration of the dots on the letters but is also extended to the alteration of the letter itself. Ibn aṣ-Ṣalāḥ says that there are

The *muḥarraf* (distorted) is that in which some of the vowelling has been changed although the letters are unaltered.

The *mawqūf* (halted) is the words and deeds that have been narrated from a Companion, whether with an uninterrupted or interrupted chain. It is also used for other than the Companions if qualified such as "Muʿammar stopped it (*waqafah*) at Hammām," and "Mālik stopped it (*waqafah*) at Nāfiʿ."22. The *maqṭūʿ* (severed) is that which comes from the Followers: their sayings and doings [and the *isnād* of which] stops at them.

The *muʿḍal* (problematic) is that in which two or more consecutive narrators are omitted from its chain such as the saying of Mālik, "The Messenger of Allah ﷺ said. . ." or the saying of ash-Shāfiʿī, "Ibn ʿUmar said such-and-such."

The *mudallas* (misrepresented) is that in which omission [of a narrator] from the chain is subtle. Such as the transmitter narrates a ḥadīth which he had not heard from someone whom he met and with whom he was contemporary, in such a manner as to create the impression that he had heard it from him. For example someone's saying, "From so-and-so" or "so-and-so said," and this is *tadlīs al-isnād* (misrepresentation in the chain).

Teachers can also be misrepresented (*tadlīs as-shuyūkh*), such as naming one's shaykh, giving him an agnomen (*kunya*)[87] or ascription (*nisba*), or describing him in such a manner as he is not recognised. The worst form of misrepresentation is misrepresentation to make equal (*tadlīs at-taswiyah*) which is that one does not omit one's teacher but omits someone else, i.e. the teacher of one's teacher or someone further removed in the chain than him because that person is weak or a minor and his (i.e. the weak narrator's) teacher is a trustworthy narrator. He uses words that can imply direct audition from the second teacher in order to better the ḥadīth.

Al-Mursal al-khafī (ḥadīth with hidden looseness) is that which a contemporary narrates from someone whom he did not meet—i.e. it is not known whether he met him or not, in fact [it is known that] there is an intermediary between them—with a wording which could be interpreted as meaning that he actually heard it. The difference between the misrepresented (*mudallas*) and the subtle *mursal* is that the *mudallas* is particularly with respect to someone who narrates from someone—whom it is known that he met—something he had not heard from him. If he is contemporary with him but it is not known whether he met him then it is a subtle *mursal*.

The *shādhdh* (anomalous) is that which a trustworthy narrator or an utterly truthful person narrates in contrast to someone weightier than him in accuracy of retention or [weightier] because of the greater number [of narrations], or [weighter]

---

different types of misreading such as misreading caused by improper audition (*taṣḥīf as-samaʿ*), improper seeing (*taṣḥīf al-baṣar*), improper wording (*taṣḥīf al-lafẓ*) and improper understanding (*taṣḥīf al-maʿnā*).

87 i.e. a name containing *abū* or *umm* such as Abū Mūsā. Ed.

due to some other factors other than to two mentioned.[88] (a contrast which requires the rejection of that which someone weightier narrates). Its dialectical opposite is called the *maḥfūẓ* (preserved).

The *maḥfūẓ* (preserved) is that which a weightier person narrates in contrast to someone who is lower than him in terms of weightiness (a contradiction which would require the rejection of the contradicting ḥadīth).

The *munkar* (unfamiliar) is that which a weak narrator narrates in contrast to one who is acceptable (with a contradiction which would require the rejection of the contradicting ḥadīth). Its dialectical opposite is called the *maʿrūf.*

The *maʿrūf* (well-known) is that which the accepted narrator narrates in contradiction to the weak narrator (with a contradiction which would require the rejection of the *Sharḥ an-Nukhbah.*

The *mawḍūʿ* (fabricated, forged) is that which is deliberately concocted i.e. devised as a lie against the Messenger of Allah ﷺ. It is the worst type of weak ḥadīth and the ugliest, and it is the same whether its fabrication is known because of his (i.e. the narrator's) admission or because of some evidence derived from the condition of the narrator such as his being given to following the personal desires of some leaders in falsehood, or because of its (the fabrication's) occurrence in part of his (the fabricator's) chain when he is a liar and that tradition is not known except from him with no one else agreeing with him on that and there being no supportive ḥadīth for it. [Similarly the fabrication is known] from the state of the material narrated such as the weakness of its wording or its meanings, or its being contrary to some of the Qurʾān or widespread *sunna* or a categorical consensus or clear reason. It is the same whether he himself invented what he fabricated or took it from someone else's words, or it is a ḥadīth with a weak chain for which he formulated a sound chain so that it gains popularity. It is [also] the same whether he fabricated it in order to lead others into error or anticipating a reward for so doing or out of sectarian prejudice or to amaze [people with unique ḥadīth] or in order to follow the desires of a ruler, or in the case where the fabrication is because of delusion or a simple mistake.

The *matrūk* (abandoned) is that whose narrator is suspected of lying about the Messenger of Allah ﷺ because his ḥadīth contradicts known principles and it is not narrated except through him, or because his lying takes place in ordinary talk among people for which he is well known, and this is less serious than the former.

The *muʿallal* (defective) is that in which a *ʿillah* (hidden defect) is discovered, which denotes a concealed obscure cause [of defect] in the ḥadīth, although outwardly it seems to be free of it. The defect is detected because of the narrator being

88 Such as due to the understanding of the narrator (*fiqh ar-rāwī*), or a high chain (*ʿuluw al-isnād*) or due to the ḥadīth being found in a book which the general mass have accepted to be authentic and authoritative.

alone and because of others contradicting him, along with other evidence that alerts the person knowledgeable in this matter to the fact that an apparently uninterrupted ḥadīth (*mawṣūl*) is actually a *mursal* or that an [apparently] *marfūʿ* is a *mawqūf*, or that a ḥadīth has been inserted within a ḥadīth or to the mistake of someone erroneous, to such an extent that it (the mistake) is most probable in his view and so he judges that the ḥadīth is not authentic, or [to the extent that] he is uncertain and so hesitates [to pass judgement] about it.

This type is one of the greatest and more subtle types of the sciences of ḥadīth, and only those who are people of memory, experience and acute understanding are able to master it. The defect can occur in the chain and that is in the majority of cases and it may sometimes occur in the text. That which occurs in the chain may impair both the chain and the text or it may impair the chain only while the text may remain attributed to the Prophet (*marfūʿ*) and *ṣaḥīḥ*.

The *muḍṭarab* (disrupted) is a ḥadīth narrated in various equally [strong] ways, whether it is twice or more times from a single narrator or from a second narrator or from several narrators without any cause for preference. Then if one of the two or more narrations is considered weightier because of the memory of its narrator or for some other cause for preferring one over the other then the ruling goes in favour of the one which is weightier and the ḥadīth is then not considered to be *muḍṭarab*. The narrations which are outweighed are either anomalous (*shādhdh*) or unfamiliar (*munkar*) as we have seen already. Sometimes the disruption occurs in the chain and at other times in the text, and it may also occur in both together.

The *maqlūb* (mixed-up) is that in which the bringing forward or putting back [of a portion of text or names in the chain] occurs mistakenly. Similarly [when] alteration or exchange occurs either in the chain by ascribing the name of the narrator to his father or his father's name to him, such as Murrah ibn Kaʿb and Kaʿb ibn Murrah, and this is the most common, or by exchanging a narrator with whose narration the ḥadīth is famous for another narrator of the same generation. For example ascribing a ḥadīth to Nāfiʿ which is well known to be [narrated] from Sālim. If it is not due to a mistake but to purposely say something unique then it is like the fabricated (*mawḍūʿ*). It (the mixing-up) may [also] occur in the text such as the ḥadīth of Abū Hurayrah in Muslim in which there is, "...and a man who gives charity which he conceals to such an extent that his right hand does not know what his left hand has spent," which is what has been reversed by one of the narrators, and it should in fact be "... to such an extent that his left hand does not know what his right hand has spent."[89]

89 The right hand is used for spending and for other clean activities, whereas the left hand is used for impure activities such as washing after the toilet.

It may also occur in such a manner that the chain of a text is taken for another text or vice versa, and again if the intention is to make it seem unique then it is like the fabricated (*mawḍūʿ*). It is sometimes done to test the memory of the *muḥaddith* or his acceptance of prompts. The people of ḥadīth have done this. The people of Baghdād reversed one hundred ḥadīth for al-Bukhārī in order to test him and he quoted them back to them correctly and so they openly admitted his merit.[90]

Al-mazīd fī muttaṣil al-asānīd (additions to cohesive chains) is that in whose chain there has been added in a narrator. Those [narrators] who do not add him in are more meticulously careful than are those who add him in. The condition [for accepting an addition in the chain] is that clear audition is declared by [the narrator] in whose chain the additional [narrator] lacks in the position [in the chain] where the addition is found [in this chain]. If [this is not the case] then the addition is preferred and the tradition in which the addition has occured is considered to be either misrepresented (*mudallas*), or interrupted (*munqaṭiʿ*) or there is hidden loosness (*mursal khafiyy*) in it.

The *muhmal* (the neglected or overlooked) is that in which the narrator narrates from one of two people whose names are the same, whether that is a agnomen (*kunya*) or otherwise, or they have the same name and father's name, or they share those names and the grandfather's name, or all of those and their ascription as well [for example 'Kūfan'] referring to him using that [name, agnomen or other reference] which is common [between the two] and not in any way distinguished from the other. To remove [the confusion left by] his neglecting [to make a distinction between the two narrators], reference is made to substantiating evidence and the most likely probability, such as if it becomes clear that the narrator [who narrates from one of the two] is exclusive to one of them because he only narrates from him. If that (i.e. the exact identity of the narrator) is not clear, then if both of them are trustworthy narrators there is no harm [in not knowing which of them it is], or are both untrustworthy narrators then there is harm in it as is the authentic position, or if they are both unknown then the neglect is severe.

The *shāhid* (the attesting or supporting narration) is a ḥadīth which is the same as another or it resembles it in meaning alone, and the Companions [who narrate them] are different, and citing it [as supportive evidence] is called *istishhād*.

Al-Mutābaʿah (following, corroboration) is that a narrator—about whom it was

90 What this means is that if *isnād* (b) has an additional narrator (y) between (x) and (z) which is not found in *isnād* (a), then the onus is on the narrator of *isnād* (a) to prove that clear audition (*simāʿ*) has occurred between (x) and (z) thus eliminating any scope for an addition of narrator (y). If the narrator of *isnād* (a) fails to establish this direct audition (for example by using the preposition *ʿan* instead of *simāʿ*) then preference will be given to *isnād* (b) and the addition of narrator (y) will be held valid. In this instance the omission of narrator (y) from *isnād* (a) will be deemed as either mirepresentation, interrupted or a hidden loosness. Ed.

thought that he had alone narrated—is corroborated by someone else in the wording of what he narrated, with the condition that there only be a single Companion (in the agreement of someone with someone else).[91] This other person is called the *mutābiʿ* or the *tābiʿ* [follower]. *Mutabaʿah* is perfect if it occurred in favour of the narrator himself [about whom it was thought that he alone narrated] and it is imperfect if it occurred in favour of his teacher or someone beyond him [in the *isnād*]. Some people specifically define the *mutābaʿah* to be that which agrees in wording whether it is from that [same] Companion or not, and [they define] the *shāhid* [attesting narration] to be that which similarly agrees in meaning (i.e. whether from the same companion or not).[92]

The *iʿtibār* (consideration) is the investigation of the paths of transmission of the ḥadīth which is thought to a unique single transmission in order to know whether it has a chain in agreement with it (*mutābiʿ*) or an attesting narration (*shāhid*) or not.[93]

The *muḥkam* (decisive) is an accepted ḥadīth safe from contradiction from another accepted ḥadīth even if only apparently.

Mukhtalif al-ḥadīth (differing ḥadīth) are two acceptable ḥadīth which are apparently contradictory in meaning but whose meanings it is possible to reconcile without being recklessly arbitrary.

Nāsikh and *mansūkh* (abrogator and abrogated) are two accepted ḥadīth whose meanings are contradictory to such a degree that it is impossible to reconcile their meanings, but the later of the two is established either by externally[94] known history [*min khārij*] or [by history] which is known but not externally.

Paraphrasing ḥadīth (riwāyat bi 'l-maʿna)

The soundest position is that if a ḥadīth contains multiple meanings [*mushtarak*] or is in summary [*mujmal*] or is ambiguous [*mutashābih*] or is one of those concise ḥadīth containing comprehensive meanings [*jawāmiʿ al-kalim*] then it is not permissible to transmit in meaning only. If it is decisive [*muḥkam*], it is permissible for someone knowledgeable in the language [to transmit it in the meaning]. If it has an apparent meaning [*ẓāhir*] which carries other meanings such as a general ḥadīth [*ʿāmm*] which can carry specification [*khuṣūṣ*] or if it is literal but can carry a

91 This means that both the original and corroborating narrations come from a single companion and the chain of transmission branched off after the companion. If the companions are different, then the corroborating narration is a *shāhid*. Ed.

92 This is an alternative understanding of what *shāhid* and *mutābaʿah* are. According to this understanding, any agreement in wording is *mutābaʿah* and any agreement in meaning is *shāhid*. Whether the narration comes from a single companion or not is not a factor. Ed.

93 Imam al-ʿAynī in *ʿUmdat al-Qārī*, 1:8, gives some good examples of these types as does Shaykh Aḥmad Shākir in his notes to *Ikhtiṣār ʿUlūm al-Ḥadīth* of Ibn Kathīr pp. 63–66.

94 Externally known history is chronological evidence found outside the ḥadīth itself in another ḥadīth or piece of evidence.

metaphorical meaning, then it is only permissible for a person qualified to exercise independent reasoning [paraphrase the ḥadīth]. Moreover, whenever its meaning is concealed recourse to the books compiled to explain unusual words [*gharīb*][95] is required to learn individual meanings, and for knowledge of the problematic idiomatic meanings to the books compiled to explain the meanings of the traditions (*shurūḥ al-ḥadīth*).[96] The *gharib al-ḥadīth* (unusual lexicographical words) in the ḥadīth are those obscure expressions which are difficult to understand because of the rarity of their usage.

Expressions used for the narrators of ḥadīth

Ṭabaqah (generation) linguistically means people who resemble each other, and technically it means people who are close to each other in age and [their position in the] chain or in terms of [their position] in the chain alone because the teachers of this one are the teachers of the other or their teachers are close to each other.

The Companions (*Saḥābah*) are a generation (*ṭabaqah*) and the Followers are another generation and their Followers are another generation and so on. Sometimes two narrators may be from a single generation from one perspective and from two generations by another perspective, such as [the way in which] they have divided up the Companions into twelve [sub]-generations or more and the Followers into fifteen [sub]-generations and so on.

A Companion is someone who met the Prophet ﷺ while believing in him and died upon Islam even if apostasy from Islam interposed.[97] Those are excluded who saw him believing in him between [his] death and burial and died upon Islam because they are not counted as having met him, as are those who met him as a kafir and then accepted Islam but never met him as a believer, and those who met him believing in him and then apostatised and died in apostasy, and we seek refuge in Allah ﷻ.

A Follower is someone who met a Companion even if he did not believe in the Prophet ﷺ and then died upon Islam even if apostasy interposed. As to the interposition of apostasy there is the disagreement of Abū Ḥanīfah in both cases because according to him it invalidates actions unqualifiedly.

A *mukhaḍram* is someone who lived both in the Jāhiliyyah and in Islam and did not see the Prophet ﷺ while believing in him and so he is one of the oldest of the Followers whether or not it is known that he became a Muslim during the life of the Prophet ﷺ, such as the Negus.

---

95 These are books such as *an-Nihāyah* by Ibn Athīr. Ed.

96 These are books such as *Fatḥ al-Barī* by Ibn Ḥajar ʿAsqalānī. Ed.

97 Like ʿAbdullāhibn Abī Saraḥ

CHAPTER 1

Concerning the fact that ascribing weakness or trustworthiness to narrators, or judging that ḥadīth are *ṣaḥīḥ* or *ḥasan* is a speculative [*ijtihādī*] matter, and that each person has their own perspective.

IT IS QUITE valid for a narrator to be considered weak by someone but trustworthy by others, and similarly for a ḥadīth to be considered weak by some and authentic or fair by others. That is indicated by the words of ʿAllāmah Ibn Taymiyah in his book *Rafʿ al-malām ʿan al-aʾimmah al-aʿlām* in his own words, "It ought to be known that none of the Ummah's widely accepted imams deliberately contradicts the Messenger of Allah ﷺ in any matter of his *sunna* whether is a minor or major matter. Rather, if any of them are found to have a verdict against which there is a contrary authentic ḥadīth, then he must surely have had a justifying reason for abandoning it [that *ṣaḥīḥ* ḥadīth]." Then he went into explaining the reasons and their causes at some length, up until he said:

> The third reason: believing that a ḥadīth is weak because of independent reasoning (*ijtihād*) in which one is contradicted by another. There are reasons for this [contradiction], among which is that the narrator of the ḥadīth is regarded by one of them as weak while the other regards him as a trustworthy narrator. The knowledge of the narrators is a vast science, and the scholars of narrators and their states have consensus and differences of opinion just as other scholars have in their [respective] sciences.
>
> [...] "The fourth reason: his stipulating concerning the tradition narrated by a single just *ḥāfiẓ* conditions regarding which others disagree with him, such as that some of them stipulate comparing the ḥadīth with the Book and the *sunna*, and some stipulate that the ḥadīth narrator ought to be a jurist (*faqīh*) if the ḥadīth contradicts analogies derived from basic principles. Some (such as the Ḥanafīs) stipulate that the ḥadīth should be widespread and well established if it is regarding that which is commonly faced [by people], and other such things which are well known in their contexts." (Abridged).

As-Suyūṭī said in *Tadrīb ar-Rāwī* "Subtle defect (*ʿillah*) is an expression for a concealed obscure reason which impugns the ḥadīth although it outwardly appears to be free of it." Ibn aṣ-Ṣalāḥ said, "The defective (*muʿallal*) ḥadīth is that in which a defect is discovered which undermines its authenticity (*ṣiḥḥah*) although it apparently is sound. It finds its way in to the chain which apparently contains in itself all of the conditions of authenticity. The defect is detected because of an isolated narrator (*taffarud ar-rāwī*) and because others contradict him, as well as other reasons joined to that which alerts the knowledgeable person to a mistake that is most probable in his view. Hence, he passes the judgement that the ḥadīth is not authentic or he hesitates [to pass judgement] over it. Sometimes the explanation of the scholar studying the defect falls short of establishing proof of his claim [that the ḥadīth is defective], just as with the money-changer in his critical apprehension of the dinar and the dirham."[98]

Ibn al-Mahdī said, "Recognition of the science of ḥadīth is inspiration. If you were to say to the scholar [knowledgable] of the defects of ḥadīth, 'From where have you said this?' He would not have a proof, and how many people are not guided to that." (Abridged) I say that it is clear that the opinion of one person who exerts his intellect (mujtahid) is no proof to another.

The Ḥāfiẓ said in *al-Fatḥ* after mentioning Ibn Maʿīn's ascription of an error to Ibn ʿUyaynah (d. 198/813) in the chain of the ḥadīth concerning someone passing in front of a person who is praying, in his own words, "Ibn al-Qaṭṭān found fault with that and said, 'It is not certain that Ibn ʿUyaynah was mistaken in that.' I say that the imams finding defects in ḥadīth is based what is most likely in their view [*ghalabat al-ẓann*], and if they say, 'So-and-so was mistaken about such-and-such,' his mistake is not in fact absolutely certain, but on the contrary it is the weightier possibility and so is relied upon."

I say that a possible opinion being considered weightier by one person does not necessarily require it to be such according to others.

As-Suyūṭī said in *Kanz al-ʿUmmāl*,[99] "At-Tirmidhī[100] and Ibn Jarīr (d. 310/923) both said, 'Ismāʿīl ibn Mūsā as-Suddī narrated to us, "Muḥammad ibn ʿUmar ar-Rūmī informed us (*anbaʾanā*) from Sharīk from Salamah ibn Kuhayl from Suwayd ibn Ghafalah from aṣ-Ṣunābiḥī from ʿAlī who said, 'The Messenger of Allah ﷺ said, "I

98 The purpose of quoting as-Suyūṭī here is to establish that there is variation and diversity in the conclusions of scholars when researching aspects of ḥadīth including when detecting subtle defects. This further reinforces his point that these matters are speculative, and different scholars have different perspectives.

99 ʿAlī al-Muttaqī, *Kanz al-ʿUmmāl*, 6:401. Note: as-Suyūṭī did not write *Kanz al-ʿUmmāl*. The *Kanz* is a topical rearrangement by Shaykh ʿAlī al-Muttaqī al-Hindī of some of as-Suyūṭī's ḥadīth collections such as *al-Jāmiʿ al-Ṣaghīr* and *al-Jāmiʿ al-Kabīr*.

100 In his *Sunan*, 13:171.

am the house of wisdom and ʿAlī is its door.'"'" At-Tirmidhī said, 'This ḥadīth is *gharīb* [unusual],' and in one version, 'unfamiliar (*munkar*) because of being narrated by a weak narrator contrary to one who is acceptable). Some of them narrated this ḥadīth from Sharīk without mentioning in it that it is from aṣ-Ṣunābiḥī and this ḥadīth is not known from any other of the trustworthy narrators except from Sharīk, and in the chapter there is [a narration] from Ibn ʿAbbās.' Ibn Jarīr said, 'This tradition is in our view *ṣaḥīḥ* in its chain, but according to the school of others it necessarily has to be defective (*saqīm*) because of two defects: first, that this tradition is not known to have any other narration from ʿAlī from the Prophet ﷺ except in this way; second, that Salamah ibn Kuhayl in their view was one by whose narration proof could not be established; but others have coincided with ʿAlī in narrating this tradition from the Prophet ﷺ.'"

I say that the words of Ibn Jarīr show their disagreement on the conditions for the authenticity of ḥadīth and for considering the narrators trustworthy narrators.

At-Tirmidhī said in his *Jāmiʿ*, "The ḥadīth of Abū Hurayrah, and it is, 'Whatever is between the east and the west is a qiblah,' has been narrated from him in more than one way, and some of the people of knowledge discussed Abū Maʿshar with respect to his memory, and his name was Najīḥ the *mawlā* of Banī Hāshim. Muḥammad[101] said, 'I do not narrate anything from him, even though people have narrated from him.'"

I say that this shows that ascribing weakness or trustworthiness to narrators is a matter of intellectual speculation in reaching a judgement (*ijtihād*).

He said in his *ʿIlal*, "The imams of the people of knowledge differ on ascription of weakness to narrators just as they differ on other matters in knowledge. It is mentioned that Shuʿbah (d. 160/776) regarded Abu'z-Zubayr al-Makkī, ʿAbd al-Malik ibn Abī Sulaymān and Ḥakīm ibn Jubayr as weak and abandoned narrating from them, but then Shuʿbah narrted from those who had less standing in memorisation and integrity. He narrated from Jābir al-Juʿfī, Ibrāhīm ibn Muslim al-Hajarī and Muḥammad ibn ʿUbaydullāh al-ʿArzamī and more than a few others who are regarded as weak in ḥadīth. Someone said to Shuʿbah, 'You abandon ʿAbd al-Malik ibn Abī Sulaymān and yet you narrate from Muḥammad ibn ʿUbaydullāh al-ʿArzamī?' He said, 'Yes.' More than one of the imams regarded Abu'z-Zubayr al-Makkī, ʿAbd al-Malik ibn Abī Sulaymān and Ḥakīm ibn Jubayr as firm and dependable [*thabat*] and narrated from them."

Then he[102] mentioned that ʿAṭāʾ and Ayyūb as-Sakhtiyānī regarded Abu'z-Zubayr as a trustworthy narrator, and that Sufyān ath-Thawrī regarded ʿAbd al-

101 Referring to imam Muḥammad ibn Ismāʿīl al-Bukhārī who was the Shaykh of at-Tirmidhī.
102 Meaning at-Tirmidhī.

Malik ibn Abī Sulaymān as a trustworthy narrator. It is narrated of ʿAlī—al-Madīnī (d. 234/849): "Yaḥyā said, 'Sufyān ath-Thawrī and Zāʾidah narrated from Ḥakīm ibn Jubayr.'" ʿAlī [al-Madini] said, "Yaḥyā saw no harm in his ḥadīth." (Abridged)

Adh-Dhahabī said in his *Dībājah Tadhkirat al-Ḥuffāẓ*, "This is a mention of the names of the authenticated carriers of prophetic knowledge, whose *ijtihād* [exertion of intellect to arrive at a judgement] one refers to in declaring someone a trustworthy or a weak narrator, or in declaring a ḥadīth as authentic or declaring it spurious (*tazyīf*)."

In it there is a clear statement that declaring someone a trustworthy narrator or a weak narrator, and declaring a ḥadīth authentic or declaring it spurious (*tazyīf*) is a matter of speculative intellectual judgement (*ijtihād*) in which it is possible for there to be differences of opinion, so that one person's criticism of a narrator does not necessarily mean that he is disapproved of by everyone.

An-Nawawi said in his introduction to the commentary of [*Ṣaḥīḥ*] Muslim, "Detractors have found fault with Muslim because of his narrating in his *Ṣaḥīḥ* from a number of weak narrators, but there is no fault in him because of that. The answer to it is from a number of points of view which Ibn aṣ-Ṣalāḥ mentioned: first, that the [criticism] was with respect to a weak narrator from someone else's point of view whom he regarded as a trustworthy narrator, and one cannot say [in rebuttal] that invalidation (*jarḥ*) takes precedence over validation (*taʿdīl*) because that is in the case where the invalidation is firmly established and explanable [by reasons], but if that is not the case then invalidation is not [necessarily] accepted."

The Ḥāfiẓ [ibn Ḥajar] said in the introduction to *al-Fatḥ* [*al-Bārī*] in the ninth section which he composed to list the names of those narrators in the *Ṣaḥīḥ* who had been impugned, in his own words,

> Before plunging into it, every fair person ought to know that the author of the *Ṣaḥīḥ* narrating from any necessitates that he is upright in his view and that his retention is sound and he is not neglectful. This is the case when he narrated from him in the core ḥadīth. As for when he narrated from him in corroborating ḥadīth (*mutābaʿāt*) or attesting ḥadīth [*shāhid*], or in *taʿlīq* [ḥadīth that he narrated in his chapter headings omitting the *isnād*] then the rank of those from whom he narrated varied in terms of retention and other things, although their truthfulness was established in principle. At that point if we find someone else impugning them, then that impugning is opposite this imam's validation of them, and thus that impugning is only accepted if the reasons are clearly outlined, and explained by some criticism which diminishes the uprightness [*ʿadālah*] of this narrator and his retention unspecifically, or in his retention of a specific tradition, because the reasons which prompt the imams to impugn someone are various, among them being those which diminish the person's stature and those which do not. (Abridged.)

I say that the clear proclamations of the imams of ḥadīth of the fact that invalidation and validation are matters of speculative intellectual judgement [*ijtihādī*] are too numerous to be counted, and perhaps in that which we have mentioned there is enough. Thus it does not necessarily follow from one person's reckoning a ḥadīth to be authentic that it is sound according to others, nor from one person's reckoning a ḥadīth to be weak that it is weak according to others. So understand this and do not be among the neglectful.

CHAPTER 2

In explanation of what important basic principles and *uṣūl* are connected to declaring ḥadīth *ṣaḥīḥ* or *ḥasan*

He [as-Suyūṭī] said in *Tadrīb ar-Rāwī*,

> When someone says, 'This is a *ṣaḥīḥ* ḥadīth,' then the meaning of this is that, it is such a ḥadīth whose chain is uniterrupted, along with having the aforementioned attributes [of authenticity] and therefore we accepted it, acting according to the outward [correctness of] the chain. This is not [saying] that it is in fact absolutely certain, because of the fact that mistakes and forgetfulness are possible for trustworthy narrators, contrary to the position of those who say that the tradition of a single narrator makes something decisively certain.
>
> If anyone says, 'This ḥadīth is not *ṣaḥīḥ*,' (if he had said it is weak it would have been shorter) then it means its chain is not authentic according to the aforementioned conditions, not that it is actually a lie, because of the possibility of the truthfulness of a liar and the correctness of someone who makes many mistakes.

I say that it is permissible to use a weak ḥadīth as proof if there is evidence of its soundness, just as it is permissible to give up acting in accordance with an authentic ḥadīth because of evidence to the contrary, as we will see in the following extract.

The meticulous scholar [Ibn al-Humām] said in *Fatḥ al-Qadīr*,

> Muslim narrated from many in his book who were not safe from being criticised and similarly there are in al-Bukhārī a group of people who have been discussed critically. The pivot of the affair concerning narrators is on the ijtihād of the people of knowledge, as it is in the preconditions, so much so that whoever reckons a condition to be correct whereas someone else considers it of no account, then what the other narrates of that in which that condition does not exist would be in his view sufficient to contradict those which do comprise that condition. It is similar with those who regard a

narrator as weak whom others regard as a trustworthy narrator. Certainly, the heart of someone who is not a mujtahid and those who are not informed of the narrator's case will be more at ease with that which the majority are agreed upon. As for the mujtahid who exercises his independent judgement in considering the existence or absence of a condition, and the one who is informed about the narrator, then he only refers to his own view..." up until his words, "...so why is it not valid that the ḥadīth with a sound chain should be considered weak because of substantiating evidence as to its weakness in reality, or that the fair ḥadīth should be raised up to the rank of the authentic because of other substantiating evidence? Just as we have shown the practice of the great Companions [to be] in accordance with what we said, and their abandoning the requirements of that ḥadīth [because of evidence to the contrary], and the practice of the great predecessors was similar.

*

When a *mujtahid* uses a ḥadīth as proof [of a ruling etc], it is a declaration that it is authentic as is [mentioned] *in at-Taḥrīr* by Ibn al-Humām and others.[103] There is in *Tadrīb ar-Rāwī*,

> Abu'l-Ḥasan ibn al-Ḥaṣṣār[104] said in *Taqrīb al-Madārik ʿalā Muwaṭṭaʾ Mālik*, "Sometimes the jurist knows that the ḥadīth is authentic when there is no liar in its chain because of its being in accordance with a verse of the Book of Allah ﷻ or with some of the principles (*uṣūl*) of the Sharīʿah and so that brings him to accept it and to act in accordance with it."

I say that the like of this is *ṣaḥīḥ li-ghayrih* not [*ṣaḥīḥ*] of its own nature, as the words of as-Suyūṭī indicate in *at-Tadrīb* together with his abovementioned words.

The Ḥāfiẓ said in *at-Talkhīṣ al-Ḥabīr* concerning a ḥadīth about which al-Bayhaqī spoke, in his own words, "Aḥmad and Ibn al-Mundhir used this ḥadīth as evidence and in their firm assertion of that there is proof of its being authentic in their views."

I say that, similarly in the firm assertion of every mujtahid regarding a ḥadīth there is a proof of his regarding it as *ṣaḥīḥ*, so understand!

Ibn al-Jawzī said in *at-Taḥqīq*, "Whenever a ḥadīth scholar narrates a ḥadīth and a *ḥāfiẓ* uses it as proof, it will only occur to people that it is *ṣaḥīḥ*, as it is [mentioned] in *Naṣb ar-Rāyah*."

The Ḥāfiẓ [Ibn Ḥajar] said in *al-Fatḥ*, "Ibn Ḥazm narrated it using it as proof."

---

103 Ibn ʿĀbidīn, *Radd al-Muḥtār*, (Cairo: Bulāq, 1272), 4:37, this was also the view of imam al-Kawtharī as mentioned in his notes to *Shūrut al-Aʾimmah al-Khamsah* of al-Ḥazimī, pp. 56, 59.

104 He is Abū 'l-Ḥasan ʿAlī ibn Muḥammad al-Khazrajī al-Ishbīlī al-Fāsī al-Sabtī, a scholar of the Maliki school, he visited Egypt and other places. *Ḥāfiẓ* al-Mundhirī heard some of his books from him, and he resided in Makkah and passed away in Madinah in the year 611 may Allah ﷻ have mercy on him. His biography can be found in *al-Aʿlām* of al-Ziriklī, 5:151 and *Muʿjam al-Muʾallifīn* of Kaḥḥālah, 7:228.

I say that every ḥadīth which Muḥammad ibn al-Ḥasan the imam or the ḥadīth scholar *Ḥāfiẓ* aṭ-Ṭaḥāwī narrates using it as proof, then it is a sound proof based on this principle because of the fact that both of them are ḥadīth scholars and mujtahids as we will explain in its place.

The meticulous scholar [Ibn al-Humam] said in *al-Fatḥ*, "If the weak ḥadīth is supported by something from the Qur'an that shows that it is sound then it is authentic."

He also said, "Someone might say that the judgement that a ḥadīth is weak or authentic is only an outward judgement, but in essence it is conceivable for that which has been judged to be outwardly weak to be sound." i.e. if substantiating evidence should arise. With the above-mentioned words, he [Ibn al-Humam] gave an example of that in the fact that it is established that the *madhhab* of Abū Hurayrah is that it is sufficient to wash three times on account of a dog lapping a dish, [and] that [this view of his] is a piece of substantiating evidence which shows that what is narrated from him on this topic as a *marfūᶜ* ḥadīth is authentic. [It is also an example] of that which the weak narrator has narrated well [i.e. correctly and authentically].[105]

There is also in it, "In short, that which is not a *marfūᶜ* ḥadīth or that which is raised (*marfūᶜ*) but which is outweighed in certainty by another raised ḥadīth can sometimes be given priority over its counterpart if it is accompanied by substantiating evidence showing that it is authentically from him ﷺ and that he acted continuously by it."

*

A ḥadīth is sometimes judged to be *ṣaḥīḥ* if people[106] receive it and accept it, even though it may not have a sound chain.

Ibn ᶜAbd al-Barr said in *al-Istidhkār* when he narrated from at-Tirmidhī that al-Bukhārī declared the ḥadīth of the sea to be authentic, 'its waters are pure...', even though the people of ḥadīth do not regard the likes of its chain to be sound,[107] "nevertheless the ḥadīth in my view is authentic because the people of knowledge received it and accepted it."

I say that acceptance is sometimes expressed in words and at other times by acting in accordance with [the ḥadīth]. For that reason the meticulous scholar [Ibn al-

---

105 Earlier the point has been made that it is possible for the authentic narrator to make a mistake and the weak narrator to be correct. Here, an example is given of when substantiating evidence proves that what a weak narrator has narrated is in fact authentic and thus acceptable. Ed.

106 i.e. the people of knowledge. Ed.

107 Shaykh Abū Ghuddah mentioned that the people of ḥadīth actually have classified its chain and content to be *ṣaḥīḥ*, this was discussed by him in detail in the appendix to al-Laknawī's *al-Ajwibah al-Fāḍilah*, pp.228–238.

Humam] said in *al-Fatḥ*, "the statement of al-Tirmidhi 'and the practice is according to it in the view of the people of knowledge,' requires that its root is strong even if the specific [narrators] of this path are weak.

As-Suyūṭī said in *at-Taʿaqqubāt*, "The ḥadīth[108] which at-Tirmidhī narrates and about which he said, 'Aḥmad and others have declared Ḥusayn to be weak,[109] and practice is according to it in the view of the people of knowledge.' Thus he indicates by that, that the ḥadīth is strengthened by the verdict of the people of knowledge; more than a few have declared clearly that part of the proof that a ḥadīth is authentic is the verdict of the people of knowledge according to it even if it does not have a reliable chain."

Also, there is in it, "At-Tirmidhī said, 'Ibn al-Mubārak and others held the view that the *ṣalāt at-tasbīḥ* [is authentic] and they mentioned the virtues in it.' Al-Bayhaqī said, "ʿAbdullāh ibn al-Mubārak used to pray it,' and the people of right action transmitted it one to another, and in that there is support for the *marfūʿ* ḥadīth.'

In fact, if the Ummah receive and accept a ḥadīth then in our view it is in the meaning of the widespread ḥadīth (*mutawātir*). Al-Jaṣṣāṣ said in his *Aḥkām al-Qurʾān*, "The ummah made use of these two ḥadīth[110] even though they are narrated by way of solitary individuals (*āḥād*) so that they became within the scope of the *mutawātir* because whatever traditions transmitted by solitary individuals (*āḥād*) people accept, are in our view of the same meaning as if they were *mutawātir* because of that which we will make clear in its appropriate places."

*

The authentic ḥadīth is not confined to that which is in *Ṣaḥīḥ* al-Bukhārī and Muslim, but on the contrary authentic ḥadīth are also to be found in other works, as is mentioned in *Tadrīb ar-Rāwī*, "They did not comprehensively encompass all of the authentic ḥadīth in their two books nor did they undertake to do that—i.e. to encompass them completely, for al-Bukhārī said, 'I have not recorded in my book *al-Jāmiʿ* anything but that which is authentic, but I left out authentic ḥadīth for fear of being too lengthy.' Muslim said, 'I have not recorded everything which I regard as authentic here, but have only recorded what they hold consensus on.' By this he means that which he found in his view to comprise the preconditions of authentic

108 Referring to the ḥadīth of Ibn ʿAbbās "He who joins between two prayers without an excuse has committed a major sin".

109 Ḥusayn ibn Qays Abū ʿAlī al-Raḥabī also known as Ḥansh is one of the narrators of this ḥadīth, p. 80, h. 188.

110 The ḥadīth in Abū Dāwūd 2:257, and Ibn Mājah, 1:672 from ʿĀ'ishah from the Prophet ﷺ who said, "The [irrevocable] divorce of the slave woman consists of two divorces and her *ʿiddah* consists of two menstrual periods," and from Ibn Mājah, 1:672 and ad-Dāraquṭnī, 4:38 from Ibn ʿUmar who said, "The Messenger of Allah ﷺ said, "The divorce of the slave woman is done twice and her *ʿiddah* is two menstrual periods."

ḥadīth on which there is consensus even if some of them did not see their [preconditions] in some of them, as Ibn aṣ-Ṣalāḥ said.

An-Nawawī preferred the view that what is meant [by consensus] is that trustworthy narrators do not differ about the text and the chain of the same ḥadīth, not that there is no disagreement concerning the trustworthiness of its narrators. Ibn aṣ-Ṣalāḥ said, 'The proof of that is he was asked about the ḥadīth of Abū Hurayrah, "When it [Qurʾān] is recited, be silent," as to whether it is authentic. He said, "in my view it is authentic." Someone asked, "Why did you not record it here?" And so he answered in that way.'"

I say that it is permissible to counter a ḥadīth which the two of them narrated or one of them with an authentic ḥadīth which someone else narrated.

The meticulous scholar [Ibn al-Humam] said in *al-Fatḥ*,

> The fact that the contradicting narration is in al-Bukhārī does not necessarily require his [al-Bukhārī's] ḥadīth having precedence after both of them being authentic. On the contrary the factor which determines which is weightier is sought elsewhere. As for the saying of those who say that "the most authentic of ḥadīth are those which are in the two *Ṣaḥīḥ* books and then that which al-Bukhārī alone narrated and then that which Muslim alone narrated and then those which are based on both of their conditions but narrated by other narrators and then those which are based on what one of them narrated", it is arbitrariness which cannot be followed, since superior authenticity is only because of their narrators comprising those preconditions which they reckoned were important. When the existence of these preconditions in narrators of ḥadīth from books other than the two *Ṣaḥīḥ* books can be determined, then is not the ruling of greater authenticity of what is in the two *Ṣaḥīḥ* books the epitome of arbitrariness? Also their judgement or the judgement of one of them that a specific narrator unites those preconditions within himself is not something whose agreement with actual fact can be absolutely determined; it is conceivable that the facts may be contrary to it.

I say that even if we concede that whatever is in their two books is more *Ṣaḥīḥ*, this cannot be paid any attention when contradiction occurs, just as when two men establish evidence and both of their witnesses are upright, but the witnesses of one of them have more *taqwā* and scrupulousness than those of the other, his evidence does not outweigh the other's because of that after [it has been established that] both [sets of witnesses] have [principle] uprightness according to the *Sharīʿah* in common. Instead the factor which will determine which outweighs the other will be sought elsewhere.

Nevertheless, the claim that the most authentic ḥadīth are those in the two books, or that that of al-Bukhārī is more *ṣaḥīḥ* than *Ṣaḥīḥ* Muslim and others, is only a sound view in general terms and with respect to the totality and not in terms of specific details of each ḥadīth. [As-Suyūṭī] clearly stated this in *Tadrīb ar-Rāwī* where he said:

> Things can occur to a lesser ḥadīth which render it of greater rank, such as when they [al-Bukhari and Muslim] both agree on narrating a *gharīb* [unusual] ḥadīth whereas Muslim or someone else narrates a widely known (*mashhūr*) ḥadīth or one which is described as 'the soundest of chains.' That does not impugn what has been discussed earlier because that is with respect to the totality [but not specific details]. Az-Zarkashī said, "thus we know that the preference of *Ṣaḥīḥ* al-Bukhārī over Muslim and others is the preference of the totality over the totality not the preference of every individual ḥadīth of one over every single ḥadīth of the other."

There is also in *at-Tadrīb* that al-Ḥākim said,

> The *ṣaḥīḥ* ḥadīth is divided into ten categories five of which are agreed upon, and upon five of which there is disagreement. The former which are agreed upon is chosen by al-Bukhārī and Muslim—[up until his words]—the fifth are ḥadīth of a group of people narrating from their fathers from their grandfathers whose narration from their fathers from their grandfathers has not become widespread except through them, such as ʿAmr ibn Shuʿayb narrating from his father from his grandfather, Bahz ibn Ḥakīm from his father from his grandfather, and Iyās ibn Muʿāwiyah ibn Qurrah from his father from his grandfather. Their grandfathers were Companions whose grandsons were trustworthy narrators. These [narrations] are also used as proof and are narrated in the books of the imams with the exception of the two *Ṣaḥīḥ* books [of al-Bukhari and Muslim].

I say that this is also a clear proof of the existence of *ṣaḥīḥ* ḥadīth in works other than the two *Ṣaḥīḥ* books.

*

As-Suyūṭī said in the opening lines in which he categorised statements in the *Jāmʿ al-jawāmiʿ*[111] in his own words:

> I have [given reference to] al-Bukhārī by [using the sign] *'kh'* and to Muslim by *'m'* and Ibn Ḥibbān by *'ḥb'* and al-Ḥākim in *al-Mustadrak* by *'k'* and aḍ-Ḍiyāʾ al-Maqdisī in al-Mukhtārah by *'ḍ'*. Everything in these five books is authentic and so attribution to them shows that the ḥadīth is authentic, apart from those [narrations] in *al-Mustadrak* which have been critically reviewed, to which I will draw attention.
>
> Similarly that which is in the *Muwaṭṭaʾ Mālik*, *Ṣaḥīḥ* Ibn Khuzaymah and that of Abū ʿAwānah and Ibn as-Sakan, the *Muntaqā* of Ibn al-Jārūd and in the books

111 *Jamʿ al-Jawāmiʿ* and *al-Jāmiʿ al-Kabīr* are two names for the same work.

called *Mustakhraj*, attribution to which also shows that the ḥadīth are authentic. Everything in the *Musnad Aḥmad* is accepted because the weak ḥadīth that are in it are almost fair (*ḥasan*)." (Abridged from *Kanz al-ʿUmmāl*).

In *Tadrīb ar-Rāwī*,

> Third—concerning the issues related to the authentic ḥadīth, those books which are written supplying other chains of transmission for ḥadīth in the two *Ṣaḥīḥ* books—such as *al-Mustakhraj* by al-Ismāʿīlī, and by al-Barqānī, Abū Aḥmad al-Ghiṭrīfī, Abū ʿAbdullāh ibn Abī Dhuhl, Abū Bakr ibn Marduwayh on al-Bukhārī, and by Abū ʿAwānah al-Isfirāʾinī, Abū Jaʿfar ibn Ḥamdān, Abū Bakr Muḥammad ibn Rajāʾ an-Naysabūrī, Abū Bakr al-Jawzaqī, Abū Ḥāmid ash-Shārakī, Abu'l-Walīd Ḥassān ibn Muḥammad al-Qurashī, Abū ʿImrān Mūsā ibn al-ʿAbbās al-Juwaynī, Abū Naṣr aṭ-Ṭūsī, Abū Saʿīd ibn Abī ʿUthmān al-Ḥīrī on Muslim, and by Abū Nuʿaym al-Aṣbahānī, Abū ʿAbdullāh ibn al-Akhram, Abū Dharr al-Harawī, Abū Muḥammad al-Khallāl, Abū ʿAlī al-Māsarjisī, Abū Masʿud Sulaymān ibn Ibrāhīm al-Aṣbahānī, Abū Bakr al-Yazdī on each of them [al-Bukhārī and Muslim], and by Abū Bakr ibn ʿAbdān ash-Shīrāzī on both of them in one single composition. [A *mustakhraj*] has two benefits: the exaltedness of the chain and an increase in authentic ḥadīth, because these extra ḥadīth are authentic because of the fact that they have their chains [al-Bukhārī's and Muslim's].

There is also in it,

> The Ḥāfiẓ Abū ʿAbdullāh al-Ḥākim was concerned in his *Al-Mustadrak* to detail those [narrations] which are in addition to their's [i.e. al-Bukhārī and Muslim] and in accordance with their conditions or with the conditions of one of them, or simply authentic even though neither of their conditions are met. Sometimes he narrated in it what is not authentic in his view in order to draw attention to it. He [al-Hakim] is lenient in authentication. Adh-Dhahabī abridged his *Mustadrak* and critically reviewed much of it as being weak or unfamiliar (*munkar*). He compiled a volume of the ḥadīth in it which are fabricated mentioning almost a hundred ḥadīth. Therefore, whatever al-Ḥākim regarded as authentic which we found no other dependable authorities authenticating or declaring weak, then we judge that it is *ḥasan* unless a defect should emerge in it that necessarily requires that it be weak.

I say that adh-Dhahabī relieved us of the necessity of doing that; so whatever he confirmed of it is *ṣaḥīḥ*, and whatever he was silent about and did not review is *ḥasan* as Ibn aṣ-Ṣalāḥ said. I saw that al-ʿAzīzī in his commentary on al-*Jāmiʿ aṣ-Ṣaghīr* used adh-Dhahabī's affirmation of al–Ḥākim's authentication as proof. So let that be known. And Allah ﷻ knows best.

A book that is also a source of *ṣaḥīḥ* ḥadīth is *al-Mujtabā* by an-Nasāʾī and it is widely available and read in all the lands. Muḥammad ibn Muʿāwiyah al-Aḥmar who narrated from an-Nasāʾī said, "An-Nasāʾī said, 'The book *as-Sunan al-kubrā* is all authentic and some of it is defective,' but he did not explain its defect, 'and the selection called *al-Mujtabā* is all authentic.'"[112] The Ḥāfiẓ Abu'l-Faḍl ibn Ḥajar said,

> Abū ʿAlī an-Naysabūrī, Abū Aḥmad ibn ʿAdī, Abu'l-Ḥasan ad-Dāraquṭnī, Abū ʿAbdullāh al-Ḥākim, Ibn Mandah, ʿAbd al-Ghanī ibn Saʿīd, Abū Yaʿlā al-Khalīlī, Abū ʿAlī ibn as-Sakan, Abū Bakr al-Khaṭīb and others all referred to the book of an-Nasāʾī with the designation of authenticity [*as-ṣiḥḥah*].

As-Sindī said in his commentary on an-Nasāʾī,

> In general, using the term authentic for the small book [*al-Ṣaghīr*] of an-Nasāʾī, which is the well-known one, is widespread. This is also based on calling *ḥasan* ḥadīth *ṣaḥīḥ*. The weak ḥadīth [in it] are very few and appended to [the] *ḥasan* [category] if nothing else exists in that topic. This is stronger in the compiler's [an-Nasai's] view and in the view of Abū Dāwūd than the opinions of men, and Allah ﷻ, knows best.[113]

*

If there is disagreement about the ḥadīth, with some regarding it as *ṣaḥīḥ* or *ḥasan* and others regarding it as weak, then it is *ḥasan*. It is the same if people differ about the narrator, some regarding him as a trustworthy narrator and others regarding him as weak, then he is someone whose ḥadīth are *ḥasan*. He [al-Suyuti] said in *Tadrīb ar-Rāwī*,

> Note: *ḥasan* also has different ranks just as does the authentic. Adh-Dhahabī said, "The highest of its ranks is: Bahz ibn Ḥakīm from his father from his grandfather, ʿAmr ibn Shuʿayb from his father from his grandfather, and Ibn Isḥāq from at-Taymi and the likes of these about which it is said that it is authentic. This is the lowest rank of the authentic. Then after that there are those about which there is difference of opinion as to whether it is fair or weak, such as the ḥadīth of al-Ḥārith ibn ʿAbdullāh, ʿĀṣim ibn Ḍamrah, and Ḥajjāj ibn Arṭāh and the likes of them."

I say, [there are] also those such as Muḥammad ibn Abī Laylā, al-Ḥasan ibn ʿUmārah, the Qāḍī Sharīk, Shahr ibn Ḥawshab and others of those about whom there is disa-

112 *Al-Mujtabā* is what is common amongst the people and is one of the books from the six canonical collections.

113 This means that when only weak ḥadīth are available regarding an issue, an-Nasāʾī and Abū Dāwūd prefer to use them as evidence than rely on the mere opinions of scholars. Ed.

greement as to whether they are trustworthy or weak narrators, and there are many of them. adh-Dhahabī who is a person of perfect induction in the critical examination of narrators said, "No two people of the people of knowledge of this affair have ever agreed regarding authenticating a weak narrator or in regarding a trustworthy narrator as weak. It is for this reason that the opinion of an-Nasāʾī was not to abandon the ḥadīth of a narrator unless everyone was agreed on rejecting him." (Quoted in *ar-Rafʿ* from al-Sakhāwī's *Fatḥ al-Mughīth*).

Al-Mundhirī said in the introduction to his *Targhīb*, "So I say that if the narrators of the *isnād* of a ḥadīth are trustworthy narrators but among them there is someone about whom there is disagreement, then its chain is fair or it is decent [*mustaqīm*] or there is no harm in it [*lā baʾsa bih*]." He also said in the chapter which he composed to explain the narrators about whom there is disagreement in his biographical notice on Muḥammad ibn Isḥāq ibn Yasār the author of al-Maghāzī. After a long discussion, [he said] "In summation he is one of those about whom there is disagreement and his ḥadīth are *ḥasan*."

Az-Zaylaʿī said [in *Naṣb ar-rāyah*] transmitting from Ibn al-Qaṭṭān concerning the ḥadīth of Qays ibn Ṭalq from his father that, "There is disagreement about the ḥadīth and so one ought to say that it is *ḥasan* but not pass the judgement that it is authentic, and Allah ﷻ knows best." Also in it Ibn Daqīq al-ʿĪd said,

> This ḥadīth (i.e. "the two ears are part of the head") is defective for two reasons: first, there is criticism about Shahr ibn Ḥawshab; second, doubt regarding wether it is *marfūʿ*. However, Aḥmad, Yaḥyā, al-ʿIjlī, Yaʿqūb ibn Shaybah and Sinān ibn Rabīʿah regarded Shahr as a trustworthy narrator, and al-Bukhārī narrated his ḥadīth; and even though he has been regarded as somewhat weak, yet Ibn ʿAdī said, "I hope that there is no harm in him [*lā baʾsa bih*]," and Ibn Maʿīn said, "He is not strong, so the ḥadīth in our view is *ḥasan*."

In the gloss (*ḥāshiyah*) on Abū Dāwūd[114] under the ḥadīth, "Forgive the people of consistent good conduct their slips except for crimes deserving capital punishments [*ḥudūd*],"[115]

> This is one of the ḥadīth which the *Ḥāfiẓ* Sirāj ad-Dīn al-Qazwīnī criticised in the *Maṣābīḥ* of al-Baghawī and claimed that it was fabricated. Ibn ʿAdī said, "This ḥadīth is unfamiliar [*munkar*] with this chain and only ʿAbd al-Malik narrated it." Al-Mundhirī said, "ʿAbd al-Malik is weak." Al-Ḥāfiẓ Ṣalāḥ ad-Dīn al-ʿAlāʾī said, "About this ʿAbd al-Malik, an-Nasāʾī said, 'There is no harm in him.'" Ibn Ḥibbān

114 Called *Mirqāt as-Saʿūd* 2:253, the author of *ʿAwn al-Maʿbūd* quoted from it in 4:232.

115 Narrated by Abū Dāwūd, 4:13, al-Bukhārī in *al-Adab al-Mufrad*, imam Aḥmad in *al-Musnad* and an-Nasāʾī as mentioned in *Fayḍ al-Qadīr* of al-Munāwī 2:74.

declared him as a trustworthy narrator, and so the ḥadīth is *ḥasan,* if Allāh Most High wills, not least because an-Nasāʾī narrated it for he did not narrate rejected or weak ḥadīth nor from anyone who is abandoned.

The meticulous scholar Ibn al-Humām said in *al-Fatḥ*,

> ad-Dāraquṭnī narrated from ʿUbaydullāh ibn ʿAbdullāh from Ibn ʿAbbās, "The Messenger of Allah ﷺ only forbade the meat of carrion. As for the hide, hair and wool of it there is no harm in it," and he regarded it as defected because of ʿAbd al-Jabbār ibn Muslim regarded it as weak, which is unacceptable for Ibn Ḥibbān mentioned him in *ath-Thiqāt*—Trustworthy Narrators—and therefore the ḥadīth does not descend any lower than *ḥasan*.

As-Suyūṭī said in *at-Taʿaqqubāt* concerning the ḥadīth of ʿĀ'ishah which is *marfūʿ*, "It is not fitting for a people among whom is Abū Bakr that anyone else should lead them," in refutation of Ibn al-Jawzī who regarded it as defective because of ʿĪsā ibn Maymūn, [saying] that he is not considered proof worthy and because of Aḥmad ibn Bashīr, because he is abandoned. In his [as-Suyūṭī's] own words,

> At-Tirmidhī narrated this ḥadīth, and al-Bukhārī used Aḥmad ibn Bashīr in proof, and the majority regarded him as a trustworthy narrator. ad-Dāraquṭnī said that he was weak but his ḥadīth are to be reckoned with. Ḥammād said about ʿĪsā, "A trustworthy narrator." Yaḥyā said once, "There is no harm in him," but others regarded him as weak but he was not suspected of lying, and so the ḥadīth is *ḥasan*.

Al-Ḥāfiẓ said in *Tahdhīb at-tahdhīb* in the biographical notice on ʿAbdullāh ibn Ṣāliḥ who was al-Layth's scribe, "Ibn al-Qaṭṭān said, 'He is truthful, and nothing is established about him that would make one drop his ḥadīth except that there is disagreement about him, and so his ḥadīth are *ḥasan*.'"

I say that these expressions in their entirety are a proof of what we have said that if there is disagreement about a narrator then his ḥadīth are [considered] *ḥasan*. If it were not because of fear of being prolix I would produce more details of that for you. Whoever studies the books on the narrators, the defects, and the reinvestigations of fabricated ḥadith will never doubt this principle.

*

Ḥasan ḥadīth are like the *ṣaḥīḥ* in using them as proof even though they are lower in strength. For this reason a party include them as a type of *ṣaḥīḥ*, such as al-Ḥākim, Ibn Ḥibbān and Ibn Khuzaymah, along with their saying that it less than the authentic as explained earlier; he [as-Suyuti] said that in *Tadrīb ar-Rāwī*. Al-Ḥāfiẓ [ibn Hajar] said in in the commentary of *an-Nukhbah*, "This category of *ḥasan* ḥadīth share with the *ṣaḥīḥ* in being used in proof even if less than it and it resembles it in being categorised into different ranks some of which are above others."

*

If the ḥadīth which is *ḥasan li dhātih* is narrated in more than one way, even if only one other way, becomes stronger and raised up from the degree of being *ḥasan* to the degree of being *ṣaḥīḥ*. He said that in *Tadrīb ar-Rāwī* and he [Ibn Ḥajar] stated that clearly in the commentary of *an-Nukhbah*.

*

If the paths of transmission of a weak ḥadīth are numerous, even if there is only one other path of transmission,[116] then it ascends because of that to the degree of *ḥasan* and may be used as proof.

He said in *Tadrīb ar-Rāwī*, "There is no novelty in using as proof a ḥadīth which has two such paths of transmission that if either one of them is alone, it would not be considered a proof, just as is the case with the *mursal* ḥadīth if it is narrated by another path with an full chain, or if another loose [ḥadīth] confirms it with its condition, as we will see." There is also in it, "Similarly, if its weakness is because it is *mursal* or because of misrepresentation (*tadlīs*) or a narrator is unknown, then [that weakness] is removed by its being narrated through another path, and it becomes of less standing than a ḥadīth which is intrinsically *ḥasan*."

In the commentary of *an-Nukhbah*:

> When the one whose memory is bad is parrelled with one who is considered[117] and he is either higher or similar but not less than [the one with the bad memory], similarly the confused person who does not distinguish [the point of confusion], the concealed [narrator] (*mastūr*), the loose chain (*mursal*), and similarly the misrepresented (*mudallas*), then in all of these cases their ḥadīth become *ḥasan* although not intrinsically. Rather it's being described thus [i.e. as *ḥasan*] is due to taking into account the totality of both the follower (*mutābiᶜ*) and the parralled (*mutābaᶜ*), because each one of them in terms of the possibility of being correct or incorrect are equal. Then if a narration is produced by one of those to be reckoned with which accords with one of them, then one of the two probabilities outweighs the other, and that shows that the

116 The author does not mean here that any *ḍaᶜīf* ḥadīth ascends to the degree of *ḥasan* if there is another transmission. This is only the case if the weakness in the ḥadīth is because the narrator has a poor memory, gets mixed up [*ikhtilāṭ*], because of *tadlīs* [hiding a defect], or because the ḥadīth is *mursal*. On the other if the weakness is because the narrator is suspected of lying or worse, or if the ḥadīth is irregular [*shādhdh*], then the ḥadīth remains weak even with multiple transmissions. (Abridged from the footnotes of Shaykh ᶜAbd al-Fattāḥ), *Qawāᶜid*, p. 78, fn. 6.

117 Here the word *muᶜtabar* is used in a technical sense to mean the one whose narrations are considered as proof text, and not in the literal sense as to mean reliable.

ḥadīth is *maḥfūẓ* (correctly preserved and safe from corruption), and so it ascends from the degree of being a ḥadīth about which one hesitates and is in doubt to the degree of being accepted, and Allah ﷻ knows best.

According to *Mā thabata bi 's-Sunna*, transmitting from al-Ḥāfiẓ al-ʿIrāqī:

> The apparent outward meaning of al-Bayhaqī's words is that the ḥadīth on reprieve (concerning the tenth day of Muḥarram) is *ḥasan* according to the view of people other than Ibn Ḥibbān also, because he narrated it by different paths of transmission from a body of the Companions as a raised (*marfūʿ*) ḥadīth.

Then he said,

> Even if these chains are weak, yet when they are connected to each other, it brings about strength. Ibn Taymiyah's denial saying that nothing is narrated from him ﷺ about reprieve is an illusion as you have learnt. The verdict of Aḥmad that it is not *ṣaḥīḥ*—i.e. intrinsically—does not negate the fact that it is *ḥasan* because of the other [transmissions], and the ḥadīth which is *ḥasan* because of the other [*ḥasan li ghayrih*] may be used as proof as has been explained in the science of ḥadīth. (Here end the words of al-ʿIrāqī)

The meticulous scholar said in *al-Fatḥ*, "These are a number of ḥadīth, even if they were weak, the texts are *ḥasan*, and how could that not be so when among them there are those which do not descend below the degree of being *ḥasan*?" There is also in it, "These are multiple paths of transmission from more than ten Companions, even if each one of them were weak, the totality of them are firmly established as proof, and how could that not be the case when some of them do not descend below the degree of *ḥasan*?"

The author states in *Tadrīb ar-Rāwī*:

> The ḥadīth which is weak because of the narrator being a sinner or liar is unaffected by another ḥadīth being in accord with it if the other is similar to it because of the severity of its weakness and the inferiority of the supporting narration. However, with the collective of its paths of transmission it does rise above the degree of being rejected [*munkar*] or baseless [la asla lahu], which the Shaykh al-Islam—i.e. Ḥāfiẓ Ibn Ḥajar—stated clearly. He said, "Rather, often the numerous paths of transmission will make it reach to the degree of a [ḥadīth of a] concealed narrator (*mastūr*) and the ḥadīth of someone of poor memory such that if another path of transmission is found for it in which there is a similar possible weakness, it will ascend with all of that to the degrees of being *ḥasan*."[118]

118 Based on the context here it is clear that *ḥāfiẓ* Ibn Ḥajar is speaking of the ḥadīth of a sinner or

The noted savant and ḥadīth scholar, the gnostic ash-Shaʿrānī who was a pupil of as-Suyūṭī said in *al-Mīzān*,

> The dominant majority of the ḥadīth scholars have made use of weak ḥadīth in establishing proofs when there are many paths of transmission, and they have appended it to [the category of] the *ṣaḥīḥ* sometimes and to the *ḥasan* at other times. This type of weak ḥadīth is found very often in the book *as-Sunan al-Kubrā* by al-Bayhaqī, [a book] which he authored intending to support with evidence the verdicts of the imams and of their companions. This is because if he did not find a *ṣaḥīḥ* or *ḥasan* ḥadīth with which to prove the verdict of that imam or the verdict of any of those who followed his judgements [in *taqlīd*] he would begin to narrate weak ḥadīth from such-and-such paths of transmission, and suffice himself with that, and he would say, "These paths of transmission strengthen each other."

*

What Abū Dāwūd was silent about is fine for use as proof. Al-Mundhirī said in the introduction to his *Targhīb*,

> Every ḥadīth which I ascribe to Abū Dāwūd and about which I am silent, then it is as Abū Dāwūd mentioned, it does not fall lower than the degree of being good (*ḥasan*) and, at times, can possibly be according to the conditions of the two *Ṣaḥīḥ* books or one of them.

The noted scholar ash-Shawkānī said in *Nayl al-Awṭār*, "We have previously introduced the point that a body of the imamṣ of ḥadīth have clearly stated that that which Abū Dāwūd was silent about is fine for use as proof."

According to *Tadrīb ar-Rāwī*:

> One of its common sources—meaning of *ḥasan* ḥadīth– is the *Sunan* Abī Dāwūd because it has been narrated from him that he mentions in it the *ṣaḥīḥ* and that which resembles it or is close to it. That which is very weak he explains and makes clear, but that about which he mentions nothing is fine."

About the ḥadīth of Abū Dāwūd, "Allah ﷻ continues to be directed towards the slave while he is in his prayer as long as he does not look about. If he looks about He turns away from him," al-Mundhirī said,

> Abu'l-Aḥwaṣ—the narrator—is unknown, and no one apart from az-Zuhrī narrated from him. Yaḥyā ibn Maʿīn said, "He is nothing." Al-Karābīsī said, "He is not dependable according to them." An-Nawawī said in *al-Khulāṣah*, "He [Abu 'l-Aḥwaṣ] in it is

---

suspected liar rising to the degree of the two types of ḥadīth mentioned in the quote. Ed.

an unknown narrator, but Abū Dāwūd did not regard the ḥadīth as weak and so it is *ḥasan* in his view."[119] (*Az-Zaylaʿī*)

*

The extra ḥadīth[120] which the Ḥāfiẓ mentions in *Fatḥ al-bārī* and remains silent about, are *ṣaḥīḥ* or *ḥasan* in his view as he stated clearly in his introduction.[121] In his own words,

> Then I narrate secondly that which is narrated to an authentic aim in respect to that ḥadīth, such as textual and *isnād* narrated benefits that are complementary or additional, [and such as] exposing obscure matters, the clear statement of a *mudallis* that he heard [the ḥadīth suspected of being misrepresented] from his sheikh, and the corroboration of [a ḥadīth] by someone who heard from a confused sheikh[122] before his confusion; taking all of that from the core *musnad* texts,[123] ḥadīth compendiums [*jawāmiʿ*],[124] the *mustakhrajāt*,[125] the *ajzāʾ*[126] and *fawāʾid*,[127] with the prior stipulation that what I narrate of that be *ṣaḥīḥ* or *ḥasan*.

Ash-Shawkānī said in *Nayl al-awṭār* concerning the ḥadīth of Khawlah bint Ḥakīm "That she asked the Prophet ﷺ about a woman who sees in her sleep what a man sees. . .",[128] "and the Ḥāfiẓ mentioned it in *al-Fatḥ* and did not discuss it critically." He [ash-Shawkānī] also spoke about the ḥadīth of Yaʿlā ibn Umayyah, "That the Messenger of Allah ﷺ saw a man bathing in an open tract of land. . . ." "Al-Bazzār narrated the like of it in a ḥadīth of Ibn ʿAbbās at some length, and the Ḥāfiẓ mentioned it in *al-Fatḥ* and did not speak about it." In this there is an indication that the

119 Although the author has clearly stated the position that any ḥadīth that Abū Dāwūd has remained silent about is at least *ḥasan*, Shaykh ʿAbd al-Fattāḥ, in his footnotes on this work, has stressed that this is not the position of the *muhaqqiq* (meticulous) scholars. Imam Abū Dāwūd's statement that any ḥadīth he has been silent about in his *Sunan* is fine, is not to be taken as unqualifiedly as the statement itself appears to be. Rather, imam Abū Dāwūd has also narrated ḥadīth from weak and very weak narrators in the *Sunan*, sometimes because their weakness is well known among ḥadīth scholars and at other times out of error. Therefore his silence over a ḥadīth cannot always be taken as an accurate indication of a ḥadīth's acceptability, although generally it is seen to be so. *Qawāʿid*, p. 83–87, fn. 1.

120 Those ḥadīth he narrates in the commentary on the ḥadīth of *Ṣaḥīḥ al-Bukhārī*.

121 Called *Hady as-Sārī ilā Fatḥ al-Bārī*.

122 Meaning a shaykh whose memory became weak later in life but it is unclear in the case of a particular ḥadīth as to which period of his life in which the ḥadīth was narrated from him.

123 A *musnad* text is one which is indexed based on narrators rather than topics.

124 *Jawāmiʿ*, plural of *Jāmiʿ*, are ḥadīth compilations which contain all of the topics that are contained in the whole body of ḥadīth.

125 Texts that are compilations of ḥadīth that concur with the ḥadīth of other compilers such as al-Bukhārī and Muslim but with alternative chains via their shaykhs. Ed.

126 *Ajzāʾ*, plural of *juzʾ*, are ḥadīth compilations based on one specific topic.

127 *Fawāʾid*, plural of *fāʾidah*, are ḥadīth compilations of specific benefits and anecdotes. Ed.

128 i.e. a wet dream.

silence of the Ḥāfiẓ in *al-Fatḥ* is an indication or a clear proof that it is either *ṣaḥīḥ* or *ḥasan*, and Allah ﷻ knows best.

I say that similarly the Ḥāfiẓ's silence about a ḥadīth in *at-Talkhīṣ al-Ḥabīr* indicates that it is either *ṣaḥīḥ* or *ḥasan*, because ash-Shawkānī often uses his silence in *at-Talkhīṣ* as positive proof the way he uses his silence in *al-Fatḥ* as proof. This becomes clear from checking *Nayl al-Awṭār*.

*

"It does not necessarily follow when they say, 'There is nothing on this topic more *ṣaḥīḥ* than this,' that the ḥadīth is *ṣaḥīḥ*, but on the contrary what is meant is that the ḥadīth is the most authentic ḥadīth on the topic, and they very often mean this sense by this phrase." As is in *al-Jawhar an-Naqī*.

I say that it is thus possible that it could be weak but it is better than other ḥadīth. However, it is not possible for it to be fabricated.

CHAPTER 3

Concerning the ruling on acting by a weak ḥadīth and the conditions for doing so when it is only narrated by one route. If it is narrated through two or more routes we have already seen that it is sometimes to be appended to the [degree of] *ṣaḥīḥ* and sometimes to the [degree of] *ḥasan*.

According to *ad-Durr al-Mukhtār*: "It is to be acted upon in the [the ḥadīth related to the] virtues of actions."[129] His commentator Ibn ʿĀbidīn said, "[It is acted upon] in order to obtain the virtue which is the consequence of the actions." Ibn Ḥajar said in the commentary of *al-Arbaʿīn*,

> [It can be acted upon] because if it is in fact *ṣaḥīḥ* then it has been given its due of action, but if not no harm comes of it in terms of declaring something to be halal [which actually may not be] or haram [when it actually may not be], or voiding some other person's rights. It is narrated in a weak ḥadīth, "To whoever the [statement that there is a] reward for an action reaches from me and he does it, will obtain its reward even if I had not said it," or similar to what he said.[130]

As-Suyūṭī said, "the weak [ḥadīth] is acted upon in rulings [*aḥkām*][131] also if there is in it some precaution."

---

129 The 'virtues of actions' [*faḍā'l al-aʿmāl*] refers to the rewards and merits that are promised upon carrying out the actions. This should not be confused with the narrations that establish the action in principle, which must be *ṣaḥīḥ* or *ḥasan* to be accepted as proof. Acting upon these narrations means that a person carries out the action with greater zeal in the hope of achieving the rewards and virtue mentioned in such ḥadīth. Imam ʿAbd al-Ḥayy al-Laknawī has a detailed discussion regarding this issue in *al-Ajwibah al-Fāḍilah* p.36–59 with Shaykh Abū Ghuddah's footnotes, as does Imam al-Kawtharī in *Maqālat al-Kawtharī* p.44–46, Ed.

130 Shaykh Abū Ghuddah could not find from his research any such ḥadīth in the books of weak or fabricated narrations, there are narrations with similar wordings in *al-Laʾālii al-Maṣnuʿa* of as-Suyūtī 1:214–215 and in *Tanzīh al-Sharīʿat al-Marfūʿah* of Ibn ʿArāq 1:265. Al-Madāghabī in his notes to *Fatḥ al-Mubīn* p.32 quotes al-Munāwī's preference that this narration should not have been mentioned by Ibn Ḥajar al-Haytamī. Al-Munāwī in *Fayḍ al-Qadīr* 6:95 mentions Ibn al-Jawzī labelling it as fabricated in *al-Mawḍūʿāt* 1:258 and al-Suyūtī's agreement with this grading in *al-Laʾālii al-Maṣnuʿa* 1:214

131 By rulings [*aḥkām*] matters of halal and haram, *mustaḥab* and *makrūh* etc. are meant.

*

He said in *ad-Durr al-Mukhtār*,

> Note: the precondition for acting by a weak ḥadīth is that it should not be extremely weak, and that it should be comprised under a general principle, and that that ḥadīth should not be believed to be a *sunna*. As for fabricated ḥadīth it is not acceptable to act by them in any state, nor is it permitted to narrate them unless that is accompanied by explanation of their fabrication.

Ibn ʿĀbidīn said,

> Extreme weakness is that no single route of transmission is entirely free of having a liar or someone suspected of lying, which is what Ibn Ḥajar said. His saying, "That one does not believe that that ḥadīth is *sunna*," means [not believing] that it is *sunna* to act by it. As-Suyūṭī's expression in the commentary of *at-Taqrīb* [i.e. *Tadrīb ar-Rāwī*], "The third is that one does not believe while acting upon it that it is firmly established, but one believes in it as a precaution [lest it be true]."[132] As for his saying, "As for fabricated ḥadīth it is not acceptable to act according to them in any case," i.e. not even in supererogatory actions. Aṭ-Ṭaḥṭāwī said, "i.e. in the case where it contradicts principles of the Sharīʿah. As for the case in which it is comprised under a universal principle there is nothing to forbid one using it, but not by regarding it as a ḥadīth but simply because it [the content of the ḥadīth] is comprised within a universal principle." So think about it.[133]

*

He [al-Suyūṭī] said in *Tadrīb ar-Rāwī*,

> Whenever you see a ḥadīth with a weak *isnād*, then you may say that it is weak with this chain, but you may not say that the text itself is weak nor that it is weak unqualifiedly simply because of the weakness of this chain. This is because it may well have another chain which is *ṣaḥīḥ* unless an imam says that it is not narrated by any route which is *ṣaḥīḥ* or that it does not have an chain by which it is established or if he says that it is a weak ḥadīth and explains its weakness. Then if he says categorically that it is weak but does not explain his reason there is some discussion about that which we will come to later.

---

132 As-Suyūṭī's expression here appears disjointed from the surrounding text. Perhaps the Shaykh quoted it as another example of how the scholars regard the weak ḥadīth but did not use an appropriate conjunction so that continunuity would be apparent. Ed.

133 In his footnote on this point, Shaykh ʿAbd al-Fattāḥ Abū Ghuddah says, 'it is not at all permissible to mention a fabricated ḥadīth under a specific or a general principle. This opinion of the great scholar aṭ-Ṭaḥṭāwī cannot be heeded at all. Ed.

The upshot of what he has so far mentioned is that one should suspend judgement about it until its condition becomes clear.

I say that its condition sometimes becomes clear for a mujtahid if it corresponds to analogical reasoning, or the verdicts of the Companions and the Followers, or the indications of textual sources, etc. And we have indicated that in the first section, so remember that.

Ibn Ḥazm said, "All Ḥanafis are unanimously agreed that the *madhhab* of Abū Ḥanīfah is that a weak ḥadīth in his view is more suitable than theoretical opinion (*raʾy*)." So consider carefully this concern for ḥadīth and the tremendous importance of them and their place in his view. Thus it is in *al-Khayrāt al-ḥisān*.

The noted ḥadīth scholar ʿAlī al-Qārī said in *al-Mirqāt*, "Their strong *madhhab* is to give preference to a weak ḥadīth over pure analogical reasoning which may be open to falsification."

In *Tadrīb ar-Rāwī*, Ibn Mandah quoted that he heard Muḥammad ibn Saʿd al-Bāwardī saying, "The opinion of an-Nasāʾī was that he would narrate from everyone about whom it was not unanimously agreed to abandon him." Ibn Mandah said,

> Similarly, Abū Dāwūd took the same position and would narrate weak ḥadīth if he did not find anything else in that topic, because they are stronger in his view than people's opinions. This was also the view of Imam Aḥmad because he said that weak ḥadīth are preferable to him than the theoretical understandings of men since one only turns to analogical reasoning after failing to find a text.

I say that it is not intended by 'weak' those ḥadīth which are extremely weak because one does not act by such at all, as we have shown previously from *ad-Durr al-Mukhtār* and nothing is firmly established by them. On the contrary, what is meant by it is what Ibn al-Qayyim said in *Iʿlām al-muwaqqiʿīn* in which he mentioned the principles that Aḥmad used in his *fatwās*. He said:

> The fourth principle is that one passes judgement on the basis of a loose ḥadīth (*mursal*) and weak ḥadīth if there is nothing in that topic which would contradict it, and it is this he preferred over analogical deduction. He does not mean by "weak" false or unfamiliar ḥadīth (*munkar*) nor those in whose chain there is someone who is suspected (of lying), resorting to and acting by which is not acceptable. Rather, weak ḥadīth in his view are a counterpart of the *ṣaḥīḥ* and are a category of the *ḥasan*. He did not categorise ḥadīth into *ṣaḥīḥ*, *ḥasan* and weak, but into *ṣaḥīḥ* and weak. Weak ḥadīth have in his view different ranks. Thus if there does not exist on the topic a tradition which would contradict it nor a verdict of a Companion, nor a consensus to the contrary then the practice according to the weak ḥadīth in his view is better and more fitting than analogical deduction. There are none of the imams who do not,

on the whole, agree with him on this principle, because there are none of them who did not give preference to weak ḥadīth over analogical deduction.

He also said,

The companions of Abū Ḥanīfah agree unanimously that the school of Abū Ḥanīfah is that the weak ḥadīth is in his view more suitable and appropriate than analogical deduction and [one's own] opinion and that it was on that basis that he founded his school. Such as he gave preference to the ḥadīth about bursting out in laughter despite its weakness over analogical deduction and opinion, and he gave preference to the ḥadīth about doing wuḍūʾ with date-nabīdh on a journey, despite its weakness, over analogical deduction and opinion. He forbade amputating a thief's hand who had stolen something whose value is less than ten dirhams even though the ḥadīth narrated concerning this is weak, (up until he said,) Thus giving preference to weak ḥadīth and traditions from the Companions over analogical deduction and opinion was his position and the position of Imam Aḥmad. The meaning of "weak" in the terminology of the first generations is not the same as its usage by later scholars, but on the contrary that which the later scholars call *ḥasan* the earlier scholars sometimes called weak, as we have previously seen."

The Ḥāfiẓ Ibn Taymiyah said,

Affirmation of *ḥasan* is a terminological usage of at-Tirmidhī, but people other than at-Tirmidhī only have *ṣaḥīḥ* and weak. In their view weak ḥadīth are those which fall short of being *ṣaḥīḥ*. The [weak ḥadīth] can either be rejected (*matrūk*) such as when [a narrator] is suspected of lying or of making many mistakes, or they can be *ḥasan* if [the narrator] is not suspected of lying. This is the meaning of the words of Aḥmad, "Acting by weak ḥadīth is more appropriate than analogical deduction."[134] (*Iḥyāʾ as-sunan* cited from *at-Tuḥfat al-Marḍiyyah*.

I say that Ibn Taymiyah's words show that if the narrator is not suspect or excessively mistaken, then his ḥadīth are *ḥasan*.

In summary, the meaning of weak in the wordings of our people, "The weak

134 Shaykh ʿAbd al-Fattāh has inserted a lengthy discussion here. He quotes the research of his student Shaykh Muhammad ʿAwwāmah that the statement of imam Ibn Taymiyah that imam at-Tirmidhī is the pioneer of the term *ḥasan* is incorrect since it is clearly proven that earlier scholars among his own teachers such as Imam al-Bukhār have used the term. In fact, even Imam Aḥmad himself has used it. This then renders the conclusion of this paragraph incorrect and it becomes necessary to conclude that when Imam Aḥmad says that 'weak ḥadīth is preferred over opinion' he means exactly that and does not mean *ḥasan* ḥadīth. However, he means moderately weak ḥadīth that are close to *ḥasan*. If this were not true, what would be the point of indirectly asserting that *ḥasan* ḥadīth are preferred over analogical deduction when that is obvious anyway. By establishing that imam Ibn Taymiyah's assertion is incorrect, we would have to also accept that the author's subsequent conclusion in the next paragraph is also incorrect. *Qawāʿid*, pp. 100–108, fn. 2.

ḥadīth is given precedence over analogical deduction," is that which the later scholars call intrinsically weak [*ḍaʿīf li dhātih*] but *ḥasan* because of other factors [*ḥasan li ghayrih*] when it is supported by other evidences and the like. If you explore the ḥadīth which Ibn al-Qayyim mentions as examples of weak ḥadīth which Abū Ḥanīfah gave precedence to over analogical deduction, you will find that all of them are *ḥasan* either in themselves or because of other [supporting factors], as the reality of that will become clear to you by studying this book of ours inshāʾAllāh, exalted is He.

*

The difference between the weak ḥadīth (*ḍaʿīf*)and the ḥadīth which is regarded as weak (*muḍaʿʿaf*) is that the former may not be used as proof in rulings except in [narrating] the virtues of actions, but the second may be used as proof.

Al-Qasṭallānī said in *Irshād as-Sārī*,

> The ḥadīth which is regarded as weak (*muḍaʿʿaf*) is that which there is no consensus as to its weakness, but on the contrary in its text or in its chain some of them ascribe weakness and others regard it as strong. It is higher than the weak, and there are examples of them in al-Bukhārī. (From the introduction to *Musnad al-Imām al-Aʿẓam* by one of the eminent people.)[135]

I say that this refers back to what we said at first, that the ḥadīth about which there is a difference of opinion is *ḥasan*.

In *Tadrīb ar-Rāwī* there is that al-Ḥākim said, "The *ṣaḥīḥ* ḥadīth is divided into ten sub-divisions, five about which there is agreement and five about which people differ," and then he mentioned those about which there is agreement and then he said,

> As for the sub-divisions about which there is disagreement, they are: (1) the ḥadīth ascribed directly to the Prophet ﷺ by one of the Followers without mention of the Companions or Companion from whom he heard it (*mursal*), (2) ḥadīth of those who misrepresent (*tadlīs*), [but only] if they do not mention that they heard the ḥadīth directly, (3) That which one trustworthy narrator narrates with a complete chain of transmission and other trustworthy narrators narrate as a *mursal* ḥadīth [ascribed directly to the Prophet ﷺ without mentioning the Companion or Companions from whom they heard it], (4) The narrations of trustworthy narrators who are not themselves memorisers of ḥadīth (*ḥāfiẓ*) with knowledge [of the science], (5) The narrations of people of innovation (*bidʿah*) who are nevertheless truthful.

135 The eminent person intended here is the great scholar Shaykh Muḥammad Ḥasan as-Sanbhalī of India, a contemporary of Shaykh ʿAbd al-Ḥayy al-Laknawī.

Shaykh al-Islam Ibn Ḥajar said,

> As for the first and the second, they are as he said. As for the third, al-ʿAlāʾī objected by saying that in the two *Ṣaḥīḥ* books there are a number of ḥadīth about which there are different views as to whether they have continuous connected chains of transmission or they are loose (*mursal*). As for the fourth, al-ʿAlāʾī said, "There is agreement that it is acceptable and that one may use it as proof if the preconditions of acceptability exist in it, and this is not a matter about which there is any kind of disagreement, and that the person should be a memoriser (*ḥāfiẓ*) is not a precondition, because if it were then one could not use most of the narrators as proof. As for the fifth, there is disagreement about it as he said. However, in the two *Ṣaḥīḥ* books there are a number of ḥadīth from a group of innovators who were otherwise known to be truthful and whose knowledge of ḥadīth was well known; their ḥadīth were not thrown away because of their innovation." He said, "And there remains one subdivision about which there is disgreement: the narration of someone whose acceptability as a narrator [*ʿadālah*] is not known." (Abridged)

I say that two matters are summed up from this: first, that there are ḥadīth in the two *Ṣaḥīḥ* books about which people differ as to whether they are *ṣaḥīḥ*. Second, the loose ḥadīth (*mursal*), the narration of those who are known for misrepresentation (*tadlīs*) who narrate without mentioning that they did actually hear the ḥadīth directly from the first narrator, and the narration of someone whose acceptability as a narrator is unknown are sub-divisions of the *ṣaḥīḥ* ḥadīth about which people differ; some of them regard them as *ṣaḥīḥ* and some regard them as weak, and therefore they are of those ḥadīth which are considered weak (*muḍaʿʿaf*) and are not weak, so understand!

The meticulous scholar (Kamāl ibn al-Humām) stated in *al-Fatḥ*: "Recommended acts (*istiḥbāb*) are established by weak ḥadīth but not by fabricated ḥadīth (*mawḍūʿ*)." It is stated as such in *Jāmiʿ al-āthār* by our Shaykh. I say that, this is as we have previously shown from as-Suyūṭī, that one acts by weak ḥadīth in judgements and rulings also if in that there is an element of taking precaution.

*

In *At-Taʿlīq al-ḥasan* there is, "Weak ḥadīth suffice for supporting [other ḥadīth]," and in another place in that book, "Weak ḥadīth are fine for strengthening [other ḥadīth]."

I say that this is agreed upon unanimously among ḥadīth scholars because the loose ḥadīth (*mursal*) is weak in their view, but it is strengthened if it is produced as a *mursal*, or a musnad [fully connected] narration from a different weak path of transmission, as we will see. We have previously shown from *Tadrīb ar-Rāwī* that there is no novelty in using as proof a ḥadīth with two paths of transmission neither of which could be used as a proof by itself.

*

Al-Bayhaqī resolved to not narrating in his compilations any ḥadīth which he knew to be fabricated, as-Suyūṭī said this in *Tadrīb ar-Rāwī*. He [al-Suyuti] said in *al-Laʾālī al-maṣnūʿah* after defending a ḥadīth which Ibn al-Jawzī counted as fabricated, in his own words,

> When you recognise that the person mentioned in the *isnād* is Ibrāhīm ibn Zakariyyā al-ʿIjlī whom Ibn Ḥibbān mentioned in *ath-Thiqāt* not [Ibrāhīm ibn Zakariyyā] al-Wāsiṭī whom he mentioned in *aḍ-Ḍuʿafāʾ* and because of whom the ḥadīth suspected of being spurious, then you recognise that the ḥadīth emerges out from the domain of fabrication, and you recognise the high station of al-Bayhaqī in the fact that he does not narrate anything in his books which is fabricated, which is something he undertook [to achieve].[136]

I say that similarly al-Mundhirī resolved to not publish in his *at-Targhīb* those ḥadīth about which it has been said that they are proven to have been fabricated, as he stated clearly in his introduction. So it is acceptable to mention as supporting evidence those among their ḥadīth about which they are silent or which have had the judgement passed on them that they are weak.

*

Ibn al-Jawzī said,

> There are six categories of ḥadīth: first, those about which al-Bukhārī and Muslim agree, and that is the ultimate. Second, those which al-Bukhārī or Muslim alone narrated. Third, those whose *isnād*s are sound but which neither of them narrated. Fourth, those which have a minor tolerable weakness, and this is the *ḥasan* ḥadīth. Fifth, those which are seriously weak and are severely problematic; these have differing gradations according to the ʿulamāʾ some of whom regard it as being closer to those which are *ḥasan* claiming that they are not seriously problematic, and some others seeing them as severely problematic and append them to fabricated ḥadīth. About this matter I composed the book called *al-ʿIlal al-mutanāhiyah fī al-aḥādīth al-wāhiyah*. Sixth, those fabricated ḥadīth which are categorically determined as lies. We have composed on this category our book *al-Mawḍūʿāt*.

---

136 Shaykh Abū Ghuddah in his notes quotes a number of authorities who disagree with this, and state that imam al-Bayhaqī did mistakenly cite narrations which were severely weak or fabricated. *Qawāʿid*, pp. 112–114, fn. 4.

As-Suyūṭī said, "Since we have mentioned everything in his [Ibn al-Jawzi's] book, we will begin now with the additions to it. Thus among them (i.e. the fabricated ḥadīth) there is that which is categorically considered to be fabricated and that which a *ḥāfiẓ* stated that it is fabricated. I have some views in this, which I will mention so that it can be considered." (*Al-Laʾālī al-maṣnūʿah*).[137]

I say that by this you have learnt that that which Ibn al-Jawzī mentioned in *al-ʿIlal al-mutanāhiyyah* is not all of those things about which there is unanimous consensus as to the severity of its weakness, but on the contrary there is among it that about which the ʿulamāʾ have differed and have brought it closer to the *ḥasan*, so one ought to pay attention to that. It is confirmed by that that there are also two degrees of severely weak ḥadīth: first, that on which they agreed as to the severity of its weakness, and that about which they differed. The former is basically not to be used in argument, but the latter may sometimes be used in argument, so understand!

*

Among the terms utilised by the people of ḥadīth for acceptable ḥadīth there are: *jayyid* (good), *qawī* (strong), *ṣāliḥ* (suitable), *maʿrūf* (the well-recognised), *maḥfūẓ* (preserved), *mujawwad* (declared good), and *thābit* (the firmly established).

As for that which is *jayyid* (good), Shaykh al-Islām said after transmitting the words of Ibn aṣ-Ṣalāḥ,

> This indicates that Ibn aṣ-Ṣalāḥ regarded the *jayyid* and *ṣaḥīḥ* ḥadīth to be equal. There is in at-Tirmidhī 'in [the chapter of] medicine', 'This is a *jayyid ḥasan* ḥadīth.' Others said the same; there is no difference between *jayyid* and *ṣaḥīḥ* in their view, except that the genious scholar among them only moves from sahih to *jayyid* because of a subtle point;[138] as if in his view the ḥadīth rises above the degree of being intrinsically *ḥasan* but he hesitates as to whether it attains the degree of being *ṣaḥīḥ*. Thus the attribution of the degree of *jayyid* is lower ranked than the attribution of *ṣaḥīḥ*; the same is true of the [term] strong (*qawī*).
>
> As for that which is suitable (*ṣāliḥ*), it is a term which comprises both the *ṣaḥīḥ* and the *ḥasan* because of their suitability for use in proof, and the term is also used for that weak ḥadīth which is suitable for evaluation (*iʿtibār*) [either through corroboration or attestation].[139]

---

137 This paragraph can be a bit confusing and so needs to be cleared up: As-Suyūṭī has actually quoted Ibn al-Jawzī's above mentioned categorisation of ḥadīth in his book *al-Laʾālīi al-Maṣnuʿah*, the author seems to have taken the quote in conjunction with some of as-Suyūṭī comments on it. This is the link between the quote from Ibn al-Jawzī and the subsequent paragraph from as-Suyūṭī. Ed.

138 i.e. he does not use the two terms interchangeably but recognises a subtle point of difference between them. Ed.

139 Meaning the weak ḥadīth has got the capacity to function as a parallel report (*mutābiʿ*) or attest another report (*shāhid*).

As for the well-recognised (*maʿrūf*), it is the diametric opposite of the unfamiliar (*munkar*) ḥadīth *Maḥfūẓ* ḥadīth are diametrically opposite to anomalous (*shādhdh*) ḥadīth. The explanation of that will come in the appropriate place. The *mujawwad* (declared good) and the thābit (firmly established) also comprise both the *ṣaḥīḥ* and the *ḥasan*.

Also among their expressions is: mushabbah (comparable) which is used to denote the *ḥasan* and that which is close to it, so that in respect to it (the *ḥasan*) is like the relationship of the jayyid (good) to the *ṣaḥīḥ*. (*Tadrīb ar-Rāwī*)

*

Often I will mention weak ḥadīth in *al-Iʿlāʾ* [*as-sunan*] or in its marginal notes for which I have not found anyone who regards them as strong; intending by that the reinforcement of my arguments rather than using them as [independent] proof. I may also mention in the marginal notes ḥadīth from *Kanz al-ʿUmmāl* and other books of this science whose state I do not know in terms of whether they are *ṣaḥīḥ*, *ḥasan* or weak. My intention in mentioning them is to support what is in the text itself by the numerous paths of transmission, or to draw attention to the fact that the issue does have a source in the ḥadīth even though we may not have come across details of its chain.

When we find in the books of *fiqh* a verdict with which a ḥadīth agrees that has been narrated by one of the imams of the subject, it predominates in our view that it had reached our imams, and that it is very likely that they came across it with a chain suitable to be used in proof. Our failure to come across it does not necessarily require that it is weak or that it should be rejected, because of our shortsightedness and the paucity of our resources. This is because there are many books of ḥadīth and the narrators of ḥadīth whose name only remains in this age of ours and we cannot even find a trace of them. Even if the weakness of a ḥadīth is conceded, the agreement of the analogical deduction of *fuqahāʾ* with it is an evidence which makes its acceptability more probable as we have indicated before. We will mention the proof of that in the coming sections. May Allah ﷻ reward with the best reward whoever aids us in this noble endeavour, and Allah ﷻ is sufficient for us and an excellent Guardian.

CHAPTER 4

On the ruling on ascription of ḥadīth to the Prophet ﷺ (*raf*ʿ), on statements made by Companions without such ascription (*waqf*), on ḥadīth whose chains are fully connected (*muttaṣil*) and those which are interrupted (*munqaṭi*ʿ), and on the suitability of using as proof the verdicts of the Companions and the great Followers, and concerning the ruling on the addition of a reliable narrator.[140]

We read in *Tadrīb ar-Rāwī*,

> If some of the trustworthy narrators who are exact in narration of ḥadīth narrate a ḥadīth as a loose ḥadīth (*mursal*) and others narrate it as a *muttasil* (uninterrupted); or the same narrator narrates it as a raised ḥadīth (*marfū*ʿ) or *muttasil* on one occation but narrates is as a *mursal* or a *mawqūf* on another occation, then the authentic position according to the people of ḥadīth, *fiqh* and jurisprudence (*uṣūl al-fiqh*) is that the judgement on it belongs to the person who narrates it as a *muttaṣil* or a *marfū*ʿ. [This is irrespective of] whether or not the person who differs is the same as him in terms of memorisation and attention to detail or better than him, because that, i.e. the ascription [to the Prophet ﷺ] or its having an uninterrupted chain is an addition of a reliable narrator (*thiqah*) which is accepted.

An-Nawawī said in the introduction to the commentary of Muslim,

> If one of the exact and trustworthy narrators narrates the ḥadīth as a *muttasil* and another narrates it as a *mursal*, or one narrates it as a *mawqūf* and another as a *marfū* or if he the same narrator narrates it as a *muttasil* or *marfū*ʿ at one time and a *mursal* or *mawqūf* at another time, then the sound position which has been held by the critical judges of ḥadīth, the *fuqahā*ʾ and the experts in jurisprudence, and which al-Khaṭīb al-Baghdādī confirmed as sound, is that the judgement is given in favour of the person who narrates it as a *muttasil* or a *marfū*ʿ ḥadīth. [This is irrespective of]

140 This is when a trustworthy narrator adds something to the text or chain that has not been narrated by others.

whether the person who disagrees with him is of the same status or better or better in memorisation because it is an addition of a reliable narrator which is acceptable.

He also said (in the chapter on the prayer at night),

> The sound position and indeed the correct one on which the *fuqahāʾ*, the scholars of the principles [of ḥadīth and *fiqh*] and the critical judges of ḥadīth from among the ḥadīth scholars all agree is that if a ḥadīth is narrated as a *marfūʿ* and *mawqūf* or a *muttaṣil* and *mursal* then it is judged to be *marfūʿ* and *muttaṣil* because that is an addition of a reliable narrator, regardless of whether the one who ascribes it to the Prophet ﷺ or gives it as an uninterrupted chain is more or less in terms of memorisation [than the one who differs from him] or such narrators are more numerous.

By this it becomes obvious to you that ascription to the Prophet ﷺ (*rafʿ*) or its having a connected *isnād* (*wasl*) is an addition that is not contradictory to its being *mursal* and *mawqūf* [in another version], otherwise it would not be acceptable even if the person ascribing it to the Prophet ﷺ as a *marfūʿ* ḥadīth was a reliable narrator since the addition of a reliable narrator is only accepted if it is not inconsistent with the narration of the larger body, as we will see.[141]

As-Suyūṭī said in *at-Tadrīb*, "Al-Māwardī said, 'There is no contradiction between that which is narrated as raised (*marfūʿ*) one time and as the statement of a Companion another time since it may be such that he narrated it and is now giving a *fatwā* on the basis of it.'"

Ad-Dāraquṭnī said concerning the ḥadīth of Ibn ʿAbbās which he ascribed to the Prophet ﷺ (*marfūʿ*) "The two ears are a part of the head," that, "Its chain is wrong, and it is only a ḥadīth ascribed to the Prophet ﷺ by one of the Followers (*mursal*)." ʿAbd al-Ḥaqq concurred with him and he said, "Ibn Jurayj upon whom the ḥadīth pivots narrates from Sulaymān ibn Mūsā from the Prophet ﷺ as a *mursal* ḥadīth (without mention of the Companions from whom he heard it)." Ibn al-Qaṭṭān investigated further saying that this is not a criticism of it, and there is nothing to prevent there being two ḥadīth, one of which is with a chain and the other of which is *mursal*; Ibn al-Qaṭṭān said, "Its *isnād* is *ṣaḥīḥ* because of its being connected back and because of the trustworthy nature of its narrators."[142] In that there is proof that

141 This simply means that the apparent contradiction between *marfūʿ* and *mawqūf*, and *muttaṣil* and *mursal* in different paths of the same ḥadīth is not to be regarded as the same as the contradiction between a *shādhdh* (irregular) and *maḥfūdh* (properly memorised) ḥadīth. That contradiction is reconcilable by the simple realisation that the addition in the *marfūʿ* and *muttaṣil* is accepted because it is the addition by a reliable narrator. If another transmission does not have the addition, then we assume it is missing due to oversight or mistake. Ed.

142 Ibn Ḥajar has a lengthy discussion spanning three pages regarding this narration in his work *an-Nukat ʿalā Muqaddimat Ibn aṣ-Ṣalāḥ*, his conclusion being that there was some basis for this ḥadīth.

there is no inconsistency between a ḥadīth being *mursal* and a ḥadīth ascribed to the Prophet ﷺ with an *isnād* (*marfūʿ*).

The Ḥāfiẓ said in the introduction to *al-Fatḥ*,

> The defect mentioned with respect to the two of them is not injurious because the narration of Ḥusayn comprised both ascription to the Prophet ﷺ (*rafʿ*) and being a statement of a Companion without ascription (*mawqūf*) at the same time. Thus if another narration only comprises being a statement of a Companion without ascription then it would be comprising an addition which does not contradict the other narration and is thus accepted by the scholars of ḥadīth.

*

Al-Ḥāfiẓ said in the commentary of *an-Nukhbah*,

> The extra addition of a narrator in them—i.e. the *ṣaḥīḥ* and *ḥasan*—is accepted as long as there does not occur anything which contradicts a narration from someone more trustworthy than those who do not mention this additional extra. This is because an addition either does not contain a contradiction between itself and a narration of someone who does not mention it, in which case it is unqualifiedly accepted. [This is] because the judgement on it is that of a separate ḥadīth which a trustworthy narrator uniquely narrates and no one else narrates it from his shaykh; or else it is contradictory in that it necessarily entails that if one accepts it one has to repudiate the other narration. This is the case in which it has to be seen whether it or the one which contradicts it is the weightier, and thus the weightier is accepted and the less weighty is repudiated. It is also famous of a group of the ʿulamāʾ that they gave the verdict that the addition is to be accepted unqualifiedly without detail.

I say that his words show the acceptance of additions of a narrator of *ḥasan* ḥadīth also. That which as-Suyūṭī said in *at-Tadrīb* and an-Nawawī in the commentary of Muslim and elsewhere that it is accepted if one of the trustworthy narrators with attention to detail narrate it, he meant that which applies generally to narrators of both the *ṣaḥīḥ* and the *ḥasan*. The narrator of the *ṣaḥīḥ* is an irreproachable person (*ʿadl*) with complete attention to detail (*ḍābiṭ*), and the narrator of the *ḥasan* is someone whose attention to detail is less but who yet retains all the other preconditions of someone who narrates *ṣaḥīḥ* ḥadīth, as is in *Sharḥ an-Nukhbah*.

We have already seen that someone about whom there is a disagreement of opinion as to whether he is a trustworthy narrator or a weak narrator is also *ḥasan* in narration of ḥadīth, and so his additions are accepted in view of the fact that he is someone who narrates *ḥasan* ḥadīth, so one ought to pay attention to that.

In *Nūr al-Anwār* there is:

> If there is an addition in one of two traditions, then if the narrator—i.e. the Companion—is one person, one acts by the one which affirms the addition. If there are different narrators [Companions] then they are treated as two separate traditions and both are acted upon, as is our *madhhab* concerning the fact that an unqualified [text] is not interpreted according to a qualified [text] in two rulings.

I say that this is qualified by [saying that] this is as long as the addition is not contradictory, as is obvious, and there is extra detail about that as will follow.

*

The isolated narration of someone who narrates *ṣaḥīḥ* and *ḥasan* ḥadīth is not accepted if it contradicts that which a group of trustworthy narrators transmit, and that is called irregular (*shādhdh*).

The Ḥāfiẓ said in the commentary of *an-nukhbah,* "The irregular report is that which someone acceptable narrates contradicting that which someone more fitting than him narrates. This is what is reliable in the definition of the irregular report according to technical usage."

Ibn al-Ḥanbalī said in *Qafw al-athar,* "By analogy on what has preceded, the additional material of a weak narrator is not accepted if it contradicts that of a trustworthy narrator."

Some of the people of ḥadīth have taken the position of categorically refuting additional material, and that is narrated of the greater number of the companions of Abū Ḥanīfah. However, the chosen position according to Ibn as-Sāʿānī and others of the Ḥanafis is that if someone upright (*ʿadl*) is alone in transmitting additional material that is not contradictory, such as if he narrated that he peace be upon him "entered the house" and he added "and he prayed", then if the assemblies [in which the different versions of the ḥadīth were heard] are different, it is accepted by unanimous agreement. If it is one [assembly] and others [who he contradicted] are such a number that it is inconceivable that they could have neglected the material which he has added, then it is not accepted. However, if they do not amount to such a number, then the dominant majority take the position that the additional material is acceptable, contrary to some of the scholars of ḥadīth and Aḥmad in one narration from him. If the state of the assembly is unknown then it is more appropriate to accept it than when it is one assembly with that precondition.[143] As for if the additional material is contradictory, then it is obvious that they are incompatible.

By this you recognise that the Ḥanafis also do not accept the additional material

143 i.e. with the precondition that the those other than him are not such a number that it is inconceivable that they could have neglected the material which he has added. Meaning that when the state of the assembly is unknown it is a better scenario than the above in which the addition is accepted. Ed.

of the trustworthy narrator when it is not contradictory without certain conditions, and not unqualifiedly.

Supplement

If one finds a corroborating narrator (*mutābiʿ*) or supporting narration (*shāhid*) for an irregular ḥadīth (*shādhdh*) then that removes its irregularity and it becomes acceptable as proof. The narration of the one who by himself would not be used as proof and indeed would be counted among weak narrators is comprised under [such] corroborating and supporting evidence. In the two books of al-Bukhārī and Muslim there are a body of weak narrators whom they mention in corroborating and supporting transmissions. However not every weak narrator is valid for that, as will be seen. For this reason ad-Dāraquṭnī and others say about weak narrators, "So-and-so is to be considered, but so-and-so is not to be considered."[144] It is thus in *Qafw al-Athar* and there is something similar in *Tadrīb ar-Rāwī* and other works.

*

Disconnection (*inqiṭāʿ*) [in *isnāds*] is of two types: outward and inward. The outward one is like the *mursal* tradition and the explanation of it will come soon. The inward is also of two types:

First, that which is outwardly connected but from another respect has deficiency in it, i.e. that it lacks some preconditions which narrators ought to have. Its ruling is that a tradition from a kāfir, a deviant, a child, an insane person or someone whose inattention is extreme, cannot be accepted (and this is the weak ḥadīth in all its ranks,[145] and we have already mentioned its rulings. Some remaining things about it will appear among the principles of invalidation and validation (*jarḥ wa taʿdīl*))

Second, that in which defficiency appears due to its contradicting a proof which is superior to it in comparison, in that it contradicted the Book [of Allah ﷻ] where the Book is definitive in its meaning (*qaṭʿī ad-dalāla*); [in such an instance] the tradition is rejected and [treated as] disconnected. As for if the Book is not definitive in its implication and the ḥadīth has been narrated with a *ṣaḥīḥ isnād* then in that case the ḥadīth is not abandoned but on the contrary the āyah is interpreted and the tradition acted upon. It is thus in *Nūr al-Anwār* along with its commentary.

*

Similarly, the ḥadīth is not accepted—meaning the narration of a single person—

144 The Arabic words are '*yuʿtabaru*' and '*lā yuʿtabaru*'. Ed.

145 Meaning that every ḥadīth with a weak narrator is an inwardly disconnected (*munqaṭiʿ*) ḥadīth which may have a physically connected chain of transmission but the absence of preconditions from a narrator or narrators makes it inwardly disconnected. Ed.

when it is contrary to the well known *sunna* whether it is transmitted by numerous chains of transmission (*mutawātir*) or transmitted with two chains of transmission (*mashhūr*).

*

Similarly, it is not accepted if it is narrated concerning a well known occurrence contrary to that which the community transmit, such as when the community narrate that he ﷺ used to say the *basmalah* silently but one person narrates that he did so aloud, then that is not accepted. That is because the event of the prayer was continuous and well known, with thousands of men attending it, and if only one man heard it then this is strange. There is in *at-Tawḍīḥ* "and either the disconnection is because of the fact that it is an irregular text (*shādhdh*) concerning a matter of general concern."

*

Similarly, if the imams of the first generations overlooked it, i.e. the Companions, because if they discussed among themselves from their own opinions but did not turn to the ḥadīth, that is a sign of its being disconnected. All of this is mentioned in *al-Manār* and *Nūr al-Anwār*.

I say that similarly, the Companions' not showing concern for an action despite many a reason for it indicates to the fact that it is disapproved, even if lightly, and to the weakness of what is transmitted in it, because their lack of concern for it and their overlooking it cannot be imagined whilst it is legislated [as part of Sharīʿah, i.e. something permissible] let alone whilst it is recommended.

Similarly action by a ḥadīth being abandoned in the age of the Companions or the Followers is a sign of its abrogation or its weakness, as the aforementioned words in *al-Manār* show. And he stated that explicitly in *at-Talwīḥ* by saying,

> As for the second, which is disconnection due to contradiction because of the overlooking [of the ḥadīth] by the Companions; this is due to the fact that it contradicts their consensus in not accepting it and in not acting by it, in which case it is interpreted as an error [of the narrator who narrated it] or as abrogated. It is clear that what is meant is the agreement of anyone other than this narrator [who narrated the abandoned ḥadīth], he is by all means of course an adherant of it. (Abridged)

The upshot of that is that along with the trustworthiness and exactness of the narrator it is preconditional in our view for the authenticity of a ḥadīth that the the ḥadīth does not contradict a definite [*āyah*] of the Book or a well known *sunna* and that it should not be overlooked or action by it abandoned in the first generations, and that it should not be an irregular text (*shādhdh*) concerning a matter of general concern, but is on the contrary conspicuous and widespread, so remember this point because it is very useful. The people of principles (*uṣūl*) among our companions [the Ḥanafīs] have relieved us of the need for establishing proofs for it, because they have already accomplished that in their books.

*

Know that the wording 'as-*sunna*' is comprised in the *marfūʿ* [ḥadīth which are ascribed by a Companion to the Messenger of Allah ﷺ] according to them. Ibn ʿAbd al-Barr said in *at-Taqaṣṣī*, "Know that when a Companion uses the term '*sunna*' unqualifiedly the '*sunna*' of the Prophet ﷺ is meant by it, and it is similar when others use it unqualifiedly as long as it is not ascribed to someone such as when they say, "The *sunna* of the two ʿUmars," etc." (As quoted by az-Zaylaʿī).

It is similar with when he (i.e a Companion) says, "You have achieved the *sunna*," or "... the *sunna* of Abu'l-Qāsim". There is in *al-Maḥāsin* of al-Bulqīnī the Shāfiʿite, "Note that it (i.e. such a statement) is in the same sense as the statement, 'To do such-and-such is of the *sunna*,' or that he says, 'We used to do such-and-such,' without ascribing it to his epoch ﷺ." The chosen position of as-Sirāj al-Hindī among us[146] is that if he ascribes it to him, it is a *marfūʿ* [ḥadīth ascribed by a Companion to the Messenger of Allah ﷺ] and an absolute proof, but if not then the apparent meaning by 'We used to do such-and-such,' or 'They used to do such-and-such,' is confirmation [*taqrīr*], so the apparent meaning would be that it is a *marfūʿ* [ascribed to the Messenger of Allah ﷺ] and a proof. It is thus in *Qafw al-athar*.

I say that it is likewise judged as a *marfūʿ* if a Companion who has not taken from the ancient books makes a statement in which there is no place to exercise *ijtihād*[147] and it is not connected to the explanation of a linguistic usage or the commentary on an unusual usage of a word, as is in *Qafw al-athar* also. And if a Follower (*tābiʿī*) of the same state[148] said the same, then it is also judged as a *marfūʿ*, but however it is a *mursal*[149] because of the omission of the name of the Companion. The proof of that is what is in *Tadrīb ar-Rāwī*: "As for the verdict of he who says that the *tafsīr* of a Companion is *marfūʿ* [ascribed to the Messenger of Allah ﷺ], such a person being al-Ḥākim who said in *al-Mustadrak* that, "the student of ḥadīth ought to know that the *tafsīr* of a Companion who witnessed the revelation is, according to the two

146 Meaning the Ḥanafīs.

147 Meaning that it is a statement about something that could only have come from the Prophet because it narrates to an act of worship or matter of faith or other such matter that falls beyond the reach of speculation and inference. Ed.

148 I.e. he does not take from ancient scripture and he makes a statement in which there is no place to exercise *ijtihād*.

149 I.e. a hadīth ascribed directly to the Prophet ﷺ by one of the Followers without his mentioning the Companion or Companions from whom he heard it.

Shaykhs, a ḥadīth with an *isnād* (i.e. *marfūʿ*)," then that is with respect to an explanation connected to the causes of revelation of an *āyah* and the like which could not have been taken from anyone other than the Prophet ﷺ and in which there is no space for the exercise of opinion. Anything other than that is a *mawqūf* [statement of a Companion without attribution to the Prophet ﷺ]. I say, the same is said about a Follower except that the *marfūʿ* [ḥadīth ascribed to the Messenger of Allah ﷺ] with respect to him is a *mursal*."[150] (Abridged) And it is clear that that in which there is no space for opinion, *tafsīr* and anything else are equal in it.

*

If a Follower said, "They used to do such-and-such," and, "they used to say such-and-such," and, "they saw no harm in that," then it would appear to be an ascription to the Companions unless a proof is established otherwise. This is obvious upon reflection. It is the same if he said, "The *salaf* used to do..." or "say such-and-such," for the use of the 'salaf' in the usage of the Followers is only about the Companions, and in the case of those who came after them it refers to the Companions and the Followers both.

*

The verdict of a Companion who was a *mujtahid* about something for which there is no text is in our view a proof for which one would abandon analogical deduction (*qiyās*), then if it became widespread and they were tacit in approval then it is unanimously agreed that one must follow it. It is unanimously agreed that it is not obligatory to do so with respect to that about which they differed because that is the same as the differences of opinion of the mujtahids. So it is legitimate for those after them to act by whichever one of them they wish without taking a third (combined or compromised) position, because it would be false by the unanimous consensus formed from these two differing views.[151] If they differ, then everything on which the two Shaykhs agreed is obligatory for us to follow. If one does not know whether they agreed or disagreed then that is a proof in our view because of the possibility of it having been heard from the Prophet ﷺ. If one submits that it has not been heard from him but that on the contrary it is a view, then the view of a Companion is stronger than another person's view. It is thus in *Nūr al-anwār* and the like of it is in *at-Tawḍīḥ maʿa 't-Talwīḥ*.

---

150 I.e. ḥadīth ascribed directly to the Prophet ﷺ by one of the Followers without his mentioning the Companion or Companions from whom he heard it.

151 I.e. since the whole body of the companions take one of the two differing positions their consensus is on one of the two. A third position combined out of the two would be outside this concensus and thus unacceptable. Ed.

Our people and most of the Shāfiʿīs ascribed to Imam ash-Shāfiʿī that he said, "None of them are to be followed [in *taqlīd*] whether what he said is grasped by analogical deduction or not. However, his words in *ar-Risālah al-Baghdādiyyah* which al-Ḥasan ibn Muḥammad az-Zaʿfarānī narrated from him states something different from that, for he declared clearly in it that the views of the Companions are more praiseworthy for us and more appropriate than our own opinions. He said in the narration of ar-Rabīʿ from him, "*Bidʿah* is what contradicts the Book or the *sunna* or a tradition from one of the Companions of the Messenger of Allah ﷺ," and so he regarded whatever contradicted the verdict of a Companion as a bidʿah. Ibn al-Qayyim mentioned it in *Iʿlām al-Muwaqqiʿīn*.

In it he also mentioned,

> And if one Companion did not contradict another, then either his verdict was well known among the Companions or it was not. If it was well known, then the position of the dominant majority of the different parties of jurists is that it is a consensus and a proof. If his verdict was not well known or it is unknown as to whether or not it was well known, then people differed as to whether or not it is a proof. The dominant majority of the ummah took the position that it is a proof. This is the verdict of the dominant majority of the Ḥanafis which Muḥammad ibn al-Ḥasan declared and it is mentioned of Abū Ḥanīfah textually, and it is the school of Mālik and his companions, as his usage of it in his *Muwaṭṭa'* is a proof. It is also the verdict of Ishaq Ibn Rāhawayh, Abū ʿUbayd, and it is textually stated from Imam Aḥmad in more than one place, and is the chosen position of the dominant majority of his companions, and it is textually stated of ash-Shāfiʿī in both his old and new schools.[152]

Then he went to great lengths in mentioning the verdicts of ash-Shāfiʿī and his texts which show that the verdicts of the Companions are in his view valid proof, so let the reader refer to that.

*

The verdict of a senior Follower whose *fatwā* appeared during the time of the Companions is in our view a proof just as is that of a Companion, as is in *at-Tawḍīḥ*. Ibn al-Qayyim said in *Iʿlām Muwaqqiʿīn*,

152 Imam ash-Shāfiʿī is famous for having two schools of thought: the old Baghdadi school and the new Egyptian school. Most of what we know of the school of Imam ash-Shāfiʿī, or when we refer to the opinions of imam ash-Shāfiʿī we are actually referring to his later Egyptian school. The old Baghdadi school is no longer in vogue and therefore a lot of imam ash-Shāfiʿī's earlier opinions have been lost. Al-Ḥasan ibn Muḥammad az-Zaʿfrānī is the one who transmitted the old school from the imam whilst ar-Rabīʿ and al-Muzanī are transmitters of the new school. In this respect imam at-Tirmidhī's *Sunan* is importatant because most of the opinions in the *Sunan* that Imam at-Tirmidhī quotes from al-Shāfiʿī are by way of az-Zaʿfrānī meaning ash-Shāfiʿī's old school. Ed.

> The right-acting first generations differed about that. Some of them said that it is obligatory to follow a Follower in that on which he gave *fatwā* and in which a Companion or another Follower did not contradict him. This is the verdict of some of the Ḥanbalīs and Shāfiʿīs, and ash-Shāfiʿī stated clearly in one place that he said it in emulation (*taqlīd*) of ʿAṭāʾ. This is from the perfection of his knowledge and understanding because he could only find the verdict of ʿAṭāʾ on the matter, and so his verdict in his view was the strongest thing found on the matter. Anyone who reflects upon the books of the imams and those after them will find them laden with taking the explanation of the Followers as proof." (Abridged)

*

The verdict of Ibrāhīm an-Nakhaʿī is a proof according to us (hanafis) if he does not contradict the verdict of a Companion or above [i.e. the Prophet ﷺ], because even if he was not one of the senior Followers yet he was one of the senior Followers in terms of *fiqh* according to the Imam (Abu Hanifa),[153] so much so that he said to al-Awzāʿī, "Ibrāhīm has more *fiqh* than Sālim." And also because Ibrāhīm was one of those who most held to Ibn Masʿūd[154] and his companions, and he was their mouthpiece in his time without departing from that way except in a very few instances, and even in those instances not departing from the verdicts of the Companions: ʿAlī and ʿUmar. The ḥadīth scholar of India[155] said in *Ḥujjat Allah al-Bālighah*,

> Saʿīd ibn al-Musayyab was the one who most expressed the position of the People of Madīnah and he was the most knowledgable (by memory) of ʿUmar's judgements and Abū Hurayrah's ḥadīth. And Ibrāhīm was the one who most expressed the position of the jurists of Kūfa, ʿAbdullāh ibn Masʿūd and ʿAlī ibn Abī Ṭālib and their companions. Thus when the two of them spoke, i.e. Saʿīd and Ibrāhīm, giving a verdict about anything without ascribing it to anyone, then in the main they are ascribed to one of the right-acting first generations either explicitly or implicitly or the like. Thus the jurists of their two cities united around them and took their verdicts from them, they got to understand them thoroughly and then issued their judgements according to that, and Allah ﷻ knows best.

He said in another place,

> Imam Abū Ḥanīfah ؓ was the one who most adhered to the school of Ibrāhīm and

153 He is also one of the Shaykhs of Imam Abū Ḥanīfah as discussed in the introduction of ʿAllāmah Abū 'l-Wafāʾ al-Afghānī to the book *al-Āthār* of Imam Muḥammad ibn Ḥasan al-Shaybānī, 1:30.

154 This gives the impression that he met and learnt from Ibn Masʿūd (RA), however this is not the case as clarified by Shaykh Abu Ghuddah. What is meant here, probably, is that he held to the *fatwas* and opinions of Ibn Masʿūd (RA) based on what he learnt from his companions. Ed.

155 Meaning Shāh Walīullāh ad-Dehlawī.

his contemporaries without exceeding that except in what Allah ﷻ willed, and he played a great part in deriving judgements according to his [Ibrāhīm's] school, and he was very finely attuned in all the aspects of deriving judgements [on that basis], coming to the derivative rulings in the most perfect manner. If you wish to know the reality of what we have said, then summarise the verdicts of Ibrāhīm and his contemporaries from the *Kitāb al-Āthār* by Muḥammad and the *Jāmiʿ* of ʿAbd ar-Razzāq and the *Muṣannaf* of Ibn Abī Shaybah, and then compare them with his *madhhab* and you will not find him departing from that way except in a very few instances, and even in those instances he will not depart from that position which the *fuqahāʾ* of Kūfa took.

Ibn al-Qayyim mentioned in *Iʿlām al-Muwaqqiʿīn* the following,

> Ibn Jarīr said, 'Among (the Companions) there was no one other than Ibn Masʿūd who had companions who were well known and who accurately recorded his *fatwā*s and the positions he took in *fiqh*. And he would abandon his own verdict in favour of ʿUmars verdict, and would hardly contradict him in any of the positions he took, and he would revert from his own verdict in favour of his [Umar's] verdict.

Al-Aʿmash said about Ibrāhīm, "He would not consider anything equal to the verdict of ʿUmar and ʿAbdullāh ibn Masʿūd if they were in agreement, but if they differed the verdict of ʿAbdullāh was more pleasing to him since he was gentler."[156]

Ad-Dāraquṭnī said in his *Sunan*,

> Although this narration is *mursal*, nevertheless Ibrāhīm an-Nakhaʿī was the most knowledgeable among people of ʿAbdullāh and his view and *fatwās* for he had learnt that from his maternal uncles ʿAlqamah, al-Aswad and ʿAbd ar-Raḥmān the two sons of Yazīd, and others of the senior companion of ʿAbdullāh. He [Ibrāhīm] was the one who said, 'If I say to you that ʿAbdullāh ibn Masʿūd said something then that is [narrated] from a large number of his companions from him. If I heard it from one man then I will name him for you.

He also said, some lines before that,

> And ʿAbdullāh ibn Masʿūd had too much *taqwā* of his Lord and eagerness for his *dīn* than to narrate from the Messenger of Allah ﷺ that he gave judgement in some case and then give judgement contrary to it. Something like this could not be imagined of ʿAbdullāh ibn Masʿūd, and he is the one who said about a case which was brought to him about which he had heard nothing from the Messenger of Allah ﷺ and about

156 The word used here is *altaf* which can also mean subtler or finer. One would indicate a contrast from ʿUmar's hard disposition; the other would indicate finer and more subtle understanding on the part of Ibn Masʿūd.

> which nothing had reached him from him ﷺ, 'I will give my verdict on it according to my own view, and if it is correct then it is from Allah ﷻ and His Messenger ﷺ, but if it is mistaken then it is from me.' Then afterwards it reached him that his *fatwā* was in accordance with the judgement of the Messenger of Allah ﷺ on a similar case. His companions saw him at that moment rejoicing as they had never seen before because of the agreement of his *fatwā* with the judgement of the Messenger of Allah ﷺ."

I say that when this was the state of Ibn Masʿūd ؓ and he followed the judgement of the Messenger of Allah ﷺ first of all, and if he did not find such then he passed judgement according to the verdict of ʿUmar ؓ as we have seen, and since Ibrāhīm was the most knowledgeable of people of Ibn Masʿūd ؓ and his views and judgements and the one who most closely adhered to his school; so Abū Ḥanīfah ؓ chose the way of Ibrāhīm and became the person who most adhered to him and to his contemporaries. Thus when he found a verdict from him[157] which the verdict of a Companion or the like did not contradict, then he chose the verdict of Ibrāhīm and because of it abandoned analogical deduction and he would use it as a proof, as will be clear to whoever studies *Kitāb al-āthār* of Muḥammad.

That is only because of the fact that in the main his verdicts are ascribed to one of the right-acting first generations explicitly or implicitly, in fact Abū Ḥanīfah often took as proof the verdict of Ibrāhīm despite the existence of the verdict of one of the Companions to the contrary, and that was in those cases about which the imam knew that the verdict of Ibrāhīm with respect to them was indeed the verdict of ʿAbdullāh or ʿUmar or ʿAlī, and was not merely because of his personal opinion.

In summary, the verdict of Ibrāhīm is a proof even if our people [the Ḥanafīs] did not declare it so explicitly, nevertheless their action shows it.

---

157 Meaning Ibrāhīm an-Nakhaʿī.

CHAPTER 5

Concerning the rulings on the *mursal* ḥadīth, the *mudallas*,[158] the *muʿallaq*,[159] the *munqaṭiʿ*[160] and the *muʿḍal*.[161]

Ibn al-Ḥanbalī said in *Qafw al-Athar*,

> The chosen position in detail is to unanimously accept the *mursal* ḥadīth[162] of the companion and the *mursal* ḥadīth of the second generation.[163] Unqualified accepatance of the third generation according to us (the Ḥanafīs) and according to Malik, but according to ash-Shāfiʿī (the *mursal* of the third generation is accepted) if it fulfils one of five conditions: that someone else transmits it as a *musnad* (i.e. with an uninterrupted chain to the Prophet ﷺ), or that someone else also transmits it as a *mursal* ḥadīth but their shaykhs are different, or if the verdict of a Companion supports it, or if the verdict of most of the ʿulamāʾ supports it, or if it is known that he only omits reliable narrators (in the *mursal* ḥadīth).[164]

*

As for the *mursal* ḥadīth of those who come after these, then they are acceptable according to some of our people but rejected according to others unless trustworthy

158 The ḥadīth in which the mention of a narrator has been omitted.

159 The ḥadīth in which there is omission of one or more narrators from the beginning of the *isnād*.

160 The ḥadīth from the middle of whose *isnād* one or more narrator omitted.

161 The ḥadīth from which there are two or more consecutive narrrators missing

162 The ḥadīth ascribed directly to the Prophet ﷺ by one of the Followers without mention of the Companion or Companions from whom he heard it.

163 Meaning the *tābiʿīn* (the Followers), the third generation being *atbāʿ at-tābiʿīn* (the followers of the Follwers). These are the three generations that the Prophet ﷺ declared as the best generations.

164 There is a slight complication here that one must be aware of. We have come to know that a *mursal* ḥadīth is when a *tābiʿī* narrates a ḥadīth ascribing it directly to the Prophet ﷺ without mentioning the Companion. When someone from the third generation omits a narrator, it may be that a Follower and a Companion have been omitted. If this is the case, then the author is using the term *mursal* in a broader sense ecompassing the omission of a second generation *tābiʿī* and a third generation *atbāʿ at-tābiʿīn*. Ed.

narrators narrate their *mursal* ḥadīth as they have narrated their *musnad* (fully connected) ḥadīth (in which case it would be unanimously accepted). However, if the narrator omits in his *mursal* ḥadīth narrators who are reliable as well as those who are not, then it is narrated from Abū Bakr ar-Rāzī of our own people [the Ḥanafīs] and from Abul Waleed al-Bājī of the Mālikīs that there is consensus that such a person's *mursal* ḥadīth are unacceptable, as is also in *Qafw al-Athar*.

I say that by this one knows that the fact that someone omits in *mursal* ḥadīth trustworthy narrators and from others is an impugnment with respect to the *mursal* ḥadīth of anyone after the first three generations. As for the people of the first three generations, their *mursal* ḥadīth are unqualifiedly acceptable to us as we have seen.

ʿAllāmah Sayf ad-Dīn al-Āmidī al-Uṣūlī ash-Shāfiʿī said in his book *al-Iḥkām*,

> They differ about accepting traditions which are *mursal*, the format of which is that someone who did not meet the Prophet ﷺ but whose testimony is valid says "The Messenger of Allah ﷺ said such-and-such": Abū Ḥanīfah, Mālik and Aḥmad ibn Ḥanbal, in the better known of the two narrations from him, accepted it as did the dominant majority of the Muʿtazilah, but ʿĪsā ibn Abān [of the Ḥanafīs] made the distinction that he unqualifiedly accepted the *mursal* ḥadīth of the Companions, the Followers and the Followers of the Followers and those who are imams of transmission but not from those apart from them.
>
> As for ash-Shāfiʿī, he said, "If the *mursal* ḥadīth is from the *mursal* ḥadīth of the Companions or it is a *mursal* ḥadīth which someone else narrates with a full *isnād*, or another person narrates it as a *mursal* ḥadīth but from shaykhs different from the former's, or it is supported by the verdict of a Companion or the verdict of most of the people of knowledge, or if the person transmitting the *mursal* ḥadīth is recognised to be one who does not transmit *mursal* ḥadīth from someone who has a defect such as ignorance etc, such as the *mursal* ḥadīth of Saʿīd ibn al-Musayyab; then (in all such cases) is is acceptable, but otherwise [if it does not fulfil these conditions] then no."[165] Most of his companion agreed with him about that as did Qāḍī Abū Bakr and a large body of the *fuqahāʾ*.
>
> The chosen position is the unqualified acceptance of the *mursal* ḥadīth of the reliable person and the proof of that is found in consensus and in reason:
>
> As for the consensus, it is that the Companions and Followers agreed unanimously to accept *mursal* ḥadīth from someone who is reliable. As for the Companions, they accepted the traditions of ʿAbdullāh ibn ʿAbbās despite the great number of narrations that he made when it has been said that "He only heard four ḥadīth from the Messenger of Allah ﷺ because of his young age."[166] There is also that which

165 Refer to these conditions discussed in detail in the book *ar-Risālah* of imam ash-Shāfiʿī, pp. 461–464.
166 Shaykh Abū Ghuddah mentions that his own research into the number of ḥadīth Ibn Abbas ﷺ

is narrated of al-Barāʾ ibn ʿĀzib that he said, "Everything we report to you we did not hear from the Messenger of Allah ﷺ, but we heard some of it and our companions narrated some of it to us." As for the Followers it was their custom to transmit traditions as *mursal* ḥadīth, which is shown by that which is narrated of al-Aʿmash that he said, "I said to Ibrāhīm an-Nakhaʿī, 'When you narrate to me, give me an *isnād*.' So he said, 'If I say to you, "So-and-so narrated to me from ʿAbdullāh," then he is the one who narrated it to me, but if I say, "ʿAbdullāh narrated to me," then a large group of people (*jamāʿah*) narrated it to me from him.'" That is also shown by what is well known of Ibn al-Musayyab, ash-Shaʿbī and others narrating *mursal* ḥadīth, and that continued to be well known among the Companions and the Followers without anyone repudiating it and is thus a consensus (*ijmāʿ*).

As for a logical [explanation], it is that if the trustworthy reliable narrator says, "The Messenger of Allah ﷺ said such-and-such," expressing certainty of that, then what is obvious from his position is that he would not regard (saying) that as permissible unless he knew or thought very strongly that the Prophet ﷺ had (in fact) said it. This is because if he thought that the Prophet ﷺ had not said it, or if he had a doubt about it then he would not have considered it permissible for himself in his *dīn* to transmit it decidedly from him. [This entails] lying and deceiving the audience, and that necessitates that he regards the person he narrates from to be authentic, for if not he could not know or have a strong belief in being truthful in his narration.

Then al-Āmidī went to great lengths in replying to what it is likely that objectors might produce against his words, so refer to that.

There is in *Tadrīb ar-Rāwī*,

Someone other [than the author] said, "The locus of its being acceptable according to Ḥanafīs is if the narrator of the *mursal* ḥadīth is from the people of the first three meritorious generations, and if it is not from them then no, because of the ḥadīth, 'Then lying will become widespread,' which an-Nasāʾī declared *ṣaḥīḥ*. Ibn Jarīr said, 'All of the Followers agreed unanimously that *mursal* ḥadīth are acceptable[167] and no repudiation of that is reported of them or of any of the imams after them up until the end of the first two hundred years.' Ibn ʿAbd al-Barr said, 'As if he meant that ash-Shāfiʿī was the first to reject it.'"[168]

---

narrated directly from the Prophet ﷺ reached over 40 ḥadīth. This view of Shaykh al-Āmidī is a very unusual one. *Qawāʿid*, p. 140, fn. 1.

167 Ibn Ḥajar in his *an-Nukat ʿalā Ibn aṣ-Ṣalāḥ* and his student as-Sakhāwī in *Fatḥ al-Mughīth*, p. 57, disagree with the claim that there was unanimous agreement.

168 Although Ibn ʿAbd al-Barr makes this clarification, he himself seems to imply the weakness of Ibn Jarīr's assertion of a consensus in *at-Tamhīd* by saying it was his *claim* (and so not established or accepted fact). Ed.

*

The *mursal* ḥadīth is in our view less than a connected (*marfūʿ*) ḥadīth with an *isnād*, contrary to that which one of them said, "Whoever gives an *isnād* has referred you to another [whose authenticity you have to look in to yourself], and someone who gives you a *mursal* ḥadīth has vouched [for it] to you."[169]

Ibn al-Ḥanbalī said in *Qafw al-Athar* explaining the degrees of *ṣaḥīḥ* and *ḥasan* ḥadīth,

> If there is in it all the qualities of a *ṣaḥīḥ* ḥadīth wihout any disagreement then it has precedence over that which has them [qualities] but with some disagreement about the existence of one of them. Similarly if the disagreement is over whether it is a precondition for authenticity after agreeing that it lacks it, such as connectedness (*ittiṣāl*) with respect to those who regard *mursal* ḥadīth of the people of the first three generations as *ṣaḥīḥ*—which is our Ḥanafī people—and such as ability to retain meticulously (*ḍabṭ*) with respect to those who regard as *ṣaḥīḥ* that which someone who is trustworthy transmits even if he is not meticulous in retention.

Thus when a *mursal* ḥadīth and one with an *isnād* contradict each other then the one with an *isnād* is given precedence unless the *mursal* ḥadīth has support in one of the five ways which ash-Shāfiʿī mentioned. The jurists added among the conditions which support it that analogical deduction should agree with it, as is in *Tadrīb ar-Rāwī*. Thus it would become like a ḥadīth with an *isnād*, indeed better than it in some cases. He said in *Tadrīb ar-Rāwī*,

> If the narration of a *mursal* ḥadīth is *ṣaḥīḥ* by its being produced by another route with an *isnād* or as another *mursal* ḥadīth which someone transmits from narrators other than the narrators of the first *mursal* ḥadīth then it is *ṣaḥīḥ*. It becomes clear from this that the *mursal* ḥadīth is *ṣaḥīḥ*, both it and what supports it. If they are both contradicted by a *ṣaḥīḥ* ḥadīth from one route and if it is impossible to reconcile them, we will prefer them over it because of multiple paths of transmission. (Abridged)

Al-ʿAynī said in *ʿUmdat al-qārī*, "If two *ṣaḥīḥ mursal* ḥadīth contradict a ḥadīth with a full *isnād* it is more appropriate to act according to the two *mursal* ḥadīth."

*

That which ash-Shāfiʿī mentions about the *mursal* ḥadīth being supported by a

---

169 This means by giving all the names in the *isnād*, the onus remains on the reader to verify the authenticity of the ḥadīth, whilst if a name has been omitted then one can assume that the missing link is authentic.

ḥadīth with an *isnād*, then what is meant by a ḥadīth with an *isnād* in his words is that which is not a *ṣaḥīḥ* ḥadīth that can stand by itself. He said in *Tadrīb ar-Rāwī*, "Ar-Rāzī and other jurists illustrated that the ḥadīth with an *isnād* that acts as a support should not be one that can stand on its own with an *isnad*. This is so that the proof is established by means of both of them, otherwise the proof would be established by means of the ḥadīth with an *isnād* alone."[170]

*

The ḥadīth scholars consider as *ṣaḥīḥ* the *mursal* ḥadīth of some of the imams among the Followers of which we would mention:

The *mursal* ḥadīth of ash-Shaʿbī. Adh-Dhahabī said in *Tadhkirat al-ḥuffāẓ*, "Aḥmad al-ʿIjlī said, 'The *mursal* ḥadīth of ash-Shaʿbī are *ṣaḥīḥ*, he just about always narrated *mursal* ḥadīth that were *ṣaḥīḥ*.' And it is thus in the *Tahdhīb at-Tahdhīb* in which there is also, 'Al-Ājurrī said from Abū Dāwūd, "The *mursal* ḥadīth of ash-Shaʿbī are more favored to me than the *mursal* ḥadīth of an-Nakhʿī."

The *mursal* ḥadīth of an-Nakhaʿī. There is in *Naṣb ar-Rāyah*, "Ibn ʿAdī narrated with an *isnād* from Ibn Maʿīn that he said, 'The *mursal* ḥadīth of Ibrāhīm are *ṣaḥīḥ* except for the ḥadīth about the merchant from Baḥrayn[171] and the ḥadīth about the loud laughter.'"

And there is in *Tadrīb ar-Rāwī*, "As for the *mursal* ḥadīth of an-Nakhaʿī, Ibn Maʿīn said, 'The *mursal* ḥadīth of Ibrāhīm are more favored to me than the *mursal* ḥadīth of ash-Shaʿbī.' There is also from him, 'They are more agreeable to me than the *mursal* ḥadīth of Sālim ibn ʿAbdullāh, al-Qāsim, and Saʿīd ibn al-Musayyab.' Aḥmad said, 'There is no harm in them.'"

The *mursal* ḥadīth of Ibn al-Musayyab. And there is in it also from al-Ḥākim in *ʿUlūm al-ḥadīth*, that he said, "The most *ṣaḥīḥ* of them as Ibn Maʿīn said are the *mursal* ḥadīth of Ibn al-Musayyab because he was one of the children of the Companions, he met ten of them, he was the *faqīh* of the people of Ḥijāz and their *muftī*, and he was the first of the seven *fuqahāʾ* whose consensus Mālik reckons to be the consensus of all people."

I say that we have seen previously that Ibn Maʿīn said about the *mursal* ḥadīth of an-Nakhaʿī, "They are more pleasing to me than the *mursal* hadīth of Sālim ibn ʿAbdullāh, al-Qāsim, and Saʿīd ibn al-Musayyab," and thus there is a contradiction

---

170 Ar-Rāzī and others are clarifying ash-Shāfiʿī's position that the *musnad* ḥadīth which supports the *mursal* ḥadīth that he is referring to should not be one that can stand alone i.e. be a *ṣāḥīḥ* or *ḥasan* ḥadīth, or else the proof will be established through it and not the *mursal*. Ed.

171 Recorded by Ibn Abī Shayba: Ibrāhim narrates from the Prophet that a person came to the Prophet ﷺ and said, Prophet of Allah, I'm a merchant, I frequent Bahrain.' The Prophet ordered him to pray two rakats i.e. *qaṣr*. *Muṣannaf* Ibn Abī Shaybah, 2:448.

in his judgements on the preference of the *mursal* ḥadīth of an-Nakhaʿī and Ibn al-Musayyab, and Allah ﷻ knows best.

The *mursal* ḥadīth of Shurayḥ the Qāḍī. I say that the *mursal* ḥadīth of Shurayḥ the Qāḍī ought also to be considered *ṣaḥīḥ* just as the *mursal* ḥadīth of Ibn al-Musayyab and an-Nakhaʿī, because he was a trustworthy narrator who had lived during the life of the Prophet ﷺ but without meeting him (*mukhḍaram*) and one of the most magnificent of the senior Followers. ʿUmar, ʿUthmān and ʿAlī had sought from him to accept the position of qāḍī, he narrated *mursal* ḥadīth from the Prophet ﷺ and the majority of his narrations were from the Companions. Abū Nuʿaym mentioned him in his book on Comapanions which indicates that he had met the Messenger of Allah ﷺ, and Ibn as-Sakan narrated it in the same way in his own book (also called) *aṣ-Ṣaḥābah* and he said, "I have not found anything about him that indicates that he met the Messenger of Allah ﷺ except for this, and because of that the Ḥāfiẓ (Ibn Ḥajar) mentioned him in *al-Iṣābah* in the first category of the Companions.

Thus the *mursal* ḥadīth of a Follower who may have been a Companion is more likely to be *ṣaḥīḥ* than the Followers because his narration of a ḥadīth as *mursal* is close to a Companion's narration of a ḥadīth as *mursal*, so understand this. We will soon see something from Ibn Ḥibbān which shows the unqualified acceptability of the *mursal* ḥadīth of the senior Followers because of the fact that they would only omit the mention of the companions in *mursal* ḥadīth.

The *mursal* ḥadīth of al-Ḥasan. As for the *mursal* ḥadīth of al-Ḥasan, Ibn al-Madīnī said, "The *mursal* ḥadīth of al-Ḥasan that trustworthy narrators narrate from him are *ṣaḥīḥ*; how few are those (ḥadīth) that fall short of this!" Abū Zurʿah said, "For everything in which *al-Ḥasan* said, 'The Messenger of Allah ﷺ said...' I have found a firmly established source except for four ḥadīth." Yaḥyā ibn Saʿīd al-Qaṭṭān said, "Never did *al-Ḥasan* say, 'The Messenger of Allah ﷺ said...' except we found sources for it, with the exception of one or two ḥadīth."

The *mursal* ḥadīth of Ibn Sīrīn. I say that similarly the *mursal* ḥadīth of Muḥammad ibn Sīrīn are also *ṣaḥīḥ*, for there is in *al-Jawhar an-Naqī*, "Abū ʿUmar said in the beginning of *at-Tamhīd*, 'The *tadlis* (concealment of gaps in the *isnād*) and the *mursal* of every person about whom it is known that he only took from trustworthy narrators are acceptable, so the *mursal* ḥadīth of Saʿīd ibn al-Musayyab, Muḥammad ibn Sīrīn and Ibrāhīm an-Nakhaʿī are in their view *ṣaḥīḥ*.'"

The *mursal* ḥadīth of Muḥammad ibn al-Munkadir. Similarly the *mursal* ḥadīth of Muḥammad ibn al-Munkadir are also *ṣaḥīḥ*. Ibn ʿUyaynah said, "I have never seen anyone more fitting to say, 'The Messenger of Allah ﷺ said [so-and-so]' without being asked 'from whom is it' than Ibn al-Munkadir," meaning because of his (excellent) investigation.

The *mursal* ḥadīth of a party of the reliable Followers and their Followers. There is in *Tadrīb ar-Rāwī*, "And Yaḥyā ibn Saᶜīd[172] said, 'The *mursal* ḥadīth of Saᶜīd ibn Jubayr are more preferable to me than the *mursal* ḥadīth of ᶜAṭāʾ.' Someone said, 'Are the *mursal* ḥadīth of Mujāhid more preferable to you than the *mursal* ḥadīth of Ṭāwūs?' He said, 'How close they are! And the *mursal* ḥadīth of ᶜAmr ibn Dīnār are more preferable to me,[173] and the *mursal* ḥadīth of Muᶜāwiyah ibn Qurrah are more preferable to me than the *mursal* ḥadīth of Zayd ibn Aslam, and the *mursal* ḥadīth of Mālik ibn Anas are most preferable to me and there is no one among the people more *ṣaḥīḥ* in ḥadīth than him."

*

The ḥadīth scholars have clearly stated that the *mursal* ḥadīth of some of the Followers and their Followers are weak.

The mursal ḥadīth of ᶜAṭāʾ. Ibn al-Madīnī said, "ᶜAṭāʾ[174] used to take from every sort. The *mursal* ḥadīth of Mujāhid[175] are more preferable to me than his *mursal* ḥadīth by a great deal.

The *mursal* ḥadīth of az-Zuhrī.[176] Ibn Maᶜīn and Yaḥyā ibn Saᶜīd al-Qaṭṭān said, "It (i.e. his *mursal* ḥadīth) is nothing," and ash-Shāfiᶜī spoke similarly.[177] He said, "Because we find him narrating from Sulaymān ibn Arqam."[178] Al-Bayhaqī narrated that Yaḥyā ibn Saᶜīd said, "The *mursal* ḥadīth of az-Zuhrī are worse than the *mursal* ḥadīth of others because he was a ḥāfiẓ and whenever he was able to name [his narrators] he did so, and he only left out those whom he did not want to name."

The *mursal* ḥadīth of Qatādah. Yaḥyā ibn Saᶜīd used not to regard the *mursal* ḥadīth of Qatādah as anything, and he would say, "He is like the wind."

The *mursal* ḥadīth of Abū Isḥāq al-Hamdānī, al-Aᶜmash, at-Taymī and Ibn Abī Kathīr. And he said, "The *mursal* ḥadīth of Abī Isḥāq al-Hamdānī, al-Aᶜmash, at-Taymī and Yaḥyā ibn Abī Kathīr resemble nothing."

The *mursal* ḥadīth of Ismāᶜīl ibn Abī Khālid, Ibn ᶜUyaynah and Sufyān ibn Saᶜīd. "The *mursal* ḥadīth of Ismāᶜīl ibn Abī Khālid are nothing, and the *mursal* ḥadīth of Ibn ᶜUyaynah resemble the wind, and Sufyān ibn Saᶜīd [ath-Thawrī]." Thus it is in *Tadrīb ar-Rāwī*.

I say that this discussion does not proceed according to our principle, for each

---

172 He is Yaḥyā ibn Saᶜīd al-Qaṭṭān.

173 It would have to be assumed that what is meant here is that the *mursal* ḥadīth of Mujāhid and Ṭāwūs are equal while those of ᶜAmr ibn Dīnār are more preferable compared to their's. Ed.

174 He is ᶜAṭāʾ ibn Abī Rabāḥ al-Makkī.

175 He is Mujāhid ibn Jabr al-Makkī.

176 He is Muḥammad ibn Shihāb az-Zuhrī.

177 In *ar-Risālah*, p. 469, *al-Kifayah* of *Khaṭīb* al-Baghdādī, p. 386 and Ibn Abī Ḥātim in *Adab al-Shāfiᶜī*, p. 82.

178 Sulaymān ibn Arqam is weak and abandoned (*matrūk*) by the consensus of the ḥadīth scholars. Az-Zuhrī would sometimes narrate ḥadīth that were received through him as *mursal*. Ed.

one of these is from the people of the second or third generation, and their *mursal* ḥadīth are unqualifiedly acceptable in our view.

The fact that a narrator of *mursal* ḥadīth takes from every sort is only a criticism against the *mursal* ḥadīth of people of lesser rank than these as we have seen previously. Also, it will become clear to you in what is forthcoming that the narration of *mursal* ḥadīth and concealment of gaps in the chain of narration (*tadlīs*) have the same judgement, and yet many of those whose *mursal* ḥadīth the ḥadīth scholars regard as weak they accept their concealment of gaps in the chain of narration, thus there is no meaning to rejecting their *mursal* ḥadīth.

The Ḥāfiẓ (Ibn Ḥajar) said in *Ṭabaqāt al-mudallisīn*, "The second rank comprises those whose *tadlīs* the imams tolerate and they narrate from them in the *ṣaḥīḥ* collections because of their imamate and the small amount of their *tadlīs* in comparison to that which they have narrated (in total), such as ath-Thawrī, or those who only concealed (did *tadlīs* of) trustworthy narrators, such as Ibn ʿUyaynah."

This shows the acceptability of concealment of gaps in the chain of narration as practised by ath-Thawrī and Ibn ʿUyaynah in their view, therefore their narration of *mursal* ḥadīth should be the same, and similarly the narration of *mursal* ḥadīth of other imams on whose imamate the people of knowledge agree upon such as az-Zuhrī, Qatādah, ʿAṭāʾ ibn Abī Rabāḥ and the likes of them.

As for the fact of their taking from every sort of person, that does not seriously impair the *ṣaḥīḥ* nature of their *mursal* ḥadīth because they did not definitely assert the ascription of a word or deed to the Prophet ﷺ unless they knew or predominantly believed that the Prophet ﷺ had said that or had done that. That requires that the intermediary they did not name must have been someone they deemed to be reliable, for if not they would not have known or predominantly believed in his truthfulness in his narration, and thus it would not have been valid for them to be definite about that as we have seen previously in the statement of al-Āmidī in some detail.[179]

*

The chief Qāḍī (Ḥāfiẓ Ibn Ḥajar) said, "The judgement on those about whom it is established that they conceal gaps in the chain of narration, is that if they are people who are reliable, then only that in which they state definitely that it was narrated to

---

179 To put that simply, it cannot be permissible for people of the calibre of those mentioned to say definitively that the Prophet ﷺ said or did something without being certain of the reliability of the source. If we assume that they were not, they would have grossly erred in their definitive attribution of a ḥadīth to the Prophet ﷺ, and thus their own reliability would come in to question. Since everyone accepts them to be reliable, they will also have to accept that their *mursal* ḥadīth are also reliable. Either both they and the *mursal* ḥadīth are reliable or both are unreliable. Since everyone considers them to be reliable, we will also have to extend that consensus to their *mursal* ḥadīth. Ed.

them[180] is accepted, according to the soundest position." As for our view (Ḥanafīs) it has been said, "His narration has the same status as the *mursal* ḥadīth and you already know its judgement in our view." It is thus in *Qafw al-Athar*.

I say that if the person practising concealment of gaps in the chain of narration is one of the trustworthy narrators of the three generations then his omission of gaps in the chain of narration is unqualifiedly accepted just as is his narration of *mursal* ḥadīth, but if he is of a lesser rank than them, there is more detail to it which we have very recently examined. And there is in *Tadrīb ar-Rāwī*,

> The dominant majority of those who accept the *mursal* ḥadīth say, "The person who practises concealment of gaps in the chain of narration is unqualifiedly acceptable," as al-Khaṭīb cited. The author [al-Nawawī] transmitted in *Sharḥ al-muhadhdhab* following al-Bayhaqī and Ibn ʿAbd al-Barr, that there is agreement on the rejection of that which he (the concealer) narrates using *ʿanʿanah* ("from so-and-so from so-and-so…"). That is interpreted as referring to the agreement of those who do not use *mursal* ḥadīth as proof.

Useful Point

Ibn ʿAbd al-Barr[181] cited the imams of ḥadīth as saying,

> The concealment of gaps in the chain of narration by Ibn ʿUyaynah is accepted because when he was stopped (and asked about who he left out of the chain)[182] he referred to people such as Ibn Jurayj, Maʿmar and their likes. Ibn Ḥibbān expressed his preference of him saying, "This is something that only belongs in this world to Ṣufyān ibn ʿUyaynah because he used to narrate with concealment of gaps in the chain of narration but he would only do so concealing proficient trustworthy narrators," and then he likened that to the *mursal* ḥadīth of the senior Followers who only omitted Companions in *mursal* ḥadīth. The way that al-Bazzār expressed it was, "Whoever concealed trustworthy narrators (by practicing *tadlīs*), then his concealment in the chain of narration is acceptable to the people of knowledge."

I say that Ibn Ḥibbān's likening the *mursal* ḥadīth of the elder Followers to the concealment of gaps in the chain of narration of Ibn ʿUyaynah shows the acceptability of their *mursal* ḥadīth according to the hadīth scholars because of the fact that they

---

180 Stating definitely means that they specifically say 'he narrated to me,' or 'he told me', or I heard from him '*samiʿtu*' etc. Prepositions such as *ʿan* (from so and so, known in ḥadīth terminology as *ʿanʿana*) would be unacceptable in this scenario as the preposition does not give any indication of the mode of transmission and reception. Ed.

181 *At-Tamhīd* 1:31.

182 Ibn ʿAbd al-Barr cites examples in *at-Tamhīd* in which people ask Ibn 'Uyaynah 'who is before such and such', and having been asked he would disclosed a narrator or narrators he had omitted. These narrators were always reliable people. Ed.

omitted the Companions in *mursal* ḥadīth. We alluded to that before in the section on the *mursal* ḥadīth of Shurayḥ.

Useful Point

The most authentic position is that concealment of gaps in the chain of narration (*tadlīs*) is not an impugnment; it has been shown that the concealment of gaps in the chain of narration (*tadlīs*) is not *ḥarām* in that which Ibn ʿAdī narrated from al-Barāʾ who said, "There were no cavalry among us on the day of Badr except for al-Miqdād." Ibn ʿAsākir said, "His saying, 'among us' means the Muslims since al-Barāʾ was not present at Badr."

I say that it is more appropriate that narration of *mursal* ḥadīth is [also] not an impugnment since concealment of gaps in the chain of narration is worse than it, as cannot be hidden from anyone.

Al-Baghawī said, "Aḥmad ibn Ibrāhīm al-ʿAbdī narrated to us, 'Muḥammad ibn Muʿādh narrated to us, "Muʿādh narrated to us from Shuʿbah that he said, 'I have never seen any of the people of ḥadīth who did not conceal gaps in the chain of narration except for Ibn ʿAwn and ʿAmr ibn Murrah.'" It is thus in *Ṭabaqāt al-Mudallisīn*.

Useful Point

Al-Bayhaqī said in *al-Maʿrifah*, "We have narrated from Shuʿbah that he said, 'I have spared you[183] from the concealment of gaps in the chain of narration (*tadlīs*) of three: al-Aʿmash, Abū Isḥāq[184] and Qatādah.'"

I say that this is an excellent principle in the ḥadīth of these three, that if they come to us by way of Shuʿbah, then that shows that they were heard, even if they come in the form of "from so-and-so from so-and-so" (*muʿanʿanah*). The like of that is, "Al-Layth narrated to us from Abu 'z-Zubayr from Jābir," because he (al-Layth) only heard from him what he had heard from Jābir.[185]

I say that a better principle than that is that which the Ḥāfiẓ mentioned in *al-Fatḥ* that Shuʿbah only conveyed *ṣaḥīḥ* ḥadīth from his shaykhs.

Ibn al-Qayyim said in *Iʿlām al-mūwqqiʿīn*, "How can that not be so, when Shuʿbah carries the banner for this ḥadīth, and when one of the imams of ḥadīth has said, 'If you see Shuʿbah in the *isnād* of a ḥadīth then take hold of it with both hands.'" So every ḥadīth in whose *isnād* there is Shuʿbah is safe from concealment of gaps in the chain of narration, confusion of the narrators, and his insinuations (*talqīn*)[186] etc., on condition that the *isnād* leading up to Shuʿbah is *ṣaḥīḥ*.

183 I.e spared you from having to look into or be suspicious of.... Ed.

184 Meaning Abu Isḥāq al-Sabīʿī.

185 Ibn Ḥajar, *Tabaqāt al-Mudallisīn*, p. 21.

186 *Talqīn* is when a narrator approaches a shaykh with a ḥadīth compilation, recorded either in

The Ḥāfiẓ said in *al-Fatḥ* also,

> Al-Ismāᶜīlī also showed the authenticity of the hearing [of ḥadīth] of Abū Isḥāq from ᶜAbd ar-Raḥmān [ibn al-Aswad ibn Yazīd] by the fact that Yaḥyā al-Qaṭṭān narrated it from Zuhayr, and he said after narrating it by way of him, "Al-Qaṭṭān would not agree to take from Zuhayr what had not been the direct hearing of Abū Isḥāq." It is as if he recognised that by observation of the action of al-Qaṭṭān or by a clear statement in his own words.

*

The *muᶜallaq* (hanging) is that [ḥadīth] from the beginning of whose *isnād* one or more consecutive [narrators] are dropped without deliberate concealment of gaps in the chain of narration (*tadlīs*) whether or not the rest [of the narrators] are dropped.

And the *muᶜḍal* is that from whose *isnād* two or more consecutive [narrators] are dropped, wherever the omission may be.

And the *munqaṭiᶜ* is that from whose *isnād* one or more are dropped without them being consecutive, wherever the omission may be.

So between each of the *muᶜḍal* and the *munqaṭiᶜ* and between the *muᶜallaq* there is commonality in one respect.

One of our fellow hanafis, as-Sirāj al-Hindī transmitted that the *mursal* ḥadīth in the technical usage of the ḥadīth scholars is the saying of a Follower, "The Messenger of Allah ﷺ said..." and that (ḥadīth) from whose narrators one narrator before the Follower is omitted is called *munqaṭiᶜ*, and if more are omitted it is called *muᶜḍal*. Thus he did not mention the *muᶜallaq* (as narrated) from them not because its name was not heard from them but because it is either *munqaṭiᶜ* or *muᶜḍal*. And he (also) said, "All of them are called *mursal* by the jurists (*al-uṣulıyyun*)." You have already learnt the judgement on the *mursal* ḥadīth of the people of the three generations and those after them according to the chosen position among us, for that is the unqualified ruling on the *mursal* ḥadīth according to the people of *uṣūl*. (Abridged)

I say that there is also comprised in this section the *balāghāt* (those traditions in which someone of the later generations simply says, "It has reached me [*balaghanī*] that the Messenger of Allah ﷺ said..."), for the *balāghāt* of the trustworthy narrators of the people of the three generations are acceptable in our view unqualifiedly, such as Imam Malik, Abū Ḥanīfah, ash-Shāfiᶜī, Muḥammad ibn al-Ḥasan, Abū Yūsuf and

---

writing or by memory, and seeks his permission to read them to him after giving him the impression that the ḥadīth are the shaykh's narrations when in fact they are not. He may insinuate by saying to the shaykh, 'are you not the shaykh who narrated these ḥadīth?' When the shaykh is someone whose recollection of his own narrations is poor, he may say yes, and authorise the reader to narrate the ḥadīth from him. This was one way in which fabricators could seek credibility for their fabrications. This is an impugnment against both the insinuator and the shaykh who accepts it. Ed.

the likes. The *balāghāt* of someone after these if transmitted [from him] by trustworthy narrators just as they narrate his fully connected narrations, such as al-Bukhārī, Aḥmad and others, are acceptable unanimously if transmitted using words of conviction, but if he used to omit trustworthy and other (non-trustworthy) narrators in the mode of *mursal* ḥadīth then it is unanimously agreed that they are not acceptable, although they have mentioned, as is in *Radd al-Muḥtār* and elsewhere, that the *balāghāt* of Muḥammad are (to be treated as) fully connected (*musnad*). Thus it is in *at-Ta ͑līq al-Mumajjad*.

Muḥammad ibn ͑Abd al-Bāqī az-Zurqānī said in *Sharḥ al-Muwaṭṭā ͗*, "The *balāghāt* of Mālik are not weak since all of them have been followed up and found to have *isnād*s by other routes than him," as is in *Ghayth al-ghamām* by the ḥadīth scholar al-Laknawī.

As for the ruling on the *mu ͑allaq* traditions of al-Bukhārī and Muslim then that which is expressed using words denoting conviction such as, "So-and-so said, did, ordered, narrated or mentioned..." then that is their judgement that it is *ṣaḥīḥ* from the person to whom it is ascribed, and some of it is that which is according to their preconditions (and thus *saḥīḥ*), and some of it is *ṣaḥīḥ* but not according to their conditions.

And as for that which is not expressed with conviction such as, "It is narrated, mentioned, cited, said to be so, or it has been narrated, mentioned or cited from so-and-so that such-and-such..." or "there is in the chapter from the Prophet ﷺ", then there is no ruling in this that it is *ṣaḥīḥ* from the person to whom it is ascribed. Occasionally they apply that in that which is *ṣaḥīḥ*. However, that which is referred to using words indicating (possible) weakness, and we have said that its authenticity cannot be decided, is not extremely weak because they (al-Bukhari and Muslim) have included them in the book termed as *Ṣaḥīḥ*. It is also expressed thus in *Tadrīb ar-Rāwī* in an abridged form.

CHAPTER 6

The *muḍṭarab* ḥadīth (contradictory), which is one that is narrated in different ways,[187] and the contradiction in it sometimes occurs in the *isnād* and at other times in the text, and it may occur in both together.

The Ḥāfiẓ said in the introduction to the *al-Fatḥ*,

> For the *ḥuffāẓ*, differences in the ḥadīth do not necessarily require that it be contradictory (*muḍṭarab*) except in two conditions: first, the points of difference are equal (on either side). However, when one of the two statements is considered weightier it is given precedence and the *ṣaḥīḥ* [*isnad*] does not become defective because of the outweighed [*isnād*]. Second, alongside equality [in the points of difference) it is impossible to reconcile them according to the principles of the ḥadīth scholars and one's preponderant view is that the ḥāfiẓ did not detail that ḥadīth exactly, in which case the judgement is passed on that narration alone that it is contradictory.

There is also in it, "The ascription of a defect because of a simple disagreement is not itself something that invalidates, since a mere disagreement does not necessitate a contradiction that would cause weakness."[188]

*

According to *al-Jawhar an-Naqī*:

> And when a trustworthy narrator establishes an *isnād* it is relied upon and one does not worry about disagreements. Many ḥadīth of the two *Ṣaḥīḥ* books are not safe from disagreements such as this. Al-Bayhaqī did the same as this in the beginning of the book in the ḥadīth of, "Its waters are pure..." in which he explained the differ-

187 The ḥadīth is narrated with different paths of transmission but they irreconcilably contradict each other. Ed.

188 This means that although many ḥadīth have differing paths, this does not mean the ḥadīth fall in to the *muḍṭarab* category, it is only such if the contradictory elements in the differing paths are all equally strong and there is no way to consolidate them based on the principles of the ḥadīth scholars. Ed.

ences that occur in it, and then he said, "Except that the one who established its *isnād* is a trustworthy narrator, and that is Mālik, and he put it in *al-Muwaṭṭaʾ* and Abū Dāwūd narrated it in *as-Sunan*."

[as-Suyūṭī] said in *at-Tadrīb*:

Shaykh al-Islām [Ibn Ḥajar] said that "The contradiction may co-exist with soundness, and that is if the contradiction occurs in the name of a single man, his father and ascription, etc., and he is a trustworthy narrator, and so the ḥadīth is judged to be *ṣaḥīḥ* and the disagreement about what we have mentioned causes no harm despite the fact that it is called '*muḍṭarab*'. Az-Zarkashī stated that unequivocally in his *Mukhtaṣar* saying, 'Inversion (*qalb*), irregularity (*shudhūdh*), and contradiction (*iḍṭirāb*) can at times enter into the categories of *ṣaḥīḥ* and *ḥasan*.'"

CHAPTER 7

On the principles of invalidation and validation and their wordings, and the causes of invalidation.

VAGUE INVALIDATION (*al-jarḥ al-mubham*) is not accepted but it is accepted when it is about someone whom no one has validated.

Authentication may be accepted when it is vague without explanation of the reason, because the reasons may be too many and thus too onerous to mention. As for invalidation, it is only accepted if it is explained and the reason for invalidation made clear, since invalidation can result from a single reason which is not difficult to mention, and because people differ about the reasons for invalidation, and thus some of them will invalidate based on that which he believes is invalidation but which in reality is not invalidation. For this reason it is necessary that one explains the reason for invalidation so that it becomes clear as to whether it is critical or not.

Ibn as-Salāh said,

> This is obvious and confirmed in *fiqh* and in its principles, and *al-Khaṭīb* mentioned that it is the school of the imams among the *ḥuffāẓ* of ḥadīth such as the two shaykhs[189] etc. For that reason al-Bukhārī used as proof a group of people whom others had invalidated such as ʿIkrimah and ʿAmr ibn Marzūq, and Muslim used as proof Suwayd ibn Saʿīd and a group of people about whom disparagement is well known, and Abū Dāwūd did similarly. This shows that they took the position that invalidation is not established unless the reason for it is explained."

Aṣ-Ṣayrafī said, "It is the same when they say, 'So-and-so is a liar'; it must be explained because (linguistically) 'lying' may be used to mean 'being mistaken' such as when one says, 'Abū Muḥammad lied,' meaning 'he was mistaken.'"

Having regarded this verdict as correct, Ibn aṣ-Ṣalāḥ then asked himself this question:

189 i.e. imams al-Bukhārī and Muslim. They are referred to as the two shaykhs (al-Shaykhayn). Ed.

> Someone may ask, "People only depend in their invalidation of narrators and rejection of their ḥadīth upon the books compiled by the ḥadīth critics. [These critics] rarely turn to explain the reasons [in their books] and only confine themselves to the bare statement, 'So-and-so is weak,' or 'So-and-so is nothing' etc., or 'This is a weak ḥadīth', or 'a ḥadīth which is not established' etc., and so stipulating that one explains the reason for invalidating someone would lead to paralysis in that activity and would close the door of invalidation in the great majority of cases."

Then, in short, he answered that question by saying:

> Even if we do not rely on this in confirming the invalidation and passing judgement to that effect, we may rely on it in hesitating to accept the ḥadīth of those about whom something like this is said, based on the fact that it creates a strong doubt within us the like of which requires us to hesitate. Later, if the doubt about him leaves because of our investigation of his circumstances, we will accept his ḥadīth without hesitation, such as the ones affected by such invalidation whom the authors of the two *Ṣaḥīḥ* books and others used in proof. So understand that, because it is a good way out (of that ojection) (*makhlaṣ*).

Thus it is in *Tadrīb ar-Rāwī* and in *ar-Rafʿ wa't-Takmīl* transmitted from *Muqaddimah* Ibn aṣ-Ṣalāḥ.

The upshot is that if no one considers a narrator as a trustworthy narrator, and one person invalidates him unclearly (*mubham*) then one hesitates to accept his ḥadīth. If anyone regards him as a trustworthy narrator, then vague invalidation of him is not accepted, but on the contrary it is vital that the reason for it be explained. This is the meaning of what we have previously said, that the person about whom there is disagreement (i.e. that person about whom there is both unclear validation and unclear invalidation) his ḥadīths are regarded as accepted (*ḥasan al-ḥadīth*). What is mentioned of the two (i.e. validation and invalidation) in the biographical dicitionaries of narrators is predominantly thus, so that one accepts the validation but not the invalidation and his ḥadīths are used as proof. You have already learnt that their verdict of weakness or "he is nothing" or "entirely weak" (*wāhin bimarrah*) and other things, are all obscure invalidations, thus that has no effect on those whom anyone has authenticated and said that they are trustworthy narrators.

The Ḥāfiẓ said in the introduction to *al-Fatḥ*, "ʿAbd al-Malik ibn aṣ-Ṣabbāḥ al-Mismaʿī al-Baṣrī was one of the companions of Shuʿbah. Abū Ḥātim said, 'capable (*ṣāliḥ*)',[190] and the author of *al-Mīzān* mentioned him and then transmitted from al-Khalīlī that he said about him, 'Suspected of stealing ḥadīth,' and this is an obscure invalidation."

---

190 The term *ṣāliḥ* here is a technical ḥadith term which means having the capability of being used as a proof (*ṣālihun lil iḥtijāj*) and not the lexical meaning of being upright. Ed.

I say that they did not pay heed to this invalidation after Abū Ḥātim had declared him to be a trustworthy narrator, and al-Bukhārī, Muslim and an-Nasāʾī used him in proof.

And he said in the biographical notice on Saʿīd ibn Sulaymān al-Wāsiṭī, "Abū Ḥātim said, 'He was a reliable and trustworthy narrator,' but ʿAbdullāh ibn Aḥmad said narrating from his father, 'He was someone who made many mistakes,' and ad-Dāraquṭnī said, 'They speak [critically] about him.' I say that this ascrption of weakness is obscure and is not accepted." And the Ḥāfiẓ inclined in *Sharḥ an-Nukhbah* and the introduction to *Lisān* (*al-Mizan*) to accepting obscure invalidation about those whom nobody considered trustworthy narrators, and he said,

> Rather, the correct position is to provide details, so that if the invalidation is explained while the condition is thus (i.e. some of them considered him a trustworthy narrator and others considered him invalid), then [the invalidation] is accepted, but if not one acts by the validation. And the statement of those who give precedence to validation is to be interpreted on this basis. As for someone whose state is unknown and nothing is known about him apart from the verdict of one of the imams of ḥadīth that he is weak , or abandoned (*matrūk*), or dropped (*sāqiṭ*)[191] or that he is not used in proof and the like, then the verdict is according to his verdict and we do not require of him the explanation of that, since even if he explained it and it was not a critical aspersion, ignorance of the state of that man would prevent us using him in proof; how can it not be so when he has been declared weak?

I say that it ought not to be accepted according to the one who uses as evidence an unknown narrator (*mastūr*) of the three generations even if no one declared him to be a trustworthy. Invalidation does not affect [his standing] unless it is explained, since even if he explained it and it is not a critical aspersion, ignorance of his state does not prevent us from using him in proof.[192]

If there is both invalidation and validation for a narrator, which has precedence?

If both invalidation and validation are present for a narrator, then if they are both vague the validation is given precedence over the invalidation as we have seen before. If the invalidation is explained and the validation is vague the invalidation is given precedence. This is the most correct position according to the *fuqahāʾ* and the jurists, and al-Khaṭīb transmitted it from the dominant majority of the scholars. This is because the person who invalidates [the narrator] has extra knowledge which the one authenticating him has not discovered. If the validation is also detailed (*mufassar*) in that the person doing it says, "I know the reason which the person invalidat-

191 *Sāqiṭ al-Iḥtijāj*, his ḥadīths are dropped from making use as proof texts. Ed.
192 Because of the simple fact that he is from the earliest three generations. Ed.

ing him has advanced, but the [narrator] has repented (*tāba*) and his state became good," then the validation is given precedence, as is implied in the *Tadrīb ar-Rāwī*.

I say that it is similar if the person who authenticates him says, "So-and-so is a trustworthy narrator and those who spoke about him critically have done him wrong," or he says, "Some of them spoke against him without proof," etc., and in these cases the validation is also given precedence, because it is of the same ruling as the [validation] with an explanation because it shows that the person doing the validation knew the verdicts of those who invalidated [the narrator] and that it had no effect on him. Upon pondering over their words, it becomes obvious that this is detailed validation (*taʿdīl mufassar*), in particular the words of the Ḥāfiẓ in the introduction to *al-Fatḥ* where he answered the aspersion of some ḥadīth scholars against narrators from the *Ṣaḥīḥ* [collections] so refer to that.

An example of that is the saying of Ibn ʿAbd al-Barr about ʿIkrimah, "He is one of the noble ʿulamāʾ, and the words of those who speak against him have no effect, since none of those who spoke against him have any proof." The Ḥāfiẓ mentioned it in his Introduction [to *al-Fatḥ*] using him as a proof.

Yaʿqūb[193] said, "Aḥmad ibn Ḥanbal said to me, 'My position about the narrators is that I do not abandon a ḥadīth narrator's ḥadīth until the people of a city concur that one should abandon his ḥadīth.'"

He whose trustworthiness and whose imamate is firmly established with the ummah is unaffected by invalidation even if it is explained

Someone whose trustworthiness is firmly established whose imamate the Ummah has concede voluntarily, then invalidation has no effect on his standing even if it is explained, and his ḥadīth are *ṣaḥīḥ* and not only *ḥasan*.

Abū Jaʿfar ibn Jarīr (aṭ-Ṭabarī) said,

> No one can reject ʿIkrimah's precedence in knowledge of *fiqh*, and the Qurʾān and its interpretation, and his abundant narrating of traditions, and the fact that He knew his master[194] [ʿAbdullāh ibn ʿAbbās ﷺ], and the praise lavished on him by the great companions of Ibn ʿAbbās; such (is the standing of his companions) that it would establish a man's trustworthiness even if one of them had testified (to it) and he would be worthy of that testimony. And whoever's trustworthiness is established then invalidation of him is not accepted, and trustworthiness does not diminish by conjecture.

I say that a number of the early generation invalidated him, but the ḥadīth schol-

193 He is Yaʿqūb ibn Sufyān al-Fārsī al-Fasawī the Hafidh, passed away in the year 277 (AH).

194 Meaning his master Sayyidunā ʿAbdullāh ibn ʿAbbās ﷺ.

ars never turned to their words because of the clear establishment of his trustworthiness and of his imamate, and they counted his ḥadīth among the *ṣaḥīḥ*.

Ibn Jarīr said, "If it were that everyone against whom a claim were made [that he held] a wrong belief, and [by the simple matter of the claim alone] it was to be confirmed against him and by that his trustworthiness was to diminish and his testimony nullified, it would be necessary to abandon the majority of the ḥadīth scholars of the lands because some people have ascribed unworthy things to every one of them."

The opinion of every person who regards someone as invalid is not taken, even if that invalidator is one of the imams. At times certain obstructions will prevent the invalidation from being accepted

It is not permissible to accept the verdict of every ḥadīth critic against any narrator, even if that critic is one of the imams or one of the most famous scholars of the ummah, for often there are matters which prevent the acceptance of his invalidation, at which point the ruling is that his invalidation is to be rejected. This has many forms which are not hidden to those who are expert:

One form is that the critic is himself invalidated [by someone else], in which case one does not immediately accept his invalidation [of the other], and likewise his validation unless someone else accords with him, such as al-Azdī because he had a sharp tongue and was excessive in his invalidation. Adh-Dhahabī said in his biographical notice of Abān ibn Isḥāq al-Madanī after transmitting from Abū'l-Fatḥ al-Azdī that he is to be abandoned, "I say that he is not to be abandoned, because Aḥmad and al-ʿIjlī declared him to be a trustworthy narrator, and Abu'l-Fatḥ is excessive in his invalidation. He has a very large compilation which goes to the limit about those invalidated, and he himself invalidated a large number of people whom no one pre viously had spoken about [critically], while he himself is criticised."

The Ḥāfiẓ said in *Tahdhīb at-Tahdhīb* in the biographical notice on Aḥmad ibn Shabīb al-Ḥabaṭī al-Baṣrī after transmitting about him from al-Azdī that he was not well received, "I say that no one has turned to this verdict, for on the contrary al-Azdī is not well received."

He also said in the Introduction to *al-Fatḥ* in the biographical notice of ʿIkrimah, "As for the first reason, then the verdict of Ibn ʿUmar (on him) is not firmly established as coming from him since it is the narration of Abu Khalaf al-Jazzār from Yaḥyā al-Bakkāʾ that he heard Ibn ʿUmar saying that, but Yaḥyā al-Bakkāʾ's ḥadīth are abandoned.[195] Ibn Ḥibbān said, 'It is impossible for someone who is trustworthy to be invalidated by the words of someone who is himself invalidated.'"

Another form of it is that the critic is stubborn and severe in his invalidation There

195 He is Yaḥyā ibn Muslim al-Azdī, his biography is in *Mizan*, 4:382, 408, and *at-Tahdhīb*, 11:278

are a number of the critics who have some severity in this area, and so they invalidate a narrator for the least reason, and they make pronouncements against him which ought not to be made. The validation of someone like this is taken into account but their invalidation is not as long as they do not accord with others who are fair and who are themselves to be reckoned with. Among the severe are Abū Ḥātim, an-Nasāʾī, Ibn Maʿīn, Abu'l-Ḥasan ibn al-Qaṭṭān, Yaḥyā ibn Saʿīd al-Qaṭṭān, Ibn Ḥibbān and others, because they are well known for being excessive in invalidation and severe in it.

Adh-Dhahabī said in *al-Mīzān* in the biographical notice of Ṣufyān ibn ʿUyaynah, "Yaḥyā ibn Saʿīd al-Qaṭṭān was extremely severe on the narrators." He also said in his biographical notice on Sayf ibn Sulaymān al-Makkī, "Even with his severity Yaḥyā al-Qaṭṭān narrated from Sayf."

He also said in the biographical notice of al-Ḥārith al-Aʿwar,[196] "The ḥadīth of al-Ḥārith are in the four *Sunan*, and an-Nasāʾī despite his severity about narrators has used him in proofs and strengthened his affair."

Adh-Dhahabī said in his biographical notice on ʿUthmān ibn ʿAbd ar-Raḥmān aṭ-Ṭarāʾifī, "As for Ibn Ḥibbān he was harsh (*taqaʿqaʿa*)[197] as was his custom."

The Ḥāfiẓ said in *al-Qawl al-Musaddad fi 'dh-Dhabb ʿan Musnad Aḥmad*, "Ibn Ḥibbān sometimes invalidated a trustworthy narrator so much so that it was as if he did not know what was coming out of his head." Thus it is in *ar-Rafʿ wa't-Takmīl.*

Adh-Dhahabī said in the biograhical notice on Muḥammad ibn al-Faḍl as-Sadūsī ʿĀrim the shaykh of al-Bukhārī, after mentioning his having been declared a trustworthy narrator by ad-Dāraquṭnī, "I say that this is the verdict of the Ḥāfiẓ of the age the like of whom has not appeared since an-Nasāʾī. So how does this verdict compare to that of Ibn Ḥibbān the brash inferior one (*khassāf*)?"

The Ḥāfiẓ said in the Introduction to *al-Fatḥ* in the biographical notice on Muḥammad ibn Abī ʿAdī al-Baṣrī, "Abū Ḥātim has severity [in his view]." And he said in *Badhl al-māʿūn fi faḍl aṭ-ṭāʿūn*, "It is sufficient to regard him (i.e. Abū Balj Yaḥyā al-Kūfī) as strong that an-Nasāʾī and Abū Ḥātim declared him a trustworthy narrator despite their severity."[198]

Adh-Dhahabī said in *Tadhkirat al-Ḥuffāẓ* in the biographical notice on Abu'l-Ḥasan ibn al-Qaṭṭān after citing praise of him, "However, he was severe on the conditions of the narrators and was unfair in as much as he took to considering Hishām ibn ʿUrwah and the like of him to be lenient." He said in *al-Mīzān* in the biographical notice of Hishām[199] after declaring him a trustworthy narrator, "One does not

196 He is al-Ḥarith ibn ʿAbdullāh al-Aʿwar al-Hamdānī. Shaykh Abd al-Aziz al-Ghumari has a treatise called *al-Bāḥith ʿan ʿIlal aṭ-Ṭan fi 'l-Ḥīrith* in which argues that he is a trustworthy narrator.

197 Literally *taqaʿqaʿa* means to rattle on; what is meant here is that he makes excessive criticism. Ed.

198 Al-Laknawī, *ar-Rafʿ*, p. 179.

199 Meaning Hishām ibn ʿUrwah. Adh-Dhahabī, *Mīzān*, 4:301–302.

take into account that which Abu'l-Ḥasan ibn al-Qaṭṭān said, so do not be rash, and give up mixing well established imams with weak narrators and confused people. For he is the Shaykh of Islam, but may Allah ﷻ make our equanimity towards you good, Ibn al-Qaṭṭān."

As-Sakhāwī said in *Fatḥ al-Mughīth*,

> Adh-Dhahabī categorised those who spoke concerning narrators thus: (1) A category who spoke about all narrators, such as Ibn Maʿīn and Abū Ḥātim. (2) "A category who spoke about most of the narrators such as Mālik and Shuʿbah. (3) A category who spoke about one man after another (i.e. half of them) such as Ibn ʿUyaynah and ash-Shāfiʿī. He said all of them are also in three categories:
>
> 1. A category of them who were severe in invalidating and thorough in validation, criticizing a narrator for two or three mistakes. So if this one declares a person to be a trustworthy narrator then take hold of what he says as strongly as you can, and cling to his validation. But if he declares a narrator weak then look and see if anyone else has agreed with him in his ascription of weakness, and if they have whilst none of the skilled and proficient scholars have declared that man to be a trustworthy narrator then he is weak. If someone does declare him to be a trustworthy narrator, then this is the person about whom they said: 'invalidation of him is not accepted without explanation', meaning that the verdict of Ibn Maʿīn, for example, 'that he is weak' is not enough if he does not explain the reason why he is weak, and then (it transpires that) later al-Bukhārī and others come and declare him to be a trustworthy narrator.
> 2. A category of them who are lenient such as at-Tirmidhī and al-Ḥākim.
> 3. A category of them who are moderate and well balanced such as Aḥmad, ad-Dāraquṭnī and Ibn ʿAdī.[200]

Ḥāfiẓ ibn Ḥajar said in his *Nukat ʿalā Ibn aṣ-Ṣalāḥ*,

> No generation of scholars who criticise the narrators is free of extreme and moderate [ones]. Of the first, there are Shuʿbah and Sufyān ath-Thawrī, and Shuʿbah is more severe than him. Of the second, there are Yaḥyā al-Qaṭṭān and Ibn Mahdī and Yaḥyā is more severe than him. Of the third, there are Yaḥyā ibn Maʿīn and Aḥmad ibn Ḥanbal, and Yaḥyā is more severe than Aḥmad. Of the fourth, there are Abū Ḥātim and al-Bukhārī, and Abū Ḥātim is more severe than al-Bukhārī.[201]

---

200 Shaykh ʿAbd al-Fattāḥ has mentioned that the inclusion of Ibn ʿAdī among the moderate critics is questionable as al-Laknawī has explained in *ar-Rafʿ wa 't-Takmīl* (pp. 208–216), as have other scholars. He seemed particularly severe in his criticism against the hanafis. Ed.

201 al-Laknawī, *ar-Rafʿ*, pp. 187–188.

Among the severe later scholars there are: (1) Ibn al-Jawzī the author of *al-Mawḍūʿāt* and *al-ʿIlal al-Mutanāhiyah*. (2) ʿUmar ibn Badr al-Mawṣilī the author of *Risālah fi 'l-Mawḍūʿāt* which is an abridgement of the *Mawḍūʿāt* of Ibn al-Jawzī. (3) Ar-Raḍī aṣ-Ṣāghānī the linguist who has two treatises on fabricated ḥadīth. (4) Al-Jūzaqānī author of the book *al-Abāṭīl*. (5) Shaykh Ibn Taymiyah al-Ḥarrānī the author of *Minhāj as-Sunna*. (6) Al-Majd the linguist and author of the *Qāmūs* and *Sifr as-Saʿādah* etc. They are severe in invalidation of ḥadīth. They haste to pass judgement that a ḥadīth is fabricated or that it is weak because of some impairment, even if slight, in its narrator or because of its contradicting another ḥadīth; how may a strong ḥadīth have they passed judgement on that it was fabricated or weak, and how many a ḥadīth which suffered some slight weakness have they passed judgement on as being strongly invalidated. It is incumbent on a person of knowledge to not hastily accept their verdicts without checking their judgements. It is thus in *ar-Rafʿ wa't-takmīl*.

I say that among the critics there are those who are severe in invalidating the people of some lands or of some *madhhab*s in particular and not others:

Such as al-Jūzaqānī who is severe in invalidating the Kūfans in particular. The Ḥāfiẓ said in *Tahdhīb at-Tahdhīb*, "Al-Jūzaqānī is not taken into account in his belittling the Kūfans."

Such as adh-Dhahabī, because of his ascetism and his extreme scrupulousness he was very profuse in invalidation of the Ṣūfīs and Ashʿarīs. At-Tāj as-Subkī said in *Ṭabaqāt ash-Shāfiʿīyah*,[202] "This Shaykh of ours adh-Dhahabī has knowledge and dīn, but he takes too much on himself against the people of the *sunna*, so it is not permissible to rely on him even though he is our Shaykh and our teacher, except that the truth has more right to be followed, and he has reached a degree of excessive prejudice which one is embarrassed of."

Such as ad-Dāraquṭnī and the likes of him from the later scholars of ḥadīth, because they were severe on Abū Ḥanīfah and his people as is not hidden from those who study their books.

The ʿAllāmah and ocean of knowledge said in *Fawātiḥ ar-Raḥamūt*,[203] "The person who declares narrators to be reliable must himself be upright and knowledgeable of the reasons for invalidation and validation, and he ought to be fair and sincere, not partisan and conceited about himself because no account is taken of the verdict of someone who is partisan, such as how ad-Dāraquṭnī impugned Imam Abū Ḥanīfah as being weak in ḥadīth. What abomination is worse than this?" . . . up until he said, "The truth is that the verdicts which issued from them with respect to

202 1:190, Shaykh Abu Ghuddah felt that some of the criticisms of imam adh-Dhahabī by his student were a little harsh.

203 Referring to Mulla ʿAbd al-ʿAlī al-Laknawī, *Fawātiḥ*, 2:54.

this high minded Imam all issue from partisanship and are unworthy of attention, and the light of Allah ﷻ is not extinguished by their mouths, so safeguard it."

And such as al-Khaṭīb al-Baghdādī author of *Tārīkh Baghdād*. The author of *Tanwīr aṣ-ṣaḥīfah*[204] said, "Do not be dazzled by al-Khaṭīb's words, because he has prejudice against a group of the scholars such as Abū Ḥanīfah and Aḥmad and some of his companions, and he attacked them in every way. One of them compiled *As-Sahm al-muṣīb fī kabid al-Khaṭīb* about that."

As for Ibn al-Jawzī he followed al-Khaṭīb," as is in *ar-Rafᶜ wa't-takmīl*.

I say that Ibn al-Jawzī's following *al-Khaṭīb* is astonishing for as-Sarūjī[205] transmitted from Ibn al-Jawzī that he said, "One ought not to accept al-Khaṭīb's invalidation or his validation, because his verdict and his transmission show little dīn, as al-ᶜAynī said in *al-Bināyah*."

At-Tāj as-Subkī said in *Ṭabaqāt ash-Shāfiᶜīyyah*,

> Beware! Beware of understanding their principle (that invalidation has precedence over validation) unqualifiedly, for on the contrary the correct position is that someone whose imamate and uprightness are firmly established, and whom a great many people praise and very few people impugn, and along with that there is substantiating evidence that shows the reason for his being invalidated, such as *madhhab* based prejudice or some other reason, then one does not pay attention to his being invalidated.

In it there is also,

> We have familiarised you with the fact that invalidation is not accepted from a critic—even if he explains it—about someone whose acts of obedience greatly outweigh his acts of disobedience, and the people who praise him outnumber those who are his detractors, and those who affirm authenticity outnumber those who invalidate him if there is such substantiating evidence which the intellect testifies that the like of it can provoke an attack on the one being invalidate, such as *madhhab* based prejudice or worldly competitiveness as may happen among peers, etc. Thus one does not pay heed to the words of ath-Thawrī and others about Abū Ḥanīfah, nor the words of Ibn Abī Dhiʾb and others about Mālik, or Ibn Maᶜīn about ash-Shāfiᶜī or an-Nasāʾī about Aḥmad ibn Ṣāliḥ al-Miṣrī, etc.
>
> If we use the precedence of invalidation unqualifiedly we will not be left with a single imam who was untouched, since there is no imam but that critics have impugned him, and those who were to perish did so [by attacking him].

---

204 He is Imam Yūsuf ibn Ḥasan ibn Ahmad ibn ᶜAbd al-Hādī al-Ḥanbalī passed away in 909 (AH).

205 He was the chief judge of Egypt Abū ᶜAbbās Aḥmad ibn Ibrāhīm ibn ᶜAbd al-Ghanī ibn Abū Isḥāq al-Sarūjī al-Ḥanafī (d. 720 (AH)), a biography of him can be found in al-Qurashī's *al-Jawāhir al-Muḍīyyah*, 1:53 and al-Laknawī's *al-Fawāʾid al-Bahiyyah*, p. 13.

Adh-Dhahabī said in *Tadhkirat al-Ḥuffāẓ*[206] in the biographical notice on Ḥāfiẓ Abū Nuʿaym, "Ibn Mandah's statement about Abū Nuʿaym is atrocious and I do not even like to quote it, and I do not accept the verdict of either of them about the other, for both of them are acceptable to me. . ." up until he said,

> No importance is attached to the words of peers about each other, particularly if there is a hint that it stems from enmity, *madhhab* affiliation or envy, and no one is free from these things except those whom Allah ﷻ protects. I know of no age whose people are free of that apart from the prophets and utterly truthful (*ṣiddīqūn*) and if I wanted to I could fill notebooks for you, enumerating that.[207]

In summary, if invalidation issues from partisanship, enmity, aversion or the like, then it is rejected invalidation, as is the invalidation of peers about each other if it is without proof or glaring evidence and is based on partisanship and aversion. If it is not this or that, then it is acceptable.

Stipulated qualities a narrator must have in order for his narrations to be acceptable, and mention of accidental circumstances that are not intrinsically harmful

The dominant majorities of the imams of ḥadīth and *fiqh* agreed unanimously that it is a precondition that a narrator should be someone who is upright (*ʿadl*) and who is meticulous in the retention (written or by memory) of what he narrates. [Furthermore, to be] Muslim, adult, sane, free of causes of deviation and those things which detract from a person's honour (*murūʾa*).[208] [The narrator should also be] alert and attentive and not careless, a memoriser if he narrates from memory, meticulous in safeguarding his writing from alteration and change if he narrates from it, knowledgeable of what will change the meaning if he narrates it, as is in *Tadrīb ar-Rāwī*. The transmission of a disbeliever, an insane person, a child, an idiotic person, a simpleton or a deviant is not accepted. What is meant by his being meticulous (*ḍabṭ*) is that his memorisation of what he hears outweighs his failure to memorise, and his recollection of it outweighs his forgetfulness, as is in *Uṣūl al-Āmidī*. The occasional unexpected occurrence of forgetfulness or negligence and surmise (*wahm*) are not detrimental, because no one is free from this, as is in the ḥadīth, "I am only a mortal; I forget just as you forget."[209]

---

206 Shaykh ʿAbd al-Fattāḥ points out that this reference is an oversight on the part of the author, may Allah ﷻ have mercy on him, adh-Dhahabī actually said this in *al-Mīzān* in the biographical note on Abu Nuʿaym.

207 *Ar-Rafʿ wa 't-Takmīl*, pp. 267–270.

208 *Murūʾah* is one's sense of honour and dignity which serves as an obstacle in front of all things undignified and dishonourable. It encourages a person to be truthful, chaste, and generally upright. One description given is 'that you do not do in secret anything that you would be ashamed to do in public.' (*Līsān al-ʿArab*). Ed.

209 Al-Bukhārī, 1:422, Muslim, 5:61–62, Ibn Mājah, 1:380.

There is in *al-Lisān*,

> Ibn al-Mubārak said, "Who is safe from surmise?" Ibn Maʿīn said, "I am not suprised at someone who narrates and makes a mistake, but I am only surprised at someone who narrates and gets it right."[210] I say that this is something over which one ought to hesitate, so that if a man is invalidated because of the fact that he made a mistake in a ḥadīth or surmised or was the only person who narrated it, that invalidation is not confirmed and his ḥadīth are not rejected for that reason.

What is meant by being free from the causes of deviation is that he does not commit major wrong actions nor persevere in minor wrong actions, the details of which are in the lengthier works (*al-muṭawwalāt*).

Explanation of that which is not an invalidating factor in a narrator

Invalidation is only significant if it is in one of the aforementioned preconditions and nothing else. Thus none of the following are a cause for invalidation: narration of *mursal* ḥadīth, concealment of gaps in the chain of narration (*tadlīs*), being busy with *fiqh*, entering into the sulṭān's employment if that is legitimate according to the *Sharīʿah*, horseriding, racing animals, excess in permissible talk, scarcity of narration, a lesser number of shaykhs, a lack of journeys undertook [in search of knowledge], etc., because they do not cause any harm to the uprightness and meticulousness of the narrator. The jurists (*uṣūl*) among our people and the thorough ḥadīth scholars among us and others have stated that clearly, and expansive details are in the exhaustive works (*al-muṭawwalāt*).

Al-Āmidī said in *al-Iḥkām*,

> It is [not seen as] a criticism that passing judgement on the basis of his testimony was abandoned because of the fact that it is possible that could have been due to a cause other than what is considered a valid impugnment. [Similarly] testimony of adultery and (testimony of) anything that necessitates the captial punishment against the person witnessed against when the requisite number of witnesses is not complete [is not seen as an invalidating criticism],[211] since he did not explicitly commit slander but only came to that position by way of testimony.[212] [Likewise the narrator is not invalidated as a result of indulging] in those matters in which *ijtihād* is possible

210 i.e. gets it right always.

211 This is because, according to Sharīʿah, when witnesses against a crime are below the number that is required (for example 4 witnesses are required for the *ḥadd* of fornication), the testimony is rejected and the witnesses are charged with slander, thus losing their standing as credible witnesses. The point here is that this does not necessitate that their ḥadīth narrations are also rejected. Ed.

212 In other words, it is possible that the witness's testimony is truthful and thus the charge of slander is only technical as a result of the required number of witnesses not coming forward. Ed.

and which some imams have given judgement in favour of, such as playing chess and drinking *nabīdh* etc., nor is concealment of gaps in the chain of narration [a cause of invalidation] because it is not lying, but is only an allusion (*maʿāriḍ*) which spares one from lying.

And in *al-Manār* and its commentary *Nūr al-Anwār*,

> Vague aspersions (*aṭ-ṭaʿn al-mubham*) from imams of ḥadīth do not invalidate a narrator in our view, such as when he says, 'This ḥadīth is invalidated or denounced' or something like that, unless it occurs with clarification of a factor of invalidation that everyone agrees upon, not one in which there is disagreement, so that it is invalidation according to some but not others. Along with that it issues from someone whose pure intention is well known and who is not known for being partisan. So aspersions such as concealment of gaps in the chain of narration, that he narrated *mursal* ḥadīth, that he raced animals, joked, was young, was not accustomed to narrating, or sought to abundantly engage in *fiqh* cases are not accepted.

The Ḥāfiẓ said in the Introduction to *al-Fatḥ*,

> The second category of those who have been declared weak because of some rejected matter such as prejudice, obstinate excessiveness, or that the person who is declaring [the narrator as] weak is not one of the scholars of critical evaluation, or because of the fact that he has little knowledge of the statements of the people who spoke about that person or his state, or because of his coming at a much later age etc. Added to that is also someone who is criticised for a matter that does not harm all of his ḥadīth, such as someone who is regarded as weak with respect to some of his shaykhs but not others. It is similar in the case of somone who became confused or his capacity for memorisation altered, or someone who is precisely detailed in his writing but not when he speaks from memory, because none of these can have the term "weak" applied to them unqualifiedly, but rather it is correct in their regard to be detailed.

The ruling on the narrator who denies his narration

If the person narrated from denies the narration, and the denial is outwright by words like, "You have lied about me, and I did not narrate this to you," then one drops acting by that ḥadīth by unanimous agreement. If the denial involves some doubt or hesitation by words like, "I do not remember narrating this ḥadīth to you," or "I do not recognise it," then according to Abū Yūsuf, al-Karkhī and Aḥmad ibn Ḥanbal one drops acting by that ḥadīth, but according to Muḥammad, ash-Shāfiʿī and Mālik one does not drop it. It is thus in *al-Manār* and *Nūr al-Anwār* along with its marginalia.

The ruling on when the narrator acts contrary to his narration

If the narrator acts contrary to his narration after narrating it in such a way that the contradiction is certain, then acting by that ḥadīth is dropped in our view. If he did that before narrating it, or its chronology is unknown then that is not a reason for invalidation [of the narration]. It is thus in *al-Manār* and its commentary. The narrator's specification of one of its probable meanings, if it carries more than one meaning, so that he acted on an interpretation of his own does not prevent someone else acting by it according to another interpretation. It is also thus in it (in *al-Manār*). The narrator's abstaining from acting by his narration is the same as his acting contrary to it, which he also declared in *al-Manār*.

The ruling on a Companion acting contrary to a ḥadīth

The practice of the Companions or a Companion contrary to a particular ḥadīth necessitates its being impugned if the ḥadīth was clear and didn't carry any obscurity for them or him. If it does contain a lack of clarity then that does not necessitate a cause for impugnment in it. It is thus *in al-Manār* and its commentary. Similarly, their acting according to the requirements of a ḥadīth shows that it is *ṣaḥīḥ* as ash-Shāfiʿī said about *mursal* ḥadīth when it is supported by the verdict of a Companion, "It is used as proof, and similarly his action (is also a proof). And we have mentioned this previously.

Explanation of the anonymity of the narrator (jahālah) that is harmful [to the ḥadīth] and that which is not

The Companion being unknown does not damage the authenticity of the ḥadīth because they were all reliable so there is no need to clarify the unknown narrator by citing numerous narrators, as is in *Tadrīb ar-Rāwī*. Al-Āmidī said in *al-Iḥkām*. "The dominant majority of the scholars agree on the reliability of the Companions."

As for the anonymity of a narrator apart from the Companions, there are two types: either he is anonymous or not:

As for the anonymous, there is disagreement as to the acceptability of his ḥadīth. What ought to be our *madhhab* is that it is acceptable even if he is left anonymous without the titles of validation,[213] but with the same condition that we considered in the *mursal* ḥadīth, as is in *Qafw al-Athar,* which is that he is of one of the three generations and no other.

The one who is not anonymous may be both unknown himself (*ʿayn*) and his

213 Ambiguity with the wording of validation is when the narrator says, 'a reliable person narrated to me', and without the wording of validation is when the narrator says, 'a shaykh told me,' or 'one of them told me,' or 'so and so told me', and so on, without mentioning the narrator's name. (abridged from Shaykh ʿAbd al-Fattāḥ's footnotes, 203, fn., 4). Ed.

state unknown (*ḥāl*) and the ruling on that will come soon. Or his state may only be unknown whereas he himself is known. Similarly he may appear to be reliable but his inward is unclear, it is said about him that he is the "veiled" (*mastūr*) according to them. The position of ash-Shāfiʿī, Aḥmad ibn Ḥanbal and most of the people of knowledge is that narrations of the person whose state is unknown are not acceptable, on the contrary there must be internal information about his state. Abū Ḥanīfah and his followers say that outward manifestation of Islam and apparent freedom from deviation are sufficient for acceptance of a narration, as is in *Uṣūl al-Āmidī*.

And there is in *Qurrat al-ʿayn fī ḍabṭ asmāʾ rijāl aṣ-ṣaḥīḥayn*,[214]

> Someone whose state is unknown is unacceptable, and he is of three types: First, someone whose reliability is unknown outwardly and inwardly and so is not acceptable according to the dominant majority. Second, someone whose reliability is unknown inwardly but not outwardly, and this is the veiled one (*mastūr*), and the chosen position about him is that he is acceptable. Sulaym ar-Rāzī asserted that categorically, and this is the practice in most of the well known books of ḥadīth concerning those whose time is long past and (detailed) knowledge of whom is impossible. Third, someone who is himself unknown, and this is someone whom the scholars do not know and whose ḥadīths are unknown except through one single narrator.

There is in the introduction to the *Musnad al-Imam al-Aʿẓam* by one of the eminent scholars,[215]

> Al-Qasṭalānī said in *al-Irshād*, "Some people accepted the veiled person (*mastūr*) which is the position Ibn aṣ-Ṣalāḥ regarded as the weightiest." Ibn Ḥajar said in *Sharḥ an-Nukhbah*, "A large group accepted his narration without any restriction," and it is transmitted from ʿAlī al-Qārī[216] that he said, "Ibn Ḥibbān chose this position in conformity with al-Imam al-Aʿẓam since someone whose testimony is valid in his view is that person about whom no invalidation is known. He [Ibn Ḥibbān] said, 'And people in all their different states are right-acting and reliable until that which necessitates invalidation becomes evident about them, and people are not made responsible for what is unseen to them and are only made responsible for ruling by outward appearance.'"

There is in *Tadrīb ar-Rāwī*,

> The narration of someone veiled, and that is the person who is apparenty reliable but inwardly his reliability is unknown, is used in argument and proof by some of those

---

214 By ʿAbd al-Ghanī al-Baḥranī, p. 8.

215 He is the great ḥadīth scholar Muḥammad Ḥasan as-Sanbhalī.

216 In his book *Sharh Sharh al-Nukhbah*, p. 154.

> who reject the first,[217] and it is the verdict of some of the Shāfiʿīs. The Shaykh Ibn aṣ-Ṣalāḥ said, 'And it appears that the practice is based on this in many of the books of ḥadīth regarding a body of narrators who are of distant times and it impossible to have internal information about them. Similarly the authordeclared it *ṣaḥīḥ* in *Sharḥ al-muhadhdhab*.

> Adh-Dhahabī said in *al-Mīzān* in the biographical notice on Mālik the Egyptian,[218]

> Ibn al-Qaṭṭān said, "He is one of those whose reliability is not established," meaning that no one stated that he is a trustworthy narrator. And among the narrators of the two *Ṣaḥīḥ* books there is a large number of whom we do not know that anyone has stated that they are trustworthy narrators. And the dominant majority agree that any shaykh from whom a body of people have narrated and who has not done something for which he was repudiated, then his ḥadīth are *ṣaḥīḥ*.

And in the *Fatḥ al-mughīth* by as-Sakhāwī transmitting from *Ḥāfiẓ* Ibn Ḥajar there is,

> If the narrator whose state is unknown has not been invalidated nor authenticated, all of his shaykhs and those who narrate from him are trustworthy narrators and he has not brought any repudiated ḥadīth, then he is a trustworthy narrator in his [i.e. Ibn Ḥibbān's] view. And in the *Kitāb ath-thiqāt* there are many of such a description, and for that reason those who did not know his technical terminology opposed him in his regarding them as trustworthy narrators, but there is no objection against him because he cannot be challenged in that.

He mentioned the same as that in *Tadrīb ar-Rāwī*.

So by this you have probably come to know of the agreement of many of the ḥadīth scholars with Abū Ḥanīfah on accepting the narration of someone who is veiled, so be attentive to that.

The pivot of (the matter of) the anonymity (*jahālah*) or recognition (*maʿrifah*) of the person according to ḥadīth scholars rests on those who narrate from him, so that someone from whom one person alone narrates is a person who is unknown according to them while someone from whom two reliable people narrate becomes known and his anonymity is lifted from him, as is in *Tadrīb ar-Rāwī*. But according to us it is (acceptable) irrespective of the quantity or the paucity of those who narrate from him as will follow.

Moreover, know the narrations of the person who is unknown (*majhūl al-ʿayn*),

---

217 By the first he means the narration of someone whose reliability is unknown both outwardly and inwardly.

218 He is Māik ibn Khayr al-Zabadī al-Miṣrī, see *al-Mizan*, 3:426.

and he is someone from whom only one person narrates, are not rejected unanimously by the ḥadīth scholars, but on the contrary there is disagreement in this. Some say that he is not acceptable absolutely, and some say that he is absolutely acceptable and this is the position of those who stipulate nothing more for a narrator than his being a Muslim. Some say that if only one such person has narrated from him who only narrates from a reliable narrator—such as Ibn Mahdī and Yaḥyā ibn Sa ͑īd—then he is acceptable, but otherwise not. Some say that if he is well known outside of knowledge such as for his abstinence from the world or his firmness (*najdah*) then he is acceptable, but otherwise not, Ibn ͑Abd al-Barr chose this position. Some say that if any of the imams of invalidation and validation declared him free from defect along with a single person narrating from him then he is acceptable, but otherwise not, Abu'l-Ḥasan ibn al-Qaṭṭān chose this position, and Shaykh al-Islam i.e. *Ḥāfiẓ* ibn Ḥajar, declared it correct, as is in *Tadrīb ar-Rāwī*.

As for in our view, then only one person transmitting from him is not an invalidating cause; this is clearly declared in *Musallam ath-thubūt* and its commentary *Fawātiḥ ar-Raḥamūt*.

The unknown—i.e. the unknown person[219]—in our view is someone who is only known for one or two ḥadīth and his reliability is unknown, whether or not one person narrates from him or two or more. The ruling about it is that if this unknown person is a Companion then his being unknown does no harm as we have seen previously. If he is not a Companion, then either his ḥadīth appeared in the second generation or not, if it did not appear it is valid to act by it in the third generation but not after it. And if it appeared (in the second generation), and if the right-acting first generations testified to the authenticity of the ḥadīth or if they were silent and did not cast aspersions on it then it is accepted, but if they rejected it it is rejected. And if some of them accepted it and some rejected it along with trustworthy narrators narrating from him, then if it accords with analogical reasoning it is accepted, but if not then it is rejected, as is in *Qafw al-Athar*, along with some slight alteration of expression.

If the narrator is well known in narration and in reliability then it is unqualifiedly accepted, whether or not he was well known for *fiqh*, and whether or not his ḥadīth accorded with analogical reasoning, and whether or not one, two or more narrated from him. Making a distinction between the person who is known for *fiqh* and the person known as reliable is the school of ͑Īsā ibn Abān. As for according to al-Karkhī and those who followed him of our own companions, the *fiqh* of the narrator is not a precondition for the ḥadīth being preferred over analogical reasoning, but on the contrary the tradition of every person who is reliable is preferred

219 As opposed to the unknown state (*majhūl al-ḥāl*). Ed.

over analogical reasoning as long as it is not contradictory to the Book and the well known *sunna*, as is in *Nūr al-Anwār*.

The statements of our companions concerning the person who is veiled (*mastūr*) differs: so it is known from the words of al-Āmidī and ʿAlī al-Qārī—aforementioned—that he is accepted in our view unqualifiedly. And he said in *Qafw al-athar*, "As for the veiled one, and he is in our view someone who outwardly is reliable but whose reliability is unknown inwardly, whether only a single person or two or more narrate from him, the ruling on such a person's ḥadīth is that it is inwardly disconnected (*inqiṭāʿ*)[220] and that it is not accepted except in the first generations," meaning the first three generations whose goodness has been testified to, as he declared clearly in the chapter on severed ḥadīth (*inqiṭāʿ*).[221]

And he[222] transmitted in the introduction to the *Musnad al-Imam* also from al-Qārī in which he said,

> And [chapter] eighteenth: that which is transmitted from him (Imam Abū Ḥanīfah), "And the upshot of the disagreement[223] is that the veiled one (*mastūr*) among the Companions, the Followers and their Followers is accepted because of his [the Prophet] testifying for them in his saying, 'The best of generations is my generation, then the one succeeding them and then the one succeeding them,'[224] and others are only accepted by authentication, and this is a good way of detailing (the matter)."

What appears to me from the words of our *fuqahā*ʾ is that what is meant by the acceptability of the narration of a veiled person who is not one of the Companions in their view is that it is permissible to act by it but it is not incumbent, and it is the same with the person who is unknown (*majhūl al-ʿayn*) outside of the Companions, and Allah ﷻ knows best.

*

Someone whose person (*ʿayn*) and reliability are known, but his name and lineage are unknown may be used in proof (by unanimous agreement). And there are many examples of that in the two *Ṣaḥīḥ* books. And if he said, "So-and-so or so-and-so informed me," because of doubt [as to which it was] but both are reliable then it is used as proof, but if the reliability of either is unknown or if he said, "So-and-so or

---

220 This means that although apparently connected this ḥadīth would be treated as disconnected (*munqaṭiʿ*) for the lack of clarity about the unknown narrator which is an internal below-the-surface reason. Ed.

221 *Qafw al-athar*, p.15.

222 ʿAllāmah al-Sanbhalī in *Tansīq al-Niẓām fī Musnad al-Imām*.

223 Between Abū Ḥanīfah and his students Abū Yūsuf and Muḥammad regarding the *mastūr* as mentioned in *Sharḥ Sharḥ an-Nukhbah*, p.155.

224 Al-Bukhārī, 5:191, and Muslim, 16:81 with a similar wording.

someone else" without naming him, then it cannot be used as proof because of the possibility that the (actual) narrator is the unknown person, as is in *Tadrīb ar-Rāwī*.

I say that our aforementioned disagreement also applies to the narrator whose reliability is unknown.

The establishment of the reliability of a narrator by abundance (of narrations) and fame, and mention of those imams whose reliability is well known

Reliability is also established by abundance of narrations and fame, so that someone whose reliability has become well known among the people of knowledge from the people of ḥadīth and others, and praise of him is very widespread then that is enough to establish it—i.e. his being reliable—and there is no need along with that to have someone who ascribes reliability to him explicitly.

The Qāḍī Abū Bakr al-Bāqillānī said, "The witness and informant only require a validation if they are not well known for reliablility and people's contentment with them, and if their affair is ambiguous and confused." He said, "The proof of that is in the fact that the knowledge of the exposure of their private affairs and the fame of their reliability is stronger [evidence] to people than the validation of one or two people who may conceivably lie or be partisan." As is in *Tadrīb ar-Rāwī* in an abridged form.

I say that as the likes of Abū Ḥanīfah, Mālik, the two Sufyāns, al-Awzaʿī, ash-Shāfiʿī, Muḥammad ibn al-Ḥasan, Abū Yūsuf, Aḥmad ibn Ḥanbal, al-Layth, Shuʿbah, Ibn al-Mubārak, Wakīʿ, Ibn Maʿīn, Ibn al-Madīnī and those like them in reputation and integrity, then one does not need to enquire into their reliability. One only enquires into the reliability of those whose condition is concealed. As for these [famous scholars], their reliability is well known to ḥadīth scholars, the *fuqahāʾ* and the people of knowledge.

Adh-Dhahabī said in *al-Mīzān*, "Similarly, I will not mention in my book any of those imams who are followed in derivative rulings because of their majesty in Islam and their high standing with people, such as Abū Ḥanīfah,[225] ash-Shāfiʿī and al-Bukhārī."

The Ḥāfiẓ Ibn ʿAbd al-Barr expanded on it and said, "Every bearer of knowledge who is well known for being endowed with it is reliable, and his affair is predicated upon reliability until a cause for invalidation becomes evident," and Ibn al-Mawwāq among later scholars agreed with him about that, as is in *Tadrīb ar-Rāwī*.

That which lifts anonymity of person (jahālat al-ʿayn) from a narrator

Anonymity of a person is lifted by the narration of two reliable narrators according

225 Shaykh Abū Ghuddah in his notes to *ar-Rafʿ*, p.101–104 has a lengthy discussion proving the forgery of disparaging comments regarding imam Abū Ḥanīfah in adh-Dhahabī's *Mīzān*.

to the dominant majority but reliablity is not established by that. Ad-Dāraquṭnī said, "Anyone from whom two trustworthy narrators have narrated, then his anonymity is lifted and his reliability is established," as is in *at-Taʿlīq al-Ḥasan* transmitting from *Fatḥ al-Mughīth* by as-Sakhāwī.

Ibn al-Qayyim said in *Zād al-Maʿād* concerning the ḥadīth of Abū Rukānah about separating [a couple] because of impotence,

> There is no defect in this ḥadīth except Ibn Jurayj's narration of it from one of Banī Abū Rāfiʿ, who is unknown, but who is a Follower and Ibn Jurayj is one of the trustworthy, upright imams, and the narration of a reliable narrator from someone is validation of that person as long as no invalidation is known of him, and lying had not become manifest among the Followers.

He said, "It is not suspected of Ibn Jurayj that he conveyed it from a liar nor from someone who was not in his view a trustworthy narrator and did not make clear his state."

This shows us that the state of being unknown is lifted from a narrator by the narration from him of one reliable person if he is from the generations whose goodness has been testified to [by the Prophet ﷺ] and this is close to the school of our Ḥanafī masters, so remember it.

The *Ḥāfiẓ* Ibn Ḥajar said in *al-Fatḥ* concerning the ḥadīth "So are you two blind?" of Umm Salamah,[226]

> Its *isnād* is strong and the most that has been said in finding fault with it is that az-Zuhrī alone narrated it from Nabhān, but this is not a damaging criticism because someone whom az-Zuhrī recognises and describes as being Umm Salamah's mukātab slave and who no one has invalidated, his narration is not rejected.

He said in *Tadrīb ar-Rāwī*,

> And when a reliable person narrates from someone whom he names, that is not considered validation according to the majority of the people of ḥadīth and others, and that is the sound position. It has been said that it is validation, since if he had known some cause for invalidation of him he would have mentioned it and if he did not mention it (despite knowledge of it) that would be an act of deception in the dīn. It has been said that if the reliable person who narrated from him only narrated from reliable people then his narrating from him is validation of him, but if not then it is not, and the people of *uṣūl* such as al-Āmidī, Ibn al-Ḥājib and others preferred this position.

226 Narrated by Abū Dawūd in his *Sunan*, 4:63, and at-Tirmidhī, 10:230.

I say that the first position is more precautious, but the second is stronger and more reliable in terms of evidential basis but it ought to be confined to the three generations, and the third position is more accurate and balanced and there is no need to restrict it to any particular generation.

In it there is also,

> If he said, "A trustworthy narrator narrated to me," or something similar without naming him, it is not enough for validation according to the authentic position until he names him. It has been said that it is categorically enough just as if he had specified who he was, because he is equally trusted in both cases.[227]

I say that if the narrator who says, "A trustworthy narrator narrated to me," is himself trustworthy then what ought to be our *madhhab* is that we accept this validation with respect to those of the first three generations because the unknown person of those generations is a valid proof for us, therefore the one left unknown with a statement of validation is more fittingly accepted, but in other than them [the first three generations], then no.

*

Mention of a group of scholars all of whom only narrated from trustworthy narrators

Yaḥyā ibn Saʿīd al-Qaṭṭāna and Ibn Mahdī. Both of them only narrated from trustworthy narrators as we saw previously quoting from *Tadrīb ar-Rāwī*. Similarly, Mālik, Shuʿbah (Ḥāfiẓ declared that clearly in the introduction to *Tahdhīb at-tahdhīb*), Saʿīd ibn al-Musayyab, Muḥammad ibn Sīrīn and Ibrāhīm an-Nakhaʿī. He said in *al-Jawhar an-Naqī*,

> Abū ʿUmar said at the beginning of *at-Tamhīd*, "Every person about whom it is recognised that he only took from trustworthy narrators, then his concealment of gaps in the chain of narration (*tadlīs*) and his narration of *mursal* ḥadīth are acceptable. Thus, the *mursal* ḥadīth of Saʿīd ibn al-Musayyab, Muḥammad ibn Sīrīn and Ibrāhīm an-Nakhaʿī are *ṣaḥīḥ* according to them."

I say, and similarly Yaḥyā ibn Maʿīn even if I know of no one who clearly stated this. However, his stature is more majestic and more elevated than that he should narrate from someone who was not a trustworthy narrator without clarifying it, because he used to repel lies about the Messenger of Allah ﷺ, and he would get together with Aḥmad and Ibn al-Madīnī and the likes of them, and he would be the one who would select the ḥadīth for them, none having excelled over him, as is

227 i.e. if his validation is trusted when he names someone and validates him, he should also be trusted when he says that his narrator is trustworthy without naming him. In both cases he is the one that is relied upon. Ed.

in *at-Tahdhīb*, so may Allah ﷻ reward him on our behalf and on behalf of all of the Muslims with the best, most complete and most bountiful of rewards.

Similarly, Yaḥyā ibn Abī Kathīr aṭ-Ṭāʾī about whom Abū Ḥātim said, "Yaḥyā is an imam who does not narrate from any but trustworthy narrators." It is thus in *at-Tahdhīb*.

I say that Ṣufyān ibn ʿUyaynah is the same, because they accepted his concealment of gaps in the chain of narration (*tadlīs*) which was only because of his avoidance of weak narrators as we have already seen.

Similarly, Aḥmad's shaykhs all of whom were trustworthy narrators. *Ḥāfiẓ* al-Haythamī said[228] concerning Thābit ibn al-Walīd ibn ʿAbdullāh ibn Jumayʿ, "Aḥmad narrated from him, and his shaykhs were trustworthy narrators."[229]

I say that it is the same with the shaykhs of our Imam al-Aʿẓam Abū Ḥanīfah ؓ, they are trustworthy narrators.[230]

The Imam ʿAllāmah ash-Shaʿrānī the pupil of Ḥāfiẓ as-Suyūṭī said in *al-Mīzān*,

> Allah ﷻ, granted me the gift of being able to study the three *Musnads* of Imam Abū Ḥanīfah from a *ṣaḥīḥ* copy that had the handwriting of ḥadīth memorisers (*ḥuffāẓ*) on it, the last of them being *Ḥāfiẓ* ad-Dimyāṭī. I saw that he only narrated ḥadīth from the best of the Followers who were reliable and trustworthy narrators, such as al-Aswad, ʿAlqamah, ʿAṭāʾ, ʿIkrimah, Mujāhid, Makḥūl, al-Ḥasan al-Baṣrī and the likes of them. Thus, all of the narrators between him and the Messenger of Allah ﷺ were reliable, trustworthy, most notable and select. There are no liars among them nor any who are suspected of lying. My brother, it is sufficient proof of their reliability that Imam Abū Ḥanīfah ؓ was satisfied enough with them to take the rulings of his dīn from them given the intensity of his scrupulousness and his caution.

I say that the strictness of the Imam in the area of narration is well known, so much so that he said, "A man ought not to narrate a ḥadīth unless he has retained it in memory from the day he heard it up until the day he narrated it." At-Ṭaḥāwī transmitted it: he said, "Sulaymān ibn Shuʿayb narrated to us: My father narrated to us, and he said: Abū Yūsuf dictated to us and he said: Abū Ḥanīfah said it [the previous quote]."[231] We will bring you what will show you the knowledge of the Imam concerning narrators and his critical evaluation of them. So whomever Abū Ḥanīfah narrates from without explaining any invalidation of him is a trustworthy narrator.

---

228 *Majmaʿ az-Zawāʾid*, 1:80.

229 Shaykh ʿAbd al-Fattāḥ has commented that this is mostly true but not absolutely as put here. Imam Aḥmad narrated from the likes of ʿAmir ibn Ṣāliḥ and ʿAlī ibn Mujāhid al-Kābulī who were among the abandoned (*matrūk*) and suspected of lying, p. 218, fn. 5. Ed.

230 Here again, Shaykh ʿAbd al-Fattāḥ points out that this is true in the dominant majority of cases but not always. He also on the rare occasion narrated from weak narrators, p. 220, fn. 1. Ed.

231 *Jawāhir al-Muḍiyyah*, 1:31.

It is similar with those from whom the honoured Imam and chief of the *fuqahā'*, leader of the ḥadīth scholars and Amīr al-Mu'minīn in the sciences of the *Sharīʿah* in his time, Muḥammad ibn Idrīs ash-Shāfiʿī al-Muṭṭalibī, the scholar of Quraysh narrated and was silent about; such people are trustworthy narrators. He was one of the imams to whom people refer about ḥadīth and invalidation (*jarḥ*) and validation (*taʿdīl*).

This is so, even if some of his companions differed with us and did not regard his narration from someone as his validation of them as a trustworthy narrator, because of his narrating from al-Aslamī,[232] whose state is open for all to see. However, we esteem him too much to think that he would narrate from someone suspect without clarifying his condition, for his rank is higher and more elevated than that. As for his narration from al-Aslamī, he was, in his view, trustworthy in ḥadīth even if others regarded him as weak. Ash-Shāfiʿī knew him himself and accompanied him, so he must have found in him that which made narration from him palatable to him.

Similarly, everyone from whom Ibn Abī Dhi'b narrated is a trustworthy narrator except for Abū Jābir al-Bayāḍī, Ibn Maʿīn and Aḥmad ibn Ṣāliḥ said this, as is in *Tahdhīb at-tahdhīb*.

Likewise, those from whom an-Nasā'ī narrated are trustworthy narrators. Adh-Dhahabī said in *al-Mīzān*, narrating from al-Khaṭīb in the biographical notice on Abu'l-Walīd Aḥmad ibn ʿAbd ar-Raḥmān al-Busrī, "Abu'l-Walīd's state in our view is not that which Abū Bakr al-Bāghandī mentioned from as-Sukrī, but on the contrary he was truthful, because an-Nasā'ī narrated from him and that is sufficient for you."

Similarly, anyone from whom an-Nasā'ī narrated in al-Mujtabā about whom he was silent, then he is a proof, because he had a precondition about narrators that was more strict than those of al-Bukhārī and Muslim. Ḥāfiẓ Ibn Ḥajar said, "Abu'l-Faḍl ibn Ṭāhir reported, saying, 'I asked Saʿd ibn ʿAlī az-Zanjānī about a man and he declared him a trustworthy narrator. I said to him, "An-Nasā'ī did not use him as proof," and he said, "Son, Abū ʿAbd ar-Raḥmān had a precondition about narrators that was stricter than those of al-Bukhārī and Muslim."'" It is thus in *Zahr ar-Rubā*.

Similarly, those from whom al-Bukhārī narrates are trustworthy narrators because he only narrates from those who are in his view trustworthy narrators both in the *Ṣaḥīḥ* and in his other works. Muḥammad ibn Abī Ḥātim narrated from him that he said, "I wrote down from one thousand and eighty people among whom there were only people of ḥadīth." He also said, "I only wrote down from people who said, 'īmān consists of both word and deed,'" as is in the introduction to *al-Fatḥ*.[233]

Similarly, those whom al-Bukhārī mentions in his Histories, without casting

232 He is Ibrāhīm ibn Abī Yaḥyā al-Aslamī al-Madanī.

233 This statement actually has nothing to do with validation but was mentioned because that is what Ibn Ḥajar said of him. Ed.

aspersions on them, are trustworthy narrators, because it was his habit to mention the cause for invalidation and those invalidated, as Ibn Taymiyah said.[234] It is thus in *Nayl al-Awṭār*.

Similarly, everyone from whom Muslim narrated or (whose ḥadīth) he compiled are trustworthy narrators, because he also would only narrate from those who were trustworthy narrators in his view, and he would only use trustworthy narrators as evidence.

Similarly, Abū Dāwūd. *Al-Khaṭīb* al-Baghdādī said. "That which al-Bukhārī, Muslim and Abū Dāwūd used as proof from those about whom there are known to be aspersions from other people are taken to mean that the aspersion was not established with its reason explained," as is in the introduction to Muslim by an-Nawawī. Ibn al-Qaṭṭān said, "And Abū Dāwūd only narrates from those who in his view are trustworthy narrators," as is in *az-Zaylaʿī*.

I say that similarly those about whose ḥadīth Abū Dāwūd was silent in his *Sunan* are good. Adh-Dhahabī said in *al-Mīzān* in the biographical notice on Ibrāhīm ibn Saʿīd al-Madanī narrating from Nāfiʿ, "His ḥadīth are disclaimed and he unknown, and he has a single ḥadīth on *iḥrām* which Abū Dāwūd narrated and about which he was silent, and so he is of a middling condition." So he regarded him as of a middling condition because of the silence of Abū Dāwūd about him. We have already seen that the silence of Abū Dāwūd informs the fitness of a ḥadīth for use as proof, and it is similar with the fitness of its narrators, and Allah ﷻ knows best.

I say that it is similar with Baqī ibn Makhlad who only narrated from trustworthy narrators. The Ḥāfiẓ said in *Tahdhīb at-Tahdhīb* in the biographical notice on Aḥmad ibn Jawwās al-Ḥanafī, "And Baqī ibn Makhlad narrated from him," and he had already said, "He only narrated from trustworthy narrators."

Similarly, the shaykhs of Ḥarīz ibn ʿUthmān all of whom were trustworthy narrators, about which the Ḥafiẓ made a clear statement in *al-Lisān*.

Similarly, those shaykhs of aṭ-Ṭabarānī who were not declared weak in *al-Mīzān* are trustworthy narrators, which al-Haythamī stated clearly in *Majmaʿ az-Zawāʾid*.

I say that the basis of it[235] in my view is on what adh-Dhahabī mentioned in the preface to the *Mīzān*, "I did not think it conceivable to omit the name of anyone of those mentioned as slightly weak in the books of the aforementioned imams[236] for fear of being taken to task, not because I mention him for some weakness he has in my view." Otherwise, we do not find in the *Mīzān* anything that shows the special nature of those shaykhs of aṭ-Ṭabarānī about whom he did not mention that they

---

234 Referring to Majd ad-Dīn ibn Taymiyah who passed away in 652 (AH) as opposed to his more famous grandson Taqī ad-Dīn ibn Taymiyah. Ed.

235 The above opinion of al-Haythamī regarding the shuyūkh of aṭ-Ṭabarānī. Ed.

236 Meaning the compilers of the six ḥadīth collections.

are trustworthy narrators. So it would appear that al-Haythamī only passed judgement that they were trustworthy narrators on the basis of the general nature of this statement. On this basis then it is permissible for us to pass the judgement that every narrator who is not declared weak in the *Mīzān* is a trustworthy narrator, whether or not he is a shaykh of aṭ-Ṭabarānī.[237]

With respect to this, the Ḥāfiẓ mentioned at the end of the *Lisān al-Mīzān* right after the section on miscellaneous things what implied that every narrator who is not in his *Lisān* or *Tahdhīb at-tahdhīb* is either a trustworthy narrator or veiled (*mastūr*).

I say that we have already shown the ruling on the veiled person[238] according the Ḥanafīs so refer to that.

Innovation is of two types: that which is effective in rejecting [a narrator's] narration and that which is not

As for innovation, someone who is attributed it will either be among those who are declared kāfir because of it or among those who are declared deviant (*fāsiq*) because of it.

That declaration of kufr for which a person is declared a *kāfir* must be agreed upon on the basis of the principles of all of the imams, as is the case in the extremist shīʿah groups because of the claim some of them make of the incarnation of divinity in ʿAlī or someone else. Or their belief in his return to the world before the Day of Rising (or [their belief in] the occurrence of alteration in the Qurʾān or their ascription of suspicion (of adultery) to Sayyidah ʿĀʾishah aṣ-Ṣiddīqah, may Allah ﷻ be pleased with her and may He curse the one who slanders her. So the narration of the likes of these is categorically rejected.)

Those innovations for which a person is declared a deviant are like those of the Khawārij and the shīʿah groups who do not go to those extremes, and other groups who clearly contradict the principles of the *sunna* but [their contradiction] can be traced back to an interpretation which is outwardly acceptable (*sāʾigh*). The *ahl as-Sunna* differ about the acceptance of the ḥadīth of those who take this way if they are known for being extremely cautious about lying, and well known for being free from those things which detract from their honour (*murūʾah*), and who are described

237 What the author means here is that al-Haythamī seems to be basing his opinion that the shuyūkh of aṭ-Ṭabarānī who have not been declared as weak by adh-Dhahabī as trustworthy in the *Mīzān* fall under the general category of many scholars that adh-Dhahabī did not declare weak. And since adh-Dhahabī did not single out the shuyūkh of aṭ-Ṭabarānī, this then must be a general rule which can be applied to any scholars that adh-Dhahabī mentions in the *Mīzān* but did not declare them as weak. As to why adh-Dhahabī mentions scholars that he does not deem to be weak, in a book written for the purpose of documenting the weak narrators, then he answers this question in the above quation. Ed.

238 Someone the validity of whose testimony is unknown inwardly but not outwardly.

with the qualities of religious devoutness and worship. It has been said that they are accepted unqualifiedly, and it has been said that they are rejected unqualifiedly. A third position is to detail as to whether or not he calls others to his innovation, so that the ḥadīth of someone who does not invite others [to his innovation] are accepted and the ḥadīth of someone who does invite others are rejected.

This position is the most balanced and groups of the imams adopted it. Ibn Ḥibbān claimed that there is a consensus of the people of transmission about it, but that claim is objectionable. Then the people who took that detailed position differed: some of them regarded it as unqualified, but some added further detail to it and said, "If the narration of the one who does not call [to innovation] comprises something that would strenghten and support his innovation and make it appear more attractive then it is not accepted, but if it does not comprise such material then it is accepted. It is thus in the introduction to *al-Fatḥ* by the Ḥāfiẓ.

It is said in *Qafw al-athar*,

> According to us—i.e. Ḥanafīs—if it leads to kufr, then its proponent's narration is not accepted, in concordance with most of the jurists. However, if it leads to deviation then some say that its transmitter's narration is accepted if he is an upright and a trustworthy narrator who does not invite [others to his innovation].

He (author of *Qawf al-athar*) declared afterwards that this is the chosen position.

The Ḥāfiẓ said in the introduction to *al-Fatḥ*,

> Know that sometimes a group cast aspersions on another group because of their differing about *ʿaqīdah*, so one ought to be aware of that and not take it into account except where it is true.
>
> Similarly, a group of those who are scrupulous found fault with a group who entered into the affairs of the world, and they regarded them as weak because of that, but that ascription of weakness has no effect when there is truthfulness and thorough accuracy [in the narrator], and it is Allah ﷻ who grants success.
>
> Even further from being worthy of any consideration, is the action of someone who declared a narrator weak because of a reason which actually applies to someone else[239] or because of rivalry between peers.
>
> And worse than that is those who regard as weak other people who are more trustworthy than themselves or of a higher rank or more knowledgeable of the ḥadīth, so none of this is to be given any consideration.

---

239 The Arabic text here is somewhat ambiguous and can be understood to mean that the reason for the declaration of weakness can be interpreted to mean something else, or it means that the declaration is based on a reason that actually is not a weakness in the person impugned but rather it is a weakness in another person. For example, a person is regarded as weak because a weak narrator narrated from him. Ed.

*

Irjāʾ [being one of the Murjiʾah] is of two sorts. *Tashayyuʿ* (attributed as having shīʿa tendencies) is [also] of two kinds.
The Ḥāfiẓ said in the introduction to *al-Fatḥ*,

> *Irjāʾ* literally means deferral and delay, and according to them it is of two sorts: Some of them mean by it: to delay passing judgement as to who was correct of the two parties that fought each other after ʿUthmān. Some of them meant by it: delaying passing judgement about someone who does major wrong actions and abandons the obligatory acts that they will go to the Fire, because *īmān* in their view is verbal admission and belief, and with that [wrong] action does no harm.
>
> *Tashayyuʿ* is love of ʿAlī and giving him preference over the Companions. Thus someone who gives him preference over Abū Bakr and ʿUmar is excessive in his Shīʿism and the term *rāfiḍī* (rejectionist) is used for him, but if not then merely Shīʿī. Then if he adds cursing to that or declares his hatred [for Abū Bakr and ʿUmar] openly then he is excessive in being a rejectionist, and if he believes in the return [of ʿAlī] to the world then he is even more extreme.

He said in *at-Tahdhīb*,

> Shīʿism in the usages of the earlier generations was to believe in the superiority of ʿAlī over ʿUthmān, and that ʿAlī was correct in his wars and that those who opposed him were wrong, but accepting the precedence of the two Shaykhs [Abū Bakr and ʿUmar] and their superiority. Some of them believed that ʿAlī was the best of creation after the Messenger of Allah ﷺ. If the person who believed that was scrupulous in his *dīn*, truthful and a *mujtahid*, then his narration is not to be rejected particularly if he did not invite others [to his position]. As for Shīʿism in the usage of the later generations it is purely rejectionism (i.e. cursing and abusing), so the narration of an extreme rejectionist is not accepted nor is he honoured.

I say that it is not unclear that *irjāʾ* in the first sense is in no sense an error, but—by Allah ﷻ!—on the contrary it is scrupulousness and prudence. It is more fitting to be silent about those disagreements that occurred among the Companions. So not everyone about whom the term *irjāʾ* has been used is suspect in his dīn or outside of the *sunna*. On the contrary, one must investigate his condition: if he is someone whose *irjāʾ* was about the matter of the Companions—those who fought each other—deferring judgement to Allah ﷻ, and abstaining from declaring either of the two parties correct, then he absolutely is one of the people of the *sunna* and one of the party of the scrupulous. Those about whom the term is used because they say that wrong actions do no harm, they are suspect in their dīn.

In the *Sharḥ al-maqāṣid* by at-Taftāzānī,

> It is well known of the *Muʿtazilī* school that the person who does a major wrong action without turning to Allah ﷻ in *tawbah* is eternally in the Fire even if he lives in īmān and obedience [to Allah ﷻ] for a hundred years. They made no distinction as to whether he has done one or numerous major wrong actions, and whether they occurred before the acts of obedience or after them or in between them. They regarded refusal to take a categorical position that such a person will be punished and surrendering of the judgement on the matter to Allah ﷻ—Who will forgive if He wishes or punish, as is the school of the people of the truth—as *irjāʾ*, in the sense that it is deferral of the matter and lack of conviction about punishment and reward. By this consideration, Abū Ḥanīfah and others were regarded as *Murjiʾah*.

Ibn Ḥajar al-Makkī said in the thirty-seventh section of his book *al-Khayrāt al-ḥisān*,

> A group counted Imam Abū Ḥanīfah as one of the *Murjiʾah* and this statement is not literally so. Firstly, because the commentator on *al-Mawāqif* said, "Ghassān the *Murjiʾite* used to transmit *irjāʾ* from Abū Ḥanīfah and count him as one of the *Murjiʾah*, but this is a fabrication against him by which Ghassān intended to make his own *madhhab* more saleable by ascribing it to this majestic Imam."
>
> Secondly, al-Āmidī has said, 'The *Muʿtazilah* in the early generations used to name as *Murjiʾah* those who contradicted their position about the Decree, or because when he (Abū Ḥanīfah) said, "Īmān does not increase or decrease," it was thought of him that he was *Murjiʾah* because of his separating (*taʾkhīr*) action from īmān.'"[240]

I say that many of the ḥadīth scholars use the term *irjāʾ* for those who do not say that īmān increases and decreases, and who do not admit that action enters into its [īmān's] reality, but it is not an aspersion in reality, as is clear to people skilled in the *Sharīʿah*. The dispute in that is merely verbal, as the meticulous scholars of the first and later generations have observed.[241]

That which is in *Lisān al-Mīzān* by the Ḥāfiẓ in the briographical notice on Imam Muḥammad ibn al-Ḥasan, the companion of Abū Ḥanīfah, testifies to what we have mentioned,

> Ibn ʿAdī transmitted from Isḥāq ibn Rāhuyah, "I heard Yaḥyā ibn Ādam saying, 'Sharīk—the *qāḍī*—used to not permit the testimony of the *Murjiʾah*. Then Muḥammad ibn al-Ḥasan testified before him and he rejected his testimony, and

240 *Ar-Rafʿ*, p.227.

241 Imām al-Kashmīrī in his work *Fayḍ al-bārī ʿalā Ṣaḥīḥ al-Bukhārī*, 1:53–54 has an excellent discussion regarding this issue.

so someone spoke to him about that. So he said, "I do not permit the testimony of someone who says that prayer is not a part of īmān.""

This is a clear statement from him that he only applied the term *irjāʾ* to Muḥammad because he did not regard prayer as being a part of the reality of īmān. [This is] despite his view that it (*īmān*) was perfected by acts of obedience and weakened by acts of disobedience, and despite his view that acts of obedience are beneficial and acts of disobedience are harmful,[242] and it is well known that this is in no way an error. If that had been the case, we would have been justified in accusing ḥadīth scholars of being *Muʿtazilīs* because of their verdict that actions are comprised in īmān which necessarily requires that someone who perpetrates a major wrong act is a disbeliever, and far removed are they from that![243]

So pay attention and be alert in understanding the words of those who validate and invalidate, and do not be among the negligent, because the books of Imam Abū Ḥanīfah such as *al-Fiqh al-akbar* and *Kitāb al-waṣiyyah* call out at the top of their voices that his position on the topic of īmān and its derivative rulings is not that position which the *Murjiʾah*, *Jahmiyyah* and other wrongdoers took. Similarly, the books of the Ḥanafīs testify to the falsehood of the position of the *Murjiʾah* and of every position which contradicts the *sunna*, and that Abū Ḥanīfah and his companions are absolved of that. And Allah ﷻ, is the One Responsible for guidance Who guides whomever He wills to a straight path.

Remember Ibn Jarīr's statement, "If every claim against someone that they belong to an ignoble way of thought was thus established [by the simple matter of the claim alone], his being reliable discarded, and his testimony invalidated by that, it would be necessary to abandon the majority of the ḥadīth scholars of the lands, because there is none among them who has not been ascribed something that would turn people away from him."

I say that this imām of the ḥadīth scholars al-Bukhārī also did not escape accusations of innovation. Adh-Dhuhlī accused him of holding the opinion of the creation of the Qurʾān as is elaborated on in the introduction to *al-Fatḥ*, so refer to that, and then apply that to others.

---

242 Which is clearly contrary to the view of the *murjiʾah* who believed sin was harmless as long as a person believed. This story clearly shows that there was genuine misunderstanding of the position of imam Abū Ḥanīfah and his companions among earlier scholars, despite the fact that it makes absolute sense when the issue is looked at carefully, as shaykh Abdul Fattah points out in a lengthy comment, *Qawāʿid*, pp. 235–39, fn. 3. Ed.

243 The wording of the *muʿtazilites* and the ḥadīth scholars on this issue—Iman is belief and action—is exactly the same, but the outcome is different. The same is true of Imam Abū Ḥanīfah and the *murjiʾah*, the wording is the same but the outcome is different. Somehow, people saw the distinction between the positions of the former two groups but not the latter two. In terms of outcome, the position of Imam Abū Ḥanīfah and the ḥadīth scholars are exactly the same, both believe that sins are harmful to faith and that they do not lead to disbelief. Ed.

Phrases of validation and invalidation, their levels and the ranks of their phrases

First, and this is the highest degree of validation and the most elevated among ḥadīth scholars: to describe in a manner indicating exaggeration, or which is expressed in superlatives such as "the most trustworthy of people",[244] "the most precise of people"[245] or "the most reliable of people",[246] or something similar such as "he reached the furthest limit in reliability", or "there is no one more reliable than him", or "who is like so-and-so?" or "I do not recognise him to have any equals" and "one does not ask about so-and-so".

Second, is the case when there is repetition of the word of validation such as "a trustworthy narrator, a trustworthy narrator",[247] or "a trustworthy and reliable narrator"[248] or "a trustworthy narrator who is a decisive proof",[249] or "a trustworthy narrator who is a memoriser",[250] or "reliable, a sure proof",[251] or "reliable, a *ḥāfiẓ*",[252] or "a trustworthy narrator, precise",[253] and the like of them such as "one does not ask about so-and-so".[254]

Third, that description in which there is no repetition such as "a trustworthy narrator", or "precise", or "reliable", or "a sure proof", or "upright" (*ʿadl*), or "*ḥāfiẓ*", "accurate" (*ḍābiṭ*) or "it is as if he were a written copy of the Qurʾān (*muṣḥaf*)" or "an imām". But "sure proof (*ḥujjah*)" is stronger than "trustworthy narrator" (*thiqah*).

Someone about whom [one of the above phrases] is said is one of those whose ḥadīth are used as proof and are included in the *ṣaḥīḥ* even if he alone narrated them.

Fourth, there is "utterly truthful", or "his rightful place is truthfulness" or "there is no harm in him" (*lā baʾsa bih* and *laysa bihī baʾs*)[255] according to other than Ibn Maʿīn, "cohesive" (*mutamāsik*) or "a trustworthy narrator inshāʾAllāh" or "trusted" (*maʾmūn*) or "the best" (*khiyār*) or "the best of people" (*khiyār al-khalq*) and the like.

Fifth: "a shaykh", "close to the truth",[256] "[someone] of excellent hadīth" (*jayyid al-ḥadīth*), "[someone] of good ḥadīth" (*ḥasan al-ḥadīth*), "utterly truthful with a

244 *"Awthaq an-nās"*.

245 *"Aḍbaṭ an-nās"*.

246 *"Athbat an-nās"*.

247 *"Thiqatun thiqatun"*.

248 *"Thiqatun thabt"*.

249 *"Thiqatun ḥujjah"*.

250 *"Thiqatun ḥāfiẓ"*.

251 *"Thabtun ḥujjah"*.

252 *"Thabtun ḥāfiẓ"*.

253 *"Thiqatun mutqin"*.

254 This has been mentioned twice, this is either an oversight or an indication that there is difference of opinion as to whether this particular wording belongs to the first level or the second. It is true that some scholars have mentioned it in the first level while others have mentioned it in the second. Shaykh ʿAbd al-Fattāḥ mentioned this in his comments, p. 242, fn. 3 and p. 243, fn. 1 respectively. Ed.

255 *lā baʾsa bihī* and *laysa bihī baʾs* both mean the same thing and they are both considered of the fourth level by scholars other than Ibn Maʿīn. Ed.

256 *"ilā aṣ-ṣidq mā huwa"* i.e. "he is not far from the truth".

bad memory", "utterly truthful but made suppositions",[257] "utterly truthful but made mistake s", "utterly truthful but he changed towards the end", "utterly truthful but he was charged with being *Shīʿah* or *Murjiʾah* etc., "people narrated from so-and-so", "an in-between person whose ḥadīth are of medium quality", and the like.

Sixth, "[someone] of acceptable ḥadīth" (*ṣaliḥ al-ḥadīth*), "utterly truthful inshāʾAllāh", "I hope that there is no harm in him", "I know of no harm in him", "slightly acceptable (*ṣuwayliḥ*)",[258] "accepted", "he is not far from being correct", "his ḥadīth are narrated", "his ḥadīth are written" and the like.

Those people about whom phrases [from the fourth to the sixth rank] is used, their ḥadīth are recorded and reflected upon because these expressions do not give the sense of accurate retention (by memory or writing), and so their ḥadīth are reckoned based on their agreement with those who do pay attention to detail, as is in *Tadrīb ar-Rāwī*.

There is from Yaḥyā ibn Maʿīn, "When I say "there is no harm in him", then he is a trustworthy narrator, but if I say that he is weak, then he is not a trustworthy narrator and his ḥadīth are not recorded", as is in *Tadrīb ar-Rāwī*.

As for wordings expressing invalidation, they also have six degrees:

1. The least of them is the one which is close to validation, so when they say, "lenient in ḥadīth" (*layyin al-ḥadīth*), then his ḥadīth are written and examined carefully. Ad-Dāraquṭnī said, "If I say 'weak', he is not omitted [to the extent] that his ḥadīth [are] to be abandoned, but he is invalidated to a degree which does not diminish his uprightness (*ʿadālah*)." This is a first degree and it includes that which al-ʿIrāqī mentioned: "in him there is some leniency", "some things have been said about him", "one recognises and disclaims", "he is not that" (*laysa bidhāka*), "he is not strong", "he is no proof", "he is unreliable", "he is not satisfactory", "he is close to weakness",[259] "concerning him there is a difference of opinion", "they spoke [critically] about him", "they cast aspersions on him", "he is someone on whom aspersions have been cast", "he had a bad memory", "in him there is some weakness", "in his ḥadīth there is some weakness", "he is not that strong".

2. There is also in it (i.e. in *Tadrīb ar-Rāwī*), "when they say, "he is not strong" (*laysa biqawiyy*), his ḥadīth are also recorded for further examination, and this is lower than lenient (*layyin*)." This is the second degree.

3. When they say "weak in ḥadīth" (*ḍaʿīf al-ḥadīth*), it is less than "he is not strong" and is not discarded but it is also given consideration; and this is a third

---

257 This is the translation of two statements *ṣadūqun yahim and ṣadūqun lahu awhām. Ed.*

258 *Ṣuwayliḥ*, in the diminutive, used in an affectionate sense, and occasionally in a derogatory meaning; here it indicates someone who is acceptable but to a slightly lesser degree than the one who would be described as *ṣāliḥ*. Ed.

259 *"Li 'ḍ-ḍuʿf mā huwa"* i.e. he is not far from weakness.

level. Examples of it are that which al-ʿIrāqī[260] mentioned: "weak", "[someone] of disclaimed ḥadīth" (*munkar al-ḥadīth*) and "his ḥadīth is disclaimed (*ḥadīthuhu munkar)* [both] according to people other than al-Bukhārī,[261] "weak" (*wāhin*), "they regarded him as weak", "[someone] of inconsistent ḥadīth" (*muḍṭarib al-ḥadīth*), "he is not used in proof" (*la yuhtajj bih*), "unknown" (*majhūl*). ʿAbd al-Bārī

4. The fourth is "[his] ḥadīth are rejected", "they rejected his ḥadīth", "extremely weak", "someone whose ḥadīth are rejected" (*mardūd al-ḥadīth*), "clearly weak" (*wāhin bimarrah*),[262] "they discarded his ḥadīth", "discarded" (*muṭarraḥ*), "one whose ḥadīth are discarded" (*muṭarraḥ al-ḥadīth*), "toss it away", "he is nothing" (*laysa bi shayʾ*), "he does not equal anything", "no thing" (*la shayʾ*), and the like.

5. The fifth level is "so-and-so is suspected of lying or fabrication," "omitted" (*sāqit*), "destroyed" (*hālik*), "gone" (*dhāhib*), "one whose ḥadīth have gone" (*dhāhib al-ḥadīth*), "abandoned" (*matrūk*), "one whose ḥadīth are abandoned" (*matrūk al-ḥadīth*), "they abandoned him", "about him there are objectionable views" (*fīhi nadhar*) according to al-Bukhārī, "and they were silent about him" according to him also, "he is not given consideration", "his ḥadīth are not given consideration," "he is not the trustworthy narrator", "he is not a trustworthy narrator", "not a trustworthy narrator and not trusted", and the like.

Someone about whom that is said, i.e. any statement from the fourth or fifth level, is omitted (*sāqiṭ*) and his ḥadīth are not recorded, he is not given any consideration, and not cited (as evidence or supporting argument).

6. The sixth level is the worst of them and it is that someone says "so-and-so is a liar" (*kadhdhāb)* or "he lies", "imposter (*dajjāl*)", "fabricator" (*waḍḍāʿ*), "he fabricates", "he fabricated a ḥadīth" as is in *Tadrīb ar-Rāwī* and *ar-Rafʿ wa't-takmīl.*

I say that someone about whom it is said—i.e. one of the phrases of the sixth level—then it is not permissible to narrate his ḥadīth unless it is to clarify his state and to refute him. Comprised in that also is the "person whose ḥadīth are rejected" (*munkar al-ḥadīth)* according to al-Bukhārī, as we will see.

When the expressions of evaluators differ about a narrator and some of them validate him with phrases used for validation and others invalidate him using some of the phrases used for invalidation, then the ruling about him is as we have explained previously, that the validator is preferred unless the invalidator provides explanation of his invalidation. This is because all of these phrases are examples of ambiguous invalidation in which there is no attempt to explain the cause, except when they

260 In *Sharḥ al-Alfiyyah* 2:10–12.

261 i.e. people other than al-Bukhārī consider them to be of this level, al-Bukhārī regards such statements to be of lower rank. Ed.

262 This statement is difficult to translate, al-Sakhāw said in *Fatḥ al-Mughīth* that it means 'weak i.e. in one statement without hesitation' as if to say the narrator's weakness is clear and can be declared without hesitation.

say, "swindler", "fabricator", "he fabricates", "he fabricated a ḥadīth", which are [self] explanatory.

Someone could say, "This also is vague until he explains which ḥadīth he fabricated, so that it can be known whether the responsibility for it is his or someone else's, so understand!

ADDITIONAL NOTES

In explanation of al-Bukhārī's usage of the words concerning a narrator: "about him there are some objectionable views" (fīhi naẓar) or "they were silent about him"

Al-Bukhārī uses the phrases "about him there are some objectionable views" and "they were silent about him" for those whose ḥadīth they abandoned. And he uses the phrase "[one] whose ḥadīth are ignored" (*munkar al-ḥadīth)* for those from whom narrating is not permissible, as is in *Tadrīb ar-Rāwī*.

I say that according to others, "[one] whose ḥadīth are ignored" (*munkar al-ḥadīth*) is of the degree of "weak in ḥadīth" (*ḍaʿīf al-ḥadīth*) which is the third level of invalidation, so that his ḥadīth are recorded for consideration. And "about him there are objectionable views" (*fīhi naẓar*) and "they were silent about him" are from the first or second levels, and I found no one who stated that clearly.[263]

On the difference between their statements, "a disclaimed ḥadīth" (ḥadīthun munkar), "[one] whose ḥadīth are disclaimed" (munkar al-ḥadīth) and "he narrates disclaimed ḥadīth"

There is a difference between the statement of the later scholars: "this is a disclaimed ḥadīth" and when earlier scholars say the same thing. The later scholars use it for the narration of a weak narrator who has contradicted trustworthy narrators. The earlier generations often use it purely for that which a narrator solitarily narrates even if he is one of the trustworthy narrators, in which case his ḥadīth is *ṣaḥīḥ* but unusual (*gharib*).

The Ḥāfiẓ said in the introduction to *al-Fatḥ* in the biographical notice of Muḥammad ibn Ibrāhīm at-Taymī after mentioning Aḥmad's verdict on him that "He narrated disclaimed ḥadīth", "I say Aḥmad ibn Ḥanbal and a group use 'disclaimed' for a unique ḥadīth with which has no supporting narration (*mutābiʿ*); this (verdict on at-Taymī) will be interpreted according to that, and the Group[264] used

263 Shaykh ʿAbd al-Fattāḥ mentions several scholars who did clearly mention the rank of these two words: adh-Dhahabi mentions in *Mīzān* (1:4) that they are in the third level of the five levels of invalidation in his view; al-ḥafiẓ al-Irāqī clearly mentioned their rank in *Sharḥ al-Alfiyyah* (2:11) and places them in the second level of the five levels of invalidation according to him, which is the same as al-Bukhari's ranking of them, p. 258, fn. 3. Ed.

264 The group (*al-jamāʿah*) is a term used by ḥadīth scholars to refer to the compilers of the six sahih

him in proof." He said in another place in it,[265] "Aḥmad and others use 'disclaimed' for completely solitary individuals."

I say that similarly there is a difference between the statement of the dominant majority: "so-and-so's ḥadīth are disclaimed", and Aḥmad making that same statement, because the dominant majority use it for weak narrators who contradict trustworthy narrators in their narrations and Aḥmad uses it for someone whose ḥadīth are solitary (*gharīb*) among his peers.

The Ḥāfiẓ said in the introduction to *al-Fatḥ* in the biographical notice on Yazīd ibn ᶜAbdullāh ibn Khaṣīfah after quoting Aḥmad as saying, "[His] ḥadīth are disclaimed", "I say that Aḥmad uses this phrase for someone whose ḥadīth is solitary (*gharīb*) among his peers [even if he does not contradict them], which is known from investigating his state, and Mālik and all of the imams used Ibn Khaṣīfah for proof."

I say that "one whose ḥadīth are disclaimed" (*munkar al-ḥadīth*) according to Aḥmad is the opposite of its usage by al-Bukhārī, so understand that.

Sometimes they use "[one] whose ḥadīth are disclaimed" (*munkar al-ḥadīth*) for someone who narrated a disclaimed ḥadīth but didn't do it a great deal, so that the narrator does not become weak because of that. Similarly, they sometimes used it for someone who narrated disclaimed ḥadīth from weak narrators whereas he himself is a trustworthy narrator.

Az-Zayn al-ᶜIrāqī in *Takhrīj al-Iḥyā᾿* said, "They often use the term 'disclaimed' (*munkar*) about a narrator because he narrated a single ḥadīth." As-Sakhāwī said in *Fatḥ al-mughīth*, "sometimes that is used about a trustworthy narrator when he narrates disclaimed ḥadīth from weak narrators." Al-Ḥākim said, "I asked ad-Dāraquṭnī, 'And Sulaymān ibn bint Shuraḥbīl?' He said, 'A trustworthy narrator.' I said, 'Does he not have disclaimed ḥadīth?' He said, 'He narrates them from weak narrators, but as for him, he is a trustworthy narrator.'" It is thus in *ar-Rafᶜ wa't-takmīl*. Adh-Dhahabī said in *al-Mīzān* in the biographical notice on Aḥmad ibn ᶜAttāb al-Marwazī, "Aḥmad ibn Saᶜīd ibn Maᶜdān said, 'A right-acting shaykh who narrates [ḥadīth about] the merits of actions (*faḍā᾿il*) and disclaimed ḥadīth.' I say, "not everyone who narrates disclaimed ḥadīth is regarded as weak."

I say that there is also a difference between their statement, "[one] whose ḥadīth are ignored" (*munkar al-ḥadīth*), and "he narrated disclaimed ḥadīth" (*rawā al-manākir*) or "he narrates disclaimed ḥadīth" (*yarwī aḥadīth munkarah*).

As-Sakhāwī said in *Fatḥ al-mughīth*,

> Ibn Daqīq al-ᶜĪd said, "Their verdict, 'he narrated disclaimed ḥadīth' (*rawā manākir*)

---

books. Ed.

265 In the biography of Burayd ibn ᶜAbdullāh, pp. 390, 2:118.

does not necessarily require in itself the abandonment of his narration until disclaimed ḥadīth among his narrations increase and he is eventually declared, '[one] whose ḥadīth are ignored' (*munkar al-ḥadīth*), because '*munkar al-ḥadīth*' is the description used of a person whose ḥadīth are deservedly abandoned, but the other expression does not denote persistence. How can that not be so when Aḥmad ibn Ḥanbal said about Muḥammad ibn Ibrāhīm at-Taymī, 'He narrates disclaimed ḥadīth, but he is one of those upon whom the two shaykhs are agreed, and he is the source to which one refers for the ḥadīth 'Actions are only by intentions.'"

From *ar-Rafʿ wa't-Takmīl*.

Explanation of what Ibn Maʿīn meant by his verdict on a narrator "He is nothing"

When Ibn Maʿīn says about a narrator, "He is nothing" (*innahu laysa bishayʾ*) he does not mean that he is strongly invalidated. The Ḥāfiẓ said in the introduction to *al-Fatḥ* in the biographical notice on ʿAbd al-ʿAzīz ibn al-Mukhtār al-Baṣrī, "Ibn Maʿīn declared him to be a trustworthy narrator in one narration and said in another, 'He is nothing'. I say that the Group[266] used him for proof, and Ibn al-Qaṭṭān al-Fāsī mentioned that what Ibn Maʿīn meant by his statement about some narrations,[267] 'He is nothing', is that his ḥadīth are very few."[268]

Ascription of weakness to a narrator may be in relation to someone who is stronger than him

Often they regard a narrator as weak in relation to someone else who is more reliable among his peers as the Ḥāfiẓ said in the introduction to *al-Fatḥ* in the biographical notice on ʿAbd ar-Raḥmān ibn Sulaymān ibn ʿAbdullāh ibn Ḥanẓalah who is better known as Ibn al-Ghasīl, after citing that Ibn Maʿīn and others regarded him as a trustworthy narrator, "I say that their ascription of weakness to him is in relation to others among his peers who are more reliable than him. Indeed, the Group[269] except an-Nasāʾī used him in proof."

He (Ibn Ḥajar) also said in *Badhl al-Māʿūn fī Faḍl aṭ-Ṭāʿūn*,

> Yaḥyā ibn Maʿīn, an-Nasāʾī, Muḥammad ibn Saʿd, and ad-Dāraquṭnī have declared him a trustworthy narrator, and Ibn al-Jawzī narrated from Ibn Maʿīn that he regarded him to be weak. If that is confirmed, it may be that he was asked about him and about someone superior to him and so he regarded him weak in relation to him.

266 I.e the compilers of the six authentic collections.

267 The qualification, 'some narrations' is important here as some scholars have made the error of stating this point generally. In the vast majority of cases this statement has been used by ḥadīth scholars, including Ibn Maʿīn, as a verdict of strong impugnment. Ed.

268 Refer to Shaykh Abū Ghuddah's important addition to this point which can be found in his notes to *ar-Rafʿ wa't-Takmīl* pp.153–155, and p.382–389.

269 I.e the compilers of the six authentic collections.

This is an important principle concerning those about whom the transmissions from Ibn Maʿīn differ. Abu'l-Walīd al-Bājī pointed this out in his book *Rijāl al-Bukhārī*.

His pupil as-Sakhāwī said in *Fatḥ al-Mughīth*, "Most of the disagreement transmitted in the words of the scholars of invalidation and validation should be interpreted in this way.

For this reason one ought to cite the verdicts of the people of validation and invalidation in order to make clear what is probably concealed from many people. Sometimes the disparity (in the same validator's opinions) is because of an alteration in *ijtihād*."[270]

Abū Ḥātim's declaration of a narrator as 'unknown' is intended to mean his attributes are unknown and not he himself, and he declared "unknown" some people whom others knew. The verdict regarding his declaration of someone as "unknown". Mention of the declaration of some narrators of the two Ṣaḥīḥ books as "unknown" when they are well known;and Ibn Ḥazm's declaration of some famous imams as "unknown"

When Abū Ḥātim says about a narrator, "He is unknown," he predominantly means unknown in attribute not in person. adh-Dhahabī transmits that from him in *al-Mīzān* a great deal, such as when he said in the biographical notice on Abān ibn Ḥātim, "Know every person about whom I say that he is unknown without attributing it to a source, then its source is Abū Ḥātim, and there will be a great deal of that."

As-Sakhāwī said in *Fatḥ al-Mughīth*,

> [...] regarding the opinion of Abū Ḥātim that a narrator is unknown, he does not mean by it that only one person transmitted from him. This is proved by the fact that he said about Dāwūd ibn Yazīd ath-Thaqafī that he is unknown despite the fact that a group narrated from him. For that reason adh-Dhahabī said right after that, "This verdict makes clear to you that a man may be unknown to Abū Ḥātim (i.e. his condition is unknown) even if a group of trustworthy narrators narrate from him."[271]

I say that similarly Abū Ḥātim declared some narrators unknown whom others knew and declared trustworthy. Thus his invalidation of someone by declaring them unknown cannot be trusted until another evaluating scholar agrees with him in that. And you have already learnt that adh-Dhahabī in *al-Mīzān* mainly follows

270 I.e. his opinion or knowledge of the narrator changed later in life so that at one point he validated him and later invalidated or vice versa. If the chronology of the opinions is known, then the later one should be acted upon, if not then one should hesitate. This is the opinion of al-Zarkashī in his *Nukat ʿalā ibn aṣ-Ṣalāḥ*. However, the author of this work quotes from Ibn Ḥajar, as we will see towards the end of the book, that preference will be given to validation and a specific interpretation will be made of the invalidation. Shaykh ʿAbd al-Fattāḥ concludes that this is a better perspective. Ed. *ar-Rafʿ wa't-Takmīl* p.172–174.

271 *Ar-Rafʿ wa 't-Takmīl*, pp.164–165.

Abū Ḥātim in his passing judgement on someone as unknown, so whoever studies the *Mīzān* should pay attention to that.

As-Suyūṭī said in *Tadrīb ar-Rāwī*,

> A group of ḥāfiẓ scholars declared some narrators unknown because of their own lack of knowledge of them when in fact they were people well known to others for reliability. I will enumerate what is in the two *Ṣaḥīḥ* books of that:
>
> Aḥmad ibn ʿĀṣim al-Balkhī whom Abū Ḥātim declared unknown but Ibn Ḥibbān declared a trustworthy narrator and said about him, 'The people of his city narrated from him'.
>
> Ibrāhīm ibn ʿAbd ar-Raḥmān al-Makhzūmī whom Ibn al-Qaṭṭān declared unknown but whom others recognised and Ibn Ḥibbān declared a trustworthy narrator.
>
> Usāmah ibn Ḥafṣ al-Madanī whom Abu'l-Qāsim al-Lālakāʾī declared unknown, but about whom adh-Dhahabī said, 'He is not unknown; four people narrated from him'.
>
> Asbāṭ Abu'l-Yasaʿ whom Abū Ḥātim declared unknown but whom al-Bukhārī recognised.
>
> Bayān ibn ʿAmr whom Abū Ḥātim declared unknown but whom Ibn al-Madīnī, Ibn Ḥibbān and Ibn ʿAdī declared to be a trustworthy narrator, and from whom al-Bukhārī and Abū Zurʿah narrated.
>
> Al-Ḥusayn ibn al-Ḥasan ibn Yasār whom Abū Ḥātim declared unknown but whom Aḥmad and others declared to be a trustworthy narrator.
>
> Al-Ḥakam ibn ʿAbdullāh al-Baṣrī whom Abū Ḥātim declared to be unknown but whom adh-Dhuhlī declared a trustworthy narrator and from whom four trustworthy narrators narrated.
>
> ʿAbbās al-Qanṭarī whom Abū Ḥātim declared unknown but whom Aḥmad and his son declared a trustworthy narrator.
>
> Muḥammad ibn al-Ḥakam al-Marwazī whom Abū Ḥātim declared unknown but whom Ibn Ḥibbān declared a trustworthy narrator.

Similarly Ibn Ḥazm declaring someone unknown cannot be trusted until someone else agrees with him. Because he says about each of Abū ʿĪsā at-Tirmidhī, Abu'l-Qāsim al-Baghawī, Ismāʿīl ibn Muḥammad aṣ-Ṣaffār, Abu'l-ʿAbbās al-Aṣamm and other famous people, "He is unknown," as as-Sakhāwī said in *Fatḥ al-mughīth* as is in *ar-Rafʿ wa't-takmīl.*

Explanation of what they mean by saying about a narrator, "He is not like so-and-so"

If they say about a narrator, "He is not like so-and-so" or "someone other than him is preferable to me" then this is not invalidation. The Ḥāfiẓ said in *at-Tahdhīb* in the biographical notice on Azhar ibn Saʿd as-Sammān, "Al-ʿUqaylī cited in *aḍ-Ḍuʿafāʾ* that Imam Aḥmad said, 'Ibn Abī ʿAdī is preferable to me than Azhar.' I say that this is not an invalidation which requires that he be counted among the weak narrators."

When they say, "The strangest (ankar) that so-and-so narrated was such-and-such", it does not necessitate that the ḥadīth or the narrator are weak

When they say, "The strangest that so-and-so narrated is such-and-such", then it does not necessarily follow that either the ḥadīth or the narrator are weak, because they also often use this expression for *ḥasan* and *ṣaḥīḥ* ḥadīth simply on the basis of the narrator being the only person to narrate it.

As-Suyūṭī said in *Tadrīb ar-Rāwī*,

> There occurs among their expressions "the strangest that so-and-so narrated was such-and-such," even when that ḥadīth is not weak. Ibn ʿAdī said, "The strangest that Burayd ibn ʿAbdullāh ibn Abī Burdah narrated was, 'When Allah ﷻ wishes an ummah good He takes their prophet in death before them.'" He said, "This is a good route (*isnād*) whose narrators are trustworthy narrators, and which some people have included in their *Ṣaḥīḥ* collections." And the ḥadīth is in *Ṣaḥīḥ* Muslim.
>
> Adh-Dhahabī said, "The strangest ḥadīth that al-Walīd ibn Muslim has is the ḥadīth on the memorisation of the Qurʾān,[272] but it is in at-Tirmidhī who declared it *ḥasan*, and al-Ḥākim declared it *ṣaḥīḥ* according to the conditions of the two Shaykhs."
>
> So do not be deceived by the verdict of adh-Dhahabī in the *Mīzān* or Ibn ʿAdī in the *Kāmil*, "This ḥadīth is one of the disclaimed (*manakir*) ḥadīth of so-and-so" or "one of the strangest that he narrated" and do not pass the judgement on it that it is weak simply because of this verdict, because they only mean by that the simple fact of his being unique in narrating it, and nothing more. The Ḥāfiẓ said in the introduction to *al-Fatḥ*, "Part of his habit"—meaning Ibn ʿAdī—"was that he would narrate ḥadīth that had been declared the strange, whether from a trustworthy narrator or someone who was not a trustworthy narrator."

Their verdict concerning a narrator that he has or makes suppositions (lahū awhām aw yahim) in his ḥadīth, or he made mistakes in them (aw yukhṭiʾ) does not make him fall from the degree of being a trustworthy narrator

When they say about a narrator that he has or makes suppositions, or makes mistakes (*yukhṭiʾ*) in his ḥadīth then this does not cause him to descend from the degree of

272 At-Tirmidhī, 13:75 with the commentary of Ibn al-ʿArabī, 4:274 in *Tuḥfat al-Aḥwadhī* where al-Mubārakpurī discusses its chain at length. Also narrated by al-Ḥākim in *al-Mustadraak*, 1:316 though although adh-Dhahabī criticizes the chain and mentions that it maybe fabricated.

being a trustworthy narrator, because a slight degree of supposition does not harm, and no one is free from it.

Adh-Dhahabī said in the *Mīzān* in refutation of al-ʿUqaylī for including ʿAlī ibn al-Madīnī among the weak narrators,

> So do you not have an intellect (*ʿaql*) ʿUqaylī? Do you realise about whom you are talking? I only wish you to show me who is the reliable trustworthy narrator who has not made a mistake and has not uniquely transmitted that in which no one else followed him.
>
> Moreover, not every person who has lapses or wrong actions is impugned to such an extent that his ḥadīth are weakened, nor is it a precondition of being a trustworthy narrator that one should be completely protected from wrong action and error. However, the benefit in our mentioning many of the trustworthy narrators in whom there is the least innovation or who have slight suppositions in among the great volume of their knowledge is so that it be known that other people are weightier than them and more trustworthy as narrators in the cases where they contradict them or differ from them. Thus weigh things up with justice and scrupulousness. (Abridged and cited selectively)

I say that by this it is known that the existence of the least innovation in a narrator also does not harm and does not cause him to descend from the degree of being a trustworthy narrator.

It is also similarly known that the fact that a narrator is mentioned in the *Mīzān* does not necessitate that he is weak, because adh-Dhahabī mentioned many of the trustworthy narrators in it in order to defend them, just as he mentioned ʿAlī ibn al-Madīnī in it for that purpose, or to distinguish them from the weak narrators if their names resemble each other. He stated that in the introduction to the *Mīzān* and in its conclusion in which he said:

> Moreover, (this book of mine comprises) reliable trustworthy narrators who have innovations, or trustworthy narrators about whom such people have made critical statements whose critical comments about that trustworthy narrator are not given any attention because they were obstinately harsh about him and went against the dominant majority of the people of critical evaluation and accuracy, because we do not claim absolute protection from forgetfulness and mistakes for anyone other than the prophets, peace be upon them.
>
> Moreover, (it comprises) sincere ḥadīth scholars or shaykhs whose reliability is unknown inwardly but not outwardly (*mastūr*) in whom there is the slightest leniency and who did not reach the degree of being meticulously reliable. Then, (it comprises) ḥadīth scholars who are weak in respect of their memories and have mistakes

> and suppositions but whose ḥadīth are not abandoned but on the contrary what they narrate as supporting narrations (*shawāhid*) and for the purpose of [parallel] analysis (*iʿtibār*) are accepted. (Abridged and cited selectively)

He said at the end of it,

> Its author said: may Allah seal his destiny with right actions and forgive him, 'its principle focus and its subject is the weak narrators but in it there are a large number, as we mentioned in the introduction, of trustworthy narrators whom I mentioned in order to defend them or because the criticisms regarding them do not cause any weakness.

He said under the letter *mīm*, "Muḥammad ibn Khuzaymah [narrated] from Hishām ibn ʿAmmār a false tradition." and this can almost not be recognised. As for Muḥammad ibn Khuzaymah, the shaykh of aṭ-Ṭaḥāwī, he was a well known trustworthy narrator." Thus he mentioned the Shaykh of aṭ-Ṭaḥāwī simply to distinguish him from weak narrator [with the same name].

The invalidation of al-ʿUqaylī and Ibn al-Qaṭṭān of a narrator with that which is not invalidation

Often al-ʿUqaylī casts aspersions on someone and invalidates him with the words, "So-and-so is not corroborated by anyone in his ḥadīth." This is not invalidation at all, and the scholars have refuted him in many places because of his invalidating trustworthy narrators in that way.

Adh-Dhahabī said in *al-Mīzān*,

> I only wish you to show me who is the reliable trustworthy narrator who has not made a mistake and has not uniquely transmitted that in which no one else corroborated him. On the contrary, when the trustworthy narrator who is a *ḥāfiẓ* is alone in narrating some ḥadīth, his status is further exalted and perfected and it shows his concern for the science of tradition, and his retention apart from his peers of things which they did not know, unless it is clear that he made a mistake or had suppositions about something and it is thus recognised.
>
> So first of all, look at the Companions of the Messenger of Allah ﷺ, both the senior and the junior among them, there are none who did not solitarily narrate a *sunna*. Would one say about [any of them], "this is a ḥadīth that no one else corroborated?" It was similar with the Followers, for each of them had some knowledge that none of the others had, and this is not the goal, because this is confirmed as what is necesasry in the science of ḥadīth. A trustworthy narrator who is precise and accurate narrating something uniquely is counted as *ṣaḥīḥ* and unusual (*gharīb*).

The Ḥāfiẓ said in the introduction to *Fatḥ* in the biographical notice on Thābit ibn ʿIjlān al-Anṣārī, "Al-ʿUqaylī said, 'He is not corroborated in his ḥadīth.' Abu'l-Ḥasan ibn al-Qaṭṭān followed that up by saying that that does not harm him unless there is a great deal of disclaimed narrations and contradiction of trustworthy narrators, and it is as he said."

Similarly, Abu'l-Ḥasan ibn al-Qaṭṭān often invalidated someone by saying, "His state is unknown," or "His being reliable is not established." But do not think of him that this narrator is unknown or not a trustworthy narrator, because in these expressions of Ibn al-Qaṭṭān he has a technical usage which which no one else accords with.

Adh-Dhahabī said in the *Mīzān* in the biographical notice on Ḥafṣ ibn Bughayl,

> Ibn al-Qaṭṭān said, "His state is not known." I say that I do not mention this type in this book of mine because Ibn al-Qaṭṭān speaks about every person about whom an imam contemporary with that narrator did not speak or who took from someone contemporary with him that which would show his being reliable. There are many of this type in the two *Ṣaḥīḥ* books whom no one declared weak and who are not unknown.

He said in biographical notice on Mālik ibn al-Khayr al-Miṣrī,

> Ibn al-Qaṭṭān said, "He is of those whose reliability is not established," meaning that no one said clearly that he was a trustworthy narrator, yet among the narrators of *ṣaḥīḥ* ḥadīth there are a large number about whom we do not know of anyone stating expressly that they were trustworthy narrators. The dominant majority take the position that if a group of people narrate from a shaykh who did not produce that which was repudiated of him, then his ḥadīth are *ṣaḥīḥ*.

When is their verdict on a narrator "he changed or became confused at the end" invalidation?

Often they invalidate a narrator by saying "he changed at the end [of his life]" or "he became confused" but this is not invalidation as long as he did not do that a lot.

Adh-Dhahabī said in the *Mīzān* in the biographical notice on Hishām ibn ʿUrwah after declaring him a trustworthy narrator,

> No account is taken of that which Abu'l-Ḥasan al-Qaṭṭān said, that he and Suhayl ibn Abī Ṣāliḥ became confused and changed. Yes, a man changes a little, and his memory does not remain as it was in the state of his youth, and so he forgets some of what he had memorised or makes mistakes, so what is that? Is he completely protected from forgetfulness? When he came to Iraq at the end of his life he narrated altogether a great deal of knowledge in the midst of which were a few ḥadīth which he did not handle perfectly, but the like of this happened to Mālik and to Shuʿbah

> and to Wakī[c] and to great trustworthy narrators. So avoid random [accusations] and give up mixing up reliable imams with weak narrators and those who are confused, because he is Shaykh al-Islam.

If he mixed up things a great deal, then that which his older companions narrated from him is decisive proof, and that which his later companions narrated is not unless it is known historically that his hearing from him was before he became mixed up, as is obvious from the introduction to the *Fatḥ* by the Ḥāfiẓ.

Explanation of the state of those who became confused and from whom al-Bukhārī or Muslim narrated

When al-Bukhārī narrates from someone who became confused towards the end of his life, the Ḥāfiẓ said in the introduction to the *Fatḥ*, "Apparently he only narrated from those who he had heard from before his becoming confused."

I say that it is the same with Muslim because he undertook to commit to authenticity (*ṣaḥīḥ*) as did al-Bukhārī, so that if a narration comes from someone who became confused by way of someone from whom the two Shaykhs narrated then it is a proof which shows that that narrator heard from him before he became confused.

One ought to mention ascriptions of being weak or trustworthy about a narrator and that it is not correct to confine oneself to mentionining only one of them

If there is a difference of opinion about a narrator, with some declaring him a trustworthy narrator and others declaring him weak, then to confine oneself to mentioning the ascription of weakness and remaining silent about the ascription of trustworthiness or vice versa is a serious fault. Unless the person is someone whose reliability is firmly established and whose imamate the ummah acknowledges, in which case there is no harm in confining oneself to the ascription of his being a trustworthy narrator. In fact, it is incumbent [to confine to ascribing his trustworthiness] if it is clear that the source of his invalidation is someone who is partisan, harsh, is himself invalidated, who attacks him because of his being a contemporary or because of worldly aversion, or if he is someone whose opinion is not heeded because he is ignorant of the state of the narrator. All of this is obvious after considering what we have mentioned already about the principles of invalidation and validation.

Adh-Dhahabī said in the *Mīzān* in the biographical notice on Abān ibn Yazīd al-ᶜAṭṭār, "The ᶜAllāmah Abu'l-Faraj ibn al-Jawzī counted him among weak narrators without mentioning the sayings of those who declared him to be a trustworthy narrator, and this is one of the defects of his book that he quotes the invalidation but is silent about validation."

If they say in the books on weak narrators or fabricators, "This ḥadīth is not ṣaḥīḥ or is not established," it means that it is fabricated, but if they say it in the books on juristic rulings it means to deny its technical status of being ṣaḥīḥ

It does not necessarily follow from their saying, "This ḥadīth is not *ṣaḥīḥ* or is not established," that it is fabricated or weak. Similarly, it does not follow from their saying, "Nothing on this topic is *ṣaḥīḥ* or established," that there are no *ḥasan* ḥadīth in it.[273]

Az-Zarkashī said in his *Nukat ʿalā Ibn aṣ-Ṣalāḥ*,

> Between our verdict that something is fabricated and our verdict that it is not *ṣaḥīḥ* there is a huge gap, because the former is affirmation of lying and fabrication, but the latter is to inform that there is no reliability from which it does not necessarily follow that it does not exist. This is the case with every ḥadīth about which Ibn al-Jawzī said that it is not *ṣaḥīḥ* and the like. He also said, "It does not necessarily follow from it that it is fabricated, because what is established (*thabit*) comprises what is *ṣaḥīḥ* and the weak ḥadīth [comprises that] which is less than it."

ʿAlī al-Qārī said in *Tadhkirat al-Mawḍūʿāt* "...along with the fact that the statement of as-Sakhāwī, 'It is not *ṣaḥīḥ*" does not negate the weak and *ḥasan* [ḥadīth]."

Az-Zurqānī said in *Sharḥ al-Mawāhib* after his transmitting the authentication of the ḥadīth, "Allah ﷻ looks down on the middle night of Shaʿbān..." from al-Qasṭalānī from Ibn Rajab, "Ibn Ḥibbān declared it *ṣaḥīḥ*" [and said] "in that is refutation of the statement of Ibn Diḥyah, 'Nothing *ṣaḥīḥ* has been transmitted concerning the middle night of Shaʿbān,' unless (in saying 'nothing *ṣaḥīḥ*') he means to negate the technical soundness (*ṣiḥḥaḥ*), because this ḥadīth of Muʿādh is *ḥasan* but not *ṣaḥīḥ*.

As-Samhūdī said, "It does not necessarily follow from the saying of Aḥmad concerning the ḥadīth about being generous to ones dependents on the day of ʿĀshūrāʾ that it is not *ṣaḥīḥ* (*lā yaṣiḥḥ*), that it should be false, for it may not be *ṣaḥīḥ* but yet be fine for use in proof since *ḥasan* is a rank between the *ṣaḥīḥ* and the weak."[274]

The forgetfulness of a narrator or his accepting insinuation (talqīn) is harmful to him if he did not narrate from a ṣaḥīḥ source

A great amount of forgetfulness on the part of a narrator or his accepting insinuation (*talqīn*) in the ḥadīth is only harmful if he did not narrate from a *ṣaḥīḥ* source, contrary to the case when he does narrate from it then one does not take in to account a great deal of forgetfulness since one relies then on the source and not on his memorisation, as is in *Tadrīb ar-Rāwī*.

---

273 Shaykh Abū Ghuddah mentions an important condition for the use of this statement in his introduction to Mulla ʿAlī al-Qārī's *al-Maṣnūʿ fī maʿrifat al-*ḥadīth *al-Mawḍūʿ*, p.10–15.

274 *Ar-Rafʿ*, p.137–140.

CHAPTER 8

On the principles of contradiction between different proofs and the preferring (*tarjīḥ*) of some over others

THERE CANNOT be mutual conflict in *Sharīʿah* proofs in actual fact, otherwise it would necessitate internal contradiction and frivolity which the Lawgiver is pure of. On the contrary, contradiction is assumed outwardly at first glance because of ignorance of dates or mistakes in understanding what is meant. The ruling for [apparent contradictions] is abrogation if the [chronologically] earlier and the later are known, and they are compatible with that judgement, but if not then [the judgement is] that one is preferred (*tarjīḥ*) if that is possible, because abandoning the preferred is contrary to reason and consensus. if [preference is not possible] then one tries to reconcile contraries as much as possible out of necessity, and if it is not possible to reconcile, then they both are nullified, and when both are nullified one systematically proceeds to proofs of a lower level than them, if they exist.

Thus, if there is conflict between two āyāt then one proceeds to the traditions of single individuals (*khabar al-wāḥid*), and if between two traditions then one proceeds to the verdicts of the Companions or analogical deduction, as is in *Fawātiḥ ar-raḥamūt sharḥ musallam ath-thubūt*.

Then there is a difference of opinion as to whether the verdicts of Companions have priority or analogical deduction. Al-Karkhī said, "They are equal, so that it is incumbent that one act by either of them on the precondition that one strives to investigate (the most correct option)." Fakhr al-Islām[275] said, "The verdicts of the Companions have precedence over analogical deduction, whether or not they are matters that can be grasped by analogical deduction." And if one is incapable of proceeding to something lesser than the two of them then one has to confirm the principles, i.e. to confirm everything on its principle and leaving it as it is, as is found in *Nūr al-anwār* and its gloss.

275 Meaning Fakhr al-Islām al-Bazdawī. Ed.

*

That which a Companion who accepted Islam later narrates contradicting someone who adopted Islam earlier is not counted as abrogating, unless he states clearly that he heard it from the Prophet ﷺ and he had not received anything from him ﷺ before becoming a Muslim, and that the earlier adopter of Islam had heard it before he had heard him, as is in *Qafw al-athar*.

The historical precedence of one tradition over the other may sometimes be known clearly from history, in which case the later must abrogate the earlier. Sometimes it may be known by inference such as when a forbidding [ḥadīth] and a permitting [ḥadīth] come together in a ruling without one knowing which is historically older, in such a case they hold the forbidding to be later than the permitting by inference so that it does not necessitate that abrogation takes place twice. There is greater prudenc in it too because there is no harm in avoiding what is permissible and no sin if it were that the permitting [ḥadīth] had been later, but in acting by a permitting [ḥadīth] there would be a problem if it were that the forbidding [ḥadīth] was later, as is in *Fawātiḥ ar-raḥamūt*.

*

The reconciling of two contradictory general (*ʿāmm*) rulings is achieved by means of variation (*tanwīʿ*) so that the ruling of one of the two is particularlised for some situations and the other for others; in two [contradictory] unrestricted [*muṭlaq* texts], it is [achieved] by means of the restriction (*taqyīd*) of each of them by a different restriction from the other; in two contradictory specific rulings [reconciliation is achieved] by division (*tabʿīḍ*) in that one is interpreted as referring to a condition and the other to a different condition or by interpreting one of them as being metaphorical (*majāz*) and allowing the other to remain as literally true (*haqīqah*). In case of apparent contradiction between a general text and a specific text, reconciliation is achieved through particularizing the general text, practising upon it in the area that lies beyond the specific, and practising upon the specific text whilst still allowing for the possibility of error, but not a manner akin to the particularization of the Shafiʿīs, which is that the general categorically denotes the area beyond the specific. In this specific sense the argument that particularization is possible only where there is simultaneity, whereas simultaneity remains unknown where there is contradiction, may not be raised against the Hanafis.[276]

---

276 Prior to particularization, the denotation of a general text is believed to be *qatʿī* (categorical) by the Hanafis, and *ẓannī* (speculative) by the remaining madhāhib including the Shāfiʿīs. While there has been considerable discussion around whether the denotation of a general text post-particularization is *haqīqah* (literal) or *majāz* (figurative), nothing in the existing accessible *uṣūl* literature gives reason to believe that the Shāfiʿīs hold the denotation of a particularized general text to be anything but *ẓannī*.

You have already learnt that reconciliation of contradictory reports comes after preference of one over the other, for wherever the preference of one over the other is known one does not engage in reconciliation, so be aware of that.

*

Affirmation is to be preferred over negation if they contradict each other according to al-Karkhī as is in testimony, and Imam ʿĪsā ibn Abān said, "The two are contradictory."[277] The chosen position according to Imam Fakhr al-Islām and other investigators is that if the narrator of the negation has sufficed himself with [denial of] the original fact (*bi 'l-aṣl*)[278] then the affirmation is given precedence in the same way as the preference of the invalidation over the validation, because the negation at that point is without proof. If the negation is of that which is known with its proof and not by the [denial] of the original fact, then they contradict each other since both of them constitute information based on [evidenced] knowledge, and so the negation is like the affirmation[279] and the preponderant judgement is sought (from outside).

If both of them are possible, i.e. the information [about the negation] coming forth with evidence or by [negation of] the original fact, then it is examined and the negating informant is enquired about, if he says, "the informing of negation was basd on [negation of] of the original fact then one acts by the affirmation, and if he informs that it was by evidence, then they [are deemed to be] contradictory. And presumption of continuity (*istiṣḥāb*) is a preponderant (*murajjiḥ*) and so the princi-

---

Furthermore, the authoritative Ḥanafī position is that the post-particularization denotation of a general text is identical to the pre-particularization position of the Shāfiʿīs. (See *Uṣūl al-Bazdawī* on the margins of *Kashf al-Asrār*, vol. 1 p. 308) It is therefore highly implausible that the Shāfiʿī-Ḥanafī difference alluded to in *Fawātiḥ ar-Raḥamūt* pertains to the epistemological dichotomy of *qatʿī* and *ẓannī*. A more likely locus for the difference might be the issue of *tanāwul*, i.e. the question as to whether or not the text actually applies to what it apparently denotes. The Shafiʿī answer to this question is decidedly unequivocal, while the margin of error allowed by the Ḥanafīs produces a degree of ambivalence. I am very much indebted to Shaykh MT Karaan (South Africa) for providing the translation to this passage as well as the above notes and the many discussions we had over this paragraph. Ed.

277 Thus the proof for preference will be sought from an external source. Ed.

278 This is termed as *al-ʿadam al-aṣīi* elsewhere, which means that the text simply says he didn't say or do something that another text affirms, i.e. the actual original fact is negated, in which case the affirmation is given preference, because the negation can simply be based on lack of awareness or knowledge. For example, the affirmer says, 'the Prophet said or did such and such' and the negator says, 'he did not say or do it', thus negating the actual fact of the saying or action. However, if the negation demonstrates proof or can itself be seen as an affirmation, then it is treated differently, as will follow. Ed.

279 For example, the affirmer says that the Prophet permitted something, and the negator said the prophet prohibited it. Here, the negation is not just a denial of the original fact, as it shows that the negator is not just denying the existence of something but rather affirming the negation of something: he is not saying the prophet did not permit it, but rather the Prophet forebade it, thus his negation is an affirmation of the prohibition and thus the two will be seen as contradictory. This is what is meant by negation based on or with proof or knowledge. Ed.

ple is acted on because although presumption of continuity (*istiṣḥāb*) is not a proof it is nevertheless beneficial in establishing preponderance (*tarjīḥ*). And if one does not know (by investigation and enquiry that the basis of the negation is on negation of the original [fact] or on the evidence) and is ignorant of the condition then one acts by the affirmation because it is strongest at that point. It is thus in Fawātiḥ ar-Raḥamūt along with some small alterations in expression.

*

Two actions never contradict each other because of the differences of time, so that there is one action at one time and its opposite at another, unless the two traditions give the sense that this action was repeated such that it became a custom or habit whether it was one of the incumbent acts or something else. When they contradict each other in this way then the second is the abrogating (*nāsikh*) or the particularising (*mukhaṣṣiṣ*) [of a general rule] according to the difference between the two statements of the Ḥanafīs and Shāfiʿīs (i.e. the later abrogates the earlier according to us, but is a particularisation of it according to the Shāfiʿīs). If the date [the *nāsikh* and *mansūkh*] is unknown the ruling that they are contradictory is established and the preponderant judgement is sought. As is in *Fawātiḥ ar-raḥamūt.*

*

If deed and word contradict each other then there are four categories: (a) Either the action issues without any evidence of repetition and without it being incumbent to follow it. (b) Or together with the existence of both of them, i.e. both the evidence of repetition and the evidence of following. (c) Or together with evidence of repetition alone without evidence of following. (d) Or together with evidence of following alone without evidence of repetition.

According to the first (a), which is when the action is not accompanied by evidence of repetition and evidence of following, then either the saying is particularly to do with him ﷺ just as the action is presupposed to be particular to him,[280] then [in such a case] if the saying is later than the action there is no contradiction between them. If the saying is earlier than the action then the action is regarded as abrogation before capacity to carry out the action (*tamakkun*), but if the date is unknown then the majority choose to hesitate for fear of taking an arbitrary position with respect to him ﷺ, because one of them is definitely abrogating with respect to him ﷺ, and to specify either of them without decisive evidence is not at all permissible. A preponderance based on conjecture is not enough because it is not connected to worship

280 It is presupposed because of the fact that there is no evidence of repetition or following, thus it is most likely that the action is specific to the Prophet ﷺ. Ed.

and that is obvious, because the presumption is that the saying and the act are both particular to his purified essence ﷺ.[281]

Otherwise, the saying is particularly to do with the ummah or it is broadly to do with us and with him ﷺ, in which case there is no contradiction with respect to us because the ummah do not share in the action.[282] Thus the saying would be foremost for us. And as for with respect to him ﷺ, then the aforementioned three scenarios (in the last paragraph) [apply].

According to the second (b), which is when the action is accompanied by evidence of repetition and following, then if the saying is particular to him ﷺ then there is no contradiction with respect to us, but rather the action is given precedence, but as for with respect to him ﷺ then the three aforementioned scenarios remain in effect. If the saying is particular to us then the later of the two of them abrogates the earlier whether it is a saying or a deed. Then if the obligation of following that action is established by particular (*khāṣṣ*) evidence then there is no disagreement as to its suitability for abrogating the saying; however if it is established by a general evidence such as "You have an excellent model in the Messenger of Allah"[283] then there is a difference of opinion regarding its suitability to abrogate a saying. If the date is unknown then the chosen position of the majority is to act by the saying, because its implication is more apparent than the implication of the deed. Ibn al-Humām said, "The most appropriate thing is to give preference to that in which there is prudence."

If the saying encompasses him and us then the later abrogates with respect to him and us because of the existence of the precondition of abrogation. And if the history is unknown then the chosen position of the majority is to act by the saying with respect to us, and to abstain with respect to the Prophet ﷺ for fear of passing judgement on him by conjecture.

According to the third (c), which is when the action is accompanied by evidence of repetition only, then if the saying is particular to us or encompasses him ﷺ and us then there is no contradiction with respect to us and the saying is given preference because the presopposition is that there is no following, and so the action is particular to him ﷺ, and the three aforementioned forms apply with respect to him.

According to the fourth (d), which is when the action is accompanied by proof of following alone without repetition, then if the saying is particular to him ﷺ then there is no contradiction with respect to us, but as for with respect to him then it is as we have previously seen. If it is particular to us then the later abrogates whichever

281 Thus, because it does not involve us, it is not enough to make preference based on conjecture, it is safer to abstain from an opinion if evidence does not exist. Ed.

282 Due to lack of evidence of repetition and following as already mentioned, so it is presupposed that the action only applies to the Prophet ﷺ. Ed.

283 Sūrat al-Aḥzāb: 33:21.

it may be, but if the later is unknown then the chosen position is to act by the saying, and the most fitting thing is to take [a position] based on prudence.

And if it encompasses him ﷺ and us then the later of the two abrogates, but if that is not known then the chosen position with respect to us is the saying and with respect to him ﷺ to abstain, as is in *Fawātiḥ ar-raḥamūt* along with alteration of the title for the purpose of facilitation.

*

Preference is not valid on the basis of a greater number of evidentiary proofs according to us. Thus if in one of two contradictory traditions there are an increased number of narrators but few in the other, neither tradition attains preponderance over the other because of this distinction because what is taken in to account in this area is reliability and that does not change because of quantity. How many an upright group is better than a large disobedient group.

Yes, if there is on one side a single person and on the other two, the tradition of the two is preponderant over the tradition of the single person (analagously to testimony) as is in *Nūr al-Anwār* in this sense.

*

Assigning preponderance according to us is to show in one of two similar but contradictory [traditions] such an added element over the other which does not constitute an independent proof if it is alone. Some of it refers to the *isnād* and to the narration, and some refers to the text, and some to the meaning and the judgement, and some to an external matter.

Assigning preponderance in the text may be by strength of meaning, for example that which is categorical (*muḥkam*) is preponderant over that which is interpreted (*mufassar*), and that which is interpreted is preponderant over unequivocal text (*naṣṣ*) and unequivocal text is preponderant over probabilistic text (*ẓāhir*) and obscure text (*khafī*) is preponderant over difficult text (*mushkil*). And it is not correct to make the ambivalent (*mujmal*) contradict its counterparts except after explanation and thus it becomes clear in meaning. The meaning of the ambiguous (*mutashābih*) is not known, thus it is not at all correct to make it contradict any one of the counterparts.

Consensus (*ijmāʿ*) is preponderant over text because consensus does not abrogate and is not abrogated.

The unparticularised general (*al-ʿāmm al-ghayr al-makhṣūṣ*) is preponderant over the particularised general ruling because of the fact that the former is categoric (*qaṭʿī*) and the latter is presumptive (*ẓannī*).

The emphasised ruling is preponderant over other rulings because the emphasised does not carry the possibility of interpretation or it is unlikely in it contrary to what is not emphasised.

Narration in exact wording is preponderant over narration in sense because of the possibility of mistakes in transmission of the meaning.

What happened in his ﷺ presence about which he was silent is preponderant over what reached him about which he was silent.

The one which carries the least possible interpretations is preponderant over the one which requires the more.

The closer figurative expression is preponderant over the more remote because it is more easily understood. And the figurative expression which is better known in terms of association and usage is preponderant over others.

A general statement in the form of a precondition (*sharṭ*) and result (*jazāʾ*) is preponderant over a general statement which is negative and indefinite (*an-nakira al-manfiya*) and other general expressions because the form of the precondition provides a reason for the ruling which is connected to it. Sometimes the indefinite which follows the negative *"lā"* which negates the genus[284] may become specific because it is more clear in its generality than the form of the precondition. This is the more evident position.

A plural with the *lām* and the relative pronoun is preponderant over a singular which is defined by the *lām* or by the genitive construction (*iḍāfa*).

And verbal statements are preponderant over deeds because those who disagree about the implication of the deed and the permissibility of using it for proof do not disagree about oral statements (except if the deed is coupled with evidence of following (*taʾassī*), and then they contradict each other as has passed.)

That which was heard audibly from the Prophet ﷺ is preponderant over that in which there is citation about that which transpired in his assembly or in his time and about which he was silent.

That whose danger is graver and there is silence about it outweighs that whose danger is less grave because of being silent about it.[285]

That whose affliction is not general (*ʿumūm al-balwā*) outweighs a single report which is reported about something in which the affliction is general.[286]

---

284 I.e. *la allati li nafy 'l-jins*. Ed.

285 This means that if there are two acts about which the Prophet ﷺ remained silent the one which carries more dangerous implications in doing it or refraining from it will be given preference. Ed.

286 This means that if a ḥadīth (*khabr wāhid*) is available about a particular practice which affects the whole community, and another ḥadīth which discusses a practice which does not affect the whole community then the latter will be given prefence than the first ḥadīth. This is because if the practice affects the whole community, logic dictates that more than one person should narrate (i.e. to be *mashhūr* or *mutāwātir*) this ḥadīth. The fact that only one person (*khabr wāhid*) is reporting this practice makes it suspicious and thus not preferred.

When one of two reports indicates its meaning based on legal (*sharʿī*) convention and the other based on linguistic usage and both of them (the two conventions) are used in the Sharīʿah, then it is more appropriate to act by the linguistic expression; unless the Lawgiver has borrowed it for a particular meaning for which it has become known convention so that the original linguistic meaning is avoided on the basis of Sharīʿah, in that case the legal meaning is more appropriate.

They differed as to whether a great many routes of transmission for the ḥadīth is one of the signs of preponderance or not. Most of the Ḥanafīs and some of the Shāfiʿīs took the second position, and they said, "One of the two evidences does not outweigh the other by its multiple number as long as it does not come out of the sphere of single transmissions (*āḥād*) into the sphere of those which are transmitted by several or numerous chains of transmission (*mutawātir*), or those that have become prevalent (*mashhūr*).

Most of the Shāfiʿīs and Abū ʿAbdullāh al-Jurjānī from among our people (the Ḥanafīs) and Abū 'l-Ḥasan al-Karkhī, in one narration, took the former position. There is in *Musallam ath-thubūt* along with its commentary by Walī Allāh al-Laknawī, "There is no preponderance because of multiplicity of narrations according to Abū Ḥanīfah and Abū Yūsuf, contrary to most of the ʿulamāʾ such as the three imams (Mālik, ash-Shāfiʿī and Aḥmad) and among them Muḥammad according to whom it becomes preponderant with multiple proofs and narrators even if it does not reach the level of *mashhūr*.

As for the *fiqh* of the narrator, al-Ḥāzimī[287] said, "The twenty-third reason for preponderance is that the narrators of one of the two ḥadīth, despite their being equal in memorisation and mastery, should be *fuqahāʾ* who are knowledgeable (*ʿārifūn*) in gathering rulings from productive expressions. Thus to rely upon the ḥadīth of the *fuqahāʾ* is more appropriate.

It is narrated that ʿAlī ibn Khasram said: "Wakīʿ asked us, 'Which of the two *isnād*s do you prefer: al-Aʿmash from Abū Wāʾil from ʿAbdullāh or Sufyān from Manṣūr from Ibrāhīm from ʿAlqamah from ʿAbdullāh?' We replied, 'al-Aʿmash from Abū Wāʾil from ʿAbdullāh.' He exclaimed, 'Glory be to Allah ﷻ! Al-Aʿmash is a shaykh and Abū Wāʾil is a shaykh but Sufyān is a *faqīh*, Manṣūr is a *faqīh*, Ibrāhīm is a *faqīh*, and ʿAlqamah is a *faqīh*; a ḥadīth to pass the hands of the *fuqahā'* is better than for it to pass the hands of shaykhs." Al-Ḥākim transmitted that in *Maʿrifat ʿulūm al-ḥadīth*.

According to *at-Tadrīb*, the third aspect of preponderance is the understanding (*fiqh*) of the transmitter, whether the ḥadīth is transmitted by meaning or the actual words, because when a faqīh hears that which cannot be taken in its literal meaning,

---

287 Al-Ḥāzimī, *Al-Iʿtibār fī 'n-nāsikh wa 'l-Mansūkh min al-akhbār*, p.9.

he investigates it until he uncovers that which removes the complexity, which is not the case with an ordinary person."

In the commentary on *Musallam ath-Thubūt*[288] there is: "Someone other than a faqīh is not capable of that and so he [merely] transmits what he heard. This is exactly what demands the preponderance of someone with greater understanding (*fiqh*) over someone with less *fiqh*. So a transmission by someone with greater understanding outweighs that of anyone with a lesser rank."

After mentioning a debate between Abū Ḥanīfah and al-Awzāʿī, may Allah ﷻ have mercy on both of them, [the author of] *Fatḥ al-Qadīr* states: "Abū Ḥanīfah accorded preponderance based on the understanding [*fiqh*] of the transmitters, as al-Awzāʿī accorded preponderance based on the loftiness of the *isnād*. In our view, giving preponderance to the understanding of transmitters is the stronger school." Something similar is found in *Ḥalbat al-Mujallī*, the commentary on *Munyat al-Muṣallī* by Ibn Amīr Ḥājj.[289]

Requiring one metaphor is better than requiring two metaphors.

That which indicates a meaning by congruity (*muṭābaqah*) is better than that which indicates it by necessity (*iltizām*).

That whose implication is by requirement of the text (*iqtiḍāʾ an-naṣ*)[290] is better than whose evidence is understood implicitly (*bi 'l-mafhūm*).

That which implies its meaning based on the harmonious implication (*mafhūm al-muwāfaqah*)[291] is better than that which implies based on the contrary implication (*mafhūm al-mukhālafah*).

That which is implied by something pronounced (*manṭūq*) is better than that implied by something not pronounced.

Preponderance in respect of the judgement and the meaning can sometimes be based on importance so that the ruling given based on one of them is more important in the opinion of the Lawgiver than the ruling derived from another. The more important outweighs others, for example the requisitive ruling (*al-ḥukm at-taklīfī*) outweighs a declaratory ruling (*al-ḥukm al-waḍʿī*).[292]

---

288 By Walīullāh al-Laknawī as in *al-Ajwibah al-Fāḍilah*, p.211.

289 The chain of narration for the debate between al-Awzāʿī and Abū Ḥanīfah is mentioned by al-Laknawīi in *al-Ajwibah al-Fāḍilah*, p. 213 and al-Muwaffaq al-Makkī in *Manāqib al-Imām al-Aʿẓam*, 1:130.

290 This is when an assumption has to be taken for granted because without it the text would not make sense, for example 'ask the village' (*isʾal al-qaryah*) has to be understood as 'ask the dwellers of the village' by requirement of the text, because a village cannot be asked. Ed.

291 This is the meaning that is in agreement with the obvious implication of the text. For example, in the command 'stay awake', the *mafhūm al-muwāfaqah* is its obvious implication telling one to remain awake, however 'do not sleep' is its *mafhūm al-mukhālafah*. Ed.

292 *Al-ḥukm al-waḍʿī*—declaratory ruling, is a ruling which narrates to a condition which regulates the proper implementation of an act, such as intention as condition for a valid act of worship; it does not take in to account one's ability to carry it out. *Al-ḥukm at-taklīfī*, is a ruling narrated to an act that has

That which is affirmed by necessity (*iqtiḍāʾ*) because the words are truthful and logical outweighs that which is affirmed by necessity because it is legally prescribed (*mashrūʿ*), because that which is truthful is more important.

A prohibition outweighs a command, because averting evil is more important than accruing benefit.

Making something *ḥarām* has preponderance over other rulings for the same reason; and it has been said that permissibility has preponderance because the Prophet ﷺ preferred to make things easy for his Ummah. That is what is preferred by ash-Shaykh al-Akbar, the author of *al-Futūḥat*, may his secret be sanctified. The preferred position is the first since it is more important and cautious.

The more difficult ruling takes precedence over the easier because it is more probable that it came after the easier. The Sharīʿah began with making things easy, and then rulings were revealed gradually.

That which affirms averting the ḥudūd punishments is more preferable than that which establishes that they be imposed because averting is more important.

That which necessitates divorce and emancipation has preponderance over what which negates them because that which necessitates them is of the same strength as that which establishes prohibition (as mentioned earlier).

A justified ruling (*al-ḥukm al-muʿallal*)—a ruling whose cause is mentioned—outweighs one whose cause is not mentioneA ruling which requires particularisation (*takhṣīṣ*) is preferred over one which requires interpretation because particularisation is more common compared to interpretation.

That which is in harmony with analogy (*qiyās*) is better than that which contradicts it.

Negation outweighs affirmation in that which was most likely to be well known but it didn't become so.

That by which the Rightly-guided Khulafāʾ acted is preferred over that by which others acted.

Preponderance based on *isnād* and transmission [occurs by way of the understanding (*fiqh*) of the transmitter, the strength of his accuracy (*ḍabṭ*) and his scrupulousness. There is no preponderance in our view based on the elevated rank of the *isnād* (*ʿuluww al-isnād*) and fewer number of intermediaries] as opposed to the Shāfiʿīs, [nor [is there preponderance] based on habitual narrating (*iʿtiyād*) accord ing to *Shams al-aʾimmah*] because habitual narrating plays no part in truthfulness or accuracy. There are many people who are habitual transmitters who are negligent, indeed who lie, while there are many who do not habitually transmit who give proper importance to the ḥadīth.

been commanded to be done or not, this takes in to account one's ability to carry it out, for example the command to pray or fast etc. Ed.

Preponderance is accorded on account of someone's knowledge of Arabic. Thus someone who is familiar with Arabic is preferred over someone who is ignorant of it.

Someone who transmits a ḥadīth from memory is preferred over someone who transmits it from a book.

And [preponderance is accorded] by the transmitter being from among the senior Companions in understanding and perception.

Someone directly involved with what he narrated is preferred over someone who is not directly involved.

Someone who was closer to the Prophet ﷺ when he heard the report is preferred over someone who was further away.

Someone who became Muslim earlier is preferred over someone who became Muslim later, unless the one who became Muslim early on did not actually listen [to the Prophet] after he became Muslim, and the one who became Muslim later clearly stated that he himself listened to him; then the later one is stronger.

Someone who learned something after having attained adulthood is preferred over someone who learned something while he was still a child.

The same is true of someone who learned something after becoming Muslim; he is preferred over the one who learned something before he became Muslim.

A ruling which came after the Hijra is preferred over one which came before it.

Someone whose name is not confused with someone weak is preferred over someone whose name is confused with one of those who are weak.

A report with an *isnād* is preferred over the *mursal.*

A narration clearly stated as being heard (*simāʿ*) and connected is better than the one narrated using [the preposition] *ʿan* (from) when it is from one of those guilty of *tadlīs.*

A report whose attribution to the Prophet (*rafʿ*) is firmly decided is stronger than one about whose attribution to the Prophet (*rafʿ*) they disagreed, except that [ḥadīth content] in which there is no scope for opinion.[293] In such a case, a *mawqūf* (which stops at the Companion) is the same as *rafʿ.*

Transmission from men is stronger than transmission from women when it does not concern rulings which are connected to women's affairs.

A ḥadīth with an *isnād* to one of the books of the ḥadīth scholars is preferred over one which is confirmed by way of reputation (on people's tongues).

(*Mutawātir* and *mashhūr* reports are preferred over single (*aḥad*) reports. This is evident.)

A *mursal* report from a Tābiʿī is better than *mursal* reports from those later than him.

---

293 Such as a matter narrated to the unseen, or the hereafter, or a prophecy, etc which one cannot use *ijtihad* to infer and deduce. Ed.

A report whose transmitter is known for his integrity and lineage is preferred over one with a transmitter who is not like that.

Someone who has many people validating him is preferred over someone who has a few validators. This is also the case with those whose good character is clearly stated; such a person is stronger than those whose validation is based on transmission from them or on account of a judgement given through his testimony. Validation on account of a judgement given through his testimony is stronger than basing that on transmission from him.

Preponderance based on an external factor can occur for various reasons:

One is when one of the reports has been acted on by some of the Ummah. It is better than one which has not been acted upon by anyone in the Ummah.

One is when one of them agrees with another piece of evidence from the Book, the *sunna*, consensus, analogy (*qiyās*), logic or sensory perception when the other does not. The one which is in agreement is stronger.

When both indicate a judgement and a reason, however the indication of a cause in one is stronger, then it takes precedence.

When both reports are general (*ʿāmm*) but there is agreement to act on one of them in a case, which is not the case with the other. The one on which it is agreed that one acts takes precedence in our view, which is not the case with the Shāfiʿīs.

When one of them is intended to clarify a judgement about which there is disagreement, then it takes precedence over that which does not intend to clarify that judgement.

That which is closer to prudence and fulfilment of responsibility takes precedence over that which is further from that.

A ḥadīth on which its transmitter acted takes precedence over one on which its transmitter did not act.

When one of two transmitters mentions the reason why that text exists, and the other does not, then the one which mentions the reason is stronger.

CHAPTER 9

On the biographies of our three Imams

THE BIOGRAPHY OF THE FIRST IMAM, ABŪ ḤANĪFAH

HOW EXCELLENT Abū Ḥanīfah is! The Imam of the imams, the Lamp of the Ummah, the Remover of Grief, Possesser of many virtues, His knowledge extended through the east and the west of the lands of Islam. He had the virtue of being one of the Tābiʿūn in his time. His status as an Imam was proclaimed and his esteem was acknowledged by great and notable scholars. He was praised for his vast knowledge, excellent memory, and accurate understanding by a group of those who validate narrators and a group of ḥadīth scholars. They also described him as possessing asceticism and total scrupulousness, as well as general acceptance by both the elite and common people.

Let us say something about his lofty circumstances and give an adequate account of his majestic virtues for the sake of blessing and success, not for the sake of ascertaining good character (*tazkiyah*) or validation (*taʿdīl*), because he, may Allah ﷻ be pleased with him, is greater and exalted in stature beyond any need of praise from detractors. Anyone who wants greater details about his states and virtues and his rank in knowledge, especially in ḥadīth, should consult our treatise, *Injāʾ al-Waṭan ʿan al-Izdirāʾ bi Imām az-Zaman*. We will summarise it for you here. In this section, every statement that we have attributed to someone but have not mentioned the source in terms of which book or page, it is mentioned in *Injāʾ al-waṭan* with the source and pages specified. One can consult that. We did this for the purpose of brevity.

Confirmation of the fact that Abū Ḥanīfah was one of the Tābiʿūn

Know that most ḥadīth scholars are of the opinion that a person becomes a Tābiʿī by simply meeting and seeing [a Companion] and do not stipulate that that he kept company with the Companion for any length of time. Al-Ḥāfiẓ stated in the commentary of *an-Nukhba*, 'This is the preferred [position].'

It is confirmed that our Greatest Imam saw some of the Companions, but there is disagreement as to whether he actually transmitted from them. Imam ʿAlī al-Qārī said, 'The reliable position is that that it (i.e. his transmission) is confirmed.'

The fact that he saw Anas and that he was a Tābiʿī according to the preferred position has been clearly stated by an immense number ḥadīth scholars and people who have knowledge of [historical] reports, including Ibn Saʿd, the author of *aṭ-Ṭabaqāt*, al-Ḥāfiẓ adh-Dhahabī in *Tadhkirat al-ḥuffāz*, al-Ḥāfiẓ Ibn Ḥajar in a reply to *fatwās* which were presented to him about that,[294] al-Ḥāfiẓ al-ʿIrāqī, ad-Dāraqutnī, Imam Abū Maʿshar ʿAbd 'l-Karīm ibn ʿAbdi'ṣ-Ṣamad aṭ-Ṭabarī al-Muqrī ash-Shāfiʿī—who also affirmed his transmission from the Companions,[295] al-Ḥāfiẓ as-Suyūtī—who judged that [the fact of his] transmission [from the companions] is not false, al-Ḥāfiẓ Abuʾ 'l-Hajjāj al-Mizzī, al-Ḥāfiẓ al-Khaṭīb al-Baghdādī, al-Ḥāfiẓ Ibn al-Jawzī, al-Ḥāfiẓ Ibn ʿAbd al-Barr, al-Ḥāfiẓ as-Samʿānī in his *Kitab al-Ansāb*, Imam an-Nawawī, al-Ḥāfiẓ ʿAbd al-Ghanī al-Maqdisī, Imam al-Jazarī, at-Tūrbishtī, the author of *Kashf al-kashshāf*,[296] the author of *Mirātu 'l-Jinān*—Imam al-Yāfiʿī, al-ʿAllāmah Ibn Ḥajar al-Makkī ash-Shāfiʿī, al-ʿAllāmah Ahmad al-Qasṭallānī since he counted him to be one of the Tābiʿūn, al-ʿAllāmah al-Aznīqī in *Madīnat al-ʿulūm*, and al-ʿAllāmah Badr ad-dīn al-ʿAynī al-Ḥanafī.

There is therefore no doubt that Abū Ḥanīfah was a Tābiʿī and is included in the words of the Almighty, 'Those who have followed them (i.e. the companions) in doing good: Allah is pleased with them and they are pleased with Him.'[297]

Abū Ḥanīfah, the trustworthy imam and ḥāfiẓ who transmitted a great deal of ḥadīth and the praise by ḥadīth scholars of him

As-Samʿānī stated in *al-Ansāb*: "[Abū Ḥanīfah] was preoccupied himself in seeking knowledge and went to great lengths in it until he achieved what no one else had achieved. One day he visited [the Caliph] al-Manṣūr (d. 158/775) while ʿĪsā ibn Mūsā was with him. [ʿĪsā] told al-Manṣūr, 'This is the [pre-eminent] scholar of the world today.'"

Makkī ibn Ibrāhīm[298] mentioned Abū Ḥanīfah and said: "He was the most knowledgeable of the people of his time." Al-Qāḍī Abū Yūsuf said, "I have not seen

294 As-Suyūṭī, *Tabyīḍ al-Ṣahīfah*, pp. 4–5.

295 The names of the companions that Abū Ḥanīfah heard from are mentioned in *al-Jawāhir al-Muḍiyyah fī Ṭabaqāt al-Ḥanafiyyah* of al-Qurashī, 1:28.

296 He is Sirāj al-Dīn ʿUmar ibn Ruslān al-Bulqīnī, the Shaykh al-Islam of his age and the shaykh of Ibn Ḥajar. He passed away in the year 805AH.

297 *Sūrat at-Tawbah*, 9:100.

298 He is from the students of Abū Ḥanīfah and one of the prominent Shaykhs of al-Bukhārī, the

anyone who possessed greater knowledge of the interpretation of ḥadīth than Abū Ḥanīfah." Yazīd ibn Hārūn[299] said, 'I have met a thousand men and I wrote [knowledge] from most of them. Among them I have not seen anyone with more *fiqh*, scrupulousness and knowledge than five men: the first of them was Abū Ḥanīfah.' Ibn ᶜAbd al-Barr mentioned it in his book, *Jāmiᶜ Bayān al-ᶜIlm*.

Al-Khaṭīb narrated from Shaddād ibn Ḥakīm that he said, 'I have not seen anyone with more knowledge than Abū Ḥanīfah.' Muḥammad ibn Saᶜd al-Kātib said, 'I heard ᶜAbdullāh ibn Dāwūd al-Khuraybī say, "The people of Islam must make supplication for Abū Ḥanīfah in their prayers."' He stated that he mentioned that [Abū Ḥanīfah] had preserved ḥadīth and *fiqh* for them.

Imam Abū Jaᶜfar ash-Shīzāmārī narrated from Shaqīq al-Balkhī that he said: 'Imam Abū Ḥanīfah was one of the most scrupulous, most knowledgeable, and most worshipping of people.' Ibrāhīm ibn ᶜIkrima al-Makhzūmī said, "I have not seen a scholar who is more scrupulous, who possesses more piety or more knowledge than Abū Ḥanīfah.' ᶜAbdullāh ibn al-Mubārak said, 'I went to Kufa and asked its scholars saying, "Who possesses the greatest knowledge in your land?" They all replied, "Imam Abū Ḥanīfah."'

Al-Ḥāfiẓ Ibn Khusrū narrated with his *isnād* from Muḥammad ibn Salama that he said, 'Khalaf ibn Ayyūb said, "Knowledge came from Allah ﷻ Almighty to Muḥammad ﷺ, then to his Companions, then to the Tābiᶜūn, and then to Abū Ḥanīfah and his companions."'

It is well known that 'knowledge' at that time only referred to knowledge of ḥadīth and the Qur'an, and so the most knowledgeable of people at that time was the one with the most knowledge of the Qurʾān and ḥadīth.[300]

The Ummah is agreed on the fact that Abū Ḥanīfah was a *mujtahid*, *faqih* and a great imam in *fiqh*. Al-Khaṭīb narrated from Muḥammad ibn Bishr that he said, 'I used to alternately frequent Abū Ḥanīfah and Sufyān [ath-Thawrī]. I would go to Sufyān who would ask me, "Where have you come from?" I would reply, "From Abū Ḥanīfah." He would say, "You have come from the man who possesses the greatest *fiqh* among the people of the earth."' Ḥujr ibn ᶜAbd al-Jabbār said, 'Al-Qāsim ibn Maᶜn ibn ᶜAbd ar-Raḥmān al-Masᶜūdī was asked, "Are you content to be one of the lads of Abū Ḥanīfah?" He relied, "People have not sat with anyone whose gathering was more beneficial than that of Abū Ḥanīfah."'

Muhammad ibn Muzāḥim said, "I heard Ibn al-Mubārak say, 'The person who

---

majority of al-Bukhārī's tri-narrator ḥadīth are via him. His biography can be found in *Tahdhīb at-Tahdhīb*, 10:295.

299 His biography can be found in *Tahdhīb at-Tahdhīb*, 11:366–369.

300 The author is referring to the classical distinction between *ᶜilm* and *fiqh*, where by *ᶜilm* it meant knowledge of ḥadīth and by *fiqh* it meant knowledge of the law. A person who was a master of both these disciplines was known as *faqīhun ᶜālimun*. Ed.

has the most *fiqh* is Abū Ḥanīfah. I have not seen anyone like him in *fiqh*." He also said, "If it had not been that Allah ﷻ Almighty helped me through Abū Ḥanīfah and Sufyān,[301] I would have been like other people." Abū Nuʿaym[302] said, "Abū Ḥanīfah possessed depth in questions [of *fiqh*]." Yaḥyā ibn Maʿīn said, "I heard Yaḥyā al-Qaṭṭān say, 'We do not lie about Allah ﷻ. We have not heard of anyone of better opinion than that of Abū Ḥanīfah. We took most of his positions.'"

Ar-Rabīʿ and Ḥarmala said, "We heard ash-Shāfiʿī say, "In *fiqh* people are in need of Abū Ḥanīfah." (*at-Tahdhīb*)

Imam al-Isfarāʾīnī mentioned, with his *isnād* to ʿAlī ibn al-Madīnī that he said: "I heard ʿAbd ar-Razzāq state that Maʿmar said, 'I do not know of anyone after al-Ḥasan (al-Baṣrī) who spoke about *fiqh* better than him." Abū Ḥayyān at-Tawḥīdī said, "Kings are the dependants of ʿUmar when politically lead and jurists are the dependants of Abū Ḥanīfah when they employ analogy (*qiyās*)." Al-Qārī mentioned that in *al-Manāqib*. As-Suyūṭī mentioned that an-Naḍr ibn Shumayl said, "People were asleep in *fiqh* until Abū Ḥanīfah awakened them with what he opened up and elucidated."

It is clear that *fiqh* is not easy without memorizing ḥādīth, narrations, the statements and disagreements of the Companions and Tābiʿūn, recognition of abrogating and abrogated sunan and other things. When they agree that Abū Ḥanīfah has the most *fiqh* among people, they obligate the fact that he was a memorizer of ḥādīth amassing a great number of them.

The historian Ibn Khaldūn said, "Their relying on his school, dependence on it and consideration of what he rejected and accepted indicates that Abū Ḥanīfah was one of the great mujtahids in the science of ḥadīth."

Adh-Dhahabī counted him among the *ḥuffāẓ* of ḥadīth and mentioned him in *at-Tadhkira*. He stated in its preface: "This books mentions the names of those bearers of Prophetic knowledge who are considered reliable and whose *ijtihād* is referred to in assessing whether reports are sound or lies and whether men are trustworthy or weak." It is known from this that Abū Ḥanīfah was a *ḥāfiẓ* who was a reliable bearer of Prophetic knowledge. His *ijtihād* is consulted in considering ḥādīth to be sound or weak and whether men are trustworthy or dishonest.

Al-Khaṭīb narrated from Isrāʾīl ibn Yūnus that he said: "What an excellent man an-Nuʿmān[303] was! How great was his memory of every ḥadīth which contained *fiqh*! How intense he was in investigating it! How great was his knowledge of the *fiqh* it contained!" According to Ibn al-Qayyim in *Iʿlām al-Muwaqqiʿīn*: "Yaḥyā ibn

301 Meaning Sufyān al-Thawrī the *Muḥaddith*, jurist and imam.

302 He is al-Faḍl ibn Dukayn, the Shaykh of al-Bukhārī, many of the narrations in *Ṣaḥīḥ al-Bukhārī* are via him.

303 Referring to imam Abū Ḥanīfah, Nuʿmān ibn Thābit ؓ.

Ādam[304] said, 'Nuᶜmān collected all of the ḥadīth of his land, then looked for the last [position] on which the Prophet ﷺ died."[305]

Yaḥyā ibn Maᶜīn said, "I have not seen anyone who I would put ahead of Wakīᶜ. He used to give *fatwā* based on the opinion of Abū Ḥanīfah. He used to memorize all of his ḥadīths. He heard many ḥadīth from Abū Ḥanīfah." This contains evidence that the Imam knew many ḥadīths, not just a few."

Sufyān ibn ᶜUyaynah said, "The first of those who made me sit to receive ḥadīth (or the first who made me a *muḥaddith*) was Abū Ḥanīfah. I went to Kufa and Abū Ḥanīfah said, 'This man is the most knoweldgable regarding the ḥadīth of ᶜAmr ibn Dinar.' So they gathered around me and I narrated ḥadīth to them."

Muḥammad ibn Samāᶜah said, "In his books, the Imam mentioned about seventy thousand ḥadīths.[306] He selected *Āthār* from fourty thousand ḥadīths."

The authenticity of this position is proven by what is narrated from his companions like Muḥammad ibn al-Ḥasan in his six books known as *Ẓāhir ar-riwāya*[307] and other books known as *an-Nawādir*. Simarlarly [what is narrated by] Abū Yūsuf in *al-Amālī* and *Kitāb al-kharāj*; ᶜAbdullāh ibn al-Mubārak in his books, and Wakīᶜ and others among his companion, cases which are too numerous to be counted or exhausted. If you were to do a summary of those of them which agree with *marfūᶜ* ḥadīths and *mawqūf* reports in explicitly and implicitly excluding what he deduced by his *ijtihād* you will find them to be close to that [in their quantity], Allah ﷻ Almighty willing.

All these juristic cases (*masāʾil*) are [actually] ḥādīth. The Imam narrated them by way of giving *fatwā* rather than transmitting them in the form of a ḥadīth. That his *ijtihād* should be in harmony with this immense amount of ḥādīth and opinions of the Companions without his being acquainted with them is very unlikely indeed.

Furthermore, there are a very large number of the ḥadīths of Abū Ḥanīfah which he transmitted via *isnād*. They include those which were collected by the *ḥuffāẓ* in their Musnads and those which were mentioned by his companions, Muḥammad ibn al-Ḥasan in his *al-Āthār*, *al-Muwaṭṭāʾ*, *al-Ḥujaj* and other books by him; Abū Yūsuf, Ibn al-Mubārak, al-Ḥasan ibn Ziyād and others in their books; Wakīᶜ in his *Musnad*, Ibn Abī Shayba and ᶜAbdu'r-Razzāq in their *Muṣannaf* collections; al-Ḥākim

304 He was from the teachers of the Shaykh of al-Bukhārī, his narrations can be found in *Ṣaḥīḥ al-Bukhārī*, he was a contemporary of Imam Abū Ḥanīfah in Kufah.

305 Approxiametly fifteen hundred companions took up residence in Kufa, amongst them being 70 Companions who participated in the battle of Badr, refer to the work *Fiqh ahl al-ᶜIrāq wa ḥadīthuhum* of al-Kawtharī, p.42.

306 i.e. interspersed within the juristic cases (*masāʾil*) that he dictated to his students.

307 The *ẓāhir ar-riwāya* are the six core books of imam Muḥammad al-Shaybāni which form the basis of the Ḥanafī school of thought. They are (1) *al-Jāmiᶜ al-Kabīr*, (2) *al-Jāmiᶜ al-Ṣaghīr*, (3) *as-Siyar al-Kabīr*, (4) *as-Siyar al-Ṣaghīr*, (5) *az-Ziyādāt* and (6) *al-Mabsūṭ*.

in *al-Mustadrak* and other books; Ibn Ḥibbān in his *Ṣaḥīḥ*, his *ath-Thiqāt* and other books; al-Bayhaqī in his *Sunan* and [other] books; aṭ-Ṭabarānī in his three *muʿjams*; ad-Dāraquṭnī in his books, and other scholars in other books. If all of those ḥadīth were to be collated into a single volume, it would be very large indeed.

According to al-Ḥāfiẓ in *at-Tahdhīb*: "Muḥammad ibn Saʿd al-ʿAwfī said, 'I heard Ibn Maʿīn say that Abū Ḥanīfah was trustworthy, He only narrated ḥadīth which he had memorized, and he did not narrate what he had not memorised." Ṣāliḥ ibn Muḥammad mentioned that Ibn Maʿīn said, "Abū Ḥanīfah was trustworthy in ḥadīth."[308]

Ibn ʿAbd al-Barr said in his book, *Faḍāʾil ath-thalāthah al-fuqahāʾ*:[309]

ʿAbdullāh ibn Aḥmad ad-Dawraqī stated: "Yaḥyā ibn Maʿīn was asked, 'should I listen to Abū Ḥanīfah?' Ibn Maʿīn replied, 'He is trustworthy, I have not heard anyone declare him as weak. Shuʿba ibn al-Ḥajjāj wrote to him that he should narrate ḥadīth and he ordered him to do so, And Shuʿba is Shuʿba."[310]

According to Ibn ʿAbd al-Barr in his *Jāmiʿ bayān al-ʿilm*: "Ibn Maʿīn was asked, 'Abū Zakariyyā, is Abū Ḥanīfah truthful in ḥadīth?' 'Yes,' he replied, 'he is truthful.' He added, 'Shuʿba had a good opinion of him.'"

Ibn ʿAbd al-Barr said,[311] "Those who narrated from Abū Ḥanīfah and considered him to be trustworthy were more numerous than those who said things against him."

Imam ʿAlī ibn al-Madīnī said, "Abū Ḥanīfah narrated from ath-Thawrī and Ibn al-Mubārak. He is trustworthy and there is nothing wrong with him."

Al-Ḥāfiẓ Ibn al-Athīr al-Jazarī said, "He was an accepted imam in the sciences of the Sacred law."

In *al-Khayrāt al-Ḥisān* by Ibn Ḥajar al-Makkī there is: "Shuʿba said, 'By Allah ﷻ, he had excellent understanding and a good memory."

Ibn Mandah mentioned with his *isnād* to Ibn Maʿīn that he said: "I heard ʿAlī ibn Mushir say, 'Al-Aʿmash set out to perform ḥajj. When he reached al-Qādisiyya, he summoned me, and he knew that I sat with Abū Ḥanīfah. He said to me, "'Return to the city (Kufa) and ask Abū Ḥanīfah to write down the ḥajj practices for me." I returned and asked him and he dictated that to me. Then I took them to al-Aʿmash.'"

Al-Awzāʿī said, "He was the person with the greatest knowledge of difficult questions." Imam Jaʿfar ibn Muḥammad aṣ-Ṣādiq said, "Abū Ḥanīfah possessed the greatest *fiqh* among the people of his land." Sufyān ibn ʿUyayna said, "There are two things which I did not think would go beyond the bridge of Kufa yet they

308 His biography can be found in *Tahdhīb al-Tahdhīb*, 11:280–288.

309 The full title of the work being *al-Intiqāʾ Fi Fadail al-Thalātha al-Aʾimmah al-Fuqahāʾ*, p. 127.

310 He is from the teachers of the Shaykhs of al-Bukhārī and Muslim, his biography can be found *Tahdhīb al-Tahdhīb*, 4:344, 355.

311 *Jāmiʿ bayān al-ʿilm wa faḍlih*, 2:149.

reached all regions: the Qur'anic reading of Ḥamzah and the opinion of the Imam." Al-Wāqidī said, "Imam Mālik used to take his verdict, even if he did not explicitly state that."

Yaḥyā ibn Ādam said that he heard al-Ḥasan ibn Ṣāliḥ say, "An-Nuʿmān ibn Thābit was a man of understanding and knowledge who is firm in his knowledge." Ibn al-Mubārak said, "When Misʿar ibn Kidām saw him, he stood up for him. If he was seated, he sat in front of him. He esteemed him, was inclined towards him and praised him. Misʿar was one of the prides of Kufa in his memory and asceticism." As-Samʿānī reported in his *al-Ansāb* that Misʿar said, "If someone puts Abū Ḥanīfah between him and Allah ﷻ, I hope that he will not fear nor be in remiss with regards to prudence for himself."

According to Ibn Ḥajar in *al-Qalāʾid*: "Sufyān ath-Thawrī said, 'We were like sparrows in the presence of a hawk when we were in the presence of Abū Ḥanīfah. Abū Ḥanīfah was the master of the scholars." Ibn Khallikān stated in his *History*, "Ibn al-Maʿīn said, 'Reading [of the Qur'an according to me] is that of Ḥamza and *fiqh* is that of Abū Ḥanīfah. I found people adhering to that.'"

Ibn Ḥajar al-Makkī stated: "One of the imams said, 'None of the famous imams had the like of what Abū Ḥanīfah had in his companions and students. Scholars and all people did not benefit [from anyone] as much as they benefited from him and his companions in the explanation of ambiguous ḥādīth and deduced cases.'" (*Radd al-Muḥtār*)

Ibn ʿAbd al-Barr said: "Those among the people of ḥadīth who speak negatively about him mostly criticise him for delving into opinion (*raʾy*) and analogy, and it has been already mentioned that that is not a fault." Yaḥyā ibn Maʿīn said, "Our companions[312] go to excess about Abū Ḥanīfah and his companions."

ʿAbdullāh ibn Dāwūd al-Khuraybī said: "with regards Abū Ḥanīfah people are ignorant and envious. In my view the ignorant have the best state." A man asked him, "What do people disparage Abū Ḥanīfah for?" He answered, "By Allah ﷻ, I do not know that they censure him for anything but that he spoke and was correct, while they spoke and erred. I saw him running between aṣ-Ṣafā and al-Marwah while I was with him, and people's eyes were fixed on him."

Ibn Abī ʿAʾishah mentioned a ḥadīth of Abū Ḥanīfah and one of those who were present said, "We do not want it." He said, "If you had seen him, you would have wanted it. I do not know of any likeness representing him and you except that which the poet said:

Criticise them rarely. Woe to you! May you be fatherless!
Or fill the place they filled. (Al-Khaṭīb mentioned it.)

312 Meaning the scholars of ḥadīth

Al-ʿAynī said in *al-Bināya*: "A group of great imams praised Abū Ḥanīfah: like 'Abdullāh ibn al-Mubārak, Sufyān ibn ʿUyaynah, al-Aʿmash, Sufyān ath-Thawrī, ʿAbd ar-Razzāq, Ḥammād ibn Zayd, Wakīʿ who used to give *fatwās* based on his opinion, and the three imams: Mālik, ash-Shāfiʿī, and Aḥmad, and many others."

Imam ash-Shāfiʿī said: "Mālik was asked, 'Have you seen Abū Ḥanīfah?' He replied, 'Yes, I have seen a man such that if he were to tell you that he would turn this column into gold, he would produce proof for it.' As-Suyūṭī mentioned it. Ismāʿīl ibn Abī Fudayk said, "I saw Mālik holding the hand of the Imam [Abū Ḥanīfah] while they were walking. When they reached the mosque, he put the Imam forward." (al-Qārī mentioned it.)

An-Naḍr ibn Muḥammad al-Marwazī, one of the companions of Abū Ḥanīfah, said, "Yaḥyā ibn Saʿīd al-Ansārī, Hishām ibn 'Urwah and Saʿīd ibn Abī ʿArūbah came to us, and Abū Ḥanīfah told us, 'Look and see whether you find anything we can hear from these people.'" This contains proof of his seeking out ḥadīths.

Ḥibbān (ibn ʿAlī) said: "Abū Ḥanīfah would not be sought out concerning a matter of the *dīn* or the world without him having a good tradition (*athar*) in that." Al-Qurashī mentioned that in *al-Jawāhir al-Muḍiyyah*. He also states in it in the biography of Yūsuf ibn Yaʿqūb al-Imam Abū Yūsuf, that he narrated *Kitāb al-āthār* from his father from Abū Ḥanīfah. It is a very large volume."

Aṭ-Ṭaḥāwī narrated from Bakkār ibn Qutaybah that he said, "I heard Abū ʿĀṣim an-Nabīl say, 'We were with Abū Ḥanīfah in Makka and many of the people of ḥadīth and people of opinion came to him. He said, 'Will a man not go to the owner of the house so these men may part from me?' This contains evidence of his immense position in the hearts of both ḥadīth scholars and *fuqahā'*.'"

Yaḥyā ibn Zakariyyā ibn Abī Zā'idah said, "My father told me, 'Son, you must stick to an-Nuʿmān ibn Thābit. Learn from him before you miss him.'" Yaḥyā said, "I would often present his *fatwas* to my father and he would be amazed by them." Wakīʿ was asked, "Do you frequent Zufar?" He answered, "You deceived us about Abū Ḥanīfah until he died. Do you now wish to deceive us about Zufar until we come to be in need of Asad (Asad ibn ʿAmr al-Kūfī) and his adherents?'"

ʿAlī ibn al-Jaʿd[313] said, "A man used to frequent Zuhayr (ibn Muʿāwiyah) and then he did not see him. He came to him some time later and Zuhayr asked, 'Where were you?' He replied, 'I went to Abū Ḥanīfah.' He said, "How excellent is what you learned! One gathering in which you sit with Abū Ḥanīfah is better for you than coming to me for a month!" Aṣ-Ṣamīrī stated, "ʿAlī ibn Mushir was one of the companions of Abū Ḥanīfah. He is the one from whom Sufyān (ath-Thawrī) took the knowledge of Abū Ḥanīfah and he copied his books from him."

313 He is the Shaykh of al-Bukhārī, see *Injā' al-waṭan*, 1:28.

Bishr ibn al-Walīd the Qāḍī? said, "We used to be with Sufyān ibn ʿUyaynah. When a difficult case came to us he would ask, 'Are any of the companions of Abū Ḥanīfah here?' 'Bishr is," would be the reply. He would say, 'Answer it," and I would answer. He would then said, "Surrendering to the *fuqahāʾ* is safety in the *dīn*."[314]

Al-Ḥāfiẓ Ibn Mandah narrated with his *isnād* to al-Aʿmash that a man came to him and asked him about a case. He said, "You must go to the people of that [study] circle. Because when a question is presented to them, they continue to discuss it until they hit on the correct answer." He meant the circle of Abū Ḥanīfah.

Al-Khaṭīb al-Baghdādī narrated with his *isnād* from Ibn Karāmah that he said:

> One day we were with Wakīʿ ibn al-Jarrāḥ when a man said, "Abū Ḥanīfah erred." Wakīʿ said, "How can Abū Ḥanīfah have erred when he had with him men like Abū Yūsuf, Zufar and Muḥammad with their grasp of analogy and *ijtihād*, men like Yaḥyā ibn Zakariyyā ibn Abī Zāʾidah, Ḥafṣ ibn Ghiyāth, and Ḥibbān and Mandal, the sons of ʿAlī, with their memory of ḥadīth and recognition of it, men like al-Qāsim ibn Maʿn in his knowledge of language and Arabic, and men like Dāwud ibn Nuṣayr aṭ-Ṭāʿī and Fudayl ibn ʿIyād with their zuhd and scrupulousness. Someone with companions or comrades such as these would not err. If he were to err, they would return him to the truth."

Aṭ-Ṭaḥāwī narrated with his *isnād* to Asad ibn al-Furāt that he said, "There were forty men among the companions of Abū Ḥanīfah who wrote books.[315] Among the leading ten were Abū Yūsuf, Zufar, Dawūd aṭ-Ṭāʿī, Asad ibn ʿAmr, Yūsuf ibn Khalid as-Samtī, and Yaḥyā ibn Zakariyyā ibn Abī Zāʾidah. He is the one who wrote for them for thirty years."

I say that if someone has esteemed companions like these *ḥuffāẓ* whose memory and vast knowledge has been proclaimed by ḥadīth scholars, how can such a person then have very few ḥadīths?

Abū Ḥanīfah was a critic of ḥadīth, one who could do jarḥ and taʿdīl (validate and invaliate transmitters)

At-Tirmidhī narrated in *al-ʿIlal* from Yaḥyā al-Ḥimmānī that he heard Abū Ḥanīfah say, "I have not seen anyone who lied more than Jābir al-Juʿfī nor anyone who was more excellent than ʿAṭāʾ."

Al-Bayhaqī said in his *al-Madkhal* with his *isnād* from ʿAbd al-Ḥamīd al-Ḥimmānī who said: "I heard Abu Saʿd aṣ-Ṣanʿānī while he stood towards Abū Ḥanīfah and asked, 'Abū Ḥanīfah, what do you say about taking [reports] from ath-

314 *al-Jawāhir al-Muḍiyyah*, 1:166.
315 Meaning the cases which the imam dictated.

Thawrī?" He replied, 'Write from him. He is trustworthy except for the hādīths of Abū Isḥāq from al-Ḥarith and the ḥadīths of Jābir al-Juʿfī.'"

This indicates his superiority in ḥadīth among the people of his time which was so great that he was asked about Sufyān and his peers and he critically evaluated their ḥadīth. We already mentioned what Sufyān ibn ʿUyaynah said, "The first of those who had me sit for [teaching] ḥadīth was Abū Ḥanīfah." This contains evidence that his verdict about the character of transmitters (*jarḥ wa't-taʿdīl*) was accepted. When he declared someone to be trustworthy, people went to that person and devoted themselves to him.

Abū Ḥanīfah said about Zayd ibn ʿAyyāsh, "he is unknown (*majhūl*)." Al-Ḥāfiẓ mentioned it in *at-Tahdhīb*. Abū Ḥanīfah said, "Ṭalq ibn Ḥabīb used to espouse the Qadarī doctrine."[316] Yaʿqūb ibn Shaybah said, "I asked ʿAlī ibn al-Madīnī, 'What about the words of Raqabah ibn Maṣqalah which Sufyān ibn ʿUyayna narrated from Abū Ḥanīfah?' Yaʿqūb said, "ʿAlī ibn al-Madīnī recognised him and said, 'I do not find him [mentioned] with me.'"

Abū Sulaymān al-Jūzajānī reported that he heard Ḥammād ibn Zayd say, "We only learned the *kunyah* of ʿAmr ibn Dīnār through Abū Ḥanīfah. We were in al-Masjid al-Ḥarām while Abū Ḥanīfah was with ʿAmr ibn Dīnār. We said to him, 'Abū Ḥanīfah, speak to him to narrate ḥadīth to us.' So he said, 'Abū Muḥammad, narrate to them!" and he did not say 'O ʿAmr," (*al-Jawāhir al-muḍiyyah*). There is evidence in it of his knowledge of men and his superiority in the opinion of the shaykhs.

Al-Ḥāfiẓ mentioned in *at-Tahdhīb*: "Muḥammad ibn Samāʿah narrated from Abū Yūsuf that Abū Ḥanīfah said, 'Jahm went to extremes in negation (of Allah's ﷻ attributes) until he said, "He is nothing." Muqātil went to excess in affirmation until he made Allah ﷻ like His creation.'" Adh-Dhahabī mentioned in *Tadhkira al-ḥuffāẓ* that Abū Ḥanīfah said, "I have not seen anyone with greater *fiqh* than Ja'far ibn Muḥammad (aṣ-Ṣādiq)."

Aṭ-Ṭaḥāwī said: "Sulaymān ibn Shuʿayb narrated to us [and said], my father narrated to me and said, 'Abū Yūsuf dictated to us, mentioning that Abū Ḥanīfah said: 'A man should only narrate those ḥadīths which he has memorized from the day he heard the report to the day he narrates it.'" Abū Qaṭān[317] said, "Abū Ḥanīfah said to me, 'Read to me and say, 'He narrated to me (*ḥadathanī*),' and Mālik told me, "Read to me and say, 'He narrated to me (*ḥadathanī*)."[318] Aṭ-Ṭaḥāwī reported that. (In *al-Jawāhir al-muḍiyyah*).

In *Tadrīb ar-Rāwī*: al-Bayhaqī narrated in *al-Madkhal* from Makkī ibn Ibrāhīm

316 *al-Jawāhir al-Muḍiyyah*, 1:30.

317 He is ʿAmr ibn al-Haytham, a trustworthy narrator from the narrators of Muslim. Ed.

318 This shows that both imams preferred the method of narration in which the student reads to the teacher, as he will mention further. Ed.

who said: "Ibn Jurayj, 'Uthmān ibn al-Aswad, Ḥanẓala ibn Abī Sufyān, Mālik, Sufyān ath-Thawrī, Abū Ḥanīfah, Hishām and others used to say, 'Your reading to a scholar is better than the scholar reading to you.'"

There is also in it that ᶜAbdullāh ibn al-Mubārak, Aḥmad, an-Nasā'ī and others forbade the use of "*ḥaddathanā*" and "*akhbaranā*" here (i.e. when reading to a scholar). A group of ḥadīth scholars, and most of the people of Hijaz and Kufa, like ath-Thawrī and Abū Ḥanīfah, permitted it."

[The book] also mentions *munāwalah* [passing on the text by hand] and says that *munāwalah* enjoys the same strength as actual listening according to az-Zuhrī, ash-Shaᶜbī, Ibrāhīm, Rabīᶜah, ᶜAlqamah and Mālik. The sound position is that it is inferior to listening and reading, which is the position of ath-Thawrī, Abū Ḥanīfah and ash-Shāfiᶜī.

There is also in it that *mursal* ḥadīth are weak and are not used as evidence by most ḥadīth scholars and ash-Shāfiᶜī. Mālik, Abū Ḥanīfah and a group which included Ahmad said that it is sound. We already mentioned transmitting from al-Qārī and others that Abū Ḥanīfah accepted the transmission of the *mastur* ["screened", no prominent person transmitted from him], and he was followed in that by Ibn Hibbān.

There is also in it that al-Bayhaqī narrated in *al-Madkhal* that Abū ᶜIṣmah Saᶜd ibn Muᶜādh said,

> I was in the assembly of Abū Sulaymān al-Jūzaqāni when "*ḥaddathanā*" and "*akhbaranā*" were discussed. I said, "They are both the same." A man stated, "There is a difference between them. Do you not see that Muḥammad ibn al-Hasan said, 'When a man tells his slave, "If you inform me (*akhbaranī*) about such-and-such, you are free," and he then writes that information to him, he is free. [However] if he says, "If you tell me (*ḥaddathanī*) this," and he writes that to him, he is not set free."'"

I say that the case is mentioned in [*al-Fatawa*] *al-Hindiyyah* and no disagreement was mentioned about it, thus it is also the position of Abū Ḥanīfah.

There is also in it that if he finds direct listening (*simāᶜ*) in his book but does not remember it, then it is narrated from Abū Ḥanīfah and some Shāfiᶜīs that it is not permitted for him to transmit it until he remembers. The position of ash-Shāfiᶜī and most of his adherents, Abū Yūsuf and Muḥammad ibn al-Ḥasan is that it is permitted, and that is the sound position. The precondition is that the [mention, in the book, of] listening should be in his own writing or the writing of someone who is trustworthy, and that the book is well-preserved so that it is thought probable that it is free of any alteration. If there is some uncertainty about it, then it is not permitted to rely on it.

I say that it is that it is clear that the position of Abū Ḥanīfah contains caution and prudence in the matter of transmission.

In short, the positions of this imam in the area of *al-jarḥ wa't-taʿdīl* and the principles of transmission and relating ḥadīth are too many to enumerate.[319] Ḥadīth scholars have continued to transmit them and make use of them, both of old and in recent times. All of that is evidence that he was a great imam and mujtahid in the science of ḥadīth as he was in *fiqh*. All those who are equitable and have sound hearts, like adh-Dhahabī and others, have acknowledged that.

May Allah ﷻ show mercy on those who closed their eyes to all of that out of envy and aggression, or rashness and negligence. All of that makes the falsity of the statements of his detractors clear, and that [detraction] becomes like scattered dust as if it was 'something not remembered'. We have already stated in the previous sections that if someone's reliability has been established and the Ummah have proclaimed that he is an imam, no detraction is accepted about him at all. It is also confirmed in the principles that reliability is established by fame and being well-known, and the reliability of our Greatest Imam is renowned and his being an Imam is famous.

[He is] like the sun in the heart of the sky
whose light covers the lands to the east and west.

It has also already been mentioned that when there is something which indicates that the reason for deprecation of character is due to the partisanship for one's school or worldly rivalry, as occurs between peers and contemporaries, and other such things, one does not pay any attention to his deprecation. It is affirmed by the words of the imams like Ibn Maʿīn, ʿAbdullāh ibn Dāwūd al-Khuraybī, Ibn Abī ʿĀʾishah, Ibn ʿAbd al-Barr and others that he was an envied imam whose detractors were excessive and exceeded proper limits. No deprecation at all is accepted about him from such people.

The souls of the envious are ransomed for him.
They are punished both while present and absent.
In exhaustion is he who envies the sun's light,
and strives to bring it a competitor.

Remember what as-Subkī said: "If we give deprecation unqualified precedence, then none of the imams would be safe for us since there is no imam who has not been attacked by critics and in whose [unjustified disparagement] some have not perished. If you want the detailed answer to what the detractors said regarding him, then refer to our treatise, *Injāʾ l-Waṭan*; there you will find what will rest your heart and still the mind, Allah ﷻ willing.

---

319 Examples of a good number of them can be found in *Taʾnīb al-Khaṭīb* of imam al-Kawtharī, pp.152–154 and in *Fiqh Ahl al-ʿIrāq wa Ḥadīthuhum*, pp.32–39 with Shaykh Abū Ghuddah's notes.

THE BIOGRAPHY OF THE SECOND IMAM, ABŪ YŪSUF

He was the first and most esteemed of the companions of the first Imam, the Chief Qāḍī in Islam, and ḥāfiẓ of ḥadīth and the one who followed it most, he was Abū Yūsuf Yaʿqūb ibn Ibrāhīm ibn Ḥabīb ibn Khunays ibn Saʿd ibn Ḥabtah al-Anṣārī.[320] He was the first in Islam to be called the Chief Qadi (*Qāḍī al-Quḍāt*) and the first to write books on jurisprudence (*uṣul al-Fiqh*). He dictated cases [of *fiqh*] and disseminated them. He spread the knowledge of Abū Ḥanīfah through all regions of the earth.[321]

Adh-Dhahabī mentioned him in *Tadhkirat al-ḥuffāẓ* and described him as "the scholar and imam, the *faqīh* of the two Iraqs." He heard [ḥadīth] from Hisham ibn ʿUrwa, Abū Ishāq ash-Shaybānī, ʿAṭāʾ ibn as-Sāʾib and their generation. Muḥammad ibn al-*Ḥasan* the *faqīh*, Ahmad ibn Ḥanbal, Bishr ibn al-Walid, Yaḥyā ibn Maʿīn, ʿAlī ibn al-Jaʿd and another group narrated [ḥadīth] from him. Al-Muzanī said, "Abū Yusūf was the person who most followed ḥadīth." Aḥmad said, "He was just in ḥadīth." It is narrated from Ibn Maʿīn that he said, "Among the people of opinion [*ra'y*] there is no one with more ḥadīth nor anyone firmer than Abū Yūsuf."

ʿAmr an-Nāqid said, "He was a man of *sunna*." Abū Ḥātim said, "His ḥadīths were written." Maḥmūd ibn Ghaylān said, "I asked Yazīd ibn Hārūn, 'What do you say about Abū Yūsuf?' He replied, 'I narrate from him.'" Ibn ʿAdī said, "There is no one among the people of opinion who had more ḥadīth than he did, and he often disagreed with his companions and followed the [ḥadīth] reports. When he narrates from someone trustworthy and someone trustworthy narrates from him, there is nothing wrong with him." Ibn Ḥibbān mentioned him in *ath-Thiqāt* and said, "He was a meticulous shaykh."[322]

An-Nasāʾī mentioned him among the trustworthy narrators from among the companions of Abū Ḥanīfah and said, "Qadi Abū Yūsuf is trustworthy." According to as-Samʿānī in *al-Ansāb*: "Yahyā ibn Maʿīn, Aḥmad ibn Hanbal and ʿAli ibn al-Madini did not disagree about his trustworthiness in transmission, and no one preceded him in his time. He had the highest position in knowledge, judgement, leadership, and standing."

Al-Bayhaqī also said that he was trustworthy as we find in *al-Jawhar an-Naqī*. It is narrated that Aḥmad ibn Ḥanbal said, "When three men take a position on a question, any disagreement to them is not listened to." He was asked, "And who are they?" He replied, "Abū Ḥanīfah, Abū Yūsuf and Muḥammad ibn al-*Ḥasan*. Abū Ḥanīfah

---

320 Born in the year 113, passed away in 182 as mentioned in *Tadhkirat al-Ḥuffāz* 1:293.

321 *al-Jawāhir al-Muḍiyyah* 2:221 in a note form from *Tāj at-Tarājim* of Ibn Qutlubugha.

322 *Lisān al-Mīzān*, 6:300.

had the most insight into analogy, Abū Yūsuf had the greatest insight into tradition, and Muḥammad was the person who possessed the greatest grasp of Arabic."[323]

Al-Khaṭīb reported: "Yaḥyā ibn Maʿīn said, 'We wrote ḥadīths from him.'" Al-ʿAbbās said, "I heard Aḥmad ibn Ḥanbal say, 'The beginning of my quest for ḥadīth was when I went to Qadi Abū Yūsuf. Then after him I sought out and wrote from other people.2'"[324]

Al-Ghaznawī reported from Hilāl that he had a full grasp of *tafsīr*, ḥadīth and the Arab history (*ayyām al-ʿarab*). The least of his knowledge was *fiqh*. It is narrated from ʿĀṣīm ibn Yūsuf that he said, "I said to Abu Yusuf, 'People are agreed on the fact that no one precedes you in knowledge.' He replied, 'My knowledge in relation to the knowledge of the Imam is only like a small river next to the Euphrates.'"[325]

THE BIOGRAPHY OF THE THIRD IMAM, MUḤAMMAD IBN AL-ḤASAN

He was unique in his time, the sea of knowledge, the ḥāfiẓ of ḥadīth, the faqīh master of the world, Imam Muḥammad ibn al-Ḥasan ash-Shaybānī.[326] He kept close to Abū Ḥanīfah and learned *fiqh* and ḥadīth from him. He heard [ḥadīth] from Sufyān ath-Thawrī, Qays ibn ar-Rabīʿ. ʿUmar ibn Dharr, Misʿar (ibn Kidām) and others. In Syria he heard from al-Awzāʿī and others, and in Madina from Mālik and others.

Ash-Shāfiʿī narrated from him, and his narration from him is found in his *Musnad*, [so did] Abū ʿUbayd al-Qāsim ibn Sallām, Hishām ibn ʿUbaydullāh ar-Rāzī, Abū Sulaymān al-Juzajānī, ʿAlī ibn Muslim at-Tūsī, Abū Jaʿfar Aḥmad ibn Muḥammad ibn Mihrān and others.

Ash-Shāfiʿī said: "Muḥammad ibn al-Ḥasan told me, 'I stood at the door of Mālik[327] for three years and I heard from his own words more than 700 ḥadīths.' Mālik only rarely narrated verbally.[328] If Muḥammad had not remained and stayed with him, he would not have acquired that from him. He was one of those who transmitted the *Muwaṭṭāʾ* from him. Al-Ḥāfiẓ [Ibn Ḥajar] stated that in *Taʿjīl al-Manfāʿah*.[329]

There is in it also[330] that it is narrated from al-Muzanī that he heard ash-Shāfiʿī say,

323 *At-Taʿlīq al-Mumajjad*, p. 30, citing from *al-Ansāb*.

324 *Jāmiʿ al-Masānīd*, 2:579.

325 ʿAlī al-Qārī, *al-Manāqib*, 2:523.

326 Born in al-Wāsiṭ in the year 132 and passed away in Rayy in the year 189 as mentioned in *al-ʿIbar* of adh-Dhahabī, 1:302.

327 An expression meaning stayed in his company. Ed.

328 He was mostly read to. Ed.

329 *Taʿjīl al-manfāʿah*, p. 361.

330 Ibid., p. 362.

"I have not seen a plump person lighter in spirit (*khafif ar-rūḥ*)[331] than Muḥammad ibn al-Ḥasan nor anyone more eloquent than him." Ar-Rabīᶜ reported from ash-Shāfiᶜī that he said, "I took a camel-load of books from Muḥammad." Ash-Shāfiᶜī used to esteem his knowledge, and the same was true of Aḥmad [ibn Ḥanbal]. ᶜAbdullāh ibn ᶜAlī ibn al-Madīnī reported that his father said that he was truthful. Ad-Dāraquṭnī said that he is not to be abandoned. Ad-Dūrī reported that Ibn Maᶜīn said, "I wrote *al-Jāmiᶜ aṣ-ṣaghīr* from Muḥammad ibn al-*Ḥasan*."

According to adh-Dhahabī in *al-Mīzān*: "An-Nasāʾī and others said that he was weak in respect of his memory. He narrated from Mālik ibn Anas and others. He was one of the oceans of knowledge, strong in [transmitting from] Mālik, why would he not then be strong in respect of Abū Ḥanīfah, Abū Yūsuf and other shaykhs of Kufa when he kept company with them more than he did with Mālik? Is this not simple prejudice?"

Abū Dāwūd said, as quoted in *al-Lisān*: "He should not be abandoned." Ad-Dāraquṭnī said in *Gharāʾib Mālik*, "Mālik did not mention raising [the hands] at the time of *rukūᶜ* in the *Muwaṭṭāʾ*, but mentioned it outside the *Muwaṭṭāʾ*. Twenty reliable *ḥuffāẓ*, including Muḥammad ibn al-Ḥasan ash-Shaybānī and Yaḥyā ibn Saᶜīd al-Qaṭṭān, narrated it."[332] Thus ad-Dāraquṭnī considered him to be one of the trustworthy *ḥuffāẓ* as you can see.

Ibn Saᶜd the scribe said: "Muḥammad ibn al-Ḥasan's family originated from Jazirah, but he grew up in Kufa, and sought ḥadīth and heard a lot. He then went to Baghdad and settled there. People came to him and listened to ḥadīth and opinion from him." Al-Khaṭīb said, "When he narrated to them from Mālik, his house was filled, and there were so many people that there was little free space." Abū ᶜUbayd said, "I have not seen anyone with more knowledge of the Book of Allah ﷻ than him."

It is narrated from Ibrāhīm al-Ḥarbī that he said, "I asked Aḥmad (ibn Ḥanbal), 'Where did you find these precise cases?' He replied, 'In the books of Muḥammad ibn al-Ḥasan.'"[333]

Therefore it is clear that Abū Ḥanīfah was a blessing to all the schools. Ash-Shāfiᶜī, may Allah ﷻ have mercy on him, took *fiqh* from his companion, Muḥammad ibn al-Ḥasan, and took a camel's load of books from him, and also narrated ḥadīth from him. Aḥmad learnt fine points from his books, and he first sought ḥadīth from Abū Yūsuf and was his student. It has already been mentioned that Imam Mālik used to secretly accept the position of Abū Ḥanīfah, and the same is true of Sufyān ath-Thawrī. May Allah ﷻ be pleased us and them.

331 An expression used to mean cheerfulness. It can also mean to be acutely intelligent.

332 *Naṣb ar-Rāyah*, 1:409.

333 *At-Taᶜlīq al-Mumajjad*, p.30.

CHAPTER 10

SUPPLEMENTARY ISSUES

Critical statements about a transmitter who has been declared trustworthy lower his ḥadīth from being of a ṣaḥīḥ isnad to a strong isnād

In *al-Fatḥ*, al-Ḥāfiẓ [Ibn Ḥajar] said about the ḥadīth in which it is reported that the Prophet ﷺ performed *ʿaqīqa* for himself after Prophethood,

> Abū'sh-Shaykh transmitted it via two routes. He mentioned the first and then he said: 'The second of them is the transmission of Abū Bakr al-Mustamlī from al-Haytham ibn Jamīl and Dāwūd ibn al-Muḥabbar both of whom narrated from ʿAbdullāh ibn al-Muthannā from Thumāma from Anas.' Dāwūd is weak, but al-Haytham is trustworthy, and ʿAbdullāh is one of the narrators of al-Bukhārī. The ḥadīth therefore has a strong *isnād*. If it were not that something critical was said about ʿAbdullāh ibn al-Muthannā, this ḥadīth would be *ṣaḥīḥ*.
>
> But Ibn Maʿīn said, "He is nothing." An-Nasāʾī said, "He is not strong." Abū Dāwūd said, "I do not transmit his ḥadīth." As-Sājī said, "There is weakness in him. He was not one of the people of ḥadīth. He narrated *munkar* ḥadīths." Al-ʿUqaylī said, "He is not followed in most of his ḥadīths." Ibn Ḥibbān said in ath-Thiqāt, "Sometimes he erred." Al-ʿIjlī, at-Tirmidhī and others considered him to be trustworthy.
>
> "So he is one of the shaykhs who are such that if they alone have a ḥadīth, it is not a proof. Al-Ḥāfiẓ aḍ-Ḍiyāʾ followed the apparent *isnād* and transmitted this ḥadīth in *al-Aḥādīth al-Mukhtārah mimmā Laysa fi 'ṣ-Ṣaḥīḥayn* (the chosen ḥadīths among those not mentioned in the two sahihs).

I say that certain things are deduced from these words:

When the *isnād* contains a transmitter whose ḥadīth the author of *aṣ-Ṣaḥīḥ* transmitted and yet something [negative] was said about him, then it is not stated as "*ṣaḥīḥ*"; rather one says that the *isnād* is strong, as al-Ḥāfiẓ stated.

He whose trustworthiness or weakness is disagreed upon, he alone is not an authority in anything. I have gone along with this position in some places in the book to force an argument on the opposition, following al-ʿAynī, Ibn at-Turkmānī and an-Nīmawī. They often forced an argument on the opposition using that.

However, based on our Ḥanafī principle, a sole authority like him can have the authority of a *ḥasan* proof, even if he is not an authority at the level of the *ṣaḥīḥ*. This is because validation (*taʿdīl*) takes precedence over invalidation (*jarḥ*) unless it is explained, thus when there is disagreement about whether someone is trustworthy or weak, and the invalidation is not explained, then we and most people consider the transmitter to be trustworthy and thus his sole transmission is accepted when it does not differ from the Community in a manner which would necessitate the rejection of what he narrated. Allah ﷻ. The method of Al-Ḥāfiẓ aḍ-Ḍiyāʾ tells us that someone like this transmitter is an authority in respect of what he alone has.

The validation of al-Wāqidī; criticism against transmitting the validation of the transmitter without the deprecation; the transmission of a reliable narrator from someone is not validation of him; when both validation and invalidation exist [about a narrator], does one consider the majority position or does one consider the one which validates?

According to al-Ḥāfiẓ in *al-Fatḥ*:

> Mughulṭāy was partisan about al-Wāqidī and transmitted the words of those who deemed him strong and trustworthy and did not mention those who thought him weak and suspect even though they were greater in number, more meticulous and possessed greater recognition than the first group. Among the things with which he strengthened the case of al-Wāqidī was the fact that ash-Shāfiʿī narrated from him. However, al-Bayhaqī, narrated with an *isnād* from ash-Shāfiʿī that he deemed him to be a liar. One cannot object [to this] by saying, "How then can he narrate from him?" because we would respond by saying, "the transmission of a reliable person [from someone] is not in itself validation [of him]. Abū Ḥanīfah narrated from Jābir al-Juʿfī even though it is well established that he said [about him], 'I do not think anyone lies more than he does.'"

We learn from this that when validation and invalidation both exist about the same transmitter, then one considers the position of the majority, the most meticulous, and those with the greatest knowledge of him. This is the position of ḥadīth scholars.

In our view, the Ḥanafīs, preponderance is given to validation when the invalidation is not explained, even if the detractors are greater in number, as will be clear to anyone who reads the commentary of *al-hidāya* by Ibn al-Humām and commentary of al-Bukhārī by al-ʿAynī.[334]

---

334 Al-Laknawī deals with this issue in greater depth in *ar-Rafʿ wa 't-Takmīl*, p. 94–99.

This said, Mughlṭāyy was not partisan about al-Wāqidī. He was fair. The sound position about al-Wāqidī is that of validation. In *al-Imām* Shaykh Taqiyy ad-dīn ibn Daqīq al-ʿĪd states: "At the beginning of his book, *al-Maghāzī wa 's-Siyar*, our shaykh, Abū'l-Fatḥ al-Ḥāfiẓ[335] collected the opinions of those who regarded him weak and those who regarded him trustworthy, and he gave preponderance to his trustworthiness, and he mentioned the answers to what has been said [about him].[336]

This rebuts what an-Nawawī and adh-Dhahabī said: "Al-Waqidī was weak by agreement" or "there is an established consensus that he is weak." Where is the consensus when there is disagreement about the preponderance of his trustworthiness or weakness? Allah ﷻ knows best.

A transmitter about whom there is disagreement is a proof, albeit lower than that of the one who is agreed upon

Al-Ḥāfiẓ said in *al-Fatḥ*, "There is disagreement about Muḥammad ibn Isḥāq and his shaykh (Dāwūd ibn al-Ḥuṣayn) relating from ʿIkrimah). The reply to this is that they have used *isnāds* like this as proof for a number of rulings, like the ḥadīth about the Prophet ﷺ restoring his daughter Zaynab to Abū'l-ʿĀṣ by their first marriage. Not everyone about whom there is disagreement is rejected."

Ibn al-Qayyim said in *Zād al-Maʿād*: "The Imams continue to use Dāwūd ibn al-Ḥuṣayn from ʿIkrimah as a proof."

This supports what we already said: that a transmitter about whom there is disagreement can be an authority, even if that is not like the authority of a transmitter of the *ṣaḥiḥ*.

Abū Dāwūd considers unfamiliarity (nukrah) as disagreement

Al-Ājurrī reported that Abū Dāwūd said: "We consider 'disagreement' to be when some people alone have something."[337] I say, one should be mindful of this meaning of 'disagreement' here. It is a synonym for being 'unfamiliar'. There is no deprecation in that at all if the only one who has it is trustworthy.

Adh-Dhahabī's quiescence in considering some transmitters unknown

Al-Ḥāfiẓ said in *at-Tahdhīb* in the biography of Naḍr ibn ʿAbdullāh as-Sulamī: "I saw that adh-Dhahabī had written, 'He is not recognized.'" These are the words of a quiescent (*mustarwiḥ*) scholar. If he (adh-Dhahabī) found that al-Mizzī only men-

335 It is Ibn Sayyid an-Nās in his book *ʿUyūn al-Athar*, 1:17–21.

336 Al-Ḥalabī, *Sharḥ al-Munyah*, p. 95.

337 *At-Tahdhīb*, 9:448.

tioned [the name of] one narrator [who narrates] from a [particular] man,[338] he would consider this man to be uknown (*majhūl*).[339] This person is not discarded.

I say that one should reflect on adh-Dhahabī's statement, "He is not recognized or is *majhūl*." It can only be used as an authority after confirmation since he was quiescent in considering someone unknown.

When there is any disagreement about whether someone was a Companion, then he is at least a trustworthy Tābiʿī

Al-Ḥāfiẓ says in the biography of Niyār ibn Mukram al-Aslamī in *at-Tahdhīb*: "Ibn Ḥibbān mentioned him among the Companions and also among the trustworthy Tābiʿūn. This was his custom when there was disagreement about whether someone was a Companion.

I say that every person about whom there is disagreement as to whether he was a Companion, he is at least a trustworthy Tābiʿī.

Refutation of the position of Ibn ʿAdī that any man who has not been recognised by Ibn Maʿīn is unknown; and clarification that every person best recognises the people of his town and its surroundings

Al-Ḥāfiẓ says in *at-Tahdhīb* in the biography of ʿAbd ar-Raḥmān ibn ʿAbdullāh al-Ghāfiqī, the Amir of Andalusia: "Ibn Maʿīn said, 'I do not recognize him.' Ibn ʿAdī said, 'When Ibn Maʿīn does not recognize a man, he is unknown, and one does not rely on the recognition of anyone else.'" Al-Ḥāfiẓ adds:

> This is also what Ibn ʿAdī mentioned in the biography of ʿAbd ar-Raḥmān ibn Ādam after the words of Ibn Maʿīn about both of them, "I do not recognize him," and the author concurred with him on that. This does not apply in all cases. There are many men whom Ibn Maʿīn did not recognise as trustworthy and of good character whom others recognized without having seen him. There is nothing to prevent this. This man has been recognized by Ibn Yūnus who is the reference in respect of recognition of the people of Egypt and the Maghrib; and Ibn Khalfun mentioned him in ath-Thiqāt.

I say that every man knows best the people of his town and its surroundings, and Allah ﷻ knows best.

The position of Aḥmad [Ibn Ḥanbal] regarding men is like that of the Ḥanafis; his preconditions in the Musnad; the additions by his son and al-Qaṭīʿī; the method of

338 In this case Naḍr ibn ʿAbdullāh as-Sulamī. adh-Dhahabī says that only Ibn al-Munkadir narrated from him.

339 In his work *Tahdhīb al-Kamāl*.

earlier ḥadīth scholars in their works was that they did not transmit from liars; and the value of the transmission of Ibn al-Mudhhib and al-Qaṭīʿī

Al-Ḥāfiẓ said in *at-Tahdhīb*: "Yaʿqūb said, 'Aḥmad told me, "My position regarding men is that I do not abandon the ḥadīth of any ḥadīth transmitter until the people of a city agree to abandon his ḥadīth."'" I say that this is also the position of the Ḥanafīs, as we already stated.

Ibn Taymiyah stated in *Minhāj as-Sunna*,

> Not everything Aḥmad narrated in his *Musnad* and other books is a proof according to him, but rather he narrates what the people of knowledge narrate. His precondition in the *Musnad* is that he does not narrate from those he considers to be known for lying, although there may be in it that which is weak. His preconditions in the *Musnad* are better than the preconditions of Abū Dāwūd in his *Sunan*.
>
> Then the son of imam Aḥmad made some additions and Abū Bakr al-Qaṭīʿī made further additions. There are many forged ḥādīths in the additions made by al-Qaṭīʿī and the ignorant person thought that that was part of what Aḥmad transmitted and that he himself narrated it in the *Musnad*.

There is in it (*Minhāj as-Sunna*) also that:

> There are people like Mālik, Shuʿbah, Yaḥyā ibn Saʿīd, ʿAbd ar-Raḥmān ibn Mahdī and Aḥmad ibn Ḥanbal who, in their books, do not narrate from those they know to be lying. They do not narrate from an individual who is not trustworthy in their view and they do not narrate a ḥadīth which they know to be from a liar. Thus they do not narrate the ḥadīths of liars who are known to deliberately lie, but there may be occurrences in their narrations where the author has made a mistake.
>
> Imam Aḥmad, Isḥāq and others sometimes narrate ḥadīths for the purpose of [parallel] analysis (*iʿtibār*) and for corroboration, which they consider to be weak because their transmitters were suspected of having bad memory and the like. It may be that there is evidence that the ḥadīth was properly remembered and there might be evidence that it is an error. It may be that the person who has it is inwardly a liar but is not known for lying. Rather he narrated much that is true and so his ḥadīths are narrated. Not everything that an impious person narrates is a lie, rather one must scrutinize his report, as the Almighty says, "If a deviator brings you a report, scrutinize it carefully."[340] It can therefore be narrated in order to see whether all the supporting narrations indicate that he is telling the truth or lying.

In *al-Mīzān* in the biography of al-Ḥasan ibn ʿAlī ibn al-Mudhhib there is:

> The preacher and transmitter of the *Musnad*. He used to narrate the *Musnad* of

---

340 *Sūrat al-Ḥujrāt*, 49:6.

> Aḥmad from al-Qaṭīʿī in its entirety. *Al-Khaṭīb* said, "His listening was sound except for some sections of it." It is evident that Ibn al-Mudhhib was a shaykh who was not exact. That same was true of his shaykh Ibn Mālik (al-Qaṭīʿī). It is for that reason that there are things in the *Musnad* which are not reliable in text and *isnād.*

The existence of mutabāʿah (corroborating narrations) is not a precondition of validity for every sound ḥadīth

There is in *at-Tahdhīb* in the biography of Asmāʾ ibn al-Ḥakam al-Fazarī that Al-Bukhārī said, "Only this ḥadīth and another ḥadīth which is corroborated are narrated from him." Al-Mizzī said, "This does not detract from the soundness of the ḥadīth because the existence of corroboration is not a precondition for the soundness of every sound ḥadīth."

Most of the aḥādīth of the Musnad of Aḥmad are good (jiyād); there are a few weak ḥadīths which he started to sort out. His son ʿAbdullāh only wrote from someone considered to be trustworthy by his father

Al-Ḥāfiẓ said in the preface to *Taʿjīl al-manfāʿah*:

> Some people claimed that the *Musnad* of Aḥmad is sound and that the same is true of its shaykhs. al-Ḥāfiẓ Abū Mūsā al-Madīnī wrote a book about that. The truth is that most of its ḥadīths are good (*jiyād*), while the weak ḥadīths in it are reported for corroboration (*mutabāʿah*). There are a small number of individual *gharīb* weak ḥadīths which he transmitted (and recorded) and then began to remove bit by bit and some of them remained in it after him.

Then Al-Ḥāfiẓ refuted the position of those who claimed that it contains forged ḥadīths.[341]

It also states in *Taʿjīl al-manfāʿah*, as was already mentioned, that ʿAbdullāh (ibn Aḥmad) only wrote from someone who was considered trustworthy by his father.

Mālik narrating alone from a transmitter removes ignorance of him

In *Taʿjīl al-manfāʿah* in the biography of ʿAbdullāh ibn Abī Ḥabība al-Madanī there is that Ibn al-Ḥadhdhāʾ said, "He was one of the men for whose recognition Mālik's narration form his was considered sufficient." There is in it also that the mere fact that Mālik transmitted from someone removes ignorance of him. Shuʿbah and other critical *ḥuffāẓ* are like Mālik [in that], as you will see.

---

341 Refer to Shaykh Abū Ghudda's discussion surrounding this issue in his notes to *al-Ajwibah al-Fāḍilah* of al-Laknawi, pp. 95–100 and *al-Manār al-Munīf fi 'ṣ-Ṣaḥīḥ wa 'ḍ-Ḍaʿīf* of Ibn al-Qayyim, pp. 52–53, 135–36.

Ibn Abī Ḥātim or al-Bukhārī not deprecating a transmitter renders him trustworthy
In *Taʿjīl al-manfāʿah* al-Ḥāfiẓ said in several places, "Ibn Abī Ḥātim mentioned him without mentioning any criticism of him:" on page 203 in the biography of ʿĀṣim ibn Ṣuhayb, on page 219 in the biography of ʿAbdullāh ibn al-Huṣayn, on page 223 in the biography of ʿAbdullāh ibn Saʿīd from ʿAbdullāh ibn Abī Awfa, on page 225 in the biography of ʿAbdullāh ibn ʿAbbād, on page 245 in the biography of ʿAbd Rabbihi ibn Maymūn, and on page 254 in the biography of ʿAbd ar-Raḥmān ibn ʿUqba.

His tendency indicates that Ibn Abī Ḥātim's silence from criticizing someone renders him trustworthy, as is the case with the silence of al-Bukharī.

Confirmation that al-Ḥasan heard ḥadīth from Abū Hurayra and Samurah
Al-Ḥāfiẓ said in *at-Tahdhīb*:

> There is in the *Sunan* an-Nasāʾī[342] by way of Ayyūb from al-Hasan from Abū Hurayra in *al-Mukhtalaʿāt*.[343] Al-Ḥasan said, "I only heard this ḥadīth from Abū Hurayra." He (Abū Dāwūd) transmitted it from Isḥāq ibn Rāhawayh from al-Mughīrah ibn Salamah from Wuhyab from Ayyūb. This is an *isnād* of whose narrators there is no criticism from anyone, and it supports the general fact that he listened to Abū Hurayra. His story in this regard is similar to his story with respect to Samurah in the same matter (i.e. whether he heard ḥadīth from him or not).

He also said in that book that he narrated a large amount from Samurah ibn Jundub. ʿAlī ibn al-Madinī said all of it was based on direct listening (*simāʿ*); that is what at-Tirmidhī narrated from al-Bukhārī. Yaḥyā al-Qaṭṭān and others said that it was through a book, and that does not necessitate discontinuity (of the chain). We read in the *Musnad* of Aḥmad, that al-Ḥasan said, "Samurah narrated to us: 'rarely did the Messenger of Allah ﷺ address us without commanding us to give *ṣadaqa* and forbidding us from mutilation.'" This necessitates that he heard from him more than just the ḥadīth about the *ʿaqīqa*.[344]

A group of ḥadīth scholars abandon transmitting from al-Bukhārī because of the issue of articulation [of the words of the Qurʾan]
There is in it also: Ibn Mandah mentioned on the topic of faith that al-Bukhārī used to keep the company of al-Karābīsī and that he took the issue regarding the articulation [of the Qur'an] from him.[345] There is in *al-Mīzān* that Abū Zurʿah and Abū

342 *Sunan an-Nasāʾī*, 6:168.

343 Meaning women who seek *khulaʿ* (divorce in lieu of a payment) for no reason.

344 Hafidh al-Zaylaʿī discusses the various views surrounding this in *Naṣb ar-Rāyah*, 1:89–90.

345 This is the question of whether the articulation of the words of the Qur'an is created, since that is a human action.

Ḥātim desisted from transmitting from al-Bukhārī because of the question of articulation." Al-Karābisī was inclined towards Muʿtazilism.[346]

The reason why al-Bukhārī turned from Abū Ḥanīfah

(Repeated) Al-Bukhārī also kept the company of Nuʿaym ibn Ḥammād whom ad-Dūlābī suspected of forging some stories on the virtues of Abū Ḥanīfah, all of which were lies as was mentioned in *at-Tahdhīb and al-Mīzān*. Perhaps that was the start of al-Bukhārī turning from Abū Ḥanīfah, but Allah ﷻ knows best.[347]

The Shiʿism of ʿAbd ar-Razzāq and his retraction of it

Al-Ḥāfiẓ said in *at-Tahdhīb* that Aḥmad was criticised for his transmission from ʿAbd ar-Razzāq (because of his Shiʿism.). He then mentioned that ʿAbd ar-Razzāq had retracted that. Ibn Taymiyah said in *Minhāj as-Sunna* that although ʿAbd ar-Razzāq used to incline to the Shiʿa, and narrated many reports about the virtues of ʿAlī, even if they were weak, but he was too esteemed to narrate the like of an evident lie.

Ash-Shāfiʿī's understanding of ḥadīth and the scarcity of his ḥadīths, and the scarcity of the ḥadīths of Abū Ḥanīfah and the reason for that

There is also in *at-Tahdhīb*:

> Ibrāhīm ibn Abī Ṭālib said, "I asked Abū Qudāmah about ash-Shāfiʿī, Aḥmad, Isḥāq and Abū ʿUbayd." He said, "Ash-Shāfiʿī possessed the greatest understanding among them but had few ḥadīths. Aḥmad was the most scrupulous of them, Isḥāq had the greatest memory and Abū ʿUbayd had the greatest knowledge of the dialects of the Arabs."

We read in *Taʿjīl al-Manfaʿah*:

> Many of Ash-Shāfiʿī's ḥadīths remain which are not found in this *Musnad*.[348] There is sufficient evidence of that in the statement of the Imam of the Imams, Abū Bakr ibn Khuzaymah that he did not know of any *sunna* from the Prophet ﷺ which ash-Shāfiʿī had not put in his book. How many *sunnas* which have come from the Prophet ﷺ are not found in this *Musnad*! Whoever wants to find the ḥadīths of ash-Shāfiʿī in full should consult the book *Maʿrifat as-sunan wa'l-āthār* by al-Bayhaqī for he has pursued that in the most complete manner and did not fail to mention any ḥadīth in his (ash-Shāfiʿī's) books, whether old or new.

I say that along with that, if someone considers that he had few ḥadīths, it means

346 Shaykh Abū Ghudda has a lengthy footnote regarding this. *Qawāʾid,* pp. 361–380 fn. 5.

347 Refer to Shaykh Abū Ghudda's extensive notes on this from pp. 380–84 in the above work.

348 i.e. the *Musnad* of Ash-Shafiʿī.

that he related few ḥadīths (*qalīl at-taḥdīth*) and that he did not recount the ḥadīth as ḥadīth scholars did. He mentioned ḥadīth in his books while discussing rulings and cases. This does not mean that he had little knowledge of them. He was far from that for he was a great mujtahid imam. Ijtihād is not feasile for someone who has little knowledge of ḥadīth and narrations. This is the meaning of those who say that Abū Ḥanīfah had few ḥadīths, so understand this and do not be one of the igrnorant.

Adh-Dhahabī deals in full with those who are deemed unreliable (majrūḥūn) in al-Mīzān, so if he did not mention someone he is either trustworthy or concealed

Adh-Dhahabī said in *al-Mīzān*: "I did not think that I should elide anyone who is mentioned as being weak (*layyin*) in the books of those aforementioned imams fearing I would be criticized."

This tells us that his book contains all those who are unreliable. Thus if someone is not considered weak in *al-Mīzān*, then he is either trustworthy or concealed (*mastur*). He states in the biography of Isḥāq ibn Saᶜd ibn ᶜUbadah: "He transmits but is almost unrecognized. However, I did not mention in my book all of those who are not recognized. Rather I mentioned some of them, but have comprehensively mentioned all those who Abū Ḥātim mentioned as being unknown."

If only one person narrates from someone that does not preclude that person being trustworthy and used as an authority. A few of them will be mentioned in this chapter.

Adh-Dhahabī said in *al-Mīzān* in the biography of ᶜAbdullāh ibn ᶜAmr al-Makhzūmī al-ᶜĀbidī: "I do not know of anyone who narrated from him except for Muḥammad ibn ᶜAbbād ibn Jaᶜfar. He was truthful if Allah ﷻ wills."

He marked it with the symbol of Muslim and Abū Dāwūd[349] and indicated that he was sound (by writing the letters ṣ ḥ). That is an indication that one acts on the basis that that man was trustworthy, as al-Ḥāfiẓ stated in *al-Lisān*. This tells us that a man may be trustworthy and used as an authority even if only one person narrated from him.

He said in the biography of ᶜAbd al-Akram ibn Abī Ḥanīfah reporting from his father, and from whom Shuᶜbah reports that he is almost not recognised, but the shaykhs of Shuᶜbah are excellent.

He stated in the biography of ᶜAmr ibn Khuzaymah that only Hishām ibn ᶜUrwa narrated from him, but he is considered to be trustworthy. He marked him as being [a narrator] of Abū Dāwūd and Ibn Mājah.

He said in the biography of ᶜAbdullāh ibn Aws: "Abū Sulaymān al-Kaḥḥāl alone

349 In *Mīzān al-Iᶜtidāl*, adh-Dhahabī uses letters to indicate the six authentic collections if the narrator in question has been mentioned in any of them. Ed.

reports from him; Ibn al-Qaṭṭān stated that and said that he is majhūl. I say that he is truthful." He marked him as being [a narrator] of Abū Dāwūd and at-Tirmidhī.

We already mentioned the rule of Ibn Ḥibbān about someone from whom only one person narrated that when the one transmitting from him, and his shaykh (i.e. the one he is transmitting from) are trustworthy, that he considers him also to be trustworthy.

When someone says that a transmitter errs

Adh-Dhahabī mentioned what Ibn Ḥibbān said in *ath-Thiqāt* in the biography of ʿAbdullāh ibn Insān Abī Muḥammad, who reported from ʿUrwah and whose son narrated from him about hunting sand-grouse: "He used to err." Adh-Dhahabī said, "It is not proper for al-Ḥāfiẓ to say this except in respect of someone who had narrated a number of ḥadīths. As for this ʿAbdullāh, this ḥadīth is the first and last of what he has. If he erred, then his ḥadīth is rejected according to the rule of Ibn Ḥibbān.

I say that Ash-Shāfiʿī has authenticated his ḥadīth and relied upon him; and Abū Dāwūd mentioned him as a narrator.

Female transmitters are either concealed or trustworthy

Adh-Dhahabī stated in *al-Mīzān*: "I do not know of any women who are suspect nor whom they abandoned."

The book al-Mīzān was written to mention those who are weak, but it also contains some of those who are trustworthy in order to defend them

Adh-Dhahabī also says in it:

> The author, may Allah ﷻ seal his affair with righteous actions and forgive him, said that its basic subject matter is those who are weak, but it contains some people, as we already stated in the preface, who are trustworthy. I mentioned them in order to defend them, or because the criticism against them do not bring about weakness.

Sometimes the declaration of a narrator as weak is relative in respect of someone who is stronger than him

In the introduction of *al-Fatḥ* al-Ḥāfiẓ [Ibn Ḥajar] states in the biography of ʿAbd ar-Raḥmān ibn Sulayman, known as Ibn al-Ghasīl, after mentioning the statements of those who consider him to weak: "They consider him weak in respect to those of his contemporaries who are more reliable than him." One should be aware of this.

Refutation of Ibn Saʿd's and al-Wāqidī's declaration of some transmitters as weak

Al-Ḥāfiẓ also stated in the biography of ʿAbd ar-Raḥmān ibn Shurayḥ: "Ibn Saʿd took an unusual view, claiming that he has unknown ḥadīth. I say that no one pays any attention to Ibn Saᶜd in this. Most of his material is from al-Wāqidī, and al-Wāqidī is not reliable. The Community use him [ᶜAbd ar-Raḥmān] as an authority."

The meaning of the statement of Aḥmad about a transmitter: "He is not one of the people with memory."

Al-Ḥāfiẓ also stated in the biography of ᶜAbd al-ᶜAzīz ibn ᶜUmar ibn ᶜAbd al-ᶜAzīz: "Al-Khaṭṭābī narrated that Aḥmad said, 'He is not one of the people with memory,' meaning by that that he does not have extensively memorised material,[350] for Ibn Maᶜīn has said, 'He is reliable and narrated a small amount.'"

A judgement of soundness or weakness is a matter of ijtihād in which people can disagree. Criticisms of the two Ṣaḥīḥ Collections are thus

Al-Ḥāfiẓ stated in the introduction of *al-Fatḥ*:

> An-Nawawī said in the preface to the commentary of al-Bukhārī: "Ad-Dāraquṭnī reviewed a number of ḥadīth of al-Bukhārī and Muslim, and criticised some of them. That criticism was based on the rules of some of the ḥadīth scholars which are very weak indeed and in opposition to the majority of the people of *fiqh*, *uṣūl*, and others, so do not be deluded by that."

I say that this shows you that the *fuqahā᾽* and *uṣūlīs* have rules in ḥadīth which were followed and relied upon by the two shaykhs in ascertaining the soundness of ḥadīths. It also contains evidence that a judgement of soundness or weakness is a matter of *ijtihād*.

The precedence of the shaykhs of the two shaykhs, who were imams, in the craft [of ḥadīth]

Al-Ḥāfiẓ said also in it:

> There is no doubt about the precedence of al-Bukhārī and then Muslim in recognition of the sound and faulty over the people of their time and those after them among the imams of this science. They do not disagree that ᶜAlī ibn al-Madīnī was the most knowledgeable of his contemporaries about the defects of ḥadīth, and al-Bukhārī learned that from him. Muḥammad ibn Yaḥyā adh-Dhuhlī was the most knowledgeable of the people of his time about the defects of the ḥadīths of az-Zuhrī. Both of the two shaykhs learned that from him.

I say that by that it is known that they did not precede their shaykhs and others who came before them.

---

350 Not that he does not have a strong and reliable memory. Ed.

Types of criticism [of transmitters] and faults in ḥadīth some of which have effect and some do not, and which occur in the two Ṣaḥīḥ Collections.

Disparagement (*ṭaʿn*) in ḥadīths: sometimes happens because of transmitters differing about it [one ḥadīth] by adding or removing men in the *isnād*. Detecting a defect due to the deficient path (i.e. the path from which a narrator has been omitted) is thus rejected, because if the transmitter had indeed heard it, an addition does not harm it because he may have heard it from his shaykh through an intermediary and then met the shaykh and heard it from him.[351] If he had not listened to him in the deficient path [of transmission], then the report is disconnected (*munqaṭiʿ*, missing a transmitter). The *munqaṭiʿ* falls into the category of the weak, and a weak (ḥadīth) does not render the sound (*ṣaḥīḥ*) deficient.[352]

A fault caused by an increased path of transmission (meaning the path in which there is an additional narrator) can be sound when the missing link in the deficient path is apparent. One should investigate whether that transmitter is a Companion or a trustworthy person who does not practise *tadlīs* (misrepresentation) and who clearly met the one from whom he transmits, or explicitly stated that he heard it by another path if he practices tadlīs. If that exists, then the objection is refuted by that. If it does not exist, then the break is apparent.

The author of the *Ṣaḥīḥ* may transmit the like of that in the category of that which has a corroborating (*mutābiʿ*) or attesting (*shāhid*) narration, or general contextual causes which strengthen it, and it is declared to be sound in respect to the whole.

It sometimes happens that some critics find fault in ḥadīths in which breakage (*inqiṭāʿ*) is claimed because they have not been received through audition (*simāʿ*), as is the case with ḥadīths that are transmitted by *ijāza* and through written material. This does not necessitate breakage in the view of those who permit transmission by *ijāza*. In fact that the author of the *Ṣaḥīḥ* transmits that is evidence for the validity of transmission by *ijāza* in his opinion.

Sometimes it (disparagement/*ṭaʿn*) occurs by the differing of transmitters in the ḥadīth by changing of some men in part of the *isnād*. The answer to that is that it may be possible to consolidate them so that that transmitter has the ḥadīth in both [differing] ways. This is when those who are differing in that are equal in memory and number. If it is impossible [to consolidate] because those who are differing are

351 Thus the path that seems to have a narrator omitted in fact only reflects the fact that the narrator had also heard it directly from the shaykh. So no omission has actally taken place and thus no defect exists in the ḥadīth. Ed.

352 Since one narrator has a verson that does not have the deficiency, his version is the authentic version; the one with the deficiency is the *munqaṭiʿ*. The two are entirely separate paths and thus deficiency in one does not affect the other. So one cannot argue that the ḥadīth is defective because of a different of opinion about a missing narrator because the difference need not be about the same path. Ed.

not equal, but close in memory and number, then the sound one is the preponderant and the other is ignored.

Finding fault by all of that just because of difference does not actually impair it since it is not necessary that a difference alone is an irreconcilable contradition (*iḍṭirāb*) which causes weakness, and so one must ignore that which is such.

At times it (disparagement/*ṭaʿn*) may occur because of a trustworthy transmitter alone having an addition in it contrary to those greater in number or more accurate who did not mention it. This does not render it defective unless the addition is contradictory and consolidation is not possible. However if the addition is not contradictory so that it is like a separate ḥadīth, then that is not the case, unless there are clear strong proofs that that addition is inserted into the text from the words of one of its transmitters. Whatever is of this type does have an effect.

Sometimes it may occur because one of the weak transmitters alone has the addition. Two ḥadīths of this sort are found in the *Ṣaḥīḥ*. It is clear that each of them has been corroborated.

It may occur because one of its men may be judged to be weak. Some of these weaknesses are deemed [valid] criticisms and some are not.

It may occur because of a difference in it due to an alteration in some of the words of the text. Most of this does not constitute a (valid) criticism against it since it is possible to consolidate the point of difference or give preponderance to one.

Their statement about a transmitter laysa bidhāka al-qawiyy (He is not that strong) is a soft attribution of weakness

Also in the above-mentioned introduction, al-Ḥāfiẓ stated in the biography of Aḥmad ibn Bashīr al-Kūfī that an-Nasāʾī said, "He is not that strong." He then said, "As for the fact that an-Nasāʾī declared him weak, it indicates that he was not a ḥāfiẓ. This does not necessitate that that transmitter is entirely weak."[353]

Assessment of character (jarḥ wa taʿdīl) is based on opinion; sometimes a detractor criticises in error and assumption, and examples of that

He said in the biography of Aḥmad ibn Ṣāliḥ al-Miṣrī Abū Jaʿfar ibn aṭ-Ṭabarī:

> One of the imams of ḥadīth and meticulous *ḥuffāẓ*. An-Nasāʾī had a bad opinion of him. He once mentioned him and said, "He is neither reliable nor trustworthy." Muʿāwiyah ibn Ṣāliḥ told me, "I asked Yaḥyā ibn Maʿīn about Aḥmad ibn Ṣāliḥ," and he said, "He is a liar who pursues philosophy. I saw him walking arrogantly in the mosque in Egypt." So in declaring that he was weak, an-Nasāʾī relied on what he (Muʿāwiyah ibn Ṣāliḥ)

353 This statement is a soft attribution of weakness deemed, as a disparagement, to be lower or softer than statements such as, *fulānun ḍaʿīf al-ḥadīth* (so and so is weak in ḥadīth).

> reported to him from Yaḥyā ibn Maʿīn. It is an incorrection assumption on his part which his bad opinion of Aḥmad ibn Ṣāliḥ moved him to believe.

Then he mentioned the reason which caused him to have a bad opinion of him. He mentioned that Ibn Ḥibbān said, "What an-Nasā'ī narrated from Ibn Maʿīn in respect of Aḥmad ibn Ṣāliḥ is a misgiving. That is because this Aḥmad ibn Ṣāliḥ about whom Ibn Maʿīn spoke was someone other than Ibn aṭ-Ṭabarī. He used to be called al-Ushmūnī, and was known for fabricating ḥadīths."

I say that Al-Ḥāfiẓ mentioned something similar in the biography of Aḥmad ibn Bashīr al-Kūfī after first mentioning ʿUthmān ad-Dārimī's statement that he is abandoned. He then said, "As for what ʿUthmān ad-Dārimī said, al-Khaṭīb rejected it since he confused him with another transmitter who happens to have the same name and the same paternal name. It is as al-Khaṭīb, may Allah ﷻ have mercy on him, said."

By that it is clear that assessment of character (*jarḥ wa taʿdīl*) is based on opinion. Sometimes a critic will declare someone impaired based on error and asumption, so that should be known.

Visiting a ruler out of need does not impair character

He also says in the biography of Aḥmad ibn ʿAbd al-Malik al-Ḥarrānī, that al-Maymūnī said, "I told Aḥmad, 'The people of Harran speak badly of him.' He replied, 'The people of Harran are rarely pleased with anyone. He visited the ruler because of an estate of his.'"

Aḥmad clearly states the reason why the people of Harran attacked him, which does not impair him.

The bias of the people of Madina, including al-Wāqidī and Ibn Saʿd, against the people of Iraq

He stated in the biography of Muḥārib ibn Dithār that Ibn Saʿd said that he is not used as an authority. I say that all the Imams use him as an authority, but Ibn Saʿd imitated al-Wāqidī, and al-Wāqidī followed the path of the people of Madina in being bias against the people of Iraq. Know that and you will be guided, Allah ﷻ willing

Recognition of vicissitudes (taṣārīf) in the language of the Arabs is a precondition for someone who knows jarḥ and taʿdīl

He said in the biography of ʿIkrimah, the client of Ibn ʿAbbās, quoting Ibn Jarīr aṭ-Ṭabarī:

> If someone's good character has been confirmed, then any deprecation of him is not accepted. Good character is not cancelled by supposition or by the words of a per-

son to his client, "Do not lie about me," and similar words which can have different aspects, usages and meanings other than the one assumed by stupid people and those who do not know the variations in the language of the Arabs.

I say that to understand the words of the critics it is necessary to be familiar with the variations of the language of the Arabs.

Abū Zurᶜa criticized someone without explaining the reason, and the hypercriticism of an-Nasāʾī

He said in the biography of Aḥmad ibn ᶜĪsā at-Tustarī: "Abū Zurᶜa criticized Muslim in the transmission of his ḥadīth but did not clarify the reason for that yet An-Nasāʾī used him as an authority in spite of his hypercriticism.

In corroborating texts (mutābaᶜah) one overlooks that which one does not overlook in primary texts, and al-Bukhārī only narrated from someone trustworthy

He said in the biography of Aḥmad ibn Yazīd ibn Ibrāhīm al-Ḥarrānī, whom he considered weak in reporting from Abū Ḥātim: "I met him but I did not write from him the text: 'Al-Bukhārī transmitted from him in corroborating texts, not in primary texts, although al-Bukhārī met Aḥmad and narrated from him in *at-Tāʾrīkh*, and so he knew his ḥadīths.'"

I say that it is can be known this that in corroboration, one tolerates what one does not tolerate in primary texts and that Al-Bukhārī only narrated from someone he considered to be trustworthy.

Their statement, "He is not the strongest there is" is a relative weakening

He said in the biography of Ibrāhīm ibn Yūsuf ibn Isḥāq as-Sābiᶜī that Ibn al-Madīnī said, "He is not the strongest there is." This is a relative weakening.

Recognition by al-Bukhārī is enough to render a ḥadīth ṣaḥīḥ and men trustworthy, and the same is true of those scholars like him

He stated in the biography of Asbāṭ Abū al-Yasaᶜ that Abū Ḥātim said that he is unkhown (*majhūl*). I say that al-Bukhārī recognized him.

I say that this tells us that recognition by al-Bukhārī is enough to render a ḥadīth *ṣaḥīḥ* and men trustworthy. The same is true of scholars like him or better than him, like Shuᶜbah, Mālik, Abū Ḥanīfah, ash-Shāfiᶜī, Aḥmad [ibn Ḥanbal] and others.

A later person deprecating someone is not considered when an earlier person declared someone to be trustworthy

He (Ibn Ḥajar) stated in the biography of Israʾīl ibn Yūnus ibn Abī Isḥāq as-Sabīᶜī, after mentioning the fact that the imams considered him to be trustworthy and mentioning that al-Qaṭṭān attacked him regarding the state of Abū Yaḥyā al-Qattāt saying that he narrated *munkar* ḥadīths from him, in the words:

> This is the praise said about him. After that [praise] is confirmed and his being used as an authority by the two shaykh [al-Bukhārī and Muslim], it is not appropriate for a later person who has no knowledge of the truth of the state of someone before him to deem Isra ͗īl to be weak and reject the sound ḥadīths which he always narrated, because of his (the later person's) dependence upon al-Qaṭṭān's attack on him without knowing the reason for that attack.

Ibn Abī Khaythamah said in his *Tarikh*,

> Yaḥyā ibn Ma ͑īn was told, "Isra ͗īl narrated three hundred from Abū Yaḥyā al-Qattāt and three hundred from Ibrāhīm ibn Muhājir," meaning *munkar* ḥadīths. He said, "it did not come from him but from them." Thus what al-Qaṭṭān said is taken on the supposition that the *munkar* was from him, when they were from Abū Yaḥyā, as Ibn Ma ͑īn said.

I say that this contains evidence that deprecation by a later person is not considered when someone has been praised by earlier scholars, and deprecation which is not explained has no effect when the imams' have validated good character.

One does not listen to what an innovator says about an innovator, like what a Nāṣibī says about a Shi ͑ite

He said in the biography of Ismā ͑īl ibn Abān al-Warrāq al-Kūfī after mentioning al-Jūzajānī's statement about him that: "He inclined away from the truth," in the words: "Al-Jūzajanī was a Nāṣibī who deviated from ͑Alī, so he was the opposite of a Shi ͑ite who deviated from ͑Uthmān, when the correct position is to show good will towards both, and one should not listen to what an innovator says about another innovator.

That which al-Bukhārī narrated in his Ṣaḥīḥ from the ḥadīths of Ismā ͑īl ibn Abī Uways are from his ṣaḥīḥ ḥadīths; the transmitters of the two Ṣaḥīḥ collections are not unrestrictedly used as evidence, but rather done with well known conditions

He said in the biography of Ismā ͑īl ibn Abī Uways ibn Ukht Mālik:

> The two Shaykhs used him as an authority. The rest narrated from him except for an-Nasā'ī, who took the view outright that he is abandoned. Something was narrated from Salama ibn Shabīb that requires that his ḥadīths be discarded. We narrated in

> the Virtues of al-Bukhārī with a sound *isnād* that Ismāʿīl took out his original manuscripts and gave him permission to select from them, and teach according to what he narrated so that he would narrate that and turn from other than it. This tells us that what al-Bukhārī transmitted from him is from his sound ḥadīth because he wrote from his original manuscript. According to this, none of his ḥadīths are used except what is in the *Ṣaḥīḥ* because of the criticisms of him by an-Nasāʾī and others, except for reports which are shared by others and so are considered.

I say this tells us that the transmitters of the *Ṣaḥīḥ* are not used unconditionally by ḥadīth scholars as authoritative; rather they are used with known conditions.

The two shaykhs [al-Bukhārī and Muslim] sometimes narrate that on whose weakness there is consensus in conjunction with others

He said in the biography of Asīd ibn Zayd al-Jammāl: "I did not see anyone who declared him trustworthy (rather all of them considered him weak). In *Kitāb ar-Riqāq*, al-Bukhārī narrated from him one ḥadīth in conjunction with others."

I say, if the author of the *Ṣaḥīḥ* narrated from someone in conjunction with others, he could be someone about whose weakness there is consensus, and you should know that.

The words of al-Bukhārī, "its isnād is questionable," does not necessitate that the transmitter is weak in general

He states in the biography of Aws ibn ʿAbdullāh ar-Rabaʿī: "Ibn ʿAdī mentioned him in *al-Kāmil* and narrated that al-Bukhārī said, 'its *isnād* is questionable and they disagree about.' Then Ibn ʿAdī explained what al-Bukhārī meant: 'He means that he did not hear [ḥadīth] from the likes of Ibn Masʿūd, ʿĀʾisha and others, not that he is weak in his opinion.'"

I say, al-Bukhārī's statement "it is questionable" and "its *isnād* is questionable" does not necessitate that the transmitter is unconditionally weak.

The fact that the transmitter is an innovator does not detract from his transmission unless he lied or was a caller [to his innovation]

He said in the biography of Thawr ibn Zayd ad-Dīlī: "Mālik was asked, 'How can you narrate from Dāwūd ibn al-Ḥuṣayn and Thawr ibn Zayd and others when they espoused the Qadarī view?' He replied, 'because they were such that it would be easier for them to fall from heaven to earth than lie.'"

I say thus, that the fact that a man is suspected of innovation does not affect his transmission unless he used to lie or was a missionary (*dāʿiyah*).

A person of good character (ʿadl) is not impaired by the statement of someone whose character is impaired, nor does detraction by al-Bayhaqī affect those whom the Community use as an authority

He said in the biography of Jarīr ibn ʿAbd al-Ḥamīd ibn Qurṭ aḍ-Ḍabbī:

> Abu Khaythamah said that he did not use *tadlīs* (concealment in the transmission), but ash-Shādhakūnī narrated from him that which indicates *tadlīs*. However things [critical] are said about ash-Shādhakūnī. Al-Bayhaqī said (about ʿAbd al-Ḥamīd), "He was said to have a poor memory at the end of his life." I did not see anyone else say that. Instead, the Community use him as an authoritative.

I say that a person of good character is not impaired by the statement of someone whose character is impaired, and someone ho is used as an authority by the Community is not affected by the statement of someone like al-Bayhaqī.

An example of a declaration of weakness which is rejected

He said in the biography of al-Jaʿd ibn ʿAbd ar-Raḥmān, "The five [main collections] use him as an authority. Al-Azdī took an aberrant position and said that he is questionable, following as-Sājī in that because he mentioned him among the weak, saying, 'Mālik did not narrate from him.' This declaration of weakness is rejected."

I say that one does not pay any attention to the like of this.

Types of weakness in the transmitter which are mended by corroboration

It is clear to anyone who reads the answers of al-Ḥāfiẓ about the statements of those who detract from the character of the transmitters of the *Ṣaḥīḥ* that when he narrates the statements of a detractor such as: 'he narrates *munkar* ḥadīth', 'he alone narrated some ḥadīths from so and so', 'he is weak' and 'he is not strong', he answers him by saying that the author of the *Ṣaḥīḥ* transmitted his ḥadīths for which there is corroboration (*mutābaʿah*) but did not transmit any of the ḥadīths in which he is alone.

In short, their statement that his ḥadīths are *munkar* or something similar does not affect the transmission of the transmitter unless there is no follow-up of his transmission. Understand that.

Their statement about a transmitter, "He is not strong" is a soft declaration of weakness

Al-Ḥāfiẓ said in the biography of al-Ḥasan ibn as-Sabbāḥ al-Bazzār that an-Nasāʾī said in *al-Kunā*: "He is not strong." I say, 'this is a soft declaration of weakness'.

The silence of Abū Zurʿa or Abū Ḥātim about the deprecation of a transmitter makes him trustworthy; a deprecator declaring a transmitter to be a liar has no effect on him unless the accusation is explained

He said in the biography of al-Ḥasan ibn Mudrik as-Sadūsī: "Abū ʿUbayd al-Ājurrī stated narrating from Abū Dawūd, 'He was a liar who took the ḥadīths of Fahd ibn ʿAwf and gave them to Yaḥyā ibn Ḥammād.' I say, if Abu Dāwūd's source for his lying is this action, then it does not necessitate that he was lying because both Yaḥyā ibn Ḥammād and Fahd ibn ʿAwf were both among the companions of Abū ʿAwāna. A student may ask his shaykh about a ḥadīth his companion has to ascertain whether it is part of what he heard, then he may or may not have narrated it to him. How can he be a liar because of that? Abū Zurʿa and Abū Ḥātim wrote from him, and they did not mention any deprecation of him and they are who they are in criticism.

I say that the fact that a detractor declares one of the transmitters to be a liar does not have any effect on him unless that is explained and is not unclear. The fact that Abū Zurʿa and Abū Ḥātim wrote from someone while being silent about any criticism of him renders him trustworthy, as was already mentioned.

One does not pay attention to an assumption of deprecation when there is a clear declaration of trustworthiness

He said in the biography of al-Ḥasan ibn Mūsā al-Ashyab: "One of reliable ones. ʿAbdullāh ibn ʿAlī ibn al-Madīnī narrated that his father said, 'He was at Baghdad,' as if he declared him to be weak. I say that this is mere speculation which is not authoritative."

I say that one does not pay any attention to speculation when there is a clear statement that someone is trustworthy.

Contradiction (iḍṭirāb) when it is in those who transmit from a shaykh does not affect the shaykh

He states in the biography of al-Ḥusayn ibn Dhakwān al-Muʿallim: "Yaḥyā al-Qaṭṭān said that there is *iḍṭirāb* in him. I say perhaps the *iḍṭirāb* is in those who transmit [from him] because the Imams use him as an authority."

I say, this sort of deprecation has no effect on someone the imams deem authoritative. Allah ﷻ knows best.

Ḥafṣ ibn Ghiyāth distinguishes between that which al-Aʿmash heard and his tadlīs

He states in the biography of Ḥafṣ ibn Ghiyath al-Kufi al-Ḥanafi: "Al-Bukhāri relied on this Ḥafṣ in the ḥadīths of al-Aʿmash because he used to distinguish between what al-Aʿmash clearly stated that he had heard and that in which he had concealed a narrator (*tadlīs*). Abū'l-Faḍl ibn Ṭāhir called attention to that, and it is as he said, "The Group narrated his ḥadīth."

I say, this is a distinction of Ḥafṣ ibn Ghiyāth, who was one of the eminent companions of Imam Abū Ḥanīfah.

If the person carrying out the deprecation is weak and the person deprecated is trustworthy, then no consideration is given to his deprecation. This is the case with the attacks which were made on Abū Ḥanīfah

He said in the biography of Ḥammād ibn Usāma Abu Usāma:

> He is one of the reliable imams. Al-Azdī took an aberrant position and mentioned him among the weak, he narrated that Sufyān ibn Wakīʿ said: 'Abū Usāma used to study the books of transmitters, take them and copy them. This Sufyān ibn Wakīʿ is weak and not given any consideration, as the one who quoted him, al-Azdī, is not given any consideration, even though he mentioned this from Ibn Wakīʿ with an *isnād*. The words 'Ibn Wakīʿ' are omitted from the copy which adh-Dhahabī came across of the book of al-Azdī, so he thought that he narrated it from Sufyān ath-Thawrī, and was surprised at that. Then he said, "It is a false statement."

I say that one does not pay any attention to this sort of deprecation in respect of Abū Ḥanīfah either since most of it is transmitted from the weak and unknown, so all of it is false.

The reason why al-Bukhārī changed from "So-and-so narrated to us (ḥaddathanā)" to "So-and-so told us (qāla lanā)"

He states in the biography of Hammād ibn Salama ibn Dīnār:

> He was one of the reliable imams although his memory was bad at the end of his life. Al-Bukhārī employed him [his narration] marginally[*taʿlīqan*)[354] but did not transmit from him as supporting evidence, nor in conjunction or corroboration except in one place in which he said, 'Abū'l-Walīd told us that Hammād ibn Salama narrated to him,' and he mentioned it in *ar-Riqāq*. This word ('he told us') is used by al-Bukhārī in *maqwūf* ḥadīths only, and in *marfūʿ* ḥadīths if the *isnād* contains someone whom he does not consider an authority.

So one should take note of that.

Entering the employment of the ruler, if it is permitted legally, does not impair good character

He said in the biography of Ḥumayd aṭ-Ṭawīl narrating form Yaḥyā ibn Yaʿlā al-Muḥāribī:

---

354 *Taʿlīq* are those narrations found in the the *Ṣaḥīḥ al-Bukhārī* which fall short of al-Bukhārī's conditions for a *ṣaḥīḥ* ḥadīth but nevertheless he uses them marginally such as in the title to a chapter. For example in the book of Divorce one of the chapter heading reads 'No divorce before marriage'. The chapter is void of any ḥadīth however the chapter heading itself is a ḥadith found in the *Sunan Ibn Mājah*. Methodologically al-Bukhārī was unable to include this ḥadīth in the main body of his text because of it falling short of his conditions, however he used it peripherally (*taʿlīqan*) for further support of his case. Ed.

> Zā'ida rejected his ḥadīth. I say that Zā'ida abandoned it because of his involvement in a matter pertaining to the Caliphs. Makkī ibn Ibrāhīm explained that. He said something similar in the biography of Humayd ibn Hilāl: "Al-Qaṭṭān said that Ibn Sīrīn was not satisfied with him." I say that Abū Ḥātim ar-Rāzī explained that the reason for that was that he was engaged in some employment for the Caliph. A group [of scholars] have used him as an authority.

This means that that did not impair him at all.

Extreme Shiᶜism does not cause impairment if the transmitter is trustworthy

He said in the biography of Khālid ibn Makhlad al-Qaṭawānī that he was suspected of extreme Shiᶜism: "As for Shiᶜism, we already mentioned that if he is reliable when receiving and conveying [ḥadīth], his Shiᶜism does not impair him, especially if he was not a missionary [to it]."

Thus extreme Shiᶜism does not impair the transmitter when he is trustworthy.

An example of the harshness of Ibn Ḥazm in depraction

He said in the biography of Khuthaym ibn ᶜIrāk: "Azdī took an aberrant position and stated that his ḥadīth are *munkar*. Abū Muḥammad ibn Ḥazm was careless and followed al-Azdī and was excessive. He stated, 'It is not permitted to transmit from him.' He did not know that al-Azdī was weak, so how can one accept him declaring trustworthy men to be weak?'"

I say that this shows the harshness of Ibn Ḥazm in deprecation.

A large number of deprecators is not a general cause which demands the impairment of the transmitter

He said in the biography of Rawḥ ibn ᶜUbāda al-Qaysy: "Abū Masᶜūd said that twelve men attacked him but their words had no effect on him. He is used as an authority by all of the imams."

Thus a large number of detractors does not constitute a general cause.

A difference between [the words] 'he abandoned him (tarakahu)' and 'he did not narrate from him (lam yarwih ᶜanhu)'

He said in the biography of az-Zubayr ibn Khirrīt al-Baṣrī: "Al-Bājī narrated in *Rijāl al-Bukhārī* that ᶜAlī ibn al-Madīnī said, 'Shuᶜbah abandoned him.' I say that what I saw was that ᶜAlī said, 'Shuᶜbah did not narrate from him.' There is a difference between the two expressions.

One should take note of this difference.

The fact that a transmitter is weak does not necessitate that he is weak in all his transmissions
He said in the biography of Ziyād ibn ʿAbdullāh ibn aṭ-Ṭufayl al-Āmirī: "Ṣāliḥ Jazara said, 'Ziyād is weak in himself, but he is the firmest of people in *Kitāb al-Maghāzī.*' ʿAbdullāh ibn Idrīs said, 'I did not find anyone firmer about Isḥāq (the author of al-Maghāzī) than him.' Ibn Ḥibbān was excessive and said, 'It is not permitted to use his report as an authority if he alone has it."

Thus the fact that the transmitter is weak does not necessitate that he is weak in all of his reports.

An example of deprecation arising from unsound understanding
He said in the biography of Zayd ibn Wahb al-Juhanī:

> Yaʿqūb al-Fasawī took an aberrant position and said that there were a lot of discrepancies in his ḥadīths. Then he mentioned the words of ʿUmar—in his ḥadīth—"Ḥudhayfa, by Allah ﷻ, I am one of the hypocrites?" Al-Fasawī said, "This is impossible."
>
> I say, "This is an additional form of excessiveness. This sort of thing does not render reliable scholars weak or cause sound ḥadīths to be rejected. ʿUmar said this when overcome by intense fear and sense of insecurity about being deceived. One does not pay any attention to these unsound whisperings which deem those who are reliable to be weak."

The harshness of Ibn Ḥibbān in deprecation, and his usage of words
He said in the biography of Sālim al-Afṭas:

> Ibn Ḥibbān was excessive and said about him: "He was a Murjiʾite who changed reports, and alone had puzzling reports from trustworthy scholars. He was accused of something evil and was killed in captivity." So this evil business that Ibn Ḥibbān claimed that he was accused of was the fact that he was in favour of the killing of Ibrāhīm (the Imam). As for what he said about him changing reports and other things, that is rejected because the imams consider him to be trustworthy. Ibn Ḥibbān cannot report one ḥadīth from him.

It is thus confirmed that Ibn Ḥibbān was harsh and that the likes of such accusations have no effect.

The ruling about uncertainty as to whether a transmitter listened to a report before or after he began to muddle things
He said in the biography of Saʿīd Ibn Iyās al-Jurayrī:

> Abū Ḥātim said, "He changed before he died, so if someone wrote from him in ear-

> lier times, his listening was sound." Al-ʿIjlī said: "ʿAbd al-Aʿlā was the soundest of them in relating ḥadīth from him. He listened to him eight years before he began to muddle things." Al-Bukhārī only transmitted his ḥadīth from ʿAbd al-Aʿlā, ʿAbd al-Wārith and Bishr ibn al-Mufaḍḍal. These men listened to him before he muddled things. Furthermore al-Bukhārī also took his ḥadīth from the transmission of Khālid al-Wāsiṭī from him. His position is not yet clear to me as to whether he listened to him before or after he muddled things. However, his ḥadīth from him is with a corroborating narration from Bishr ibn al-Mufaḍḍal.

I say, this is an extraordinary point, so remember it. It contains evidence that hesitation about whether a person listened to someone before or after he muddled things does not necessitate that the ḥadīth is weak.

The transmission of the seniors from among the companions of someone who muddled things is taken as sound

He said in the biography of Saʿīd ibn Abī Saʿīd al-Maqburī:

> Shuʿbah said, 'Saʿīd al-Maqburī narrated to us after he was old', and al-Wāqidī claimed that he muddled things four years before he died. Ibn Saʿd, Yaʿqūb and Ibn Ḥibbān followed him in that, while others objected to it. Ibn Maʿīn said, "Ibn Abī Dhiʾb is the firmest of people in his reports." Ibn Khirāsh said, "Al-Layth ibn Saʿd is the firmest of people in his reports." I say most of what al-Bukhārī transmitted from him is from the ḥadīth of these two men. He also transmitted the ḥadīth of Mālik, Ismāʿīl ibn Umayya, ʿUbaydullāh ibn ʿUmar al-ʿUmarī and other great men.

Thus the transmission of senior ulama from among the companions of someone who muddled things is taken to be sound.

An unclear declaration that someone is weak is not accepted

He said in the biography of Saʿīd ibn Sulaymān al-Wāsiṭī: "ʿAbdullāh ibn Aḥmad reported from his father: 'he was someone who distorted whatever you wanted.' Ad-Dāraquṭnī said, 'They said things about him.' I say this is unclear deprecation which is not accepted."

When al-Bukhārī narrated from someone who muddled things, he narrated his ḥadīths before his confusion; after the time when he became confused, he selected from his ḥadīths those on which they agreed

He said in the biography of Saʿīd ibn Abī ʿArūbah:

> Abū Nuʿaym said, "I listened to him after he muddled things." I say, al-Bukhārī only transmitted one of his ḥadīth from someone other than Qatādah (and he is the firm-

> est of people in Qatādah). As for what al-Bukhārī transmitted of his ḥadīths from Qatādah, most of it is from the transmission of those who listened to him before he muddled things. He transmitted a little from those who listened to him after he muddled, like Muḥammad ibn ʿAbdullāh al-Anṣārī, Rawḥ ibn ʿUbādah, and Ibn Abī ʿAdī. But when he transmitted from the ḥadīths of these men, he selected from them those on which they agreed. The rest use Saʿīd as an authority.

I say, this is an extraordinary point that should be remembered.

Deprecation is only accepted after confirmation
He said in the biography of Ṣāliḥ ibn Ḥayy:

> Al-ʿIjlī said in another place, "His ḥadīth are written, but he is not strong." I say this is how it is in *Tahdhīb al-kamāl* that al-ʿIjlī mentioned him in two places, but that is not the case. Rather his first words are about the subject of the biography (Salih ibn Hayy), and I have not seen anyone at all say anything about him. Aḥmad said, "He is very trustworthy (*thiqatun thiqah*)." This is the highest form of validation of character. As for his latter words, they were about Ṣāliḥ ibn Ḥayyān al-Qurashī.
>
> These two men are so similar that it was thought that they were the same person because they were contemporaries from the same land. The subject of the biography (Salih ibn Hayy) was known for transmission from ash-Shaʿbī not al-Qurashī. The Group (*jamaʿah*) accept Ibn Ḥayy as an authority.

Thus deprecation is only accepted after confirmation.

A transmitter's memorisation of ḥadīth is not a precondition for the soundness of his ḥadīth
He stated in the biography of ʿĀṣim ibn Abī an-Nujūd: "Al-Bazzār said, 'We do not know of anyone who abandoned his ḥadīths although he was not a ḥāfiẓ.'"

So memorization is not a precondition for the validity of ḥadīths.

Having an appointment in the market inspection (ḥisba) does not impair character
He said in the biography of ʿĀṣim ibn Sulaymān al-Aḥwal:

> Ibn Idrīs said, "I saw him come to the market and say, 'Take this down. Set this right.' I therefore do not narrate anything from him. Wuhayb abandoned him because he objected to some of his conduct." I say, he had charge of the [market inspection] in Kufa, as Ibn Saʿd mentioned. The Community use him as an authority.

I say, the like of that does not impair character at all.

The words of Ibn Maʿīn, "Every ʿĀṣim among transmitters is weak" is not generally applicable

He said in the biography of "ʿĀṣim ibn ʿAlī al-Wāsiṭī: "Al-Marrūdhī said, 'I told Aḥmad, "Yaḥyā ibn Maʿīn says, 'Every ʿĀṣim in this world is weak.'" He replied, "I only know good of ʿĀṣim ibn ʿAlī. His ḥadīth were sound."'"

I say this statement of Ibn Maʿīn is not generally applicable.

Deprecation arising from worldly enmity is not considered

He said in the biography of ʿAbdullāh ibn Dhakwān:

> It is said that Mālik disliked him because he worked for the ruler. Rabīʿat ar-Raʾy said, "He is not trustworthy." I say people did not pay any attention to Rabīʿah in that view because of the enmity which existed between the two of them. Instead they consider him to be trustworthy. Sufyān called him "the amir of the believers."

Thus deprecation which arises from worldly enmity is not considered.

Al-Ismāʿīlī's criticism of al-Bukhārī against his peripheral (taʿlīq) use of ʿAbdullāh ibn Ṣāliḥ al-Juhanī and the response to that

He said in the biography of ʿAbdullāh ibn Ṣāliḥ al-Juhanī:

> The scribe of al-Layth whom al-Bukhārī met and he took a lot from him. He does not meet his preconditions in the *Ṣaḥīḥ*, even though he considers his ḥadīths to be sound. He only reports one ḥadīth from him in his book, but he takes other material from him in the margins as al-Ḥāfiẓ al-Mizzī and others mentioned.

Then he mentioned the statements of those who declare his good character and those who deprecate him until he said:

> As for the marginal use from al-Layth from the transmission of ʿAbdullāh ibn Ṣāliḥ from him, there is a great deal of it. Al-Ismāʿīlī criticized al-Bukhārī for that and expressed surprise at how he used his ḥadīths as authoritative by using them additionally in the chapter headings. He said, "It is extraordinary that he used him as an authoritative when it is severed (*munqaṭiʿ*) and he is not used as authoritative when it is connected. The answer to that is, as we have already confirmed, al-Bukhārī did that because the ḥadīths that he used are sound in his view. He selected them from among his [ʿAbdullāh ibn Ṣāliḥ] ḥadīths, but they do not meet his preconditions that are the highest preconditions of soundness. This is why he does not use them in the main text of the book; this is a technical usage by him [al-Bukhārī] that has been discovered upon examination of his method. That is not objectionable.

An example of rejected unclear deprecation

He said in the biography of ʿAbd al-Aʿlā al-Baṣrī: "Ibn Maʿīn and others declared him to be trustworthy. Aḥmad said, 'He used to be accused of espousing the Qadari doctrine.' Muḥammad ibn Saʿd said, 'He was not strong.' I say this is a rejected deprecation and is unexplained; perhaps it was because of the Qadari doctrine."

An example of the relative weakening

He said in the biography of ʿAbd Rabbihi ibn Nāfiʿ: "The Group, except for at-Tirmidhī used him as an authority. It is clear that weakening on the part of those who declare him weak is in relation to his contemporaries, like Abū ʿAwāna and the likes of him."

I say, this sort of deprecation often occurs. Al-Ḥāfiẓ also mentioned something similar in the biography of ʿAbd ar-Raḥmān ibn Sulaymān, who is known as Ibn al-Ghasīl.

Among the narrators in the two Ṣaḥīḥ Collections are those who only have one narrator

He said in the biography of ʿAbd ar-Raḥmān ibn Namir al-Yaḥṣubī: "Abū Ḥātim, Duḥaym and adh-Dhuhlī said, 'Only al-Walīd ibn Muslim narrated from him.' Adh-Dhuhalī, al-Barqī and Abū Dāwūd considered him to be trustworthy. Ibn Maʿīn said that he is weak. Abū Ḥātim said that he is not strong."

I say the two Shaykhs [al-Bukhārī and Muslim], Abū Dāwūd and an-Nasāʾī narrated from him. This shows you that in the *Ṣaḥīḥ* they sometimes transmitted from those who only had one narrator.

Deprecation of a narrator is not accepted when there is doubt about his name

He said in the biography of ʿAbd al-ʿAzīz ibn ʿAbdullāh ibn Yaḥyā al-ʿĀmirī al-Uwaysī:

> Al-Khalīlī said, "They agreed that he is trustworthy," but it states in the Questions of Abū ʿUbayd al-Ājurrī that Abū Dāwūd said, "ʿAbd al-ʿAzīz al-Uwaysī is weak." If he means that then it is questionable because he declared him trustworthy in another place and narrated from him through Hārūn al-Ḥammāl. Perhaps he declared weak a specific transmission of his in which he made a mistake, or he declared someone else with the same name to be weak. In general, it is a rejected deprecation.

He means that if the name of the person criticised is not clearly stated so that there is no doubt about who it is, the deprecation is not accepted.

What Ibn Maʿīn means when he says about a narrator in some transmissions, "He is nothing" is that he has few ḥadīths

He said in the biography of ʿAbd al-ʿAzīz ibn Mukhtār al-Baṣrī: "Ibn Maʿīn said in a narration, 'He is nothing.' Ibn al-Qaṭṭān al-Fāsī mentioned that when Ibn Maᶜīn says in some transmissions, 'He is nothing,' he means that he has very few ḥadīths."

Sometimes when Ibn Maᶜīn says about a transmitter, "He is nothing" he intends to declare a specific ḥadīth of his to be weak.

Sometimes the statement of Ibn Maᶜīn about a narrator, "He is nothing," means that a particular ḥadīth of his is weak

He stated in the biography of ᶜAbd al-Mutaᶜālī ibn Ṭālib narrating from ᶜUthmān ad-Dārimī that he asked Yaḥyā ibn Maᶜīn about the ḥadīth of this man from Ibn Wahb. He said, 'This is nothing.' I say this is not a clear statement declaring him weak since it is possible that he meant the ḥadīth itself." Then he mentioned something that strengthens this possibility.

Their statement, "He was suspected of stealing ḥadīth" is an unclear deprecation

He said in the biography of ᶜAbd al-Malik ibn aṣ-Ṣabbāḥ al-Mismaᶜī: "The author of al-Mīzān mentioned him and quoted al-Khalīlī as saying about him that he was suspected of stealing ḥadīth. This is an unclear deprecation."

I say that one should take note of this point because some of those who are deficient consider it an explained deprecation.

Not memorizing ḥadīth does not tarnish a ḥadīth scholar who narrates from a book

He said in the biography of ᶜAbd al-Wāḥid ibn Ziyād al-ᶜAbdī: "Yaḥyā ibn al-Qaṭṭān indicated that he was lenient. Ibn al-Madīnī narrated from him that he said, 'I have not seen him look for ḥadīth at all. I used to discuss the ḥadīth of al-Aᶜmash with him and he would not recognize a single letter of it.' I say this does not impair him because he was a book person."

This means that he did not narrate from memory. If someone narrates from a book, his memory is of no consequence but rather his book is relied upon.

A narrator praising an innovator for what he has does not impair his character

He stated in the biography of ᶜAbd al-Wārith ibn Saᶜīd al-Baṣrī:

> What is clear to me is that they suspected him [of being a muᶜtazilī] because of his praise of ᶜAmr ibn ᶜUbayd. He used to say, "Had it not been that I know that he is truthful, I would not have narrated from him." The imams of ḥadīth used to accuse ᶜAmr ibn ᶜUbayd of lying and forbade people to sit with him. Hence ᶜAbd al-Wārith was suspected. The Group nevertheless use him as an authority.

When al-Bukhārī transmits from someone who muddled things, it is understood that he did so before he muddled things

He said in the biography of ʿAbd al-Wahhāb ibn ʿAbd al-Majīd ath-Thaqafī: "Ibn Saʿd said: 'He is a trustworthy person in whom there is some weakness.' I say, by that he meant the muddling which was held against him. It is clear that al-Bukhārī transmitted his ḥadīth from those who had listened to him before he muddled things."

This indicates what we stated earlier that when the author of the *Ṣaḥīḥ* transmits a ḥadīth from someone who muddled things: he transmitted it from those who listened to him before he muddled.

A narration of the deprecation of someone trustworthy by someone weak is weak, and the critical words of contemporaries are only accepted when they are explained

He said in the biography of ʿUthmān ibn Ṣāliḥ as-Sahmī al-Baṣrī:

> As for what Ibn Rishdīn narrated from Aḥmad ibn Ṣāliḥ that he abandoned ʿUthmān ibn Ṣāliḥ, that does not detract from him: firstly, because Ibn Rishdīn is weak and cannot be relied upon; secondly because Aḥmad ibn Ṣāliḥ is one of the contemporaries of ʿUthmān whose words about him are only accepted with a clear explanation.

The harshness of Yaḥyā ibn al-Qaṭṭān about men, especially his contemporaries

He said in the biography of ʿUthmān ibn ʿUmar ibn Fāris: "Al-Bukhārī quoted from ʿAlī ibn al-Madīnī that Yaḥya ibn Saʿīd used him as an authority. Yaḥya ibn Saʿīd was very harsh about men, especially his contemporaries."

So remember this. He deemed Abū Ḥanīfah trustworthy and followed him, as I mentioned in my treatise, *Injāʾ al-Waṭan*.

Concerning those who narrated from ʿAṭāʾ ibn as-Sāʾib before he muddled things

He said in the biography of ʿAṭāʾ ibn as-Sāʾib:

> He muddled things, so they declared him to be weak because of that. I deduce from all that the imams said that Shuʿbah, ath-Thawrī, Zuhayr ibn Muʿāwiyah, Zāʾidah, Ayyūb, and Ḥammād ibn Zayd narrated from him before he muddled things. (I say, "That is the case with Abū Ḥanīfah and he was generally senior to those scholars.") The ḥadīths of anyone other than these men who narrated from him are weak because that occurred after he began to muddle things, except for Ḥammād ibn Salama. Their position about him varies.

I say this is a useful point which should be remembered. In *Majmaʿ az-Zawāʾid* al-Haythamī stressed that Ḥammād ibn Salama also heard from him before he muddled things.

Hesitation about [whether or not] the Qur'ān [is created] does not impair a narrator
He stated in the biography of ʿAlī ibn Abī Hāshim al-Baghdādī: "Abū Ḥatim said that he is truthful. People abandoned him on account of hesitation about the Qur'an. I say, 'Abū Ḥātim explained the reason for the hesitation of those who hesitated about it, but that does not prevent accepting his transmission."

An example of nonsensical deprecation which occured from Ibn Saʿd
He said in the biography of ʿUmar ibn Nāfiʿ, the client of Ibn ʿUmar: "Ibn Saʿd said, 'He was reliable and had few ḥadīths, but they do not use his ḥadīths as authoritative.' This is a nonsensical statement. How can they not use him as authoritative when he is reliable?"

An innovator's deprecation of someone trustworthy is rejected
He stated in the biography of ʿAmr ibn Sulaym az-Zuraqī: "Ibn Khirāsh said that he is trustworthy, but there is some muddling in his ḥadīths. I say Ibn Khirāsh is mentioned as being a Rāfiḍite and innovator, so one does not pay attention to him."

When al-Bukhārī transmits from someone who muddled things that transmission was before he muddled
He said in the biography of ʿAmr ibn ʿAbdullāh ibn Abī Isḥāq as-Sabīʿī: "He was one of the reliable notable scholars before he muddled things. I did not see any transmission from him in al-Bukhārī except from his old companions, like ath-Thawrī and Shuʿbah, but not from the later ones like Ibn ʿUyaynah and others."

Ibn Ḥajar's method differs from that of al-Mizzī in mentioning the shaykhs of the subject of a biography and those who narrated from him
al-Ḥāfiẓ has said in in the introduction to *at-Tahdhīb*:

> I did not undertake to enter the shaykhs and narrators in one biography alphabetically because doing so necessitates putting the young before the old. I was keen to mention at the start of the biography the senior shaykhs of the men and those with the greatest *isnād* and memory when it is easy to ascertain that information. I was keen to finish those who narrated from him with those who are described as the last to narrate from the subject of the biography. I often clearly stated that.

I say that the order used in *at-Tahdhīb* will identify the old companions from the later ones. He also said in it:

> The aim of Shaykh al-Mizzī, may Allah ﷻ have mercy on him, was to deal in full with the shaykhs of the subject of the biography and those who narrated from him.

> However, that is something which it is not possible to deal with in full nor to catalog; it is futile. The most important benefit in that is in one thing: which is that when it is well known that only one man narrated from a person, and the one who knows that finds another narrator, that then removes the anonymity of the identity of that man by two narrators narrating from him. The pursuit and investigation of the like of that is important.

This is an excellent point derived from reading books like *at-Tahdhīb*.

The ḥadīths of Kharijite narrators are the soundest ḥadīths of the people of sects; the transmission of al-Bukhārī from ʿImrān ibn Ḥiṭṭān al-Khārijī

In the introduction to *al-Fatḥ*, al-Ḥāfiẓ stated in the biography of ʿImrān ibn Ḥiṭṭān: "He espoused the view of the Kharijites. Qatādah said, 'He is not suspect in ḥadīth.' Abū Dāwūd stated, 'In the sects, there are none sounder in ḥadīth than the Kharijites.'"

Ibn ʿAdī has extraordinary errors in his books, so one must investigate what he says

There is also in it in the biography of Ghālib al-Qaṭṭān:

> As for Ibn ʿAdī, he mentioned him among the weak and narrated ḥadīths from him, attributing them to the one who transmitted from him: ʿUmar ibn al-Mukhtār al-Baṣrī. It is one of the most extraordinary things to have occurred to Ibn ʿAdi. Perfection belongs to Allah ﷻ.

I say, do not be deceived by the fact that a man is mentioned in *al-Kāmil* or *al-Mīzān*. That is not evidence of his absolute weakness.

The strictness of ʿAlī ibn al-Madīnī regarding criticism or narrators

He stated in the biography of Fuḍayl ibn Sulaymān an-Numayrī: "ʿAlī ibn al-Madīnī narrated from him, and he was one of those who were severe [about narrators]."

I say, he declared Abū Ḥanīfah to be trustworthy as we mentioned in *Injāʾ al-waṭan*.

The strength of memory and lack of errors is a relative matter between [varying] from hafiz to hafiz

He said in the biography of Qabīṣah ibn ʿUqbah:

> Aḥmad said, "He made many errors. He was trustworthy and there was nothing wrong with him. He was more reliable than Abū Ḥanīfah, but Abu Nuʿaym was more reliable than him.' I say these conclusions are relative, for Abū Ḥātim said, 'I did not see any ḥadīth scholar who memorized and presented ḥadīths with the same words without alteration except for Qabīṣah and Abu Nuʿaym in the ḥadīths of ath-Thawrī."

An example of rejected unclear deprecation

He said in the biography of Muḥammad ibn Bashhār Bundār: "ʿAmr ibn ʿAlī al-Fallās said that he was weak but did not mention the reason for that, so they paid no attention to his deprecation of him."

Some transmitters are precise in respect of one shaykh and weak in respect of another

He said in the biography of Muḥammad ibn Jaʿfar Ghundar: "He is one of the reliable accurate companions of Shuʿbah. Abū Ḥātim said, 'His ḥadīths from other than Shuʿbah are written down, but are not used as authoritative.' This means that his ḥadīths from Shuʿbah are authoritative without a doubt."

The deprecation of a transmitter on the basis that he is one of the people of opinion is not deprecation

He said in the biography of Muḥammad ibn ʿAbdullāh ibn al-Muthannā al-Anṣārī: "One of the old shaykhs of al-Bukhārī. He is trustworthy. Aḥmad said. 'The only thing that makes him weak according to the people of ḥadīth is that he looked into opinion (*raʾy*)."

I say he was one of the students of Imam Abū Ḥanīfah.

There is no fault in them other than the fact
that their swords are notched from striking the battalions.

A judgement of general deprecation on account of a specific reason is not accepted

He said in the biography of Muḥammad ibn ʿAbdullāh ibn Muslim ibn Akhī az-Zuhrī:

> Adh-Dhuhlī said, "He had three ḥadīths without any source, all of them *mursal*, and he mentioned them." Abū Ḥātim said, "He is not strong. His ḥadīths are written." I say adh-Dhuhlī had greater familiarity with the ḥadīths of az-Zuhrī and has explained what he was criticised for, so it is clear that those who declare him to be weak do so because of those ḥadīths in which he erred.

This means that he is a trustworthy authority in the rest of his ḥadīths.

Al-Bukhārī is lenient in respect of ḥadīths which encourage good (at-targhīb) and warn against evil (at-tarhīb)

He said in the biography of Muḥammad ibn ʿAbd ar-Raḥmān aṭ-Ṭufāwī:

> Abū Zurʿa said, "His ḥadīths are *munkar*. Ibn ʿAdi reported a number of his ḥadīths." He has three ḥadīths in al-Bukhārī. There is nothing in them that Ibn ʿAdī considered to be *munkar*. The third of them is in ar-Riqāq: "Be like a stranger in this world."

> Aṭ-Ṭufāwī alone has this, and it is one of the *gharīb* ḥadīths in the *Ṣaḥīḥ*. It seems that al-Bukhārī was not strict about it since it was one of the ḥadīths which encourage good and discourage evil.

I say this contains support for the well-known fact that ḥadīth scholars are less stringent regarding ḥadīths which deal with virtues although some people have been rash by also obliging strictness in them.[355]

When a narrator sometimes errs and sometimes is correct, his ḥadīth are omitted according to Aḥmad [ibn Ḥanbal]; sometimes the narrator may be declared weak in espect of a specific ḥadīth

He said in the biography of Muḥammad ibn ʿUbayd aṭ-Ṭanāfisī:

> He was one of the shaykhs of Aḥmad [ibn Ḥanbal]. He said in one narration, "He sometimes erred and sometimes was correct." So according to Aḥmad's preference, he is someone whose ḥadīths are omitted, but he nonetheless considered him to be trustworthy in his transmission from al-Athram. I say all the imams use Muḥammad as an authority. Perhaps what Aḥmad indicated was in connection to a single ḥadīth.

I say this explains the custom of Aḥmad and shows that a declaration of weakness may concern a particular ḥadīth and not be universal.

The harshness exercised by Abū Ḥātim in narrator criticism

He said in the biography of Muḥammad ibn Abī ʿAdī al-Baṣrī: "He was one of the shaykhs of Ahmad [ibn Ḥanbal]. There is in *al-Mīzān* that Abū Ḥātim said, 'He is not used as authoritative.' One must investigate that, (because he has declared him trustworthy in a transmission), and Abū Ḥātim was harsh."

In the Ṣaḥīḥ, al-Bukhārī transmitted from weak narrators when there is corroboration (mutābaʿah)

He said in the biography of Muḥammad ibn Yazīd al-Kufi: "Al-Bukhārī and others

355 Shaykh Abū Ghuddah writes, "By quoting the above mentioned words of Ibn Ḥajar, It can be construed from the words of the author, my shaykh that al-Bukhārī was lenient with regards to ḥadīths related to virtues. Our shaykh, the erudite al-Kawtharī disagrees with him on this in his *al-Maqālāt* in the chapter 'some words regarding the weak ḥadīth', p. 45–46. He writes, 'Absolute unacceptance of weak ḥadīth was the opinion of al-Bukhārī, Muslim, Ibn al-ʿArabī, the shaykh of the Mālikīs in his time, Abū Shāma al-Maqdasī, the elder of the Shāfiʿīs in his time, Ibn Ḥazm ad-Dhāhirī and ash-Shawkānī. They have strong opinions regarding this issue which should not be disregarded.', Therefore the words of our shaykh, May Allah ﷻ have mercy on him, 'Although some people have been rash by also obliging strictness in them.', is clearly problematic." *Qawāʿid*, p. 426, f.n. 2.

declared him weak while other scholars declared him strong. It is not unlikely that what he transmitted from his ḥadīth in the *Ṣaḥīḥ* was corroborated."

I say it is thus known that in the *Ṣaḥīḥ*, al-Bukhārī transmitted from someone he considered to be weak when there was corroboration for that.

A trustworthy person is not impaired by declaring war on the ruler

He said in the biography of Marwān ibn al-Ḥakam:

> ʿUrwa ibn az-Zubayr said, "Marwān was not suspect in ḥadīth." Sahl ibn Saʿd as-Saʿīdī the Companion narrated from him, relying on his truthfulness. They were hostile towards him since he unsheathed his sword to obtain the caliphate until what we know took place [i.e. civil war]. Mālik relied on his ḥadīths and opinion as did other scholars except for Muslim.

The ḥadīths of a narrator are judged to be irregular (*shādh*) when he frequently does this.

When someone frequently relates strange and contradictory narrations his ḥadīths are judged to be aberrant

He said in the biography of Muqaddam ibn Muḥammad ibn Yaḥyā al-Muqaddamī: "Al-Bazzār, ad-Dāraquṭnī and Ibn Ḥibbān declared him to be trustworthy, but when he mentioned him in *ath-Thiqāt* he said, 'He had strange (*gharīb*) reports and contradicted.' When someone does this frequently his ḥadīths are judged to be aberrant."

I say, if the person in question does not do this frequently, then this ruling does not apply, as is clear and understood from what was said.

Al-Jūzajānī's deprecation of the people of Kufa is not accepted because of his Nāṣibī position and great deviation; an example of rejected deprecation and unexplained deprecation

He said in the biography of al-Minhāl ibn ʿAmr:

> Ibn Abi Ḥātim said, "Wahb ibn Jarīr narrated that Shuʿbah said, 'I went to al-Minhāl's house and heard the sound of a mandolin coming from it. I went back without asking him.' I asked, 'Why did you not ask him? Perhaps he did not know about it.' This is a sound objection. Al-Ḥākim mentioned that Yaḥyā al-Qaṭṭān criticised him."
>
> Al-Jūzajāni said, "He followed a bad *madhhab* and his ḥadīths were in circulation." I say, "As for al-Jūzajānī, we said more than once that his deprecation is not accepted in respect of the people of Kufa because of his great deviation and Nāṣibī position. The story of al-Ḥākim about al-Qaṭṭān is not explained."

The partisanship of Nuʿaym ibn Hammād against the people of opinion[356] (raʾy), and al-Bukhārī's transmission from him

He said in the biography of Nuʿaym ibn Hammād:

> Al-Bukhārī met him and only transmitted from him in the *Ṣaḥīḥ* in one or two places. He also narrated some additional ḥadīth (as *taʿlīq*) in the chapter headings without the *isnād*. Abū Bishr ad-Dūlābī made an attribution of fabrication to him. Ibn ʿAdī countered that by stating that ad-Dūlābī was biased against him because he was harsh towards the people of opinion.

I say since Nuʿaym was severe in opposition to the people of opinion, one must avoid those transmissions from him which dealt with Abū Ḥanīfah and his companions. Partisanship blinds people and makes them deaf. It is not unlikely that the harshness of al-Bukhārī towards the people of opinion was caused by the influence of this shaykh of his, as we already indicated.

When the statement of a critic about a narrator conflicts between deprecation and validation, then preponderance is given to validation

He stated in the biography of Hudba ibn Khālid al-Qaysī: "I read in the handwriting of adh-Dhahabī: 'an-Nasāʾī declared him strong once and weak another time.' I say perhaps he declared him weak in something particular."

I say when the statement of a critic about a man varies so that he sometimes says that he is weak and at other times that he is strong, then the practice of al-Ḥāfiẓ indicates that preponderance is given to validation of good character and the deprecation is taken to refer to a particular thing.

The division of ṣaḥīḥ into that which is sound in itself and that which is sound on account something else, and testimony to that

He said in the biography of Hishām ibn Ḥassān al-Baṣrī:

> Ibn Maʿīn said, "His ḥadīth from ʿIkrimah, ʿAṭāʾ and al-Ḥasan al-Baṣrī used to be avoided." I say the Imams used him as an authority, but they do not transmit from him from ʿAṭāʾ at all. As for his ḥadīths from ʿIkrimah, al-Bukhārī transmits a few reports from him some of which have corroboration. As for his ḥadīths from al-Ḥasan al-Baṣrī, they are in the Six Books.

---

356 The people of opinion (*ahl al-raʾy*) is a title given to imam Abū Ḥanīfah and his followers for their tendency to be relatively less superficial and literal in their understanding of the texts and seek a deeper understanding of their causes, objectives and contexts, and for their espousal and use of analogical reasoning (*qiyās*). Ed.

> ʿAbdullāh ibn Aḥmad [Ibn Hanbal] narrated from his father, "No sooner does anyone object to something of his that I find someone else who narrated it, either Ayyūb or ʿAwf."

This supports what we stated in *ʿUlūm al-ḥadīth* about there being two categories of the *ṣaḥīḥ*, some are sound in themselves, and some are sound by corroboration (*mutaba'ah*). Allah ﷻ knows best.

When al-Bukhārī transmits from someone known for tadlīs, he transmits those ḥadīths of his in which he clearly stated that he actually heard

He said in the biography of Hushaym ibn Bashīr al-Wāsiṭī:

> He is one of the imams whose trustworthiness is agreed upon, except for the fact that he was known for tadlīs, and they consider his transmission from az-Zuhrī particularly weak. As for the *tadlīs*, a group of the *ḥuffāẓ* mentioned that al-Bukhārī only transmitted from him that which he explicitly stated was related. (i.e. he used the words *haddathanā* (he told me) when narrating). As for his transmission from az-Zuhrī, none of it is found in the two *Ṣaḥīḥ* Collections.

This is a useful note which should be remembered.

The ḥadīths of Hammām ibn Yaḥyā al-Baṣrī [transmitted] at the end of his life are sounder than those which were heard from him in earlier times

He said in the biography of Hammām ibn Yaḥyā al-Baṣrī:

> It is narrated from ʿAffān that he said, "Hammām did not consult his book nor look at it. He used to diverge but still did not consult his book. Then he retracted and looked at his books and said, "Affān, we made many mistakes. We ask Allah's ﷻ forgiveness.'" I say this necessitates that the ḥadīths of Hammam at the end of his life were sounder than those heard from him earlier. Aḥmad expressly stated that. The Six Imams relied on him.

This is an extraordinary point.

The fact that the Imams rely upon a narrator weakens any statement of weakness

He stated in the biography of Waddāḥ ibn ʿAbdullāh Abī ʿAwānah: "Ibn al-Madīnī said, 'there is weakness in the ḥadīths he reported from Qatādah because his book had been lost.' I say all of the Imams relied on him," meaning that they did not pay any attention to the statements of his deprecators.

Refutation of finding fault with a narrator on account of his espousing opinion (raʾy) and acceptance of the transmission of a trustworthy Ibāḍī as al-Bukhārī accepted it in his Ṣaḥīḥ
He said in the biography of al-Walīd ibn Kathīr al-Makhzūmī: "No one declared him weak but they criticized him for following opinion. Al-Ājurrī said narrating from Abū Dāwūd, 'He is trustworthy although he is an Ibāḍī.' I say the Ibāḍīs are a sect of the Kharijites. Their position is not very atrocious and al-Walīd was not a missionary."

An example of rejected deprecation when it is criticism of a contemporary
He said in the biography of Yaḥyā ibn Zakariyyā ibn Abī Zāʾida: "ʿUmar ibn Shabbah narrated that Abū Nuʿaym said, 'He is not worthy for me to narrate from him.' This is rejected deprecation. In fact this aparently is not deprecation," i.e. because it is understood to be due to him being a contemporary.

An example of rejected unclear deprecation
He said in the biography of Yazīd ibn Abī Maryam: "The Imams considered him to be trustworthy. Ad-Dāraquṭnī said, 'he is not that.' This is a deprecation which is not explained and so it is rejected."

The caution of early scholars about negligence, even just slight
He said in the biography of Yazīd ibn Hārūn al-Wāsiṭī:

> After his eyesight deteriorated, when he was asked about a ḥadīth he did not recognize, he ordered his slavegirl to memorise for him from his book. He was criticized for that. I say early scholars were cautious about the smallest form of negligence. In truth, this does not necessitate that he is weak or lenient. The Group used him as an authority.

An example of rejected unclear deprecation
He stated in the biography of Yūsuf ibn Isḥāq as-Sabīʿī: "When al-ʿUqaylī mentioned him among the weak, he said he diverged from his ḥadīths. This is a rejected deprecation," because it is unclear.

The technical usage of al-Bardījī when he says, 'munkar al-ḥadīth', he means that it is a unique ḥadīth
He said in the biography of Yūnus ibn al-Qāsim al-Ḥanafī:

> Al-Bardījī said that his ḥadīth are *munkar*. I say I reported this so that I would not be corrected for it, otherwise the school of al-Bardījī is that *munkar* refers to a unique (*fard*) ḥadīth, whether a trustworthy or untrustworthy person has it alone. So his

> statement that "his ḥadīths are *munkar*" is not a clear deprecation. How can this be when Yaḥyā ibn Maᶜīn declared that he was trustworthy?

I say this is the meaning of "*munkar al-ḥadīth*" according to Aḥmad, as al-Ḥāfiẓ clearly stated on page 453 and 2:173. It is known from his words, "How can that be when Ibn Maᶜīn declared him trustworthy?" that his declaration of trustworthiness preponderent over the words of someone less than him and more prioritised? Allah ﷻ knows best. Ibn Maᶜīn also declared Abū Ḥanīfah to be trustworthy and so no deprecation of him is accepted from anyone less than him.

Someone trustworthy narrating some munkar ḥadīths does not cancel his trustworthiness
He said in the biography of Yūnus in Yazīd al-Aylī, the companion of az-Zuhrī:

> Wakīᶜ said, "He had a bad memory." Al-Maymūnī said that Ahmad said, "He narrated *munkar* ḥadīths." I say the majority declared him to be generally trustworthy. They only declared some of his transmissions weak where he differed from his contemporaries or narrated from memory. When he narrates from his book, he is authoritative. Aḥmad, Ibn Maᶜīn, an-Nasāʾī and the majority declared him to be unrestrictedly trustworthy. Thus this means the words of those who deprecate him are not accepted.

An example of rejected deprecation
He said in the biography of Abū Bakr ibn Abī Musā al-Ashᶜarī:

> He was an eminent Tābiᶜī. Ibn Saᶜd said, "He was older than his brother, Abū Burda. He had few ḥadīths and is considered to be weak." I say this is a rejected deprecation. The Two Shaykhs [al-Bukhārī and Muslim] transmit from him in his narration from his father. Aḥmad said that he did not listen from his father. Al-Ajurrī said that Abū Dāwūd said that he did listen to him. I say that he clearly stated that he listened to him in his transmission.

We have discussed at length here so that the student may know that deprecation does not affect the transmitter unconditionally, but rather some deprecation has an effect and some does not at all. That which does have an effect sometimes lowers the transmitter from the rank of being authoritative and sometimes it does not. Anyone who reads and reflects on this section will obtain the faculty for examination and criticism of deprecation, Allah ﷻ willing.

This tells us also that the response to the attack of those who criticise the men of al-Bukhārī and Muslim mostly only works based on the fundamental principles of the Ḥanafi imams rather than the majority of ḥadīth scholars. This is because if both aspects of the assessment of character (*al-jarḥ wa't-taᶜdīl*) are unclear, then according to them (the no-hanafis) those who are trustworthy or weak are those whom the majority declare to be so. On the other hand our position is that when the assessment of character is unclear, then validation of good character is preferred, as was stated in the chapter dealing with the fundamental principles of the assessment of character.

We should briefly mention after al that what al-Ḥāfiẓ [Ibn Ḥajar] said after his detailed discussion of this, regarding the discernment of the reasons behind criticism. From it, it becomes clear who among them can be suitably used as proof and who is not suitable. He said:

> There are two categories in this. The first is he whose weakness is because of his creed; and we already mentioned the ruling about him and explained in the biography of each of them that if he was not a missionary, or was and then repented, or his transmission is supported by a corroborating narration, then he is an authoritative proof.
>
> The second category is of the person who is declared weak by something which is rejected, like bias, harshness, not relying on someone who declares someone weak because he is not one of the people of criticism or is someone who has little information of the ḥadīths or state of the person he is speaking against or is after his time, or similar reasons.
>
> This also includes he who is cricitised for something which does not detract from all of his ḥadīths, like someone who is declared weak in respect of some of his shaykhs but not others. The same is true of someone who muddled things or whose memory deteriorated, or who was precise with his book but not precise by memory. It is not appropriate to call any of these weak without qualification. Rather, the correct position is that one goes in to detail about them, as we already explained by the praise of Allah ﷻ.

(Then al-Ḥāfiẓ mentioned in two sections the names of those narrators of the *Ṣaḥīḥ* who were accused of innovation and the like, or declared to be weak by something rejected) to the point where he said,

> All of those who are mentioned in these two sections are among those who were used as authorities by al-Bukhārī. This has not resulted in any fault being associated with him (al-Bukhari) as we explained. As for those in the two sections who are described with lack of accuracy, delusion or error or the like of that. This is a third category. He [al-Bukhārī] only used those narrations of theirs that were corroborated and which he or someone else has.

Ibn Taymiyah said in *Minhāj as-Sunna*:

> Ash-Shāfiʿī, may Allah ﷻ have mercy on him, compiled a book which deals with the disagreement of ʿAlī and Ibn Masʿūd when the people of Iraq debated a case

> with him and said, "ʿAlī and Ibn Masʿūd said...", they used the position of the two Companions as a proof [of their position]. Therefore Ash-Shāfiʿī compiled a book in which he mentioned the statements of ʿAlī and Ibn Masʿūd which [the people of Iraq] had omitted. This was a discussion with scholars who used the sources of Sharīʿah as proof from among the people of Kufa, like the adherents of Abū Ḥanīfah: Muhammad ibn al-Hasan and the likes of him.

Ash-Shāfiʿī's debate was only with Muḥammad ibn al-Ḥasan and his companions; he did not meet Abū Yūsuf

Ibn Taymiyah continues:

> Most of Ash-Shāfiʿī's debates were with Muḥammad ibn al-Ḥasan and his companions, but did not meet Abū Yūsuf nor debate with him nor listen to him. Abū Yūsuf had died before ash-Shāfiʿī went to Iraq. He died in 183 AH and ash-Shāfiʿī went to Iraq in 185 (after Mālik's death). That is why he mentioned in his books the statements of Abu Yūsuf reported from Muḥammad ibn al-Ḥasan.

The journey attributed to ash-Shāfiʿī is false

Thus the journey attributed to ash-Shāfiʿī is completely fabricated,[357] because ash-Shāfiʿī's meeting with Abū Yūsuf is mentioned in it and that he went to Iraq while Mālik was still alive.

It becomes known from these words that the School of Abū Ḥanīfah is based on the statements of Ibn Masʿūd and ʿAlī, may Allah ﷻ be pleased with both of them, narrated from the Prophet ﷺ in most cases or [are based] on their ijtihād. Abū Ḥanīfah and his adherents took a different position than Ibn Masʿūd and ʿAlī in some cases when the statements of other Companions appeared to them to be strong, as is explained in the books of our companions [the Hanafis]. Allah ﷻ knows best.

Revealing words in the tafsīr of ath-Thaʿlabī, al-Wāḥidī and al-Baghawī and their transmissions

He (Ibn Taymiyah) also said in it:[358]

> The mere attribution of a ḥadīth to the *tafsīr* of ath-Thaʿlabī or transmission of *ijmaʿ* on that from someone other than those who know transmissions and are truthful in in their transmission is not a proof as is agreed by the people of knowledge, even if

357 Arguments for the falsity of this supposed journey and meeting can be found in Imam al-Kawtharī's *Fiqh Ahl al-ʿIrāq wa ḥadīthuhum*, pp.91–92.

358 *Minhāj as-Sunna*, 4:3.

the existence of its *isnād*[359] is not known. The majority, the people of the *sunna*, do not establish anything they want to affirm using the like of this, whether it is a ruling, virtue or anything else. The same is true of the Shīʿa. Since this on its own is not a valid proof by the agreement of both groups, it is invalid to use it as evidence.

This is the position in respect of all that he quoted[360] and attributed to Abū Nuʿaym, ath-Thaʿlabī, an-Naqqāsh, Ibn al-Maghāzī and the like. The scholars of ḥadīth have agreed that ath-Thaʿlabī narrated a corpus of forged ḥadīths, like the ḥadīth which he narrated at the beginning of every sūra from Abū Umāma on the virtue of that sūra. This is why they say, "He is like someone who collects firewood at night [i.e. collects both the good and the bad]." That is also the case with his student al-Wāḥidī,[361] and those like them among Qur'an commentators who transmit both the sound and the weak.

Since al-Baghawī had knowledge of ḥadīth, more knowledge of it than ath-Thaʿlabī and al-Wāḥidī, and his *tafsīr* was a summary of the *tafsīr* of ath-Thaʿlabī, he did not mention in his *tafsīr* any of these fabricated ḥadīths which ath-Thaʿlabī narrated nor did he mention the *tafsīr*s of the people of innovation which ath-Thaʿlabī mentioned. Although there is goodness and virtue in ath-Thaʿlabī's (*tafsīr*), he had no expertise in sound and weak ḥadīths, and did not distinguish between the *sunna* and innovation in many statements."

In every branch of knowledge one consults its people and its men

He also said in it,

> We mean to mention a rule here: transmissions contain much which is true and many lies. The source [we consult] to distinguish between the two are the scholars of ḥadīth, just as we consult grammarians about the difference between correct and incorrect Arabic grammar, and linguists about what is part of the language and what is not. It is the same with scholars of poetry, medicine and other areas. Every area of knowledge has men who know it.

The elevated position of scholars of ḥadīth and their virtue over others

"The scholars of ḥadīth are more esteemed and more truthful than these men[362] and have a higher status and greater dīn. They are among the people with the greatest

---

359 It seems that Ibn Taymiyah is saying the consensus is accepted even if an *isnād* for it cannot be traced. He proves this in the subsequent sentences. Ed.

360 Ibn Taymiyah wrote *Minhāj as-Sunna* as a rebuttal against the book *Minhāj al-Karāmah* by a Shīʿī author ʿallāmah Hillī. He refers to him in this place. It seems the whole argument developed here is to refute the practice of this author in the way he used evidences and their sources. Ed.

361 The author of *Asbāb an-Nuzūl*.

362 i.e. the various categories of scholars just mentioned in the previous section. Ed

truthfulness, trustwrorthiness, knowledge and expertise in what they mention concerning assessment of character (*al-jarḥ wa't-taᶜdīl*). (Then he mentioned the names of some ḥadīth scholars,) and said, "there are many like this among the scholars of [the science of] men (*ᶜilm ar-rijāl*) and *al-jarḥ wa't-taᶜdīl*, indeed they are countless, although some of them know more of that than others and some are fairer than others in measuring their words, as is the case with people in all areas of knowledge. This is an immense science among the greatest sciences in Islam.

The disparity in the sciences of isnād among the Rafidites, Muᶜtazilites, and Kharijites; the Rafidites have the least knowledge in that

"There is no doubt that the Rafidites have the least knowledge in this area and none of the people of innovations and sects are more ignorant of it than them. Indeed the other sects, like the Muᶜtazilites and Kharijites, fall short in knowledge of this, but the Muᶜtazilites have far greater knowledge than the Kharijites and the Kharijites are far more knowledgeable than the Rafidites. Furthermore the Kharijites are more truthful than the Rafidites. In fact, we do not know of the Kharijites that they deliberately lied, rather they are among the most truthful of people.[363] The Muᶜtazilites are like all groups: some of them lie and some are truthful, but they do not have interest in ḥadīth nor knowledge to extent of what the people of ḥadīth and the *sunna* have. These people do not adhere to the dīn and so are in need of recognising what truthfulness is.[364]

The people of innovations followed another path which they innovated and relied on, and they do not mention either ḥadīths or the Qur'an in their basic principles except as supporting [evidence], not to principally rely upon.

The Rafidites have the least knowledge of and interest in this since they neither looked into the *isnād* nor other legal and rational proofs to ascertain whether whether they agree with them or not. This is why they do not have any sound connected *isnāds* at all. In fact every connected *isnād* which they have inevitably contains someone known for lying or for abundantly making errors. In that they resemble the Jews and Christians who have no *isnād*.

---

363 This is because according to the Kharijite lying is tantamount to kufr and by lying one is taken out of the folds of Islam.

364 There is a possibility that this sentence has a textual error in it as shaykh Abdul Fattah points out. It may have been altered as this particular comment does not seem to be in line with the rest of what has been said since he acknowledges that there were truthful and untruthful people among the muᶜtazilah. It seems odd that he would make such a blanket statement in the next sentence. It may be that he meant 'these people do not uphold the narrated sources and therefore are in need of recognizing what truthfulness is, based on such sources'. See *Qawāᶜid*, p. 443, fn. 1.

Isnād is one of the characteristics of Islam

"*Isnād* is one of the characteristics of this Ummah and one of the characteristics of Islam. Then within Islam it is one of the characteristics of the people of the *sunna*.[365] The Rafidites have the least concern for it since they only affirm that which agrees with their tendencies; the sign of falsehood is that something diverges from their inclination. This is why ʿAbd ar-Raḥmān ibn Mahdī stated, "The people of knowledge write down both what supports them and what opposes them; the people of sects only write down what supports them."

I say this statement of Ibn Mahdī is worthy of being written in gold ink.

The many forms of lying in transmissions

He also said, "Anyone with the least amount of knowledge and fairness knows that transmissions contain both truth and lies and that people have lied about virtues and noble qualities [of persons] as they have lied about other things. They lie in what is in agreement with them and what differs from their view. We know that they lied in much of what they narrated about the virtues of Abū Bakr, ʿUmar and ʿUthman, just as they lied in much of what they narrated about the virtues of ʿAlī. There is no sect which lies more than the Rafidites.[366] The Kharijites scarcely lie. Indeed, they are the most truthful of people in spite of their innovation and misguidance.

The stance of the people of the sunna regarding transmissions is the true stance

"The people of knowledge do not declare a transmission to be true or false by mere agreement or disagreement with what they believe. A man may transmsit many ḥadīths which contain the virtues of the Prophet ﷺ, his Community and his Companions, yet they reject them because they know that they are false and accept many ḥadīths because they are sound, even if their apparent meaning differs from what they believe, either because they believe that they are abrogated, or have an interpretation which they do not oppose, or something like that.

The principle in transmission is that one consults the imams and scholars of transmission and that one seeks evidence for its soundness or weakness in proof that is not connected to the transmission. Both are necessary. Otherwise, merely someone's statement, 'So-and-so narrated' is not used as proof either by the people of the *sunna* or the Shiʿites. There is no one among the Muslims who uses every ḥadīth narrated by every author as proof. Every ḥadīth that he uses as proof, we demand its authenticity from the outset."

---

365 i.e. the sunni community.

366 Al-Baghdādī, *al-Kifāyah*, p.126; az-Zaylaʿī, *Naṣb ar-Rāyah*, 1:357.

The custom of early ḥadīth scholars was to narrate all [they knew] about a topic, whether sound or weak

He also said:

> Abū Nuʿaym, (the author of *Ḥilya*), narrated many ḥadīths which are weak, indeed fabricated, as is agreed by ḥadīth scholars. Even though he was a trustwrothy ḥāfiẓ with many ḥadīths and extensive transmission, he narrated, as was the custom of ḥadīth scholars like him, everything in the topic so that that will be known, even if only some of them are taken to be authoritative.

Concerning a group of scholars who only narrated from someone whom they considered to be trustworthy

> "Some people in their books such as Mālik, Shuʿbah, Yaḥyā ibn Saʿīd, ʿAbd ar-Raḥmān ibn Mahdī, and Aḥmad ibn Ḥanbal do not narrate from those they know to lie. These scholars do not narrate from anyone who they do not consider to be trustworthy nor do they narrate a ḥadīth they know to come from a liar, but it may occur that someone from whom they narrate is someone who erred in it.

The practice of some scholars in following some Companions in their sunna

He also said in *Minhāj as-Sunna*,

> Aḥmad ibn Ḥanbal and many other scholars follow what ʿAlī made *sunna*, as they followed what ʿUmar and ʿUthmān made *sunna*. Other scholars, like Mālik and others, do not follow what ʿAlī made *sunna*, but all of them agree to follow what ʿUmar and ʿUthmān made *sunna*.

The false ascription of Kitāb al-Ḥiyal (legal exits) of Imam Muḥammad

Ibn Abī al-Wafāʾ al-Qurashī stated in *al-Jawāhir al-Muḍiyya* in the biography of Warrāq: "Abū Sulaymān al-Jūzajānī said, 'They lied about Muḥammad (ibn al-*Ḥasan*). He does not have a book called *al-Ḥiyal*. The book *al-Ḥiyal* was written by Warrāq.'" I say that it is not known who Warrāq is.

The false ascription to one of the imams of using forbidden legal ploys (ḥiyal)

> "How excellent al-Jūzajānī was for calling our attention to the truth and bringing us out of a blind path. This book *al-Ḥiyal*, as Ibn al-Qayyim, may Allah ﷻ have mercy on him, said,[367] contains legal ploys (*ḥiyal*) that roam between unbelief and impiety, and it is not permitted to ascribe that to any of the imams. If anyone ascribes that to

---

367 Ibn al-Qayyim, *Iʿlām al-Muwaqiʿīn*, 3:190.

one of them, he is ignorant of their principles, their capabilities and status in Islam. Even if some of these ploys are legally effective based on the principles of an imam, this is altogether different from permission [to use the ploy], deeming it permissible or teaching it. Deeming something permissible is one thing while its legal effectiveness should it be done is another thing.[368]

If one were to hypotheticaly assume that some of these ploys which are unanimously unlawful are narrated from one of the imams, then either the transmission is false, or the narrater did not exactly record his words, and so confused his *fatwā* of legal effectiveness with permissibility (*ibāḥa*), although there is a great difference between the two.

There is no disagreement between the Imams that it is not permitted to allow someone to utter the words of unbelief for some purpose unless he is forced to do so while his heart is secure in faith.

The Ḥanafīs are the most stringent in forbidding prohibited haram legal ploys[369]

"Furthermore, this is stronger in the school of Abū Ḥanīfah and his companions. They do not permit words and deeds much less than that and say that it amounts to disbelief. They said, "If an unbeliever were to tell a man, 'I want to become Muslim,' and he then said to him, 'Wait a bit,' he has disbelieved. So what would be the judgement for engendering disbelief? They said, "If someone were to use the diminutive form for a mosque (musayjid) or the Qur'an (for example muṣayḥaf), then he has disbelieved.

Thus you have come to know that these crafty individuals who give a *fatwā* allowing legal ploys which are unbelief or unlawful are not following the school of any of the Imams, and that the Imams have too much knowledge of Allah ﷻ, His Messenger ﷺ and His dīn and are too godfearing to give a *fatwā* in favour of these ploys.

I say, anyone who ascribes these ploys to the Ḥanafīs has been deceived by their ascription to Imam Muḥammad. You know that this ascription is false and a grievous lie.

---

368. An example would be utterance of three divorces at once. This is forbidden according to all imams, yet most deem it to be legally effective. Its effectiveness does not change the fact that it is haram and one who commits it will be sinful. The same goes for legal ploys, they may be legally effective according to some imams, but they are still forbidden and the imams did not permit or teach such ploys. This is a commonly misunderstood point today, to the extent that legal ploys (*ḥīla*) are permitted, promoted and deliberately administrated. Ed.

369 The author deems it pertinent to vindicate Ḥanafī's from the use of prohibitive legal ploys as they have been accused of employing it by no less authority than al-Bukhārī. See al-Bukhārī's chapter of legal ploys in his *Ṣaḥīḥ*.

ʿAbdullāh ibn Masʿūd's distinction among the Companions because of his companions and the recording of his fatwās and positions, then by their companions, and the companions of their companions among the fuqahāʾ of Kufa and Iraq

Ibn al-Qayyim said in *Iʿlām al-Muwaqqiʿīn*:

> As the Companions were the masters and imams of the Community, so they were also the masters of the muftis and scholars. Muḥammad ibn Jarīr said, "None of them had known companions who recorded his *fatwās* and positions in *fiqh* except for Ibn Masʿūd. He used to abandon his position and view for that of ʿUmar. He rarely differed with him in any of his positions and retracted his view in favour of ʿUmar's view." Ash-Shaʿbī said, "ʿAbdullāh did not do the *qunūt* in Fajr." He said, "If ʿUmar had done the *qunūt*, ʿAbdullāh would have done the *qunūt*."
>
> Then *fatwā* devolved on the companions of these Companions. The *muftīs* in Kufa were ʿAlqamah, al-Aswad, ʿAmr ibn Shuraḥbīl, Masrūq, ʿAbīda as-Salmānī, the Qāḍī Shurayḥ, Suwayd ibn Ghafala and others. These men were the companions of ʿAlī and Ibn Masʿūd.
>
> Then after them came Ibrāhīm an-Nakhāʿī, ʿĀmir ash-Shaʿbī, Saʿīd ibn Jubayr and others. Then after them came Ḥammād ibn Abī Sulaymān, Sulaymān ibn al-Muʿtamir, al-Aʿmash, Misʿar ibn Kidām. Then after them came Muḥammad ibn ʿAbd ar-Raḥmān ibn Abī Laylā, Sufyān ath-Thawrī, Abū Ḥanīfah and others.
>
> Then after them came Ḥafṣ ibn Ghiyāth, Wakīʿ ibn al-Jarrāḥ and the companions of Abū Ḥanīfah like Qāḍī Abū Yūsuf, Zufar, Ḥammād ibn Abī Ḥanīfah, Muḥammad ibn al-Ḥasan the Qāḍī of Raqqa, Qāḍī al-Ḥasan ibn Ziyad al-Luʾluʾī, Qāḍī ʿAfiyah, Asad ibn ʿAmr, and Qāḍī Nūḥ ibn Darrāj.

I say that this proves Abū Hanīfah and his companions had the greatest knowledge of the Sharīʿah in their time, since *fatwā* devolved on them at that time, and in the past no one gave *fatwā* unless he had knowledge of the Qur'an, *sunna*, and statements of the Companions and had accurate sense and judgement.

Preferring acting by the fatwā of a Companion before acting by a mursal ḥadīth in the view of Aḥmad [Ibn Ḥanbal] and the Ḥanafīs

He (Ibn al-Qayyim) also stated when clarifying the principles followed by Aḥmad in his *fatwas*: "He looked for the *fatwās* of the Companions as his adherents looked for his *fatwas*; he put their *fatwas* ahead of a *mursal* ḥadīth."

I say the same is true of the Ḥanafīs who use the statements of the Companions as evidence a great deal. This is clear to anyone well-versed in their books.

Concerning the generations whose excellence is attested

In *al-Fatḥ* al-Ḥāfiẓ discussed the ḥadīth, "The best of My Community is my generation, and the narrator's uncertainty as to whether he mentioned two or three generations after his generation." He said,

> In the ḥadīth of Jaʿdah ibn Hubayra which is found with Ibn Abī Shayba and aṭ-Ṭabarānī the fourth generation is confirmed. It reads: "The best people is my generation, then those after them, and then those after them, and then those after them, and then the others are worse." Its men are trustworthy although there is disagreement about whether Jaʿdah was a Companion.

I say the preponderant position is that he was a Companion, for he was the son of Umm Hānīʾ bint Abī Tālib who saw the Prophet ﷺ when he was young and so the fact that he saw him is true. A *mursal* report from a Companion is authoritative without a doubt and according to us so is the *mursal* report of a Tābiʿī. Therefore we are permitted to also use *mursal* reports of the fourth generation[370] as authoritative since they share with the third generation the reason why we accept *mursal* reports. Whoever wants further details of the biography of Jaʿdah should consult *al-Iṣāba* and *Tahdhīb at-Tahdhīb*.

Muslim's distinction over al-Bukhārī by preserving the exact words in narration

Al-Ḥāfiẓ also said in *al-Fatḥ* about the ḥadīth,[371] "No one should pray ʿAṣr except at Banū Qurayẓa":[372]

> Al-Bukhārī wrote it from memory and did not take care to preserve the exact words as is known that his position allows [not preserving] that, which is not the case with Muslim who often preserved the words literally. I did not allow the opposite because I agree with those who agree with Muslim about the wording in which he differs with al-Bukhārī.[373]

---

370 Shaykh ʿAbd al-Fattāḥ does not accept this line of argument in his comments. He says that in another authentic ḥadīth narrated by Ahmad and others, a fifth generation has also been mentioned. Accepting *mursal* ḥadīth on the basis of this type of extension is not a credible line of argument. See *Qawāʿid*, p. 450, fn. 3.

371 What the author tries to achieve from this paragraph and the next is to make the case for the Ḥanafī's that an established practice (*sunna*) has prominence over a lone report (*khabr wāḥid*). He does this by first establishing that Muslim is more scrupulous than al-Bukhārī when it comes to ascertaining the correct wording of particular ḥadīth since al-Bukhārī mostly paraphrases (*riwāya bi 'l-maʿna*). The scholars say that this has given Muslim an edge of al-Bukhārī. Moving on from this, the author makes the case that since paraphrasing ḥadīth is deemed to be less scrupulous than ascertaining the correct wording of the ḥadīth, on the same token something which has a more epistemic certainty (*yaqīn*) over paraphrasing ḥadīth such as the collective practice of the scholars of Madīna will be more authorative than the actual paraphrased lone report. Once the author makes this case, by analogy and appropriation the case is made for the Ḥanafī's rejection of lone reports due to the presence of evidence which has an epistemic edge over it i.e. the established practice (*as-Sunna al-Mashhūra*).

372 Al-Bukhārī 7:313, Muslim 12:97.

373 This last sentence is part of Ibn Ḥajar's wider discussion on the ḥadīth and thus may seem out of

I say this is an immense virtue by which Muslim is distinguished as he is also distinguished by the excellence of his presentation of the ḥadīth and collecting of all its paths of transmission in one place. It is from this perspective that some people prefer Muslims' book to that of Al-Bukhārī.[374]

Al-Bukhārī allows transmission of the ḥadīth by meaning; the basis of Mālik in preferring the practice of the people of Madina over single reports is when they contradict

"In it there is also evidence that al-Bukhārī permitted transmission of ḥadīth by meaning without concern for the exact wording. That may be the basis of Mālik's opinion what one should abandon single reports if they differed from the *ʿamal* of the people of Madina because the *ʿamal* of the people of Madina in the best generations has a stronger *isnād* going back to the Prophet ﷺ than the report of a single person about whom we do not know whether he accurately recorded or not, and whether he narrated the ḥadīth with the exact wording or with the meaning, and whether he understood it or not?

The basis of the Ḥanafī position that when a single report contradicts the well-known sunna it is irregular (shādhdh), it is the same when it is reported about a general need

"It [the above][375] is [also] the basis of the Hanafī position that single reports are accepted when they do not contradict the well-known *sunna*. If they contradict it, then they are irregular (*shādhdh*). That is also the case when they are reported by the transmission of solitary narrators in matters of general need (*balwā*). This is because one solitary person having knowledge of the ruling of such an occurrence is unlikely. We already indicated all of that when we discussed the fundamental principles (*uṣūl*).

A ḥadīth which was not known in the time of the four Caliphs nor in the lands that are the birthplaces of the sunna has no authority, and it is not possible for it to be one of the necessary elements of the dīn (ḍaruriyyāt ad-Dīn)

"If you recognize that, then every ḥadīṭh, which was not known in the time of the four Caliphs, or rather not known at the time of the two Shaykhs, but rather later scholars researched it and searched for it by travelling to distant lands and remote places, and

---

place here. The point about Muslim's distinction is clear. Ed.

374 Shaykh Abdul Fattah quotes Shaykh Abdul Hayy al-Kattani who said in his book *at-Tarātīb al-Idāriyyah*, "the principle according to them is that no one is given preference over al-Bukhari in refrencing. The scholars will ascribe the ḥadīth to 'the two *ṣaḥīḥs*' if it is in both of them. However, they cite the wording of Muslim because of his strict preservation of the Prophetic wording." *Qawāʿid*, p. 451, fn. 2.

375 Meaning what was said ealier about narration by meaning being the basis of Imam Malik's position regarding the practice of the people of Madina, that too is the basis for the hanafis in this regard. Ed.

it had no trace among the people of the Hijaz, the people of Madina nor the people of the two Iraqs,[376] has no authority

Such a ḥadīth is not one of the necessary elements of the dīn. This is because Islam's rise reached its limit at the time of ʿUmar ibn al-Khattāb, RA and then after him through the time of the Rightly-guided Caliphs. All of the necessary elements of the dīn must have appeared at their time in their lands. If something was hidden from them and from the people of their lands which then appeared in a distant land or remote place, then it is clear that it was an aberrant ḥadīth. If it is believed that it is sound, it is not one of the necessary elements of the dīn but something additional. This is why Muʿāwiyah RA said, "You must have the ḥadīths which were known in the time of ʿUmar. He made people fearful about [reporting] ḥadīths from the Messenger of Allah ﷺ." Adh-Dhahabī mentioned that in *Tadhkirat al-Ḥuffāẓ* from Ibn ʿUlayyah from Rajāʾ ibn Abī Salama who had heard that Muʿāwiyah said that.

ʿUmar's scrutiny of the narration of ḥadīth and his informing [people] that the existence of many paths of transmission to strengthen the ḥadīth is a good thing

"It is known that when anyone narrated from the Messenger of Allah ﷺ to ʿUmar what he did not recognise, he would ask him, "Do you have anyone who will testify for you? If not I will do something [harsh] to you." Adh-Dhahabī said, "This is evidence that when two trustworthy people narrate the report, it is stronger and has more preponderance than that which has a single narrator. That is an encouragement to have many paths of transmission for a ḥadīth so that it will rise from the level of supposition to the level of knowledge since a single person might forget or err. That is unlikely in the case of two trustworthy men when no one disagrees with.

Refuting the claim of some people that if Abū Ḥanīfah had lived until ḥadīth were codified, he would have abandoned every analogy which he used

There is no need then to say that Abū Ḥanīfah [introduced] excessive use of analogy in his school since it was at a time before ḥadīths were written down. And if he had lived until the time when the ḥadīths of the Sharīʿa were written down after the *ḥuffāẓ* had travelled to collect them in lands and ports and had obtained them, he would have taken [the ḥadīth] and abandoned every analogy he used. That is because we would say that if the Imam had obtained them, he would only have taken from them those which were known at the time of the Four Caliphs and of everything that had become known at their time nothing had escaped him. He had a thorough grasp of the knowledge of the Hijaz, Madina and the two Iraqs. This is proven

376 The two Iraqs (*al-ʿIrāqān*) refer to Basrah and Kufah. Ed.

by the great number of his shaykhs, and the fact that he was the most knowledgeable of people in his time according to the testimony of the imams, as was already mentioned. Anything else is aberrant or is not part of what is acted upon.

If we concede that some ḥadīths which must legally be acted on were concealed from the imam, we still say that Muḥammad [ibn al-Ḥasan], Abū Yūsuf, Zufar ibn al-Hudhayl, Ibn al-Mubārak, al-Ḥasan ibn Ziyād and other companions lived on until the time when ḥadīth were recorded. Then aṭ-Ṭahāwī, al-Karkhī, al-Ḥākim, the author of al-Kāfī, ʿAbd al-Bāqī ibn Qāniʿ, al-Mustaghfirī, Ibn ash-Sharqī, az-Zaylaʿī and others from among the Ḥanafī *ḥuffāẓ* and ḥadīth critics lived on to [the time of] the full examination of the ḥadīths of the Prophet and they were aware of those which were sound or weak, well-known or solitary.

Thus every analogy which Abū Ḥanīfah used which they thought to be contrary to ḥadīth was abandoned by his companions like Muḥammad, Abū Yūsuf, Zufar and al-Ḥasan. They opposed their shaykh in half of his school. The school of the Ḥanafīs is the sum of the statements of the Imam and these companions of his.

Then Ḥanafī ḥadīth scholars after them gave preponderance in some cases to the position of ash-Shāfiʿī, in others to the position of Mālik, and in others to the position of Aḥmad. They gave *fatwā* according to that which appeared preponderant to them based on proof. All of this is the School of Abū Ḥanīfah since it proceeds using his method and the principles on which he based his school. One principle is to give precedence to the text, even if it is weak, over analogy. Praise belongs to Allah ﷻ! There does not remain in our school any position which is contrary to a ḥadīth unless we have another ḥadīth which supports it. If we seem to be diverging from it, we believe that it has an interpretation which we do not diverge from. That is what all the imams and their adherents do.

No one can claim to act by all the ḥadīths. Each person acts by some of them and leaves some, either because he considers them to be weak, contrary to [Qurʾānic] text or a well-known or *mutawātir* report, or because it is aberrant (*shādhdh*), defective, abrogated or interpreted with a meaning which common people do not know, and similar reasons.

A good comprehensive statement as an argument against those who censure and forbid taqlīd

As for those who deny *taqlīd*, it is not possible for them to act by the ḥadīth according to their principle at all because acting by it is only possible by following another scholar in determining this ḥadīth to be sound and that one to be weak, that this ḥadīth must be acted on and that one need not be acted on, rather it is permitted, recommended or forbidden to adopt it. This, as you see, is all *taqlīd* in rulings because whether the ḥadīth must be adopted or the reverse, or whether it is forbidden to adopt or the reverse definitely falls into the jurisdiction of rulings.

This is why the *fuqahāʾ* mention investigating the *sunna*, what is accepted and rejected, adopted [for action] and abandoned, and the rulings of narrators in *fiqh* and its *uṣūl* since it is the subject of rulings. These people completely deny *taqlīd*, analogy and *ijtihād* (in rulings), then how can they follow ḥadīth scholars in this? How can they take their opinions and ijtihād in considering ḥadīths to be sound or weak as proof?

We have explained more than once that the soundness or weakness of a ḥadīth, and the trustworthiness or weakness of a narrator all derive from the judgement, opinion and *ijtihād* of the ḥadīth scholar. That is why disagreements arose between them about that: one scholar would declare a ḥadīth weak while another declared it sound; one would declare a man to be weak while another declared him to be trustworthy. Is this anything but disagreement of opinions? So understand and do not hasten to censure a trusted imam whose esteem has been proclaimed by the Community and whose veneration and nobility has been acknowledged by the Imams. Allah ﷻ is in charge of guiding you.

Clarification of what is meant by abrogation in the words of the Salaf; it is different from the technical usage of later scholars

Ibn al-Qayyim said in *Iʿlām al-Muwaqqiʿīn*:

> What most of the *salaf* meant by the abrogating and abrogated (*nāsikh* and *mansūkh*) is sometimes to remove a ruling altogether, which is the technical usage of later scholars, and sometimes to remove the implication of the general (*ʿāmm*), the unqualified (*muṭlaq*), apparent (*ẓāhir*) and the like either by specification, qualification, or taking something unqualified as qualified, explaining and clarifying it. They even designated an exception, precondition and attribute as "abrogation" so that it comprises the removal of the implication of the apparent meaning and the explaination of what is actually meant.
>
> So in their opinion and use of language "*naskh*" is explaining what is meant using other words, rather by using something separate from it. If anyone reflects on their words, he will see this in them countless times and it will remove difficult questions brought about by understanding their words according to later newer technical usage.

I say, the upshot is that, in their view "*naskh*" is not specific to clarifying a replacement, but includes all forms of clarification. *Naskh* is frequently used with this general meaning in the words of the critical ḥāfiẓ and imam of the ḥadīth scholars in his time, the head of the Ḥanafis in his time, Abu Jaʿfar aṭ-Ṭahāwī, may Allah ﷻ have mercy on him. Whoever is not aware of what is meant will object to him and make him the target of criticism, saying, "The claim of abrogation is only accepted through historical clarification or another additional proof, and there is no proof there." If someone is ignorant of what the speaker means he only has himself to blame. Allah ﷻ is the One who is asked for help.

Refutation of those who object to taqlīd and criticize it

Ibn al-Qayyim stated in *Iʿlām al-Muwaqqiʿīn* in refutation of the proofs of those who do *taqlīd*:

> The seventy-second reason is your statement that the Companions of the Messenger of Allah ﷺ conquered lands when people were new to Islam, and they used to give them *fatwās* but they did not tell any of them, "You must try to know the truth in this *fatwā* based on proof."
>
> The answer to this is that they did not give *fatwā* based on their opinion; they conveyed to them what their Prophet said, did and ordered. The *fatwā* they gave is the ruling and the proof. They told them, "This is the trust of our Prophet to us, and it is our trust to you." What they reported to them is the proof itself and is the ruling. The words of the Messenger of Allah ﷺ is the judgement and the proof for the judgement. That is also the case with the Qur'an. The people at that time were eager to learn what their Prophet said, did and commanded. The Companions conveyed that.

I say, the bias and cold arbitrariness in this generalisation is evident. If we were to concede that, it would necessarily mean that all the statements and *fatwās* of the Companions are *marfūʿ* ḥadīths because of your (Ibn al-Qayyim's) statement, "The *fatwā* they gave is the ruling and the proof." So the Ḥanafīs cannot be criticized when they accept the position and *fatwā* of Ibn Masʿūd in a case and leave the *marfūʿ* ḥadīth since you admit that the *fatwā* of a Companion is the ruling and is also the proof. When two ḥadīths are contradictory, one acts according to preponderance. Then if analogy or another preponderating factor [provided the basis for and] gave preference to the statement of a Companion over a *marfūʿ* report, then it should be permissible according to you to take the position of the Companion, and not permitted for you to criticise someone who does that. So, the groups who object to *taqlīd* should understand that.

Furthermore, if it is the case that the Companions, may Allah ﷻ be pleased with them, did not give people *fatwā* based on their opinions and conveyed to them what their Prophet said, did and ordered, who told you that the Tābiʿūn gave people *fatwā* based on their opinions? Why is such a claim not permitted about their *fatwās*; they only conveyed what the Companions told them, did and commanded. That was also the case with the followers of the Tābiʿūn. They conveyed to their companions what the Tābiʿūn told them, did and commanded, and so forth.

If you were to say, "Why then do their *fatwās* differ from the ḥadīths which ḥadīth scholars transmitted?" we would answer by saying, "why do the *fatwās* of the

Companions differ from the *marfūʿ* ḥadīths which these men also narrated?" That can only be denied by someone who argues with falsehood and who has blinded himself to the truth. Thus, whatever your answer is (to the last question), is [also] our answer [to yours].

In my view, although these words of Ibn al-Qayyim are not absolutely correct because the evidences stand against them and because the Companions did give *fatwā* in some questions based on their ijithād and people did not ask them for a proof which is *taqlīd* itself, they are generally correct. Indeed most of the statements of the Companions and their *fatwā*s conveyed what the Prophet ﷺ said, did or ordered. Since that is the case, it is sometimes permitted for a mujtahid to give preponderance to the *fatwā* of a Companion over an explicit *marfūʿ* report when he believes that the *fatwā* of a Companion takes preference because it is based on conveying rather than on opinion.

This said, I did not intend by these words to refute Ibn al-Qayyim, may Allah ﷻ have mercy on him. Allah forbid! He is far too esteemed and great for someone like me to speak about him. By Allah ﷻ, being the dust of his sandals would elevate our rank! Rather I wanted to refute those who use his answers to censure *taqlīd*. They should open their eyes and see what the words of their leader mean. Allah ﷻ is the One who is asked for help.

Anyone who reflects on our words just stated [above] and reads our book Iʿlāʾ as-sunan will know, Allah ﷻ willing, that we are not among those who practise the *taqlīd* which Ibn al-Qayyim censured. Rather we follow our Imam, Abū Ḥanīfah, and his companions because we know that they are the people who most followed the Qur'an and *sunna* and that they possess fundamental principles in ḥadīth as the ḥadīth scholars possessed principles. Therefore we incur no blame if we oppose them by accepting some ḥadīths and acting by them and not acting by others because the basis of the fundamental rules of the two groups is *ijtihād*, and nothing is incontestable in *ijtihād*.

Our scholars sometimes abandon the positions of their Imam for the positions of his companions if they diverge from the texts. There are numerous examples of that in the Schools as is known by anyone who examines them. They often gave *fatwā* according the positions of the Imams among whom there are the likes our imam or the likes of his companions when they saw that those scholars had the stronger proof, or for a similar reason. May Allah ﷻ be praised, we are not rigidly fixed on the position of the founder of the School by mere partisanship. Rather we and those who follow us imitate him with insight. Glory be to Allah! We are not among those who associate others with Allah ﷻ!

This type of taqlīd is necessary for everyone and the danger of abandoning taqlīd and claiming ijtihād in this time

Ibn al-Qayyim cannot dispense with this type of *taqlīd*. In fact it is necessary for everyone and there is no safety for the dīn without it. This is what Ibn al-Qayyim called following (*mutābaʿah*) and obeying the command (*imtithāl li-'l-amr*). The expressions used differ, but the meaning is the same.

> Our expressions vary while your beauty remains the same.
> And everyone indicates to that beauty.

Anyone who abandons this *taqlīd*, rejects following the pious predecessors, deems himself to be a mujtahid or ḥadīth scholar, and feels that he himself is entitled to deduce rulings and the answers to cases from the Qurʾān and ḥadīth in this time has removed the yoke of Islam from his neck, or almost done so. By Allah ﷻ, we do not see any group deviate from the dīn the way an arrow shoots from a bow except for this group who deny the *taqlīd* of the pious predecessors and criticize its people. One of their leaders spoke the truth when he said after a long experience [with them], "Abandoning *taqlīd* is the root of heresy and *zandaqa* for the common people."[377]

I say, this is also true of scholars. A scrupulous, pious, godfearing scholar who loves Allah ﷻ and His Messenger ﷺ and spends his capacity in seeking the truth is like the philosopher's stone today, only rarely found. When they abandon *taqlīd*, most of them begin to seek out allowances (*rukhaṣ*), obey their own desires and turn their passion in their god. Most of them only abandon *taqlīd* in order to argue with those who do *taqlīd*, bring about dissent and corruption among the Muslims and turn the common people into heretics. It is known that abandoning *taqlīd* for them is the root of zandaqa and heresy.

The words of one of our great elders are true: these people act by ḥadīth, but by the ḥadīth [speech] of the self, not by the ḥadīth of the Messenger ﷺ, whichever way the wind blows.

Concerning some of the weak points in the two Ṣaḥīḥ Collections and exageration in answering them

Ibn Abī al-Wafāʾ al-Qurashī said in *Kitāb al-Jāmiʿ*, which he wrote as an appendix to *al Jawāhir al-Muḍiyya*:

> People's statement that, "whoever the two Shaykhs narrated from has crossed the

377 Imam al-Kawtharī has an article on this subject in *Maqālat al-Kawtharī*, p.129–137 under the title *al-Lā madhhabiyyah Qantarah al-Lādīniyyah*.

bridge," is exaggerated glorification and is not credible. In his book, Muslim narrated from Layth ibn Abī Sulaymān and other weak people. They then say, "he narrated from them in his book for the purpose of analysis (*iʿtibār*), attestation (*shawāhid*) and corroboration (*mutābaʿah*)." This is [also] not credible because al-Ḥāfiẓ[378] said, "analysis, attestation and corroboration are matters by which the state of the ḥadīth is known. In Muslim's book he undertood [that the ḥadīth would be] *ṣaḥīḥ*, so how can the state of the ḥadīth in it be known by weak paths of transmission?"

Know that the accusative "*anna*" and the preposition "*ʿan*" necessitate that there is a break—i.e. from a person guilty of *tadlīs* (not from all narrators)—according to the people of ḥadīth, Yet this sort of thing occurs frequently in Muslim and al-Bukhārī. People say by way of exagerating the rank of those collections, 'Anything like this in other than the two *Ṣaḥīḥ* Collections is broken and what is found in the two *Ṣaḥīḥ* Collections is taken to be connected.

In his book, Muslim narrated from Abū az-Zubayr many ḥadīths from Jābir with the preposition *ʿan*. The *ḥuffāẓ* said that Abū az-Zubayr used *tadlīs* in Jābir's ḥadīths and so those that are in the form of *ʿanʿanah* (use of the preposition *ʿan*) will not be accepted.[379] Ibn Ḥazm and ʿAbd al-Ḥaqq from al-Layth ibn Saʿd that he said to Abū az-Zubayr, 'Teach me the ḥadīths which you heard from Jābir so that I can hear them from you.' He taught him the ḥadīths, and it is assumed that there were seventeen ḥadīths and he heard them from him. In Muslim there are ḥadīths other than those by the path of al-Layth from Abū az-Zubayr from Jabir by the method of *ʿanʿanah*.

Muslim also narrated in his book from Jābir and Ibn ʿUmar about the Farewell Ḥajj that the Prophet ﷺ set out for Makka on the Day of Sacrifice and performed *Ṭawāf al-ifāḍah*, then prayed Ẓuhr in Makka, and then returned to Mina. In another narration, he performed *Ṭawāf al-ifāḍah* and then returned and prayed Ẓuhr at Mina. So they glorify it and say [to consolidate the contradiction], "He repeated it to demonstrate permissibility," and other such interpretations. Ibn Ḥazm says about these two narrations, "One is a lie without a doubt."

Muslim also narrated the ḥadīth of the Night Journey in which there is, "that was before he had received Revelation." The *ḥuffāẓ* have discussed these words and said that they are weak.

Muslim also narrated, "Allah ﷻ created the earth on Saturday," when people are unanimous that there was no creation on Saturday, and that creation began on Sunday.

Muslim narrated that Abū Sufyān said to Prophet ﷺ when he became Muslim, "Messenger of Allah, grant me three things: marry my daughter Umm Habībah, make my son Muʿāwiyah a scribe, and give me command [of an army] to fight the unbeliev-

---

378 Meaning al-Ḥāfiẓ Rashīd ad-Dīn al-ʿAṭṭār in his work *al-Fawāʾid al-Majmūʿah fī Shaʾn mā Waqaʿa fī Muslim min al-Aḥadīth al-Maqṭūʿa.*

379 Meaning they will not be accepted as *muttaṣil* (connected). Ed.

ers as I fought the Muslims." The Prophet ﷺ granted him what he asked. The ḥadīth is known and famous.

There is evident error in this, for the Messenger of Allah ﷺ married Umm Habībah while she was in Abyssinia, and the Negus paid her dower on behalf of the Prophet ﷺ: four hundred dinars. He attended, gave a speech and fed them. The tale is well-known. Abū Sufyān only became Muslim in the year of the Conquest of Makka, and a number of years had passed between Abyssinia and the Conquest. Muᶜāwiyah was a scribe of the Prophet ﷺ from before. As for giving Abū Sufyān command, the *ḥuffāẓ* said that they do not recognise it. So they give futile anwers [to these discrepancies] based for the sake of glorifying [Muslim]. He (the *hafidh*) mentioned these and then said, "only some partisanship moved them to all of that."[380]

The *ḥuffāẓ* say: "When Muslim wrote his book, *aṣ-Ṣaḥīḥ*, he presented it to Abū Zurᶜa who objected to it and became angry. He said, 'You have called it *aṣ-Ṣaḥīḥ* and made a ladder for the people of innovations and others. When an opponent narrates a ḥadīth to them, they will say, "This is not in the *Ṣaḥīḥ Muslim*!"'" May Allah ﷻ have mercy on Abū Zurᶜa! He spoke the truth. This has indeed happened.

I say, the fact that Muslim and al-Bukhārī transmitted from some weak men does not detract from the soundness of their books. Their focus is on the soundness of the ḥadīths transmitted in them, not on all the narrators being narrators of what is sound. They only transmitted from weak narrators when there was corroboration, not narrations they alone had. Nevertheless, the basis of weakness and trustworthiness is ijtihād and opinion, so it is possible that these men were trustworthy according to them as opposed to the position of the majority unless they clearly stated that they are weak. In that case, it must be said that they transmitted their ḥadīths as support and corroboration. There is no doubt that what is sound is increased in strength by a large number of paths of transmission.

As for what Muslim transmitted which only weak transmitters had and whose soundness is unlikely as al-Qurashī mentioned, there is no doubt that it is weak. But every sword has a slip and every racehorse has a stumble. This does not detract from the soundness of the book in respect of the whole and in general. Likewise, it does not detract from its superior position to books other than al-Bukhārī. One does not pay any attention to a few rare instances. The truth is what we already mentioned about the superior soundness of the two books compared to other books, that it is in respect to the whole and in general, not in respect to the details of every single ḥadīth. So understand that and do not be among those who exaggerate.

May Allah ﷻ bless our master Muhammad ﷺ and his family and all his Compan-

---

380 Ibn al-Qayyim al-Jawziyya, *Jilā al-Afhām*, pp.159–168 discusses this ḥadīth at length and declares it not to be *maḥfūẓ*. Adh-Dhahabī declares it *munkar* in *al-Mīzan*, 3:93.

ions. Praise belongs to Allah ﷻ, the Lord of the Universe. I finished the rough draft of this conclusion Wednesday morning at the beginning of the blessed Ramaḍān 1347. Praise, thanks and extolment belong to Allah ﷻ.

CHAPTER 11

The special technical expressions we use in the book *Iʿlāʾ as-Sunan*, and in this preface, *Inhāʾ as-Sakan*, in all that which relates to it from *Injāʾ al-Waṭan*, and other books

If I said, "The shaykh said", "Our shaykh said" or "My Shaykh said" and the like, what is meant is my master, the Sage of the Community and Renewer of the religion, Mawlana Shaykh Muḥammad Ashraf ʿAlī, may Allah ﷻ make his praise endure and benefit us by his long life![381] Āmīn. When I use such an expression, it is what I heard from him directly or the author of *al-Iḥyāʾ* narrated in his manuscript. Otherwise I named his book from which I took it and I wrote the sign indicating the conclusion [of the quote] at the end of the words.

*

If I say, "My friend said in his appendix or his commentary," by that I mean my master, guide and beloved, our master, the ḥāfiẓ and proof, the ḥadith scholar with high *isnād* in his time, the *faqīh* of his time and age, the pole of guidance, Mawlana Shaykh Khalīl Aḥmad—may his glory and elevation endure! and what he said in his commentary on Abū Dāwūd which is called *Badhl al-Majhūd*. Sometimes I mention him by name and the commentary.

*

If I say, "al-Ḥāfiẓ said" and leave it unqualified, what is meant is the Seal of the Ḥuffāẓ, al-Ḥāfiẓ Ibn Hajar al-ʿAsqalānī—may Allah ﷻ elevate his degrees in the highest degrees of the Garden! Āmīn. If I say, "Al-Ḥāfiz said in *al-Fatḥ* or in *at-Talkhīṣ*," what I mean is what he said in *Fatḥ al-Bārī* or in *at-Talkhīṣ al-Ḥabīr*. In general when I say

381 Mawlana Ashraf ʿAlī at-Thānawī (May Allah ﷻ have mercy on his soul) was still living when Mawlana Ẓafar Aḥmad wrote *Iʿlāʾ as-Sunan*. He checked the first 9 volumes letter by letter and then left it to Shaykh Ẓafar asking him to consult him when needed. The complete twelves volumes were also published during Shaykh Ashraf's life. Ed.

al-Fatḥ or *at-Talkhīṣ*, I mean only this. When I say, "That is how it is in *at-Tahdhīb* or *al-Lisān*," I mean his books *Tahdhīb at-Tahdhīb* and *Lisān al-Mizān*. What is meant by *at-Taqrīb* is *Taqrīb at-Tahdhīb* by him. Sometimes I indicate to it by 't q'.

*

When I say, "The meticulous scholar (*al-muḥaqqiq*) said in *al-Fatḥ*," that means the shaykh and Imam Ibn al-Humām, in *Fatḥ al-Qadīr*. *Fatḥ al-Qadīr* is not meant by the expression "*al-Fatḥ*" unless it is connected to the expression *al-muḥaqqiq*, before or after it.

*

When I say, "Al-ʿAynī said," and leave it unqualified or "al-ʿAynī said in *al-ʿUmdah*," it means what he said in *ʿUmdat al-Qārī*, the commentary on al-Bukhārī. If it is someone else, I make that clear.

*

When I say, "as it is stated in *al-Jawhar* (not *jawāhir*)," I mean *al-Jawhar an-Naqī* by the scholar ʿAlāʾ ad-dīn ibn at-Turkumānī. When I say, "as is in *al-Jawāhir*," what is meant is *al-Jawāhir al-Muḍiyyah fi Ṭabaqāt al-Hanafiyyah* by the Shaykh and Imam, ʿAbd al-Qadīr ibn Abī al Wafāʾ al-Qurashī al-Hanafī. When I say "al-Qurashī" and leave it unqualified, I mean him.

*

What is meant by "*at-Tadrīb*" is *Tadrīb ar-Rāwī*, the commentary on *at-Taqrīb* of an-Nawawī by al-Ḥāfiẓ as-Suyūṭī. Sometimes I indicate it by 't d'. "*Al-Kanz*" means *Kanz al-ʿUmmāl* by as-Suyūṭī on ḥadīth,[382] not *Kanz ad-Daqāʾiq* on *fiqh*. "*Al-ʿAwn*" means *ʿAwn al-Maʿbūd*, the commentary on Abū Dāwūd by one of the excellent scholars of India.[383] "*Jāmiʿ al-Masānīd*" means *Jāmiʿ Masānīd al-Imām al-Aʿdham* by Abū al-Muʾayyid al-Khawārzimī and by "Abū al-Muʾayyid" when it is unqualifiedly mentioned al-Khawārzimī is intended. *Al-Bughya* is *Bughyat al-Wuʿāh fi Ṭabaqāt an-Nuḥāh* by as-Suyūṭī. "*Az-Zaylaʿī*" is Jamāl ad-Dīn ʿAbdullāh ibn Yūsuf, the author of *Naṣb ar-Rāyah fi Takhrīj Aḥādīth al-Hidāyah*. Sometimes I used just "az-Zaylaʿī" to refer to *Naṣb ar-Rāyah* just as "at-Tirmidhī" and "al-Bukhārī" are used to refer to their books. "*Al-Majmaʿ*" refers to *Majmaʿ az-Zawāʾid* by al-Haythamī, not *Majmaʿ al-Biḥār* on peculiar expressions in ḥadīth (*gharīb*). In most places "Abū

382 *Kanz al-ʿUmmāl* is by al-Muttaqī al-Hindī, however it is based on as-Suyuṭī's *al-Jāmiʿ al-Kabīr* and *al-Jāīʿ aṣ-Ṣaghīr*. So attributing Kanz to al-Suyuti is due to this connection. Ed.

383 Referring to Shams al-Haqq al-ʿAẓīmabadī.

Dāwūd" refers to the edition of the author of *al-ʿAwn* which is printed along the top of it, and in some places to the edition published by al-Mujtabāʾī Press in 1218 AH.

*

If I say, "Someone said in his *Iḥyāʾ*" or "Someone said," what is meant is the author of *Iḥyāʾ as-sunan*, as-Sanbhalī, in his book. He has mentioned in his book some weak objections against the Ḥanafīs and some of the Salaf out of enmity and unfairness, or ignorance and error. I have answered these and explained the foolishness of his objections, his poor understanding and lack of contemplation. By that I only meant to defend the imams who are followed in the dīn and give good advice to my Muslim brothers. If I say, "One of them said," I do not mean him but one of the scholars among the *fuqahāʾ* and ḥadīth scholars.

*

What is meant by "*ad-Durr*" is only *ad-Durr al-Mukhtār*, published on the margins of *Radd al-Muḥtār* not the version without it. It is *Radd al-Muhtār* which is meant by "*ash-Shāmiyyah*" in most places and I sometimes specify it. When I say, "*Ash-Shāmī* said," I mean the scholar and *faqīh* Ibn ʿĀbidīn, the commentator of *ad-Durr al-Mukhtār*. When I say, "That is what is stated in *ash-Shāmiyyah*," I mean in *Radd al-Muḥtār*, the commentary on *ad-Durr al-Mukhtār*. "*Al-Baḥr*" means *al-Baḥr ar-Rāʾiq* by Ibn Nujaym. "*Ad-Durar*" means *Durar al-Ḥukkām fī Sharḥ Ghurar al-Aḥkām* by Mullā Khusraw al-Ḥanafī. *Ash-Shurunbulāliyya* means *Marāqī al-Falāḥ* by Shaykh Ḥasan ibn ʿAmmār ash-Shurunbulālī with its marginal gloss by aṭ-Ṭaḥṭāwī.

*

When I say, "Aṭ-Ṭaḥāwī said," and I use it undefined, then what is meant is what he said in *Maʿānī al-Āthār*. Otherwise I explain it. Other allusions and indications are clear, Allah ﷻ willing.

So this is the final conclusion. Praise belongs to Allah ﷻ the All-Knowing for His uninterrupted kindness and bounties to this slave who is drowning in wrong actions. May the purest blessing and radiant peace be always upon the Master of the children of Ādam, our Master, the Prophet Muḥammad, and on his family and noble pious Companions until the Day of Rising, indeed as long as the Abode of Peace endures.

The book was finished Monday morning, 9th Rajab 1344 AH.[384]

The preface is complete, and praise belongs to Allah ﷻ by whose might and maj-

384 Corresponding to 24 January 1926.

esty righteous deeds are completed. I am the one in need of the mercy of the Everlasting Lord, His slave, Zafar Aḥmad al-ʿUthmānī at-Thānawī—May Allah ﷻ grant him success in preparing for the morrow and forgive him, his parents and children, his shaykhs, those he loves, and his companions. May Allah ﷻ Almighty bless our master, the Prophet Muḥammad and his family and Companions for ever.

Appendix 1

SHAYKH ʿABD AL-FATTĀḤ ABŪ GHUDDAH'S COMMENDATION (*TAQRĪẒ*) OF ʿALLĀMAH ẒAFAR AḤMAD ʿUTHMĀNĪ THĀNAWĪ'S *IʿLĀʾ AS-SUNAN*[385]

Translated by Zameelur Rahman

ALL PRAISE BE to Allāh, Lord of the Worlds, and blessings and peace be upon our leader and our master Muḥammad, and upon his family and all his companions.

To proceed: One of the most important ways in which the pure *sunna* is served is by commenting on the ḥadīths of rulings and extracting what is found in them of jurisprudence (*fiqh*) and teaching, commands and prohibitions, the lawful and the unlawful. The aspirations of the juristic ḥadīth masters vied with one another in every age and place to collect these ḥadīths on a single platform so they become a simple reference-point and easily attainable for every student of jurisprudence and seeker of benefit.

One of the best, nay *the* best, of what has been compiled on this [subject] in this fourteenth century, and the most far-reaching of them in comprehensiveness, from the perspective of the Ḥanafī masters, is the book *Iʿlāʾ as-Sunan*. This is a compilation by our teacher, the great scholar (*ʿallāmah*), the ḥadīth scholar (*muḥaddith*), the jurist (*faqīh*), the theoretician (*usūlī*), the proficient researcher, Shaykh Ẓafar Aḥmad al-ʿUthmānī al-Thānawī, which was first printed in India using [old] lithographic print in the year 1341/1923 and [later volumes continued to be printed] thenceforth, and most of it was printed there. Its printing was later completed in Karachi (Pakistan), and was published in twenty volumes.[386] These included two volumes of prologue to the book. One of them was on the sciences of ḥadīth[387] and

385 *Qawāʿid*, pp. 3–7.

386 The final volume was completed in 1357 AH (1938 CE).

387 Shaykh Abdul Fattah: This beneficial comprehensive ḥadīth-oriented introduction called *Inhāʾ al-Sakan ilā man yuṭāliʿu Iʿlāʾ as-Sunan* was printed in India in the year 1345 AH in [old] lithographic print. It was then printed in Karachi in Pakistan in the year 1383 AH in modern print. Later, Allāh, with Whom

the other on juristic principles, in view of what the book contained of noble ḥadīths in the main text (*matn*) and the juristic rulings deduced from them in the commentary (*sharḥ*), so the book by means of this comprehensiveness and meticulousness came to be at the pinnacle of what was compiled on its subject matter.

The reason for compiling this immensely beneficial book is what occurred in the course of this century when a group of people in some cities of India arose, before the partition of Pakistan, calling themselves 'Ahl al-ḥadīth', claiming that the school of the Ḥanafī masters, which is the school of the majority of Muslims in those large and expansive lands, conflicts with the Prophetic ḥadīths in many issues, just as they claimed that the Ḥanafī masters prefer analogy over the noble ḥadīth, and just as they rejected *taqlīd* of the four Imāms who are followed, and they stretched their tongues with respect to Ḥanafī jurisprudence, and more specifically, with respect to the jurist of this Ummah, Imām Abū Ḥanīfah.

Outstanding scholars from those Indian lands arose to challenge these deviant beliefs and they falsified these claims through many well-researched ḥadīth-oriented works. They explained in these [works] the reliance of the Ḥanafī masters in their jurisprudence and their school on the noble ḥadīths, and that they prefer the noble ḥadīth, and even weak ḥadīth, over analogy, and that analogy with its set conditions is amongst the proofs which must be acted upon, and the Ḥanafī Imāms are no less in deducing rulings from the *sunna* and holding firmly to it than other *imāms*, if not stronger than others in holding firmly to the *sunna* and *athar* (reports from the Companions and their successors). Rather, our teacher, the author of *Iʿlāʾ as-Sunan*—may Allāh Almighty have mercy on him and increase his rewards—established in his ḥadīth-oriented introduction, *Qawāʿid fī ʿUlūm al-ḥadīth*[388] that the Ḥanafīs prefer the statements of the Companions over analogy, due to their excessive adherence to reports from the Companions and their successors, let alone the noble Prophetic ḥadīths

Owing to this unique, comprehensive and rare book—*Iʿlāʾ as-Sunan*—and other similar ḥadīth-oriented compilations, which the scholars of India and Pakistan undertook in those lands which have now carried from the lands of the Muslims the burdens of the sciences of the *sunna*, its service and its propagation, those deviant claims against the Ḥanafīs have subsided in futility, and every arrogant, deviant or shameless pretender of knowledge has been silenced, and it has become apparent to every possessor of eyes that the Ḥanafīs are amongst the greatest adherents to ḥadīth

is grace and blessing, favoured me with serving this unique ḥadīth-oriented introduction by verifying, editing, annotating, publishing and distributing it with the title *Qawāʿid fī ʿUlūm al-Ḥadīth*. Its printing was completed in Beirut in the year 1392 in 550 pages and it became by the grace of Allāh Almighty an academic gift that is wonderful to look at and learn from, and it received the most pleasant acceptance and approval from the great scholars of this field. All praise belongs to Allāh, Cherisher of the worlds.

388 P. 289.

and reports from the Companions and their successors, while being people of analogy and research.

ʿAllāmah [Ẓafar Aḥmad al-ʿUthmānī] at-Thānawī—may Allāh reward him abundantly and raise his status and his mention before Him—exhausted in *Iʿlāʾ as-Sunan* the proofs pertinent to all the chapters of jurisprudence—from the chapter of purification to the concluding chapters of jurisprudence—with extraordinary effort and rigorous ḥadīth and *fiqh*-oriented methodology. Gazes turned to this book and the hands of the scholars from the time of its publication hastily seized it, and acquiring a copy of it came to be a major aspiration in the hearts of the scholars who knew about this book in comparison with other books or had heard about it.

It is sufficient testimony for you to know the lofty position of this book that the like of our teacher, Imām al-Kawtharī, praised it with the most wonderful praise in his book, *Maqālāt al-Kawtharī*[389] in an article in which he speaks of various lands taking turns in carrying the burdens of the sciences of the *sunna*. After referring to the efforts of the scholars of India and Pakistan and their achievements in the field of the pure *sunna* in the latter centuries, and their undertaking of the burdens of the sciences of the *sunna* since the tenth century till now, he said:

> Some of their scholars also have specific compilations on the ḥadīths of rulings in a novel original style, which is to exhaust the rulings from their sources and collect them in one place, arranged into chapters, and to comment on every ḥadīth with criticism and accreditation of its reporters and [overall] strength and weakness of the report.

After Imām al-Kawtharī loftily praised the book *Āthār as-Sunan*, written with the same objective, by the great ḥadīth master, the knowledgeable jurist, the critical analyst, Shaykh Muḥammad ibn ʿAlī, popularly known as Ẓahīr Aḥsan al-Nīmawī, the summary of what Imām al-Kawtharī said is:

> Similarly, the inimitable great scholar, the unique ocean, the teacher of the scholars of the Indian lands, the great ḥadīth master, the knowledgeable critical analyst, our master, the sage of the Ummah, Muḥammad Ashraf ʿAlī at-Thānawī, the author of works, both small and large, numbering around five hundred, nay his works numbered to more than a thousand by the time of his death, turned to this matter and he authored *Jāmiʿ al-Āthār*. A description of this book is dispensable by the mention of the great name of its author. Although it was published in India, acquiring it has become somewhat difficult since its printed copies were depleted by the great number of those interested in collecting the works of this Godly scholar (*al-ʿālim al-Rabbānī*), who is a blessing of the Indian lands, and he has a high standing amongst the scholars of India such that they call him 'the sage of the Ummah' (*Ḥakīm al-Ummah*).

389 P. 75.

This magnificent scholar instructed his student and nephew, who completed his ḥadīth studies under his tutelage and supervision, the critical ḥadīth master, the excellent jurist, Mawlānā Ẓafar Aḥmad at-Thānawī—may his achievements increase—to compile the proofs of the chapters of jurisprudence by collating the ḥadīths of rulings, [arranging them] into chapters, from the sources that are difficult to obtain, while commenting on every ḥadīth in accordance with the requirements of the science of ḥadīth of strength and weakness and acceptance and rejection, as per the varying schools. This enthusiastic scholar occupied himself with this difficult task for approximately twenty years with the utmost commitment until he completed his work with the utmost brilliance by the will and enabling of Allāh Glorified is He.

Truth be told, I was astonished by this compilation, exhaustion and this extreme comprehensiveness in commenting on every ḥadīth in accordance with the requirements of the science [of ḥadīth], in relation to the text and chain of reporters, without any apparent superficiality in support of his [Ḥanafī] school. Rather, impartiality was his principle when speaking of the opinions of the various schools. Hence, I was extremely pleased with the work. This is how the aspirations of [real] men and the earnestness of [true] heroes are. If only some of the owners of the large publishing houses in Egypt were to obtain the book from its author and print it in beautiful Egyptian type. If one of them were to do that, he would have rendered knowledge a service that would be appreciated, and he would have filled a gap in this subject. ([Here] ends the statement of our teacher, Imām al-Kawtharī.)

Indeed Allāh Almighty has shown favour by bringing this preciously noble desire to reality. For, He has enabled the publishing of this brilliant ḥadīth and *fiqh*-oriented book in the city of Karachi in Pakistan, adorned with an academically distinguished service by the great scholar, the researcher, the ḥadīth master, the perceptive jurist, the man of letters, the esteemed Shaykh Muḥammad Taqī al-ʿUthmānī,[390] the son of our respected teacher the Grand *Muftī* Mawlānā Muḥammad Shafīʿ—may his lofty shadow be lengthened in good health and happiness. That descendant, the brilliant heir, undertook the task of verifying, editing and annotating this book in a way that will complete its aims and objectives and perfect its pearls and its benefits with a lofty academic flavour and a novel typed artistic format, with a brilliant look from the beauty of modern printing. The first volume has become a wonderful academic treasure. The services of the sagacious researcher, the apple of Pakistan,[391]

390 Abu Asim Badrul Islam: This commendation (*taqrīẓ*) must have been written by Shaykh ʿAbd al-Fattāḥ Abū Ghuddah not long after our master ʿAllāmah *Muftī* Muhammad Taqi Usmani had commenced his work on *Iʿlāʾ as-Sunan*, as I know from the latter that he edited no more than the first two volumes out of the twenty-two volumes of the old Idārat al-Qurʾān (Karachi) edition.

391 ʿAbd al-Fattāḥ Abū Ghuddah: This is a title which I have designated to the verifier and editor of this book [*Muftī* Muḥammad Taqi al-Uthmani]—may Allāh Almighty protect and maintain him—while

is manifest therein, so this wonderful academic work deserves the gratitude of the students of knowledge and scholars.

Allāh is beseeched for the completion of this encyclopaedic beneficial book at his hands, so it becomes a great weight in his overflowing good deeds, Allāh willing. May Allāh reward him the best of rewards on behalf of knowledge and its people. May He also reward with goodness its distributor, publisher and all who helped in its production in this immaculate cover and beautiful printing. All praise is to Allāh by Whose grace good actions are completed.

Written by the one needy of Him Most High

ʿAbd al-Fattāḥ Abū Ghuddah
College of Sharīʿah, Riyadh
3 February 1396/1976

---

he was in the prime of his youth approximately fifteen years ago during my first trip to Pakistan in the year 1382 AH (1962 CE) when I saw in him a vigorous talent, a sharp mind, expansive knowledge, overflowing brilliance, along with a high and transparent spirit and a rare Arabic eloquence in his sermons and his extemporaneous speech. May Allāh increase him from His favour and accordance, and benefit through him [His] servants and all lands, and bless me with his righteous supplications.

Appendix 2

INTRODUCTION TO *IʿLĀʾ AS-SUNAN*

By Mufti Muhammad Taqi Usmani
Translated by Zameelur Rahman

ALL PRAISE TO Allah ﷻ, Lord of the Worlds, and blessings and peace be upon our leader and our master, Muhammad, and his family and all his companions, and on all who follow their way to the Day of Recompense.[392]

As for what follows: I cannot find in this fortunate and joyous moment any word or expression or means to express what is in my heart of the emotions of delight and gratitude to Allah ﷻ (Glorified and Exalted is He) that He has enabled me to produce this book and present it to readers in this splendid suit and wonderful dress of writing and print. It does not befit the like of me to expect such great fortune, but it is purely the grace of Allah ﷻ and only His favour on a weak and weary slave who is unable to be grateful as is deserving, and has no [option] but to borrow words from His Noble Messenger ﷺ: "I am unable to praise You—You are as You praised Yourself!"

I would like, before speaking about the book, to present to the noble reader a brief biography of the imam, the magnificent scholar, the great caller [to Allah ﷻ], the sage of the nation (*ḥakīm al-ummah*), Shaykh Ashraf ʿAlī ibn ʿAbd al-Haqq at-Thānawī, may Allah ﷻ show expansive mercy to him, for he was the first to undertake this immense academic project, and he paved its way, and called the scholars to it, and illuminated the path for them, and he remained with them for the duration of the work as a supervisor supervising them and as a guide guiding them, looking at every letter of what they wrote and assisting them by his beneficial words, and overflowing them with his sciences.

---

392 Note from the translator: This is a translation of Mufti Muhammad Taqi Usmani's introduction to ʿAllāmah Ẓafar Aḥmad al-ʿUthmānī monumental twenty-volume compendium of ḥadīth-proofs for the Ḥanafī *madhhab* called *Iʿlāʾ as-Sunan*, written in 1976 CE for his critical edition of the first volume of this book, comprising of useful biographies of Mawlana Ashraf ʿAlī at-Thānawī and ʿAllāmah Ẓafar Aḥmad al-ʿUthmānī, and a discussion on the background to the compilation of *Iʿlāʾ as-Sunan*

BIOGRAPHY OF ḤAKĪM AL-UMMAH IMAM SHAYKH ASHRAF ʿALĪ AT-THĀNAWĪ

He (Allah ﷻ have mercy on him) was from the genius and unique scholars and the righteous and sincere callers, who lit the lamps of renewal in India with bright flames and shining lights, and devoted their lives to elevating the word of Allah ﷻ and reviving the religious sciences, guarding the frontiers of Islam, remaining steadfast on calling to Allah ﷻ, and enduring what they suffered in this path.

He (Allah ﷻ have mercy on him) was born on the morning of the fifth of Rabīʿ ath-Thānī in the year 1280 after the Prophetic migration (upon its bearer be peace) (September 1863 CE) in a noble family whose lineage reached the Commander of Believers, our master, ʿUmar ibn al-Khaṭṭāb ؓ, in the village of Thana Bhawan in Muzaffarnagar District, which is considered to be from the villages which are recognised in the Indian lands for its outstanding men and its knowledgeable scholars and its great saints, like the great scholar and verifier, Shaykh Muhammad Aʿla at-Thānawī author of *Kashshāf Iṣṭilahāt al-Funūn*—that great academic encyclopaedia which has gained the praise and trust of the people of knowledge in the eastern and western regions of the globe; and like the great scholar, Shaykh Muḥammad at-Thānawī, and Hafiz Muhammad Damīn ash-Shahīd, and the knower [of Allah ﷻ], the verifier, Hājī Imdād Allāh al-Muhājir al-Makkī, who are referred to in all corners of these lands as the "three pivots" (*al-aqtāb al-thalāthah*), Allah ﷻ show expansive mercy to them.

Ḥakīm al-Ummah (Allah ﷻ have mercy on him) was born in this village that flourished with knowledge and devotion, scrupulousness and piety, and he grew up in this purely religious environment. Here, he memorised the Qurʾan, and learnt the primary Persian and Arabic [subjects] and the sciences of religion at the hands of expert teachers. From the prime of his youth, he was dedicated to [gaining] knowledge and [attending to] the scholars, devoted to acts of obedience and far-removed from useless activity. From the brittleness of his nature was that since his early childhood he could not bear to look at another's belly while it was uncovered, and when he would unexpectedly see one of the children with his belly uncovered he would be overcome by nausea, so the children would [deliberately] come before him and expose their bellies in front of him so that he would vomit, and as such he (Allah ﷻ have mercy on him) would be exhausted of vomiting again and again, and this brittleness in his nature was an existential reason from Allah ﷻ making him averse to mixing with most children, and as a consequence he was far-removed from their vain activities and their futility.

He (Allah ﷻ have mercy on him) became accustomed to night prayer when twelve years old, and the wife of his paternal uncle would sometimes wake up in the middle of the night and see him praying, and she would try to make him lessen it out of affection for him, but because of its rootedness in his soul, he was unconcerned with this and continued with his prayer.

Thus he began his education in his hometown in the primary religious sciences until he reached his fifteenth year, whereupon he travelled to Darul Uloom Deoband, which was and still is the biggest centre for religious sciences in India and an academic seminary filled with people of knowledge, virtue, recognition and piety, and a sweet pool of the pools of knowledge and devotion, from which thousands of men graduated with immense knowledge and extensive experience and deep insight and righteous works and religious firmness and sound taste in calling to Allah ﷻ and striving in His path. Thus, he (Allah ﷻ have mercy on him) was admitted into this auspicious institute, and received all the Arabic, literary, rational and transmitted sciences with teachers that recall the memories of the ancients in their extensive knowledge and their quality precision, like the imam and great warrior, Shaykh Maḥmūd al-Ḥasan ad-Deobandī, who is called "*Shaykh al-Hind*" due to his lofty rank in knowledge and piety and due to his constructive and continuous efforts in the cause of liberating India from the hands of oppressive English colonisers; and like our master, the knower [of Allah ﷻ], the verifier, Shaykh Muhammad Yaʿqūb an-Nanōtwī, who was known for his proficiency in all the sciences and arts, and his preoccupation with *dhikr* and acts of obedience; and like the imam, the philosopher, Mawlana Shaykh Muḥammad Qāsim al-Nanōtwī, the founder of Darul Uloom Deoband whose reputation for penetrating insight and deep thought and marvellous works on the science of dialectical theology (*kalām*), beliefs, jurisprudence and ḥadīth ḥspread [throughout India]; and like Mawlana Shaykh Sayyid Aḥmad ad-Dihlawī who reached the zenith in the rational sciences and he excelled in the mathematical sciences by mere [personal] study without studying them with a teacher.

In brief, Ḥakīm al-Ummah at-Thānawī (Allah ﷻ have mercy on him) stayed in Darul Uloom amongst these teachers and their peers (Allah ﷻ have mercy on them), and he acquired benefit from them, from their sciences and their service and their company. Through his entire student life he had no engagement besides studying his books and serving his teachers and professors. In Deoband, he had a number of relatives, who would often send to him invitations to eat with them, but he would make the excuse to them that he did not enter this city but for the purpose of learning and studying, so he did not visit them for the period of five years until he completed his studies.

While he was a student at Deoband, the Christians sent their missionaries to all parts of India, and they threatened the Muslims and invited them to debate and argue, so when he (Allah ﷻ have mercy on him) found the opportunity, he went out to them, debated them and overcame them with his far-reaching proofs and his clear speech, as a result of which he became well-known amongst the students and the public as a strong debater and skilled orator. However, this was in the period of his study at Deoband, and after he became an experienced scholar, he (Allah ﷺ have mercy on him) was the farthest of people from debate and argumentation, due to what he had seen that such debates and discussions lack sincerity and integrity, and rarely help in bringing people to guidance and rightness.

Thus, he (Allah ﷺ have mercy on him) studied in Darul Uloom at Deoband until he completed his studies in the year 1300 AH. It was from his humbleness that when the school board decided to inaugurate a big ceremony to distribute the certificates and turbans to the graduates, the Shaykh (Allah ﷺ have mercy on him) became frightened and he went with some of his classmates to his teacher, Mawlana Shaykh Muḥammad Yaʿqūb an-Nānōtwī (Allah ﷺ have mercy on him)—who was then the head teacher—and said:

> We heard that the school is going to present us with a certificate of completion of the sciences, and will place turbans on our heads, although the reality is that we are not deserving of this certificate and this honour, and we fear that this will be a reason for bad opinion of the school, that it produces the likes of us who have no knowledge.

However, Shaykh an-Nānōtwī replied:

> You only say this because you are in the embrace of [your] teachers, so you consider your knowledge insignificant before these [scholars]; but I bear witness that just as you leave this school, your rank will be recognised, and you will become outstanding in the field of knowledge with no comparison.

His (Allah ﷺ have mercy on him) speech came true as Ḥakīm al-Ummah at-Thānawī (his secret be sanctified) became the greatest recourse for the ulama and the commoners, and the greatest axis of learning and religion, and the ʿulama of that time confirmed that he was a marvel of his age in knowledge and piety, unequalled and unmatched.

His Teaching

In Kanpur there was a famous school called *al-Fayḍ al-ʿĀmm*, in which Mawlana Shaykh Aḥmad Ḥasan al-Amrōhowī taught, who was an advanced teacher whose reputation in all the sciences spread [throughout India], especially in the rational sciences. He had encountered some things that he disliked from the school committee, so he resigned from teaching there and founded another school.

Therefore, the owners of the school, *al-Fayḍ al-ʿĀmm*, requested from the scholars of Deoband to send to them a teacher, and Shaykh at-Thānawī had just graduated from Darul Uloom in that year, so his teachers selected him to answer their call.

Thereupon, he (Allah ﷻ have mercy on him) moved to Kanpur in the month of Ṣafar in the year 1300/1883. Thus, he began his first exodus to benefit the people at the onset of the fourteenth century. Hereof, some of the scholars considered him a reviver (*mujaddid*) of this century in the Indian lands.

In brief, he (Allah ﷻ have mercy on him) became occupied in Kanpur with teaching, calling [people to Allah ﷻ], admonishing and writing, and very soon he came to be known amongst the students for his great knowledge, brilliant teaching and powerful oration, even though he had been given the position of an experienced teacher while still in the prime of his youth. Then he founded in Kanpur another school with the name *Jāmiᶜ al-ᶜUlūm* which remains by the grace of Allah ﷻ till this day. Thus, a great multitude became his students. From the most eminent of his students are Shaykh Muḥammad Isḥāq al-Bardāwānī, who had memorised the entire *Ṣaḥīḥ* of al-Bukhārī by heart, and Mawlana Muḥammad Muṣṭafā al-Bajnūrī, the author of beneficial works in the Urdu language, and Mawlana Shaykh Ẓafar Aḥmad al-ᶜUthmānī, for whose overflowing knowledge and expansive experience *I'la al-Sunan* is sufficient proof.

His Return to his Hometown

In brief, Shaykh at-Thānawī (Allah ﷻ have mercy on him) stayed in Kanpur for a period of fourteen years, benefitting people with his lessons, his sermons and his writings. Then solitude was made dear to him, so he resigned from the school at Kanpur in Ṣafar of the year 1315/1897 and appointed his student Mawlana Shaykh Muhammad Isḥāq al-Bardāwānī as his replacement there. Then he returned to his hometown Thana Bhawan and he stayed in the *zāwiyah* (spiritual convent) of his spiritual teacher (*shaykh*), called *al-Khānqah al-Imdādiyya*, because his spiritual teacher, Ḥājī Imdād Allāh, the emigrant to Mecca, had instructed him to [do] so. Then, he remained in this *zāwiyah* till Allah ﷻ took his [soul] in the year 1362/1943. In this *zāwiyah*, Allah ﷻ produced by his hands mammoth works on religion, such [works] that large committees and global commissions are unable to [produce]. Indeed it is difficult for us to mention all of these achievements, or most of them, in this brief biography, but we will [suffice with a] selection of some of them. Allah ﷻ gives accordance.

His Writings

Ḥakīm al-Ummah shaykh at-Thānawī (Allah ﷻ have mercy on him) was the most prolific author of his time. There are none in this century who are equal to him or match him in the number of books written, as he left behind him around a thousand published books that range between large and small. There is no religious subject that Muslims are in need of in this time except he has a published book or treatise or sermon regarding it. We are unable to mention all of them in detail in this short essay, but here is a list of some of the most important of them:

As for Qur'anic exegesis, he has a marvellous exegesis in the Urdu language with the title *Bayān al-Qurʾān* in four large volumes with large size paper. It includes important academic discussions about exegesis, syntax, rhetoric, jurisprudence, speculative theology and Sufism. The value of this book will only be appreciated when a man refers to it after studying the extended books from exegetical works, for he has combined their essence and their spirit using simple academic and comprehensive expressions.He hoped to compile *Aḥkām al-Qurʾān* in the Arabic language himself, in order to collect therein the issues of jurisprudence and theology derived from the Noble Qurʾān, in particular the issues which arose in these latter times and have no mention in the earlier works. However, this was towards the end of his life when it was difficult for him to write by himself, so he delegated its composition to four scholars: my respected father, Mawlana Shaykh Mufti Muḥammad Shafiʿ and the respected Mawlana Mufti Jamīl Aḥmad (Allah ﷻ preserve them), and Mawlana Shaykh Ẓafar Aḥmad al-ʿUthmānī, the author of *Iʿla al-Sunan*, and Mawlana al-Muḥaddith Shaykh Muḥammad Idris al-Kāndihlawī the author of *at-Taʿlīq al-Ṣabīh ʿalā Mishkāt al-Maṣābīḥ* (Allah ﷻ have mercy on them). Thus, Mawlana Shaykh al-ʿUthmānī compiled two volumes of it, and my respected father Mufti Muhammad Shafiʿ compiled two volumes, and Mawlana Shaykh al-Kāndhlāwī compiled one volume. These volumes were printed in Karachi with [old] lithographic print, and the remainders have not yet been printed. May Allah ﷻ enable us to produce this book in a form pleasing to the readers.

The Shaykh also has a small treatise, *al-Taqṣīr fi at-Tafsīr*, in which he criticised some of the modern exegeses, and in which he explained valuable rules from the principles of exegesis of which many people in our time are heedless. He has twenty three other treatises on exegesis and the sciences of the Qurʾān.

As for ḥadīth, he had himself compiled *Jāmiʿ al-Āthār* and *Tābiʿ al-Āthār*, and he gave special attention to the compilation of *Iʿlāʾ as-Sunan*, and a notice on these books will come separately if Allah ﷻ wills.

In jurisprudence, he has *Imdād al-Fatāwa* in six large volumes in the Urdu language, which is a collection of his *fatwas* which he wrote himself. He (Allah ﷻ have mercy on him) was the leading authority in issuing *fatwas* in India. *Fatwa*-seekers from the eastern and western parts of the earth would refer to him and ʿulama and scholars would write to him on difficult issues, the solution to which was problematic for them, so the Shaykh answered them and solved the difficult and obscure matters with the utmost verification and scrutiny, in a manner that cooled their breasts and satisfied their thirst. Indeed *Imdād al-Fatāwa* bears witness to the depth of his insight in jurisprudence. There are valuable discussions in it related to jurisprudence and an explanation of most of the issues which arose in the latter times. This book is now considered the greatest source for muftis in Pakistan, India and Bangladesh.

He also has the book *Beheshti Zewar* (Heavenly Ornaments) which is in approximately 700 pages with large size paper, in which he assembled issues relating to all the chapters of jurisprudence, creed and spirituality. Originally, it was written for the edification of women, so in addition to religious issues, he included in it all that women need in their family life. A group of 'ulama helped him in writing this book. Although the purpose of this book was to edify women, many men have also benefitted from it, and 'ulama find it indispensible. It has been translated into a number of local languages.

He also has *Taḥdhīr al-Ikhwān ʿan ar-Ribā fi 'l-Hindustān* and *Rāfiʿ ad-Dank ʿan Manāfiʿ al-Bank* on the verification of the matter of usury; and *al-Iqtiṣād fi 't-Taqlīd wa 'l-Ijtihād* and *al-Ḥīlat an-Nājizah li 'l-Ḥalīlāt al-ʿĀjizah* in which he verified the issues relating to the wives of a lost man, an impotent man, a madman, and a cruel man, and the issues of delegating divorce (*tafwīd aṭ-ṭalāq*) and [marital] choice after puberty (*khiyār al-bulūgh*), and in most of these juristic issues he issued *fatwas* according to the *madhhab* of the Malikis, and he verified their *madhhab* by seeking *fatwa* from their scholars. He has many treatises besides these in verifying particular juristic issues.

As for beliefs and theology, he has *al-Intibāhāt al-Mufīdah fi 'l-Ishtibāhāt al-Jadīdah* which is a book unique in its field, in which he compiled the doubts which the atheists produce against Islam, and the distortions perpetrated by those who try to travel in the caravans of the Westerners, and he refuted them with a powerful and beneficial refutation; and he proved the basic Islamic beliefs using rational proofs that are convincing to all possessors of sound intellect and seekers of truth. We have just recently published with the help of Allah ﷻ Almighty an English translation. He also has *al-Maṣāliḥ al-ʿAqliyyah li 'l-Aḥkām an-Naqliyyah* and its translation in English has also been published. He has *Shahādāt al-Aqwām ʿalā Ṣidq al-Islām* in which he compiled the disbelievers' praise of Islam and its teachings. He has *Iṣlāḥ al-Khayāl, Ashraf al-Jawāb, al-Iksīr fi Ithbāt at-Taqdīr, al-Khiṭāb al-Malīḥ fi Taḥqīq al-Mahdī wa 'l-Masīḥ, Dhayl ʿalā Sharḥ al-ʿAqāʾid an-Nasafiyyah, Dirāyat al-ʿIṣmah* in refutation of philosophy, *Hidāyat al-Ḥikmah*, and many other treatises.

As for spirituality, he has *Masāʾil as-Sulūk min Kalām Malik al-Muluk* in the Arabic language, in which he derived the issues relevant to the spiritual journey (*sulūk*) and Sufism from the Noble Qur'an; and *at-Tasharruf bi Maʿrifat Aḥadīth at-Taṣawwuf*, in which he compiled the ḥadīths from which issues of Sufism are derived, and he explained them with sufficient commentary while elaborating on the principles of Sufism and its fundamental issues; and *Sharḥ al-Mathnawī li Mawlānā ar-Rūmī* in 8 volumes; and *Maʿārif al-ʿAwārif* in two volumes; and *al-Takashshuf ʿan Muhimmāt at-Taṣawwuf* and *Talkhīṣ al-Bidāyah li 'l-Ghazālī* and *Tarbiyat as-Sālik wa Tanjiyat al-Hālik* which is a collection of letters to his disciples answering their questions about spiritual illnesses, and it contains amazing anecdotes on detecting spiritual defects and treating them—no book has been compiled on this subject besides this as far as we know. He has many treatises on spirituality besides what we mentioned.

As for calling [to Islam] and giving counsel, he has *Ḥayāt al-Muslimīn*, *Taʿlīm ad-Dīn*, *Furūʿ al-Imān*, *Jazāʾ al-Aʿmāl*, *Ādāb al-Muʿāsharah*, *Huqūq al-Islām*, *Huqūq al-Wālidayn*, *Irshād al-Hāʾim fī Ḥuqūq al-Bahāʾim*, *al-Qawl al-Ṣawāb fī Masʾalat al-Ḥijāb*, *Ilqāʾ as-Sakīnah fī Ibdāʾ az-Zīnah*, *Iṣlāḥ ar-Rusūm*, *Hifẓ al-Imān* in refutation of baseless innovations and beliefs, *Aghlāṭ al-ʿAwāmm*, *Iṣlāḥ Inqilāb al-Ummah*, *Huqūq al-ʿIlm*, *Kathrat aj-Azwāj li Ṣāḥib al-Miʿrāj*, *Iṣlāḥ an-Nisāʾ* and many other books.

As for litanies and supplications, he has *al-Maʿmūl al-Maqbūl fī Qurbāt ʿind Allāh wa Ṣalawāt ar-Rasūl* in which he summarised the transmitted supplications from *al-Hiṣn al-Haṣīn* and divided them into seven sections, and this book has reached most of the Muslim houses in these lands and is recited daily; and he has *Zād as-Saʿīd* on the forms of blessings on the prophet ﷺ; and *al-Khuṭab al-Maʾthūrah* in which he collected the sermons of the Noble Prophet ﷺ and the rightly-guided caliphs; and *Khuṭbāt al-Aḥkām li Jumuʿāt al-ʿĀmm* and *Zawāl as-Sunna ʿan Aʿmāl as-Sanah*.

As for [Prophetic] biography, he compiled *Nashr aṭ-ṭīb fī Dhikr an-Nabiyy al-Ḥabīb*. And on miscellaneous rare issues: *Bawādir an-Nawādir*, *Badāʾiʿ al-Farāʾid* and *al-Laṭāʾif wa az-Zarāʾif.*

This is a short selection of some of his writings, and all this excludes his sermons published in large volumes, which will be discussed in what follows:

His Sermons

When he was a student at Deoband, the Shaykh (Allah ﷻ have mercy on him) was examined on admonishing and sermonising. A gathering would be held every Friday which the students attended, and they delivered their speeches one after another. The Shaykh (Allah ﷻ have mercy on him) was from the champions of this competition and was distinguished in this field, such that after completing his studies he became the most famous sermoniser and admonisher of his time. During his stay in Kanpur, he began to counsel the people and call them towards good. Gatherings would be held for this in every corner of the corners of the city, and then in every city from the cities of India. His sermons became famous in all the corners of the lands. For them, mounts would be saddled, and to hear them, difficulties would be endured, and opportunities would be seized. Truthfully, his sermons were like an ocean with no visible coast. There was knowledge and wisdom and proverbs and anecdotes and wonders and treasures in them which are not contained in books.

And there were insights into exegesis, ḥadīth, jurisprudence and Sufism in them which are not found in the available literature. In them, the Shaykh distributed the pearls of his gnosis that polished the hearts and illuminated the minds.

His sermons had such an impact on reforming souls and proportioning minds that nothing similar exists in this time, for how many men after listening to them withheld from what they were accustomed to of sins, and how many deviants because of them repented from innovations and passions, and how many men fumbling in doubts have been guided by them to faith and certainty?! The number of those in whom these counsels caused a transformation surpasses thousands of men and women. We praise Allah ﷻ that a large number of these counsels were recorded by his students and his disciples during his sermons, and from them twenty volumes have been published, each volume comprising of at least 700 pages.

Hence, these published counsels are continuous springs flowing to this day, not scarce and not ceasing, and not depleting and not drying up. And there are innumerable men, who did not accompany Shaykh at-Thānawī and did not see him, but they attained the benefits of his company by his published counsels, and an immense religious transformation occurred in their lives.

From his practices in admonishing was that he would not accept [anything] in exchange for it, such that if a man were to offer him anything after an admonition which apparently seemed to be in exchange [for the lecture] he would never accept it. In his admonitions, he would prefer the method of inciting hope (*targhīb*) rather than inducing fear (*tarhīb*), and he said: "I have experienced the natures of people in this time, and I found they benefit more from what gives them hope than they benefit from what puts fear in them, which is why in my admonitions I most frequently encourage hope and rarely induce fear."[393]

He would supplicate to Allah ﷻ (Glorified is He) before starting the admonition saying: "O Allah ﷻ! Grant me the ability to deliver what the attendees are in need of and what will rectify their states."[394]

Controversial issues amongst the Muslims would not interfere in his admonitions unless a controversial matter came up during [the course of] his speech, whereupon he would explain it with a sufficient explanation, gently and softly, tactfully and with good-will, not being harsh in them against his opponents, and not going into excess when criticising them as is the habit of the sermonisers of our time. Rather, he would follow the example of the Prophets (upon them peace) in soft speech[395] and good admonition.[396]

---

393 *Sīrat Ashraf*, p. 137, quoting from *Waʿẓ al-Bāṭin*.

394 Ibid, quoting from *Dhamm an-Nisyān*.

395 *Sūrat Ṭā Ha*, 20:44.

396 *Sūrat an-Naḥl*,16:125.

His Utterances (Malfūẓāt)

Every day after Zuhr, he (Allah ﷻ have mercy on him) would conduct a public gathering in the Khanqah Imdadiyyah, in which his students and disciples and the common people gathered, and he would admonish them and answer their various questions, and speak to them with whatever occurred to him without restricting [himself] to one subject and not another subject. One of the attendees in these gatherings would record his speech and whatever beneficial lessons he delivered in them. Then these speeches of his were published under the title *al-Malfūẓāt* (Utterances) in more than twenty volumes. These utterances consist of rare anecdotes of knowledge and wisdom, subtleties and wonders, stories and events, admonitions and lessons, counsels and guidance, etiquettes and characteristics, criticisms and refutations. The ʿulama of these lands have experienced that it has a strong effect in building a sound religious temperament and in encouraging towards righteous deeds.

His (Allah ﷻ have mercy on him) Pledge in the Spiritual Path

Experience has proven that mere abundance of knowledge and expansive reading are insufficient in moulding a human being to have a firm religious understanding, since rectification of the souls and purification of the hearts and perfection of the faculties and proportioning the character-traits are almost impossible to achieve for any man except by internalising in his life the example of a man from the men of Allah ﷻ, and acquiring the good fortune of his company, and acquiring benefit from his teachings, and drawing to himself those lofty capacities and that sound taste which was made possible for that man. This is why He (Glorified is He) explained the "Straight Path"[397] with His statement: "The path of those whom You have favoured",[398] indicating that the Straight Path is only the path walked upon by those favoured by Allah ﷻ, of the prophets, truthful-saints, martyrs and pious;[399] and the Prophet ﷺ explained it with his statement: "What I and my companions are upon." He (Exalted is He) said: "And follow the way of those who have turned to Me,"[400] and He (Exalted is He) said: "O you who believe! Have consciousness of Allah ﷻ and be with the truthful,"[401] indicating that a man will only be guided to the desired Straight Path by following those who turn to Allah ﷻ and by staying constantly in the company of the truthful whose souls have been refined and their internal sensibilities have been proportioned. For this [reason], the practice of the ʿulama has continuously been,

397 *Sūrat al-Fātiḥa*, 1:5.
398 Ibid., 1:6.
399 Sūrat an-Niṣā', 4:69.
400 Sūrat Luqmān, 31: 15.
401 Sūrat at-Tawbah, 9:119.

since the time of the Companions and the Followers, that they would not suffice with mere reading of books and memorisation of ḥadīths and listening to lectures, rather they would give special attention to staying in the constant company of the men of Allah ﷻ and benefiting from their company and service.

Thus, Shaykh at-Thānawī (Allah ﷻ have mercy on him) loved to accompany his teachers, and was eager to serve them, and after completing his studies, he pledged the pledge of the spiritual path to the knower [of Allah ﷻ], the perceptive, Ḥājī Imdād Allāh al-Muhājir al-Makkī, and he stayed with him for a while. Then in Shawwāl, he travelled and performed pilgrimage to the House of Allah ﷻ and visited the resting place of the Noble Prophet ﷺ, and stayed with his spiritual teacher for some time. Then he performed Hajj a second time in 1310/1893 and he stayed in the company of his spiritual teacher for a period of 6 months, and he stayed constantly with him never parting [from him] and never separating. Due to the strength of his preparation and the perfect attention of the spiritual master, in this short time he became like a mirror in which the example of his spiritual teacher shone and his characteristics and his qualities glittered until he came to be recognised in his lands for his worship and his asceticism and his scrupulousness and his excellent guidance and training. He cleansed the path of Sufism from innovated superstitions and ugly innovations and he renewed it with a [comprehensive] renewal, so we should explain his work in some detail:

His Renewal of Sufism and the Spiritual Path

People were, in the matter of Sufism and the spiritual path, between excess and negligence. Thus, one group believed that Sufism and the spiritual path is from the newly-invented innovations having no basis in the Book and *sunna*; and another believed that Sufism and the spiritual path is the name of some unveilings and ecstatic experiences and illuminations which occur to the one walking this path, and that these states and internal experiences are end-objectives of the religion, and whoever acquires them is free from the noose of the outwards laws of the Shari'ah, and the one from whom some feats and wonders emanate or to whom some unveilings and ecstatic experiences occur while awake or asleep, the people take him as an example and guide, however deviant his beliefs and however corrupt his deeds and qualities.

Thus, Ḥakīm al-Ummah at-Thānawī (Allah ﷻ have mercy on him) began to refute these two notions theoretically and practically. Theoretically, he proved in his books and his sermons and his counsels and his gatherings that Sufism and spiritual excellence (*iḥsān*) is one of the elements of religion and one of the branches of Islam, and that the laws of the Book and *sunna* divide into two categories: one category relating to the external acts which issue from the limbs and organs like prayer, fasting, charity, pilgrimage, marriage, divorce and other such laws of the Shariʿah which the jurists have expounded in their books; and a second category of the laws of the Book and *sunna* relate to the internal acts which's place is the heart and soul, and from them are commandments and prohibitions; as for the commandments, examples are: integrity and sincerity, fear and hope, desire and friendliness, patience and gratitude, humbleness and humility, love of Allah ﷻ and His Messenger ﷺ, and turning and being sincere to Him, etc; and as for the prohibitions, examples are: ostentation, seeking reputation, vanity, pride, malice, envy, hopelessness, despair, love of wealth and fame, etc.

Hence, Sufism only deals with this category of divine laws, just as jurisprudence deals with the first category of them. The Qurʾān and *sunna* are full of texts said in this context, although the laws relating to the inside of a human being are not usually possible to adopt except by training, exercise, edification and practice, because the internal diseases like ostentation, vanity etc. are hidden illnesses which often the sick person does not realise in himself, and he needs a knowledgeable experienced man inspecting his movements and stillness, his deeds and his thoughts, his ideas and his whispers, in order to detect them, and this inspector in Sufism is called a "spiritual teacher" (*shaykh*) and referral to him the "pledge" (*bayʿah*).

As for those unveilings and miracles, wonders and disposals, visions and experiences, Shaykh at-Thānawī (Allah ﷻ have mercy on him) established that they have nothing to do with Sufism. There is no doubt that Allah ﷻ often revealed some miracles at the hands of the Companions and saints, and there is no question that He (Exalted is He) had blessed some of his servants with true unveilings, but these are not the end-objectives of religion, nor are they a proof in the Shariʿah, and nor do they prove its bearer to be a saint or fearful [of Allah ﷻ] or close to Allah ﷻ, since such unveilings and disposals are not preconditioned by righteousness and piety, rather not even being Muslim and having faith, since it may occur by exercise and experience to wicked disbelieving men, as seen in the mesmerists.

Thus, the objective of Sufism is only to acquire virtuous character-traits and to avoid spiritual ailments, and the one successful in this path is he who has adorned [himself] with these virtues along with complete loyalty to the Islamic Shariʿah, and with complete adherence to the Prophetic *sunna*, and if after this Allah ﷻ gives him a share in the insight (*firāsah*) of faith or a portion of truthful unveilings, then that is an excess from Allah ﷻ. As for the one who is deprived of these virtuous character-traits and obedience to the Prophetic *sunna*, and does not stay away from spiritual ills, he is completely removed from Sufism, the spiritual path (*ṭarīqah*), sainthood and the spiritual journey (*sulūk*), whether he flies in the wind or walks on water or ascends to the heaven.

This sound and balanced vision with respect to Sufism is detailed in different books of Shaykh at-Thānawī and his sermons with its proofs from the Book and *sunna*, and their corroborants from the examples of the Companions and the saints, and their evidences from sound intellect and spiritual experience, and he repelled [in them] whatever doubts had appeared about it, and he harmonised the actions of the great Sufis with the Book and *sunna* in [a manner] that the hearts find rest and the chests find coolness, and he left no room for objection except for an ignorant denier or an obstinate feigner of ignorance.

Practically, the Shaykh refuted these two ideas by his actions conforming to the Muhammadan *sunna* and instructing his disciples according to the way of the Shari'ah. Thus, whenever anyone came to him for the pledge, he commanded him firstly to fulfil his obligations in the Shari'ah, whether from the rights of Allah ﷻ or the rights of servants. His attention to the rights of servants was stronger and more common, since he saw the condition of many people that they were persistent on rituals and did much remembrance of Allah ﷻ, but they were deficient in the rights of the servants and opposed the Shari'ah in many social interactions. Similarly, his attention to teaching social etiquettes was more [important to him] than the attention he paid to teaching litanies and remembrances, and all optional acts. He would say:

> I give most of my attention to no one being harmed by me or my disciples, whether that harm is material, like striking and argumentation, or monetary, like confiscation of rights and consuming illegally, or what is related to his honour, like disgracing a man and backbiting him, or spiritual, like leaving another in a state of conflict and confusion, or treating him in a manner he dislikes, and if any of this occurs by mistake it is necessary to immediately seek forgiveness and pardon. I give more importance to this than anything else, such that if I see anyone disobeying the Shari'ah in its outward manifestation, that causes in me a degree of pain, but when I see anyone indifferent to fulfilling these rights, it hurts me badly, and I pray to Allah ﷻ to save him from these mortal sins.[402]

In another place he said:

> The head and foundation of good character is that a man is concerned with no one being harmed because of him, and this is what the Prophet ﷺ taught by his comprehensive saying: "The Muslim is the one from whose tongue and whose hand [other] Muslims are safe." Everything that is a cause for harming another, it is included in bad character, even if its [outward] form is in the form of service or etiquette and veneration which people claim to be good character, because the reality of good character is to give rest to another, which is given priority over service, for service without giving rest is a fruit skin without a seed. Although social etiquettes are below beliefs and worship from the perspective of them being symbols of the religion, nonethe-

402 Translated from *Ashraf al-Sawanih*, 2:179.

less, they have priority over beliefs and worship from another perspective, which is that in infractions of belief and worship there is harm to a human being's self, but in infractions of social etiquette there is harm to others, and a man harming another is worse than him harming himself. Therefore, Allah ﷻ first said: "Those who walk on the earth gently, and when they converse with the ignorant, they say: Peace,"[403] in which social etiquettes are taught, and then He said: "Those who spend the night for their Lord, prostrating and standing," in which rituals are taught, so good social conduct has priority over the obligations from some perspectives. As for its priority over optional acts, it is established from all perspectives.[404]

Shaykh at-Thānawī (Allah ﷻ have mercy on him) did not possess mere theories and empty thoughts, rather these theories were manifested in his works and his life, and even in the life of his disciples. For, the Khanqah Imdadiyyah was a house of education, unique in its style in the world, in which characters were refined, and minds were edified, and individual and social etiquettes of life were taught. Muslims from all sides and corners of India come together, from them 'ulama and senior scholars, and from them doctors and engineers, and from them employers and teachers, and from them farmers and factory workers, and from them men from all walks of life. They came to him and stayed with him for long periods and they may have had with them wives and children, and the Ṣhaykh would look at their states and teach them the religion and make them learn the Islamic characteristics, and describe for them the means to acquire them and train them to [practice] the social etiquettes and explain to them their subtleties, and turn their attentions to their spiritual illnesses, and explain to them the means to rid [themselves] of them. This Khanqah had a superb rota in everything, which none could oppose; and this rota itself was a living example of Islamic social etiquettes, encouraging a man to organise his life and keep check of his moments and be concerned with fulfilling rights and avoiding harm to others.

Eventually, this Zawiyah became a great factory wherein [real] men were built, and excellent qualities and upright etiquettes were moulded. Were we to expand on these qualities and etiquettes which the Shaykh would apply and train others with, we would have a long discussion [ahead of us]. However, we wish to present to the noble reader some examples of his conduct and habit, so that this subject becomes somewhat clear:

Whenever he (Allah ﷻ have mercy on him) needed to speak to anyone, or tell him something, he would never ask him to [come] to him, rather he would walk to him himself, even if he was his student or his disciple or his younger relatives, and he

---

403 Sūrat al-Furqān, 25:63.
404 Translated from *Ādāb al-Muʿāsharah.*

would say: "It should be that the one in need goes to the one he needs not *vice versa*." One of the doctors, Hakim Muhammad Hashim, was from his disciples and close followers, who would frequently come to him, but whenever the Shaykh needed to describe to him some of the symptoms of his illness, he would go to him himself so long as that was not too difficult because of his illness.[405]

He would never give two instructions simultaneously to any of his servants, rather he would give him one instruction and then another instruction after he finished the first, and he would say: "I do this so it is not burdensome on the servant to remember the second instruction, so I bear the difficulty of remembering [it] myself, and do not burden the servant with it."[406]

He would not intercede for anyone except with justice, and if he knew or thought that that was burdensome on the one he interceded to, he would never do this, and he would say:

> The people generally take into account in the affair of intercession the right of the one interceded for, and they do not take into account the right of the one interceded to, while helping a person is a praiseworthy deed and avoiding harm is obligatory, so how is it permissible to leave an obligation to attain [something] praiseworthy?[407]

He would not insist on a guest to stay in his company for long against his will, even if the guest was from the most beloved of people to him, and his stay from the most desirable of what he enjoyed. Likewise, he would not force a guest to partake of too much food against his will so that it would not be burdensome on him.

Whenever he wrote to anyone a letter in which was a question to the one written to, he would place therein an addressed envelope along with stamps for the reply even if the one written to was from his students or his younger relatives.

Thus, he (Allah ﷻ have mercy on him) would attend to these delicate matters in social etiquettes. On this, he has a separate work. His life, and the life of his disciples, and his method in the Khanqah Imdadiyyah was a practical explanation of these Islamic etiquettes, such that the people recognised his disciples for observance of these subtleties in [their] characteristics and dealings and interactions.

In this manner, he (Allah ﷻ have mercy on him) lived for 48 years in al-Khanqah al-Imdadiyyah, benefiting people through his knowledge, his counsels, his works and his teachings, until Allah ﷻ took his [soul] in the month of Ṣafar of the year 1362 after the Prophetic migration (1943 CE), may Allah ﷻ shower him with His forgiveness and His pleasure and leave him to reside in the highest places of His gardens.

---

405 *Ashraf as-Sawanih*, 2:43.
406 Ibid.
407 *Sīrat Ashraf*, p. 280.

BIOGRAPHY OF THE AUTHOR (ʿALLĀMAH ẒAFAR AḤMAD AL-ʿUTHMĀNĪ)

As for the biography of Mawlana Shaykh Ẓafar Aḥmad al-ʿUthmānī (Allah ﷻ have mercy on him), we will suffice here with quoting what our teacher, the great and perceptive scholar, the verifier, Shaykh ʿAbd al-Fattāḥ Abū Ghuddah (Allah ﷻ preserve him), wrote in the introduction to his book *Inhāʾ as-Sakan ilā man Yuṭāliʿ Iʿlāʾ as-Sunan* which the Shaykh published with the title *Qawāʿid fī ʿUlūm al-ḥadīth*. Mawlana Shaykh al-ʿUthmānī (Allah ﷻ have mercy on him) was alive at that time, so we will firstly quote the statement of Shaykh ʿAbd al-Fattāḥ Abū Ghuddah (Allah ﷻ preserve him), and then add to it a few lines:

> He is the erudite scholar, verifier, researcher, scrutiniser, firm proof, exegete, ḥadīth-master, proficient and skilled jurist and theoretician, historian, man of letters, scrupulous, ascetic and insightful Sufi, Ẓafar Aḥmad ibn Latif al-ʿUthmānī at-Thānawī born on the 13th of Rabīʿ al-Awwal in the year 1310 AH (October, 1892 CE), in the land of his forefathers near Darul Uloom Deoband, the greatest of the institutes of learning in the Indian lands. His mother died when he was three years old, so his grandmother brought him up with the most excellent upbringing. She was a pilgrim and righteous woman. Thus, he received her righteousness and her piety from her. When he was five years old, he began to recite the Noble Qur'an with its senior memorisers in Deoband, like Hafiz Namdar, a teacher at Darul Uloom, and his deputy, Hafiz Ghulam Rasul, and Mawlana Nadhir Ahmad, who was the brother of his grandmother. When he was seven years old, he began to read Urdu and Persian books and the textbooks of numeracy and mathematics with the magnificent scholar Mawlana Muhammad Yasin who was the father of the leading scholar of Pakistan today, our master, the great scholar, Shaykh Muḥammad Shafīʿ al-Deobandi, the Grand Mufti at Karachi, and the founder of Darul Uloom al-Islamiyyah there (his lofty shadow be extended).
>
> Then he moved from Deoband to Thana Bhawan to [join] the circle of his maternal uncle Mawlana Muhammad Ashraf ʿAlī at-Thānawī (Allah ﷻ sanctify his secret), and he began to read Arabic books on morphology, syntax and literature with the able scholar Mawlana Muhammad Abdullah al-Gangohi, and he received from his uncle Ḥakīm al-Ummah something of the science of Tajwīd, and a selection of his *al-Talkhīṣāt al-ʿAshr* and [some] volumes of *al-Mathnawī* by al-Jalāl ar-Rūmī, and he read with his brother, Mawlana Saʿid Ahmad, part of *at-Talkhīṣāt*.
>
> Then, when his uncle Ḥakīm al-Ummah became occupied with compiling his immense work *Bayān al-Qurʾān* in Urdu, he brought him to Kanpur and admitted him into the school called *Jāmiʿ al-ʿUlūm* which Shaykh Ḥakīm al-Ummah

had founded when he resided in Kanpur, and he consigned its teaching to the most upright of his students, Mawlana Muhammad Ishaq al-Bardawani and Mawlana Muhammad Rashid al-Kanpuri. Thus, he read with them the books of ḥadīth that have been set in the curriculum of those lands, which are: *Ṣaḥīḥ al-Bukhārī*, *Ṣaḥīḥ Muslim*, *Sunan Abī Dāwūd*, *Sunan an-Nasāʾī*, *Sunan at-Tirmidhī*, *Sunan Ibn Mājah* and *Mishkāt al-Maṣābīḥ*, along with what strengthens their study from the books of nomenclature and ḥadīth principles. He also read with them the books of jurisprudence, exegesis and literature which are all part of the curriculum, and also some of the rational sciences.

When he attained the *sanad* in the Shariʿah and rational sciences, and was distinguished from amongst the noble students by the talents he possessed, he moved to Saharanpur and sat in the school *Maẓāhir al-ʿUlūm* and attended the lessons of ḥadīth with the knower of Allah ﷺ, the Imam, the ḥadīth-scholar, the jurist, Mawlana Khalil Ahmad al-Saharanpuri, the author of *Badhl al-Majhūd fī Sharḥ Sunan Abī Dāwūd*. After a period of close companionship with this gnostic, ḥadīth scholar and Imam, he gave him authorisation (*ijāzah*) in ḥadīth and its sciences and in all the remaining rational and transmitted sciences, and he attained a *sanad* for the completion of higher studies in the year 1328. His age at this time was 18 years, which is a young age, none reaching the pinnacle of this level at such [a young age] except the most brilliant and exceptional [students]. In this period he also attended [lectures on] some texts of logic and engineering and higher mathematics with their instructors in the aforementioned school, from them was Mawlana ʿAbd al-Latif the administrator of the school, and Mawlana ʿAbd al-Qadir al-Punjabi.

In view of his superiority and his incredible intelligence and his brilliance, he was appointed as a teacher in the aforementioned school. He taught there for a period of seven years the sciences of jurisprudence, [jurisprudential and ḥadīth] principles, logic, philosophy and other [subjects]. Then he moved to the school *Imdād al-ʿUlūm* in Thana Bhawan and was occupied with teaching the books in the curriculum of the [final] year there, which are the seven books mentioned previously, and teaching jurisprudence and exegesis. Thus, he benefitted and excelled, and a multitude of exceptional [scholars] graduated at his hands, and they propagated knowledge in those lands and they lit the paths of the Shariʿah for people.

Then Mawlana Ḥakīm al-Ummah delegated to him the compilation of the book *Iʿlāʾ as-Sunan* along with issuing *fatwa* and teaching, so he did all of this in the most excellent way. He remained compiling *Iʿlāʾ as-Sunan* for around 20 years. He compiled it in 18 parts, rather volumes, and he further compiled for it two introductions in two volumes, so this amazing book was completed in 20 volumes, and he added to it another book called *Injāʾ al-Waṭan ʿan al-Izdirāʾ bi Imām az-Zaman* in which he wrote brilliant and extensive biographies of Imam Abū Ḥanīfah and his students and their students and so forth, restricting [himself] therein to the jurists and ḥadīth-scholars. The first part of this book was published in Karachi in the year 1387.

Then Mawlana Ḥakīm al-Ummah instructed him to write *Dalāʾil al-Qurʾān ʿalā Masāʾil an-Nuʿmān* in the style of *Aḥkām al-Qurʾān* by al-Jaṣṣāṣ, and he compiled two large volumes of it ending at Surat an-Nisāʾ. It is a book that is fitting to be said of it in the language of the jurists and scholars: "Studying it is a lasting bliss, and attaining the like of it is a great victory."

He wrote a number of books in Urdu when he stayed in Thana Bhawan. From them is *al-Qawl al-Matīn fī 'l-Ikhfāʾ bi Amīn* and *Shaqq al-Ghayn ʿan Haqq Rafʿ al-Yadayn* and *Raḥmat al-Quddūs fī Tarjamāt Bahjat an-Nufūs* and *Fātiḥat al-Kalām fī 'l-Qirāʾah Khalf al-Imām* in which he verified that it is not obligatory to recite behind the imam in all prayers especially the audible ones, and as far as the silent ones are concerned, it is permissible as is a narration from Imam Abū Ḥanīfah as well. I said to the Shaykh (Allah ﷻ preserve him) during my visit to him, when he mentioned this to me: "It is also the opinion of Imam Muḥammad," and he said: "Yes, even if al-Kamāl ibn al-Humām denied it!" He has *Kashf al-Dujā* in Arabic, printed independently and as part of *al-Fatāwā al-Imdādiyyah* in which he would answer the questions of *fatwa*-seekers which reached his uncle Ḥakīm al-Ummah, of that which relates to jurisprudence and other [subjects], until it became seven large volumes. Shaykh Ḥakīm al-Ummah called it: *Imdād al-Aḥkām fī Masāʾil al-Ḥalāl wa 'l-Ḥarām.*

Then he moved to *Madrasah Muḥammadiyyah* in Rangoon, Burma, and was occupied there with propagation and admonition and lecturing for a period of two years. Later, he returned to Thana Bhawan and carried on writing *Dalāʾil al-Qurʾān* along with issuing *fatwa* and educating people. Then he travelled to Dhaka in East Pakistan [now Bangladesh] before the existence of Pakistan, and he was appointed at its university as a teacher of ḥadīth, jurisprudence and [jurisprudential and ḥadīth] principles. Subsequently, he was appointed as the head teacher in Madrasah ʿĀliyah of Dhaka, and he remained so for 8 years. There, he founded al-Qurʾāniyyāt al-ʿArabiyya University which is now the highest quality school in East Pakistan for learning the sciences of Qurʾān, ḥadīth, jurisprudence, etc.

Afterwards, he moved to West Pakistan where he now lives in Ashrafabad of Hyderabad, Sind, to Darul Uloom al-Islamiyyah, as the head teacher there, teaching ḥadīth and assuming responsibility of issuing *fatwa* to questioners and *fatwa*-seekers, and benefitting by his state, his speech and his good deeds students and seekers of benefit. May Allah ﷻ extend his noble life and bless his good deeds and his sciences, and perfect upon him the garment of safety so his benefit multiplies and his achievements are complete and he attains the great pleasure of Allah ﷻ. (End quote from our teacher ʿAllamah Shaykh ʿAbd al-Fattah Abu Ghuddah (Allah ﷻ preserve him) from the introduction to his edition of the book *Qawāʿid fī ʿUlūm al-ḥadīth*.)[408]

Mawlana Shaykh Ẓafar Aḥmad al-ʿUthmānī (Allah ﷻ have mercy on him) was alive when his book *Qawāʿid fī ʿUlūm al-ḥadīth* was published in the edition of our teacher, Allamah ʿAbd al-Fattāḥ Abū Ghuddah (Allah ﷻ preserve him), when he was the primary teacher of ḥadīth at Darul Uloom al-Islamiyyah in Ashrafabad, in which he taught *Ṣaḥīḥ al-Bukhārī*, despite his old age and his ongoing illnesses and his decreased strength. He once said to me: "Whenever I feel an increase in my illness, I intensify my teaching of *Ṣaḥīḥ al-Bukhārī*, and Allah ﷻ makes it a [means to] cure my illness."

Despite his weakness and illness, he would be constant in *dhikr* and optional prayers. He attended all the prayers in the mosque and would endure great suffering because of this. Towards the end of his life, his tongue was moist with the remembrance of Allah ﷻ in most times. In the month of Ramaḍān of the year 1394 AH, the doctors forbade him to fast due to his ongoing illnesses, however he did not agree to this and said: "ʿAbbās ؓ did not stop fasting when he was ninety years old, and he faced hardship and suffering due to fasting, such that he would sit in a container of water, and he was not happy with [paying] compensation (*fidya*), so how can I be happy with [paying] compensation?" This is how he lived, Allah ﷻ have mercy on him, until Allah ﷻ took his [soul] in Dhu al-Qaʿdah of the year 1394 AH (1974 CE), may Allah ﷻ give him rest in the safety of His mercy and pleasure. His son extracted the date of his death from [the numerical value of]: *Verily, he is in "comfort and fragrance and a garden of bliss"* (Qur'an, 56:89).[409]

Discussion about the Book Iʿlāʾ as-Sunan

Ḥakīm al-UmmahMawlana Shaykh Ashraf ʿAlī at-Thānawī (Allah ﷻ have mercy on him) had seen for [some] time that people lengthened their tongues towards imam Abū Ḥanīfah (Allah ﷻ be pleased with him), and they say that his *madhhab* is not supported by ḥadīth, and that he prefers analogy and juristic opinion over authentic ḥadīth, and other such claims which have no proof or evidence; and [he saw] that although the evidences in favour of imam Abū Ḥanīfah (Allah ﷻ have mercy on him) were detailed in many classical works, nevertheless, they were dispersed in different books and many treatises. Therefore, Ḥakīm al-Ummah (Allah ﷻ have

408 *Qawāʿid*, pp. 7–10.

409 Taking the numerical values of the Arabic *abjadī* letters, this totals to 1398 and not 1394. *Fa* 80, *ra* 200, *waw* 6, *ḥa* 8, *nūn* 50—*wa* 6, *ra* 200, *ya* 10, *ḥa* 8, *alif* 1, *nūn* 50, *nūn* 50—*wa* 6, *jīm* 3, *nūn* 50, *nūn* 50, *ta* 400—*nūn* 50, *ʿayn* 70, *ya* 10, *mīm* 40, *nūn* 50.

mercy on him) wanted to collect them into one book, so for this purpose he started [writing] a book he called *Iḥyāʾ as-Sunan* (Reviving the Traditions), in which he collected the evidences of imam Abū Ḥanīfah from the authentic ḥadīths in all the chapters of jurisprudence. However, the draft of this book was lost from the author before it was printed—and whatever Allah ﷻ wills, happens, and whatever He does not will, does not happen.

Then after a period of time, the Shaykh resumed its writing, and he changed his [earlier] method, and he called it *Jāmiʿ al-Āthār* (Compilation of Transmissions) in which he compiled the ḥadīths from which Ḥanafīs derive their *madhhab*, while paying brief attention to the quality of its chain and the ways in which evidence was deduced from them. Then he added footnotes to it with the title *Tābiʿ al-Āthār* (Complement to the Transmissions) in which he discussed the explanation of the ḥadīths which apparently contradict them. Both of them were printed in a short volume from the Qasimiyya Press in Deoband around 1315 AH with lithographic print.

However, both books were extremely brief, and did not go beyond the chapters of prayers, while he (Allah ﷻ have mercy on him) desired to compile the like of what he compiled before, and elaborate therein discussion of the ḥadīths with respect to the chain and text, narration and comprehension; whereupon Mawlana Shaykh Aḥmad Ḥasan as-Sanbhalī (Allah ﷻ have mercy on him) was ready for this task, so Shaykh at-Thānawī (Allah ﷻ have mercy on him) delegated to him the task of this compilation. Hence, in the main text [of the book] he collected the ḥadīths and reports along with a brief discussion about their chains, and he commented on them in the footnotes with respect to the text and chain with detail and elaboration. The text had the earlier title *Iḥyāʾ as-Sunan* and the footnotes had the title *at-Tawḍīḥ al-Ḥasan* (The Wonderful Elucidation), and Ḥakīm al-Ummah at-Thānawī (Allah ﷻ have mercy on him) would examine everything that Mawlana as-Sanbhalī had written letter by letter, and he changed places from it where he found the need to [do so], until he reached the Book of Hajj. Then it occurred to Mawlana as-Sanbhalī to take a second look at it, so he changed much of what he wrote previously, and he independently changed much of what Shaykh at-Thānawī highlighted without consulting him except in a few places; until the book changed from its previous style, and Shaykh at-Thānawī had not looked at any of it until its first volume was published and it became a new book, not what the Shaykh (Allah ﷻ have mercy on him) had desired, and there were many errors in it. Thereupon, the Shaykh instructed his nephew, Mawlana Shaykh Ẓafar Aḥmad al-ʿUthmānī (Allah ﷻ have mercy on him), to amend what this first volume had missing and explain the errors made in it by Mawlana as-Sanbhalī. Subsequently, Mawlana Shaykh al-ʿUthmānī wrote a volume called *al-Istidrak al-Hasan ʿalā Iḥyāʾ as-Sunan* (A Fine Amendment to the Revival of Traditions), and it was printed separately.

Then after some large and small incidents, Ḥakīm al-Ummah at-Thānawī (ﷺ have mercy on him) resolved that the remainder of what Shaykh as-Sanbhalī wrote not be printed. Rather, he instructed Mawlana al-ʿUthmānī (Allah ﷺ have mercy on him) to compile a new book. Hence, he (Allah ﷺ have mercy on him) compiled the rest of the book from the chapters of prayers to the last chapters of jurisprudence in sixteen volumes. It was from the precaution of Ḥakīm al-Ummah at-Thānawī and his attention to the rights of Mawlana as-Sanbhalī that he did not like that this book which Shaykh al-ʿUthmānī compiled remain with its earlier title *Iḥyāʾ as-Sunan*, rather he changed the title of the text to *Iʿlāʾ as-Sunan* (Elevating the Traditions) and the title of the commentary to *Isdāʾ al-Minan* (Extending Favours), so the remaining 16 volumes were published with this new title.

In brief, the end result of all of this was that the first volume of this book was published with the title *Iḥyāʾ as-Sunan*, and its addendum with the title *al-Istidrāk al-Ḥasan*, and the remainder of the book with the title *Iʿlāʾ as-Sunan*. These different titles were from that which confused the minds, so Mawlana Shaykh al-ʿUthmānī (Allah ﷺ have mercy on him) wanted, for the second edition of this book, to give it one title and incorporate the discussions of *al-Istidrāk al-Ḥasan* into the texts of *Iḥyāʾ as-Sunan* in such a way as to make it one continuous book, so he (Allah ﷺ have mercy on him) did this after the death of Ḥakīm al-Ummah at-Thānawī , and he underwent great difficulty because of this in his old age and at the end of his life. Thus, the first volume became one book which makes it a separate work of Shaykh al-ʿUthmānī and can be considered to be from his (Allah ﷺ have mercy on him) authorship, and it is fair to call it the first volume of *Iʿlāʾ as-Sunan*, which is what we are presenting before the noble reader in this volume.

Thus, this is the story behind the compilation of this book and its different names. Now the book has—and all praise is to Allah ﷺ—one title which is *Iʿlāʾ as-Sunan* by one author who is Mawlana Shaykh Ẓafar Aḥmad al-ʿUthmānī (Allah ﷺ have mercy on him).

As for the introductions to this book, three introductions were compiled for it, which should be discussed here:

The first volume of *Inhāʾ as-Sakan ilā man Yuṭāliʿ Iʿlāʾ as-Sunan* which is a valuable ḥadīth-oriented introduction to the book compiled by Mawlana Shaykh Ẓafar Aḥmad al-ʿUthmānī in which he commented on the important principles of the principles of ḥadīth. And this introduction was first printed in Thana Bhawan in lithographic print and another in Karachi with type printing. Then our teacher, the great scholar, verifier, researcher and critic, Shaykh ʿAbd al-Fattah Abu Ghuddah, produced it a third time in Halab of Sham, with his verification and his valuable footnotes, so he multiplied it in wonder and splendour and benefit, and he called it *Qawāʿid fi ʿUlūm al-*ḥadīth, may Allah ﷺ reward him with goodness and the most abundant of rewards.

The second volume of *Inhāʾ as-Sakan* which is a jurisprudence-oriented introduction to the book *Iʿlāʾ as-Sunan* compiled by Mawlana Shaykh Ḥabīb Aḥmad al-Kirānawī (Allah ﷻ have mercy on him) in which he compiled valuable discussions on the principles of jurisprudence and ḥadīth. It was printed in Karachi with lithographic print.

Injāʾ al-Waṭan ʿan al-Izdirāʾ bi Imām az-Zaman, which is a book compiled by Shaykh Mawlana Ẓafar Aḥmad al-ʿUthmānī (Allah ﷻ have mercy on him), in which he commented on the position of Imam Abū Ḥanīfah in ḥadīth and its sciences and the praise of the scholars of ḥadīth upon him, and a detailed discussion on his teachers and his students from the great ḥadīth-masters, and his services in the sciences of ḥadīth, and he answered all [the objections] that are produced against him from doubts and criticisms.

[Having said] this, this work which Mawlana Shaykh Ẓafar Aḥmad al-ʿUthmānī (Allah ﷻ have mercy on him) completed, of incorporating *al-Istidrāk al-Ḥasan* into the original book and calling all of this *Iʿlāʾ as-Sunan*, although it occurred after the death of Ḥakīm al-Ummah Shaykh at-Thānawī (Allah ﷻ have mercy on him), nonetheless, he had alluded to it in what he wrote as an introduction to the second volume of *Iʿlāʾ as-Sunan*. Given below is his statement with his wording in the second edition of the foreword to *Iḥyāʾ as-Sunan*:

Foreword to Iḥyāʾ as-Sunan in the Second Edition

> All praise to Allah ﷻ. I seek His help and I ask His forgiveness. We seek refuge in Allah ﷻ from the evils of our souls. Whoever Allah ﷻ guides, there is none to misguide him, and whoever He misguides, there is none to guide him. I bear witness that there is no deity but Allah ﷻ alone—He has no partner, and I bear witness that Muḥammad is His servant and Messenger. Allah ﷻ sent him with the truth as a bringer of good news and a warner before the [coming of] the Hour. Whoever obeys Allah ﷻ and His Messenger ﷺ, he is guided, and whoever disobeys them, indeed he harms none but himself, and does not harm Allah ﷻ in the least.
>
> To proceed: This [book] is a collection of the proofs of some of the peripherals of the *madhhab* of the earliest of the four famous *mujtahid* Imams in religion, Abū Hanīfah an-Nuʿmān (Allah ﷻ be pleased with him and them and all their followers). The need for it arose in this time when detractors lengthened their tongues towards him, so it was not possible to remain silent. I had produced a draft of parts of this some years ago in all of the chapters of jurisprudence, which I called *Iḥyāʾ as-Sunan*. However, I lost it, and praise is due to Allah ﷻ in all situations. Then after a period of time, I resumed writing some of it in a style different to the previous style, and I called it *Jāmiʿ al-Āthār*, and it has—with praise to Allah ﷻ—been published. How-

ever, it did not go beyond the chapters of prayers, and [due to some] reasons it was not possible for me to complete it, until Allah ﷻ favoured me now, since He gave me the opportunity to return to it by means of instructing one of the people who is occupied with me in serving knowledge, and he participated with me in this matter, and supported me in it in such a way that it is true to say that he is the doer and I am the assistant. I changed its style from the style of *Jāmiʿ al-Āthār* to the previous style, due to it being simple and free from difficulty, while maintaining therein the sequence of *al-Hidāyah*. In this attempt, I did not suffice with [discussing] the controversial issues which were intended for this compilation, rather I added to it some of the peripherals that are agreed upon, though few, for specific purposes.

Since this conformed to the draft of *Iḥyāʾ as-Sunan*, I felt [it was best] to call it by that earlier title, so it also becomes a revival of the lost [material], and Allah ﷻ gives accordance to complete this entire immense project. I attached to it footnotes, elucidating the meanings of the ḥadīths, and discussing their chains, and I called it *at-Tawḍīḥ al-Ḥasan ʿalā Iḥyāʾ as-Sunan*.

Moreover, know that I would examine this book till the Book of Hajj letter for letter, after the aforementioned deputy compiled it, and I changed places thereof when I found the need to [do so]. Then it occurred to him to take a second look at it, and change what needed to be changed due to his belief of his [own] expansive insight, so he corrected many places of what he wrote before and he sought my opinion in what was confusing to him in a few of these places, and he independently reviewed most of it, until the book changed from its previous style and its subject altered, and I was not aware of this until the first part of it was published and that is this [book] in your hand. For this [reason], it was in need of compiling an amendment to it, as you will find referenced in many of the Urdu places in the margins; and Allah ﷻ is asked for help.

This was begun on the last Friday of the auspicious [month of] Ramaḍān in the year 1331 after the Prophetic migration, on its bearer a million peace and greetings (1913).

This was written by the slave, hopeful of the mercy of his Mighty Lord, Ashraf ʿAlī at-Thānawī , his open and hidden sins be forgiven.

Now, given below is what he wrote as a preface to the second volume of *Iʿlāʾ as-Sunan*:

Foreword to the Second Volume of Iʿlāʾ as-Sunan

All praise to Allah ﷻ. I seek His help and I ask His forgiveness. We seek refuge in Allah ﷻ from the evils of our souls. Whoever Allah ﷻ guides, there is none to misguide him, and whoever He misguides, there is none to guide him. I bear witness that there is no deity but Allah ﷻ alone—He has no partner, and I bear witness that Muḥammad is His servant and Messenger. Allah ﷻ sent him with the truth as a bringer of good news and a warner before the [coming of] the Hour. Whoever obeys Allah ﷻ and His Messenger ﷺ, he is guided, and whoever disobeys them, indeed he harms none but himself, and does not harm Allah ﷻ in the least.

As for what follows: My dear brother! First look at the foreword to the first portion of *Iḥyā' as-Sunan* which will unveil for you the reality of the treatise. Then, secondly, understand that the need arose, due to some circumstances which there is no benefit in retelling, to delegate the task of compiling it to my nephew, the perceptive, brilliant, intelligent, Mawlawi Ẓafar Aḥmad, may Allah ﷻ keep him firm on the upright way; and to change its title from *Iḥyā' as-Sunan* to *I'lā' as-Sunan* and the title of its commentary from *at-Tawḍīḥ al-Ḥasan* to *Isdā' al-Minan*, while leaving the title of its translation as it is;[410] and to reconstructing some of the places of the first part from it which was published previously; and to call the collection of the added [notes] and that to which they were added in the first part of *I'lā' as-Sunan* as "the first part," thus this is "the second part" of it.

I set my eyes on it just like the first, letter for letter, and I found it—and all praise is to Allah ﷻ—many times better than the first in narration and comprehension and in sufficiency in its subject-matter and in the left over obligations to change some parts of it which were few. Distinguishing my speech from his speech and the like of this is just like the first. And all praise is to Allah ﷻ for what He produced and performed, and verily the latter is better for you than the former.

I am the slave, hopeful of the mercy of His Mighty Lord, Ashraf 'Alī at-Thānawī al-Ḥanafī (his open and hidden sins be forgiven), and the date is mid-1341 after the Prophetic migration, on its bearer a thousand peace and greetings (1923).

This is what Ḥakīm al-Ummah Mawlana Shaykh Ashraf 'Alī at-Thānawī (Allah ﷻ have mercy on him) wrote, and there is now no need to quote these two forewords after these tales have folded up and the entire book has become united under one title with one author, but I wished to quote them here so it serves as a good memory and clarifies the events for one who wishes to know them.

My Work in the Production of this Book

As for my work in the production of this book, it is as follows: I compared the draft of the author in which *al-Istidrāk al-Ḥasan* was incorporated into *Iḥyā' as-Sunan* with their printed original, and I correct it based on them.

410 In the margins of the first edition, there was a translation of the hadiths of *I'lā' as-Sunan* into Urdu which Shaykh [Ashraf 'Alī at-Thānawī] called *Itfā' al-Fitan* (Extinguishing the Tribulations). In this new edition, however, this translation was removed from the margins. (Mufti Taqi al-'Uthmani)

I checked the texts referenced in the book in most places and I clarified the discrepancies wherever they were

The author did not concern himself with reviewing the positions of the jurists, relying on the knowledge of the reader, so I mentioned in my footnotes these positions at the start of every chapter, drawing from the reliable recognised books to transmit the positions [of the different schools], so it becomes accessible to every reader, and he does not need [to refer to] other books while reading [it]

The author (Allah ﷻ have mercy on him) has stated in his book the page numbers of the books referenced, but these numbers differ with different prints, so I clarified in my footnote the places of those texts by using the titles of the chapters or the numbers of the ḥadīths or the subsections, which do not differ by different prints; unless its place is absolutely clear

Some books of ḥadīth were not printed at the time this book was compiled, like the *Muṣannaf* of Ibn Abī Shaybah and the *Muṣannaf* of ʿAbd ar-Razzāq and the *Ṣaḥīḥ* of Ibn Khuzaymah and others, so the author was forced to select the ḥadīths of these books from secondary sources. Thus, wherever I found a useful addition while checking the texts, I added it to the book in my footnotes

In some places I added some supporting [evidence] for the contention of the author, or some useful points, or criticisms, briefly and concisely

[Having said] this, it is necessary for me to thank a brother beloved [to me] for the sake of Allah ﷻ, the pious youth, the scholar, Mawlana Shaykh Muhammad Ishaq al-Jehlami, since he helped me for the duration of this work, a help that is appreciated, in checking the texts, chasing the sources and correcting the typing errors, and were it not for his help, it would not be possible for me to have completed this work in such a short period. May Allah ﷻ Almighty reward him with goodness and the most abundant of rewards, and give him ability to [do] what He loves and approves. *Amin*.

Finally, I have no option but to confess the shortness of my hand and the fewness of my goods [i.e. my inexperience], and that I am unable to undertake the service of this book as it deserves to be served, although I am grateful to Allah ﷻ that He has enabled me to bring it into the realm of existence. Thus, if there is anything useful in my work, it is from Allah ﷻ, and if there are errors in it, they are from me and from Satan. My success is only with Allah ﷻ. On him I rely and to Him I turn.

MUHAMMAD TAQI AL-ʿUTHMANI
Dar al-ʿUlum Karachi
18 Rabiʿ al-Awwal, 1396/1976[411]

411 *Iʿlāʾ as-Sunan*, Idarat al-Qurʾan wa 'l-ʿUlum al-Islamiyyah, Karachi: Pakistan, 1427 AH, 1:9–33.

BIBLIOGRAPHY

Abdul-Jabbar, Ghassan, *Bukhari* (New Delhi: Oxford University Press, 2007).

Ali, Mansur, 'Al-Tirmidhī and the Role of the *Isnād* in his Sunan', (unpublished Phd thesis: University of Manchester, 2009).

——, 'Review of Abū Ḥanīfah: His Life, Legal Method and Legacy by Mohammad Akram Nadwi', *Muslim World Book Review*, 4/31 (2011), 29–31.

Al-ʿAsqalānī, Ibn Ḥajar, *Fatḥ al-Bāri Sharḥ Ṣaḥīḥ al-Bukhārī*, ed. ʿAbd Allāh ibn Bāz (Riyadh Darussalam, 1997).

——, *Tahdhīb at-Tahdhīb* (Beirut Dār Ṣādir, [n.d.]).

——, *Nuzhat an-Naẓar Sharḥ Nukhbat al-Fikir* (Cairo: Maktabat al-ʿIlm, [n.d.]).

Al-ʿAynī, Badr ad-Dīn *ʿUmdat al-Qārī sharḥ Ṣaḥīḥ al-Bukhāri* (al-Munīriya, 1348).

Aʿzamī, M. Muṣṭafā, *Studies in Early Ḥadīth Literature with a Critical Edition of Some Early Texts* (3rd edn.; Indiana: American Trust Publication, 1992).

Bedir, Murtaza, 'An Early Response to al-Shāfiʿī: ʿĪsāibn Abān on the Prophetic Report (Khabar)', *Islamic Law and Society*, (2002).

Al-Bukhārī, Muḥammad ibn Ismāʿīl, *Al-Jāmiʿ aṣ-Ṣaḥīḥ*, ed. Muḥammad Zuhayr ibn Nāṣir an-Nāṣir ([n.p.]: Dār Ṭawq an-Najāt, [n.d.]).

Adh-Dhahabī, Shams Ad-Dīn, *Siyar Aʿlām an-Nubalāʾ*, ed. Shuʿayb Al-Arnāʾūṭ (Beirut: Muʾassasat ar-Risala, 1983).

Dickenson, Eerik, *The Development of Early Sunnite Ḥadīth Criticism: The Taqdima of Ibn Abī Ḥātim ar-Rāzi* (Leiden: Brill, 2001).

Dutton, Yasin, *The Origins of Islamic Law: The Qurʾān, the Muwaṭṭāʾ and Madinan ʿAmal* (London: RoutledgeCurzon, 2002).

Ibn Kathīr, ʿImad Ad-Dīn, *Ikhtiṣār ʿUlūm al-Ḥadīth* (3rd edn.: Ṣabīḥ, 1377).

Imber, Colin, *The Ottoman Empire, 1300–1640: the Structure of Power* (New York: Palgrave Macmillan, 2002).

ʿIyāḍ, Qāḍī, *Tartīb al-Madārik wa Taqrīb al-Masālik li Maʿrifat Aʿlām Madhhab Mālik* (Beirut: [n.pub.], 1967).

Al-Jawziyya, Ibn Al-Qayyim, *Iʿlām al-Muwaqqiʿīn*, ed. ʿIṣām Ad-Dīn (Cairo: Dār al-Ḥadīth, 2002).

Kamaruddin, Amin, 'Nāṣiruddīn al-Albānī on Muslim's *Ṣaḥīḥ*: A Critical Study of his Method', *Islamic Law and Society*, 11/2 (149–76).

Kāndhlawī, Zakariyyā, *Awjaz al-Masālik ilā Muwaṭṭāʾ Imām Mālik*, ed. Taqī Ad-Dīn an-Nadwī (Damascus: Dār al-Qalam, 2003).

Al-Kattāni, ᶜAbd Al-Ḥayy, *Fihris al-Fahāris wa 'l-Athbāt* (Fez 1346).
Al-Kawtharī, Zāhid, *Fiqh ahl al-ᶜIrāq wa ḥadīthuhum*, ed. Shaykh ᶜAbd al-Fattāḥ Abū Ghudda (Beirut: Muᵓassasat ar-Rayyān, 1997).
Al-Laknawī, ᶜAbd Al-Ḥayy, *al-Ajwibah al-Fāḍilah* (Aleppo, 1384).
Al-Madīnī, ᶜAlī, *Kitāb al-ᶜIlal*, ed. M. M. Aᶜzamī (Beirut: al-Maktab al-Islāmī, [n.d.]).
Al-Mizzī, Yūsuf, *Tahdhīb al-Kamāl*, ed. Bashshār ᶜAwwād Maᶜrūf (Beirut: Muᵓassasat ar-Risāla, 1985).
Nadwi, Mohammad Akram, *Abū Ḥanīfah: His Life, Legal Method and Legacy* (Leicester: Kube Publishing Ltd, 2010).
An-Nasāᵓī, Aḥmad ibn Shuᶜayb, *Sunan an-Nasāᵓī*, ed. ᶜAbd Al-Fattāḥ Abū Ghuddah (Aleppo: Maktab al-Maṭbūᶜāt al-Islāmiyya, 1994).
An-Nīmwī, *At-Taᶜlīq al-Ḥasan ᶜalā Āthār as-Sunan* (Kolkata Dār al-Ishāᶜat al-Islāmiyya, 1376).
Al-Qārī, ᶜAlī, *Sharḥ Sharḥ an-Nukhbah* (Istanbul 1327).
Al-Qazwīnī, Muḥammad ibn Yazīd, *Sunan Ibn Majah*, ed. Bashshār ᶜAwwād Maᶜrūf (Beirut: Dār al-Jīl, 1998).
Al-Qushayrī, Muslim ibn al-Ḥajjāj, *Ṣaḥīḥ with an-Nawawī's Commentary* (Cairo: al-Miṣriya, 1347).
Rahman, Fazlur, *The Living Sunna and Ahl-Sunna wa'l-Jamāᶜah*, ed. P. K. Koya (Ḥadīth and Sunna: Ideals and Realities, Kuala Lumpur: Islamic Book Trust, 1996).
Ar-Rāshidī, Badīᶜ Az-Zamān, *Inmāᵓ az-Zakan fi Tanqīd Inhāᵓ as-Sakan: Naqḍ Qawāᶜid fi ᶜUlūm al-Ḥadīth*, ed. Ṣalāh ad-Dīn Maqbūl Aḥmad (Kuwait: Dār Gharās Publication, 2003).
Ash-Shaybānī, Aḥmad Ibn Ḥanbal, *Musnad* (Al-Maymaniya, 1313).
Siddiqi, M. Z., *Hadīth Literature, Its Origin, Development and Special Features*, ed. T.J. Winter, (Cambridge: The Islamic Text Society, 1993).
As-Sijistānī, Abū Dāwūd, *Kitāb As-Sunan: Sunan Abī Dāwūd* ed. Muḥammad ᶜAwwāma (Beirut: Muᵓassasat ar-Rayyān, 1998).
——, 'Risāla ilā Ahl al-Makka', in ᶜAbd al-Fattāḥ Abū Ghudda (ed.), *Thalāth Rasāᵓil fi Muṣṭalaḥ al-Ḥadīth* (Beirut: Dār al-Bashāᵓir al-Islāmiyya, 2005).
As-Subkī, Taqī Ad-Din, *Shifāᵓ as-Siqām fi Ziyārat Khayr al-Anām* (Cairo: Būlāq, 1318).
As-Suyūṭī, Jalāl Ad-Dīn, *Tadrīb ar-Rāwi Sharḥ Taqrīb-Nawāwī* (Al-Maktabat al-ᶜIlmiyya, 1379).
——, *Ittiḥāf al-Firqa bi Rafᶜ al-Khirqah*, in ᶜAbd Allāh ibn aṣ-Ṣiddīq al-Ghumārī (ed.), *Majmūᶜ min Rasāᵓil as-Suyūṭī* (Beirut: Dār al-Kutub al-ᶜIlmiyya, 2003).
At-Thānawī, Muḥammad Aᶜlā, *Kashshāf Iṣṭalāḥāt al-Funūn* (Kolkota, 1279).
At-Thānawī, Ẓafar Aḥmad al-ᶜUthmāni, *Iᶜlāᵓ as-Sunan,* Karachi: Pakistan, 1427, ed. Taqi Usmani (Karachi: Idarat al-Qur'an wa al ᶜUlum al-Islamiyyah, 1427).
——, *Qawāᶜid fi ᶜUlūm al-Ḥadīth*, ed. ᶜAbd al-Fattāḥ Abū Ghuddah (Karachi: Idārat al-Qurᵓan wa 'l-ᶜUlūm al-Islāmiyya, [n.d.]).
At-Tirmidhī, Muḥammad ibn ᶜĪsā, *Al-Jāmiᶜ al-Kabīr* (*Sunan at-Tirmidhī*), ed. Bashshār ᶜAwwād Maᶜrūf (Beirut: Dār al-Maghrib al-Islāmī 1996).
Zaman, Qasim, *The Ulama in Contemporary Islam: Custodians of Change* (Princeton: Princeton University Press, 2002).

INDEX

compared with other sects, 227, 228